JOINING EMPIRE

The Political Economy of the New Canadian Foreign Policy

A fresh assessment of the neoliberal political economy behind Canadian foreign policy from Afghanistan to Haiti, *Joining Empire* establishes Jerome Klassen as one of the most astute analysts of contemporary Canadian foreign policy and its relationship to US global power. Using empirical data on production, trade, investment, profits, and foreign ownership in Canada, as well as a new analysis of the overlap among the boards of directors of the top 250 firms in Canada and the top 500 firms worldwide, Klassen argues that it is the increasing integration of Canadian businesses into the global economy that drives Canada's new, more aggressive, foreign policy.

Using government documents, think tank studies, media reports, and interviews with business leaders from across Canada, Klassen outlines recent systematic changes in Canadian diplomatic and military policy and connects them with the rise of a new transnational capitalist class. *Joining Empire* is sure to become a classic of Canadian political economy.

JEROME KLASSEN is a postdoctoral research fellow with the International Development Studies Program at Saint Mary's University.

Joining Empire

The Political Economy of the New Canadian Foreign Policy

JEROME KLASSEN

UNIVERSITY OF TORONTO PRESS
Toronto Buffalo London

© University of Toronto Press 2014
Toronto Buffalo London
www.utppublishing.com
Printed in the U.S.A.

ISBN 978-1-4426-4674-2 (cloth)
ISBN 978-1-4426-1460-4 (paper)

Printed on acid-free, 100% post-consumer recycled paper with
vegetable-based inks.

Library and Archives Canada Cataloguing in Publication

Klassen, Jerome, 1977–, author
Joining empire : the political economy of the new Canadian foreign policy /
Jerome Klassen.

Includes bibliographical references.
ISBN 978-1-4426-4674-2 (bound). – ISBN 978-1-4426-1460-4 (pbk.)

1. Canada – Foreign relations – 21st century.   2. Canada – Foreign
relations – United States.   3. United States – Foreign relations –
Canada.   4. Canada – Foreign economic relations.   5. Canada – Foreign
economic relations – United States.   6. United States – Foreign economic
relations – Canada.   7. Neoliberalism – Canada.   I. Title.

FC242.K58 2014   327.7109'051   C2014-903117-3

This book has been published with the help of a grant from the Federation
for the Humanities and Social Sciences, through the Awards to Scholarly
Publications Program, using funds provided by the Social Sciences and
Humanities Research Council of Canada.

University of Toronto Press acknowledges the financial assistance to its
publishing program of the Canada Council for the Arts and the Ontario Arts
Council, an agency of the Government of Ontario.

 **Canada Council   Conseil des Arts
for the Arts   du Canada**

ONTARIO ARTS COUNCIL
CONSEIL DES ARTS DE L'ONTARIO
an Ontario government agency
un organisme du gouvernement de l'Ontario

University of Toronto Press acknowledges the financial support of the
Government of Canada through the Canada Book Fund for its publishing
activities.

Violated, dishonored, wading in blood, dripping filth – there stands bourgeois society. This is it. Not all spic and span and moral, with pretense to culture, philosophy, ethics, order, peace, and the rule of law – but the ravening beast, the witches' sabbath of anarchy, a plague to culture and humanity. Thus it reveals itself in its true, its naked form.

– Rosa Luxemburg, *The Junius Pamphlet*, 1916

Contents

Figures and Tables

Figures

Tables

Acknowledgments

This book could not have been written without the financial, professional, and personal support of many individuals and institutions in Canada and around the world.

The Social Sciences and Humanities Research Council of Canada provided generous grants for this research project as well as for my doctoral work.

The MIT Center for International Studies provided an excellent environment in which to conduct research for this book. Noam Chomsky, my postdoctoral advisor, was a wonderful source of inspiration and support for this project – and for my career path and political involvements over many decades. In many ways, this book is the outcome of a chance reading of *Manufacturing Consent* as a junior high student during the first Gulf War. For this reason, it was a personal pleasure to work closely with Noam so many years later.

Many other people supported the work that went into this book. At MIT, John Tirman encouraged my research and was a great source of information on human rights and US foreign policy. At York University, where I first began to think about Canada's new imperialism, Greg Albo, Himani Bannerji, Raju Das, Sam Gindin, David McNally, John Saul, and Bruce Smardon were vital sources of information, analysis, and critique. My PhD supervisor, Greg Albo, was superb in that capacity, forcing me to study all sides of the political economy tradition in Canada and around the world.

Since graduating from York, I have been indebted to William K. Carroll, who has taught me new techniques of corporate network analysis, and supported my broader research program in invaluable ways. His seminal book, *Corporate Power and Canadian Capitalism,* is an inspiration for this one, and I hope he likes the result.

Between 2012 and 2014, the International Development Studies Program at Saint Mary's University hosted me as a Research Fellow, and in this capacity I was able to finish the manuscript. Kate Ervine, Gavin Fridell, Anthony O'Malley, and Henry Veltmeyer were superb colleagues at SMU and strongly supported my research endeavours. During my stint in Nova Scotia, I also had the pleasure of working with Andrew Biro, Rachel Brickner, and Inder Marwah at Acadia University, where I taught two courses on global politics.

Greg Albo, Aidan Conway, Murray Cooke, Adam Hanieh, Baris Karaagac, Ted Klassen Jr., Caroline Nowlan, and Justin Podur read and edited portions of the manuscript and I owe them many thanks. Anthony Fenton ploughed through the whole text and offered vital insights and analysis.

Through many conversations, David Banerjee, Peter Brogan, Irina Ceric, Dan Freeman-Maloy, Jesse Goldstein, Saseen Kawzally, Tom Keefer, Isabel Macdonald, Geoff Potvin, Tyler Shipley, David Shulman, Vince Teetart, Ryan Toews, Zhang Yun, and Rafeef Ziadah also shaped my thinking on these issues and encouraged me to write this book. Mark Gabbert, my undergraduate honours supervisor at the University of Manitoba, deserves very special thanks for turning me on to political economy, world history, and critical social theory.

In thanking these friends and colleagues, the usual caveat applies: I alone am responsible for any mistakes in the pages that follow.

On the logistical side, Casey Johnson, Bob Murray, and Laurie Scheffler helped organize my postdoctoral tenure at MIT; Cassie MacDonald and Anthony O'Malley did the same at SMU. My gratitude extends to all of them.

I am also grateful to countless individuals at Statistics Canada who helped me navigate the CANSIM II databases and answered many questions. On the research side, I also want to thank Thomas d'Aquino for granting me an invaluable interview.

Several chapters of this book were presented to academic associations, including the Congress of the Humanities and Social Sciences (Canada), the Society for Socialist Studies (Canada), the New England Political Science Association, and Fulbright Canada. The Faculty of Political and Social Science and the Center for North American Studies at the National Autonomous University of Mexico also invited me to present several chapters of this book. Needless to say, I am grateful for the feedback of all my colleagues in Canada and around the world.

Daniel Quinlan at the University of Toronto Press solicited the manuscript, and encouraged my work throughout all stages of the review and editing process. It was a pleasure to work with him on this book as well as on my previous one. Two anonymous reviewers at the University of Toronto Press also provided highly constructive suggestions for upgrading and polishing the manuscript. Barry Norris copy edited the text with expert skill and suggestions.

My family has supported my work in truly ineffable ways over many decades. To my parents, Ted and Violet, thank you for encouraging all of my interests, pursuits, and commitments. To my brothers, Carl and Ted Jr., thank you as well for supporting my work and discussing these issues at various points in time. My in-laws, Bill and Juliet Nowlan, also deserve much gratitude for allowing me to write several chapters at their house in New Brunswick during several summer stays.

Without doubt, I could not have finished, let alone started, this work without the constant support and assistance of my wife, Caroline Nowlan. With our amazing daughter, Eleanor, she inspires me to think and write about these issues in ways that point towards a better future for us and everyone else. For this and many other reasons, I dedicate this book to her.

JOINING EMPIRE

The Political Economy of the
New Canadian Foreign Policy

Introduction: Political Economy and the New Canadian Foreign Policy

While there is in Canada a rich political economy tradition, and an active community of Marxian scholars, there is ironically a paucity of Marxian analysis of Canadian foreign policy.

– Kim Richard Nossal

[T]he dominant class theory, though now quite influential, has as yet not been applied much to the study of Canadian foreign policy.

– Cranford Pratt

Over the past two decades, Canadian governments have worked to establish a new international policy approach. From the Gulf War in 1991 to more recent conflicts in Afghanistan and Libya, successive governments have been forced to contend with a new system of world order. Forged in the aftermath of the Cold War, the new international system is characterized by two key features: the global expansion of capitalism as a mode of production, and the political dominance of the United States as a de facto hegemon. These two features of the international system are closely related, establishing what many commentators have described as a new form of *empire* – a world economy and nation-state system increasingly run by transnational corporations and the political-military infrastructure of the American state (Bacevich 2002; Ignatieff 2003; Panitch and Gindin 2004). In this context, the goal of US foreign policy has been to widen and deepen the capitalist world market in ways that empower the American state and its search for global primacy (Gowan 1999; Layne 2006a; Seabrooke 2001).

In confronting this structure of world order, Canadian governments have been forced to adjust their international policies accordingly. If

Canada had previously positioned itself as a middle power in the Cold War system of international relations, and practised specialized forms of peacekeeping and conflict mediation across decades of foreign policy history, it now required a new approach, a qualitatively different strategy by which to engage the world economy and nation-state system.

This new approach has developed through two distinct stages, each of which corresponds to conjunctural shifts in the political economy of global capitalism. Throughout the 1990s, the Canadian state was a strong supporter of *neoliberalism*, the economic program associated with the deregulation of markets, the privatization of state assets, and the liberalization of trade and investment. To advance this agenda, Canadian governments of all stripes tried to reorganize both the national economy and the state apparatus in line with "free market" imperatives. They also pursued new forms of continental integration, and played a key role in the international trade and financial institutions that oversee and regulate the world economy. In the process, the Canadian market became more entwined with global circuits of capital, and Canadian firms engaged in a new wave of international investment. Although Canadian foreign policy during this period was largely dominated by economic concerns, it also included military missions in Iraq, Somalia, and the former Yugoslavia. Beyond these limited campaigns, however, few resources were dedicated to the military, and little thought was given to security and defence strategies. Instead, economic concerns were the primary interest of Canadian governments in both internal and external policy formation.

This priority changed abruptly on 11 September 2001. The terrorist attacks on New York and Washington, DC, and the US response to them, triggered a second key shift in Canada's foreign policy approach. In the years after 9/11, Canadian foreign policy was fixated on the "global war on terror" led by US President George W. Bush. In 2001, Canada gave direct support to the war in Afghanistan, and was quick to implement a variety of "national security" measures, including new antiterrorist and immigration laws. In subsequent years, Canada largely abandoned United Nations peacekeeping missions, and increased defence spending in real terms to levels not seen since the Second World War. Although Canada was not involved openly in the war on Iraq in 2003, it provided multiple forms of military assistance, and agreed to lead a mission by the North Atlantic Treaty Organization (NATO) in Kabul, Afghanistan, allowing US troops to redeploy to the Gulf (Stein and Lang 2007, 48–50). During the same period, Canada built a secret military base in the United Arab Emirates, and expanded naval operations in the Persian Gulf, the Arabian Sea, the Arctic, the Caribbean Sea, the Pacific Rim, and around the Horn of Africa. In matters of international diplomacy, Canada reneged on the Kyoto Protocol, imposed sanctions on Iran, and changed course on the Israel-Palestine conflict, giving unflinching support to Israel. In Latin America and the Caribbean, Canada established closer ties to right-wing governments, and on two occasions sent troops to Haiti, one time in support of a *coup d'état* against an elected president (Shamsie 2006).

For the first time since the end of the Cold War, then, the Canadian state has developed an integrated or systematic international policy approach, combining economic, diplomatic, and military interests. Across a number of planning documents, the Canadian state has articulated these interests as the worldwide expansion of capitalism, guaranteed access to the US market, national defence and continental security, and the global projection of military force against terrorist groups and "rogue" states. In these ways, Canadian governments in the past decade have added a second component to the new foreign policy agenda: the "global war on terror" *cum* neoliberalism. These two features of Canada's new international policy agenda have been interlaced to achieve leverage in both the world economy and the American empire.

In fusing together this new approach to global politics, Canadian governments have produced what Alexander Moens (2008) calls a "revolution in Canadian foreign policy." Within this revolution, four key trends are discernible. First, the new foreign policy bridges the economic interests of Canadian capital and the geopolitical interests of the state, and seeks *neoliberal market enforcement* at national, continental, and international scales. Second, it marks a definite *strategy of empire* by which Canada seeks to position itself in the top echelon of states, and to expand the global reach of Canadian corporations. Third, the new Canadian foreign policy is characterized by a shift away from multilateral diplomacy and UN peacekeeping towards methods of *cooperative specialization* with US foreign policy and *disciplinary militarism* towards the Third World. Finally, it entails a *continental security agenda*, which involves an internal realignment of security and defence apparatuses, and a deep integration of the Canadian state with the regional structures of US global power. Viewed together, these four trends are the axes around which Canada has organized its encounter with neoliberalism and the "global war on terror."

What lies behind these systematic changes in Canadian foreign policy, changes that have sparked so much debate and controversy both
inside Canada and around the world? The core thesis of this book is
that, to understand the new Canadian foreign policy, it is necessary
to map and analyse the process of *capitalist class formation* in Canada.
During the period of neoliberalism, the *internationalization* of the
Canadian political economy has occurred. This process entails the
cross-border interlacing of Canada's primary economic operations, so
that Canadian firms now perceive the world market as the stage upon
which capital accumulation is organized. Leading corporations in all
sectors hold trade and investment stakes across the world economy,
and thus conceive the production of goods and profits in fundamentally global terms. The upshot of this development is that a *transnational capitalist class* has formed in and around the newly globalized
circuits of capital in Canada.[1] This new social class has a vested interest
not just in the deep integration of the North American bloc, but also in
the neoliberal transformation of the world economy as a whole. In this
context, the Canadian state has been induced or impelled to develop
a new international strategy, one that embodies and secures the political and economic interests of Canadian capital. The qualitative shift in
Canada's foreign policy thus stems from what Cranford Pratt (1983/4)
calls "dominant class interests."

For this reason, the new Canadian foreign policy is a class-conscious
imperialism of the state and corporate elite. As an advanced capitalist
country with an internationalized bloc of corporate power, Canada
interacts with the world market and nation-state system in ways commensurate with empire or imperialism. It is therefore dedicated to
maximizing the profits of Canadian corporations, expanding the depth
and breadth of the global economy, gaining access to key sites of international diplomacy, and disciplining any states or political movements
that trouble this agenda. In short, Canada's new foreign policy is a
class-based effort at *joining empire*.[2]

This new class strategy, though, is shaped and modified by Canada's
particular rank and role as a secondary power in the North American
bloc. For this reason, the Canadian state tends to operate through a
security and defence alignment with US foreign policy – in particular,
through new modes of diplomatic and military specialization within
US power projections. In fact, it is through this continental alliance that
Canada seeks to secure and advance the economic interests of Canadian
capital on a global scale.

In short, it is through an integrated strategy of cooperative specialization with US power structures and disciplinary militarism towards the Third World that the Canadian state achieves a secondary position on the imperial chain as well as neoliberal market enforcement at home and abroad. To unpack this argument, in this book I develop an intersecting theory of political economy, class formation, and state restructuring. In the process, I offer a fresh understanding of the new Canadian foreign policy.

Historical Origins of Canadian Political Economy

The timeframe of this study is the two decades of neoliberalism that roughly follow the end of the Cold War. This is the period in which capitalism emerged as a global mode of production, incorporating China, the former Soviet Union, and much of the Third World. It is also the period in which US primacy was quickly established and then seemingly expanded through the "global war on terror." These dynamics at the scale of world politics provide the context for recent changes in Canadian foreign policy. To appreciate Canada's role in the world today, however, it is necessary to understand and map the historical origins of class and state formation in the Canadian political economy. Indeed, Canada's current international policy is inflected by past patterns of economic and political development. In the following brief history of the Canadian political economy, I focus especially on the intersecting patterns of economic development, class and state formation, and international relations. In tracing these dynamics across time and space, I set the context for recent debates about Canada's role in the global economy and the US empire.

The origins of the Canadian political economy lie in the colonization projects of the British and French empires of the seventeenth and eighteenth centuries. These colonial projects were structured around a particular strategy of capital accumulation – that of *merchant capital*. The object of British and French mercantilism was the accumulation of money through the trade of commodities in the world market. This project entailed the buying and selling of commodities, usually raw materials or agricultural goods, at different prices at various points in the world trading system. In the Canadian context, European mercantilism focused on the export of natural resources or staples such as fish, fur, and timber (Watkins 1963). The French colonial effort was organized through an inland trading system and a demographic project of feudal settlement. The English effort, in contrast, was organized through a "coast factory" trading system in Rupert's Land, run by the Hudson's Bay Company (HBC), a state-monopoly corporation. The HBC was a key adjunct of the North Atlantic triangle trade, and functioned economically by selling guns, rum, and wool blankets to indigenous peoples in exchange for beaver pelts and bison hides. Indigenous people were the primary labour force of the fur trade and thus were not displaced en masse from the land. At the same time, the mercantile system radically altered the social and cultural landscapes of aboriginal nations, creating new patterns of production, warfare, and religion, as well as new forms of class hierarchy, gender inequality, and national identity (Bourgeault 1988; Canada 1996; Van Kirk 1983; Satzewich and Wotherspoon 2000). Both the English and the French exploited these social and cultural dislocations to build a "system of alliances" with native nations. In 1760, the British conquered New France, and then proceeded to expand the fur trade westward. In the process, the social and political power of the merchant banks, colonial staff, and feudal landowners were entrenched in what would later become the province of Quebec (Bernier and Salée 1992).

Before the American Revolution, then, the British strategy for the northern hinterland was one of mercantile and feudal exploitation under the class power of the merchant, landed, and colonial elites. This strategy changed only after the Revolution sparked a series of political, social, and demographic transformations that British North America was unable to contain. The Revolution established a new form of republican government, which supported slavery in the South, industrialization in the Northeast, and settlement and farming – or "independent commodity production" – in the Midwest. For the British colony to the north, the Revolution meant not just a loss of land and productive investment, but also an influx of English-speaking Loyalist settlers. In response, the British declared the Constitution Act of 1791, which established a French-speaking Lower Canada and an English-speaking Upper Canada. Each colony was ruled politically by an appointed governor and executive council, as well as by an elected legislature by and for those with property. The Constitution Act also allowed for *soccage*, or private ownership of the land. In Lower Canada, private settlement and land speculation emerged in the townships southeast of Montreal, though such transformations did not displace the feudal and mercantile structures of accumulation (Bernier and Salée 1992; Coates 1999). In Upper Canada, the dominant form of settlement and production was independent farming based on private property. Loyalist farmers engaged in self-subsistence agriculture and exported grain surpluses through the mercantile trading system (McCallum 1980). By the 1820s, the farming economy was supported by manufactories in nearby towns, which were soon linked by canals, roads, and rail. Thus, although the economic structure of Upper Canada was still organized around independent commodity production and mercantile exports, it soon developed a set of independent market relations, which functioned outside the British connection.

The result was an emerging contradiction in the political economy and class structure of British North America. On the one hand, state and market structures were dominated by the colonial staff, religious establishment, feudal *seigneurs*, and merchant banks and trading companies – in particular, by the Family Compact in Upper Canada and the Château Clique in Lower Canada. On the other hand, a new system of private property and small-scale manufactory production was emerging in and around the farms and towns of Upper Canada, where English artisans, Scottish settlers, and Loyalist farmers engaged in new forms of market exchange and productive labour. The insurrections of 1837–38 were an expression of this contradiction in the social structure. Led by a popular mass of farmers, professionals, and urban workers, the uprisings called for land, democracy, and self-determination – in other words, for a "bourgeois revolution" in Canada (Ryerson 1976; Coates 1999). Although easily repressed, the rebellions had the lasting affect of achieving "responsible government" in both colonies in 1848.[3] Six years later, feudalism was abolished in Canada East, as Lower Canada had been renamed.

It is important to understand how a capitalist mode of production emerged from this context. The trigger was not simply the quantitative extension of market relations in and around private farming and world trade. Rather, the critical variable was the influx of Irish peasants into both Upper Canada and the Maritimes, and the corresponding emergence of a permanent workforce based upon *waged labour*. The emigration of hundreds of thousands of Roman Catholic Irish peasants created a "reserve army of labour" for both manufacturing and infrastructure development (Pentland 1959, 1981). This qualitative shift in social relations created a new political economy in Canada – that of *capitalism*. Between the 1840s and 1860s, a new mode of production emerged, one that was dedicated to commodity exchange for profit through a capitalist labour process. With this key transformation in social property and class relations, the economic structure of Canada was diversified away from staples exports and merchant trade towards production for profit in a domestic market economy (Panitch 1981).[4] After the abrogation of the British Corn Laws in 1846 and of the Reciprocity Agreement with the United States in 1866, the growing class of English-Canadian capitalists launched a movement for independence, which took the form of Confederation in 1867 (Ryerson 1976). This "revolution from above" was engineered to avoid absorption by the United States and to activate an industrial revolution in Canada based on railway transport and private agriculture. It also served a host of British interests, including transporting goods to and from India and China (Naylor 2006). Having suffered defeat in 1837–38, the popular masses were denied any role in shaping the state, which was directed by the Canadian corporate elite and its political supporters (Dupuis-Déri 2010; Resnick 1984).

Canadian Confederation thus engendered a new capitalist state on the northern border of the United States. To consolidate this project, the government of John A. Macdonald launched the National Policy – a strategy of national economic development through import-substitution industrialization (Smiley 1975). Broadly speaking, this strategy included the building of a transcontinental rail line, the imposition of national tariffs on manufactured imports, the dispossession of indigenous peoples through the Indian Act (1876),[5] and the emigration of white settlers into the Prairies (Daschuk 2013).[6] As a result, Canada experienced an industrial revolution between 1890 and 1913. The Canadian West developed as a major source of agricultural exports, and Canadian manufacturing firms underwent a process of concentration and centralization, creating a new structure of "monopoly capitalism" (Carroll 1986). Simultaneously, US firms crossed the tariff wall to invest in Canada's manufacturing sector, thus continentalizing the nascent methods of Fordism, including mass production, scientific management, and high-wage industrial salaries (Panitch 1981; Smardon 2010). Likewise, Canadian firms in the banking, insurance, transportation, and utilities sectors began a process of international expansion, primarily through foreign direct investments in Latin America and the Caribbean (Kaufman 1984). As a Dominion of the British Empire, Canada and its foreign policy agenda were still subordinated to the Crown, and English-speaking elites strongly supported Canada's role in British imperialism. For these reasons, Canada participated in the Boer War of 1899–1902, and automatically entered the First World War on the British side. At the same time, both wars were highly contentious, particularly in Quebec, where anti-imperialist sentiment ran strong. In 1918, for example, conscription protests in Quebec City were repressed by the military, resulting in five fatalities (Renaud and Squires 2013, 392). In the same year, French-Canadian working-class conscripts mutinied in Victoria over deployment to Siberia to fight the new Soviet government (Isitt 2006). In the first two decades of the twentieth century, then, Canada remained tightly wedded to the British Empire through financial, trading, and military relations. Yet, Canada's political economy was developing in ways that would soon rupture the links to *Pax Britannica* and call forth a new international policy and diplomatic alignment.

The inter-war years were a key period of transition for Canadian capitalism. Starting with general strikes in Vancouver (1918), Amherst, Nova Scotia (1919), Winnipeg (1919), and Victoria (1919), a militant labour movement emerged, with returning veterans playing a significant role (Heron 1998; Idiong 1997). The rise and fall of this movement followed that of the broader economy, which in 1929 sunk into a ten-year depression. With exports accounting for approximately one-quarter of Canada's gross national product, the country was highly vulnerable to the economic upheaval and experienced balance-of-payments deficits. In response to the US Smoot-Hawley Tariff Act of 1930, the government of R.B. Bennett raised taxes on US imports, and helped to redirect trade to Britain through the Commonwealth preference system.

Canada's foreign policy developed in three additional ways in the period after the First World War. First, Canadian governments were increasingly isolationist with respect to European conflicts, and pressed for more autonomy in the Empire and for separate representation at the peace conference at Versailles and at the League of Nations. In 1923, Canada gained the right to sign independent treaties. Second, Canada began to experiment with a host of new international practices, from gunboat diplomacy in Central America to armed intervention in Russia and multilateral negotiations over sanctions and war crimes in Europe. Finally, through the Balfour Report (1926) and the Statute of Westminster (1931), Canada achieved full independence in matters of domestic and foreign policy and thus became an equal member of the Commonwealth and the wider system of nation-states. As part of this process, Canada acquired its first embassies in Europe and Washington. The inter-war period was therefore a major turning point for the Canadian political economy: the formal connection to British imperialism was severed, yet new conflicts at both the national and international levels would soon embroil the country in a second world war and hasten radical changes in the domestic market, state structure, and foreign policy apparatus.

The impact on Canada of the Second World War was immense. Military production revived both the national economy and the US-Canadian trading relationship. Canada played a major role in many theatres of the conflict, and employed a "functional" strategy to gain access to Allied meetings.[7] By the end of the war, Canada possessed a strong military capacity, including the world's fourth-largest air force and fifth-largest navy (Granatstein 1993, 277). The most important change, however, was the realignment of Canada's military and defence policy with that of Washington. During the war, Canada and the United States established new forms of military cooperation – in particular, the Permanent Joint Board on Defence, established by the Ogdensburg Agreement of 1940. In the process, and through subsequent agreements on military procurement, Canadian defence policy shifted towards one of *continental convergence*. Canada became a strong ally of US foreign policy in the Cold War, and played a key role in both the founding of NATO and the conflict in Korea. As the Cold War developed, Canada also embraced – and integrated itself with – multiple scales of US nuclear strategy and infrastructure, including first-strike options and capabilities (Jockel and Sokolsky 1999).

At the same time, Canada employed a "Middle Power" strategy through which it sought to limit inter-state conflicts and rivalries, and to gain influence internationally, through multilateral processes (Keating 1993). To these ends, Canada actively shaped the new institutions of global governance, including the United Nations, the World Bank, the International Monetary Fund, and the General Agreement on Tariffs and Trade. As part of the Middle Power strategy, Canada helped to develop UN peacekeeping missions and encouraged new types of foreign aid and development assistance, especially the Colombo Plan of 1950.[8] As a result, this period is often described as the golden age of *liberal internationalism* – as the time in which Canada practised a more dedicated form of multilateral diplomacy in world affairs (Gordon 1966; Holmes 1979).

It is important to understand the political economy of this international strategy. After the war, a militant strike wave cleared the path for collective bargaining, union recognition, and welfare programs to emerge at both the provincial and federal levels (McInnis 2002). The long-term trend towards continentalism also accelerated, as US firms invested heavily in Canada's manufacturing, mining, and energy sectors (Levitt [1970] 2002). The result of this integration was a "permeable" type of Fordism in which US capital dominated key sectors of production (Jenson 1990). For this reason, there was a particular fit between the structures of class power in the Canadian economy and the political-diplomatic endeavours of the state. On the one hand, US capital was implanted as a leading class faction in Canada, thus inducing new types of foreign policy alignment (Warnock 1970). On the other hand, Canada maintained sufficient autonomy to avoid major military spending commitments and to invest productively in national infrastructure programs (Kellogg 1990, 2013). As a consequence, Canada was able to specialize in UN peacekeeping and other soft-power methods of international statecraft, while building a national infrastructure for rapid economic growth. Although its peacekeeping operations were always linked to the geopolitical interests of US foreign policy, they also reflected a class compromise *internal* to Canada – a political consensus on the primacy of social program spending over military and defence outlays. In these ways, Canada's post-war Middle Power strategy reflected not just its objective standing in the world order, but also a certain stage of development in the country's political economy and class structure.

In the late 1960s, however, this strategy began to break down. At the global level, the Cold War system fractured as US capital lost shares of world markets to Japanese and German firms and as US militarism proved unable to defeat the National Liberation Front in Vietnam (Brenner 2006a). In this context, Canada's Middle Power strategy seemed out of touch not only with global developments, but also with the nationalist turn in Canadian politics and civil society over economic and foreign policies.[9] In response, the Pierre Trudeau government launched a program of economic nationalism that resulted in the repatriation of key sectors of capital. Trudeau also tried to develop a new diplomatic strategy – the so-called Third Option – to reinforce and advance the independent interests of the Canadian state and corporate elite. Yet, despite these efforts, Trudeau employed peacekeeping and multilateralism as foreign policy tools, and still accepted the main parameters of the Cold War system.[10] A clean break with the Middle Power strategy, therefore, did not occur.

The outlines of a new strategy first emerged in the late 1980s, when the Brian Mulroney government signed a free trade agreement with the United States. The goals of this agreement were to expand the market in which Canadian firms operated; to engender new forms of competition, which might raise productivity and lower wages in Canada; and to lock in or encourage free market reforms on a continental scale (Grinspun and Shamsie 2007; McBride 2005). As well, the Mulroney government pledged to increase defence spending, and supported the first major conflict of the "new world order": the US-led Gulf War in 1990–91. But apart from these initiatives, the government made little headway in forging a new international policy approach. It began the process of neoliberal transformation in Canada, and offered diplomatic and military support for US objectives in the Middle East, but did not integrate these policies as part of a systematic strategy. In fact, facing budget deficits, it reduced defence spending and planned to close Canada's military bases in Europe.

As a result, it was left to future governments, both Liberal and Conservative, to consolidate a new international policy. In the 1990s, the strategy of neoliberal market enforcement was achieved through a mix of international, regional, and domestic initiatives, including the World Trade Organization, the North American Free Trade Agreement (NAFTA), and the Canada Health and Social Transfer. This period was also characterized by the rapid expansion of Canadian firms abroad, most notably into the United States and Europe, but also into developing countries. In this context, Canadian foreign policy was focused overwhelmingly on the globalization agenda.

After 9/11, the governments of Jean Chrétien, Paul Martin, and Stephen Harper redefined the diplomatic and security doctrines of the state in terms of the "global war on terror." In quick succession, these governments built a national security apparatus, and reorganized the foreign policy agencies around the military project of combatting terrorism, failed states, and weapons of mass destruction. These new policies were developed in conjunction with US grand strategies, and were designed in part to reinforce and secure the regional interests of Canadian capital. In such ways, Canadian governments over the past two decades have formalized a new international policy approach, one that reflects and supports both the economic interests of Canadian capital and the geopolitical interests of the state. In the process, they have transcended the Middle Power project of the Cold War period and developed a new foreign policy agenda.

From this brief historical sketch, one can draw two important conclusions. First, Canadian foreign policy has always expressed a certain mode of class and state formation in the domestic political economy. Second, Canadian foreign policy has always developed in the context of global systems of empire or imperialism. When assessing current debates on Canada's rank and role in world affairs, one must therefore be attentive to the ways in which dominant class interests are secured by the state in the context of new forms of economic development and political power at home and abroad.

Theories of Canadian State Power

Given the recent changes in Canadian foreign policy, it is not surprising that new debates have emerged in the social sciences about the nature or logic of this transformation. There are currently two broad frameworks for understanding Canadian foreign policy, each of which is variegated by internal streams or subdivisions. In the field of *international relations*, for example, research is organized into three currents: liberalism, realism, and critical theory. Likewise, in the *political economy* stream of Canadian political science, research is organized into variants of dependency or Marxist analysis. Each of these sub-models employs a different set of concepts and propositions, derived from distinct understandings of politics, economics, the state, and world order. Through a critical review of these frameworks and theories, this section sets the stage for a new conceptualization of Canadian foreign policy as a secondary form of imperialism.

International Relations Theory

Consider, first, the liberal theory of Canadian statecraft. This theory emerged in the aftermath of the Second World War, when, as we have seen, Canada developed a Middle Power strategy of building new institutions of global governance and arbitrating conflicts between Great Powers and their former colonies (Gordon 1966). This theory holds that Canadian foreign policy was guided by an ethical commitment to multilateral diplomacy, conflict resolution, and international development. In the seminal work of John Holmes (1979), Canadian diplomats such as Lester Pearson and Hume Wrong were said to have "clung, more or less, to the liberal concept ... that 'every state by pursuing the greatest good of the whole world, is pursuing the greatest good of its own citizens, and vice versa'." In this perspective, Canadian foreign policy was motivated by a genuine idealism that trumped national self-interest and overcame tendencies to war and conflict in the nation-state system. In short, Canada worked effectively at constructing a liberal world order in which new institutions would repress or contain past forms of military conflict and economic rivalry. According to Tom Keating

(1993, 10–11), "multilateralism [was] a guiding principle and operational strategy in the conduct of Canadian foreign policy across a spectrum of policy issues in the political, economic, and security arenas." In his assessment, "the active role that Canadian officials played in the late forties and their efforts to construct a multilateral framework ... offset the dominant and potentially domineering power of the United States and, at the same time, provide[d] a stable structure of peace and prosperity."

In the post-war period, then, the liberal theory of Canadian foreign policy focused on the ethical motivations of political leaders and on multilateral diplomacy as a means of achieving peace and development in world affairs. As a research program, it emphasized the decision-making processes through which Canadian politicians devised and deployed international strategies. In political terms, it was inspired by the Middle Power project of the Cold War period and the diplomatic practice of "Pearsonian idealism."

Since the end of the Cold War, liberal theory has been forced to address a new set of issues and concerns. For Michael Byers (2007, 38), the "recent pattern of law breaking by the United States" has created a new space "for an experienced, well-minded middle power [such as Canada] ... to lead the way." In his view, Canada must build upon the "middle-power tradition of multilateral leadership, which has always included promoting peace, defending human rights and championing international humanitarian law." In a more forward-looking study, Lloyd Axworthy (2003, 124) argues that Canadian foreign policy must "go global" in order to address issues of poverty, civil war, and genocide. As a Middle Power, Canada must "carve out special niches of global activity, such as peace-building or human rights work" (ibid., 74). Through the concept of "human security," Axworthy offers "a way of seeing the world and tackling global issues that derive from serving individual human needs, not just those of the nation-state" (ibid., 60). With this in mind, sovereignty must be redefined as "the responsibility [of states] to protect their own citizens. Failing that, the international community has a right to intervene" (ibid., 157). In Axworthy's view, NATO's war on Serbia in 1999 was fought for such "humanitarian principles" (ibid., 182).

In different ways, Axworthy and Byers have tried to redefine both the practice and the theory of liberal idealism. More pragmatic liberals, however, have critiqued their perspectives. According to Jennifer Welsh (2004, 159), "middlepowermanship is a *way* of conducting foreign policy.

It doesn't tell us very much about what we want to achieve through those means." As an alternative, Welsh argues, Canada must operate globally as a "Model Citizen" in two respects. First, "[a] crucial aspect of Canadian foreign policy today is simply *being what we are*: a particular, and highly successful, model of liberal democracy" (ibid., 189). Second, "[t]o achieve its goals internationally, Canada must at times be willing to engage with great powers on *their* terms" (ibid., 201). For these reasons, Welsh defends the wars in Serbia and Afghanistan, and supports the US missile defence program. In the process, she develops a more pragmatic liberalism in which the status quo values of Canadian politics are combined with the status quo structures of global power.

In the process, Welsh establishes a link to the second stream of Canadian foreign policy analysis: realism. This theory began to take shape in the 1970s in response to the crisis of the Middle Power strategy. Inspired by American theories of international relations, realism offered a critique of liberal scholarship and a new strategy by which to engage the world system in transition. Whereas liberalism highlighted the ethical postures or ideas of individual politicians in the Canadian government, realism focused on the state as an institution of military power and national security. In the realist paradigm, *states* are the primary units of analysis, and are said to be autonomous or independent of social or political moorings. As Kim Richard Nossal (1985, xii–xiii) explains, "foreign policy is formulated and conducted by government officials without input ... from societal actors." The reason is that foreign policy is "fundamentally played out between states, not between state and society." In making this argument, Nossal invokes the realist tenet that states function in a context of permanent competition with other states, and that foreign policy is fundamentally about international "power" (ibid., 9). In this context, it is not ethics or ideology that drives foreign policy, but the cold hard calculus of the "national interest."

With these notions of the state and world order, realism offered a new strategy for Canadian foreign policy. At the heart of this strategy was a new understanding of Canada's rank and role in the nation-state system. In the 1970s, the balance of power was shifting as US hegemony declined in the wake of Vietnam and the world economic crisis. In this context, Peyton Lyon and Brian Tomlin (1979, 72) argued that Canada was emerging as a "major power." In the same vein, James Eayrs (1981, 3) claimed that "the term 'middle power' no longer does justice to Canada's role in world affairs. Canada has become instead a 'foremost power' – foremost in the dictionary definition of 'most notable or prominent'." Similarly, David Dewitt and John Kirton (1983, 4) averred that "America's decline and the consequent diffusion of power in the international system have propelled Canada into a position of a principal power in the globe." In their view, principal powers "stand in the top tier of the global hierarchy of power and act autonomously in pursuit of their own interests, rather than as mediators among others or agents for them." For these writers, the rising position of the Canadian state in the global hierarchy demanded a new attention to national power projections over ethical or idealist ones.

Although these writers accepted the liberal theory of the post-war period, another line of realist scholarship critiqued the history of idealism in Canadian foreign policy analysis. For example, Nossal (1985, 58) points out that, during the Cold War, Canada was an "aligned member of the international community" on the side of the United States and the capitalist bloc. Similarly, Adam Chapnick (2000, 188) demonstrates that Canada's practice of Middle Power diplomacy in the aftermath of the Second World War was hardly an exercise of righteous idealism; rather, "[t]he history of middlepowerhood uncovers a tradition of Canadian rhetoric crafted to justify the attainment of disproportionate influence in international affairs." In other words, it was a "subtle process of nationalist self-promotion." According to Sean Maloney (2002, 246), Canada likewise supported UN peacekeeping "for reasons that are unrelated to the existing 'noble, selfless, and nice' mythology. In most of the operations ... UN peacekeeping was used by Canada as part of a Western effort to deny the Soviet Union influence and control over potential base areas they might use to degrade NATO's ability to deter and/or fight a third world war."

Through such a critique, realism became the dominant paradigm of Canadian foreign policy analysis. In the current context, this paradigm focuses overwhelmingly on the perceived threats of terrorism, rogue states, and weapons of mass destruction. Thus, Elinor Sloan (2005, 133) suggests that "[t]he primary threat to North America today is international terrorism, and specifically individuals and networks of individuals operating in terror cells dispersed around the globe, including within North America." In the same way, Nossal (2004, 756) sees the "contemporary global order" as one "marked by a state of war between Islamic extremists and those whom they believe to be their enemies and thus deserve death." Likewise, Michael Hart (2008, 104–5) contends that "[t]he most pressing threat to global security today is posed by the terrorism spawned by Islamic militants. Although the threat is global, the most immediate theatre of operations is in the Middle East. Over time, however, Europe may become a second front as the Islamification of Europe gathers speed."

In this stream of realism, racialized views of Muslims are combined with a national security doctrine that extols war and US-led militarism.[11] As Hart (2008, 335) elaborates, "[t]he time has come to bring Canadian foreign policy into the twenty-first century by grounding it in a conception of the national interest that accepts the primacy of the United States and guarantees both our national security and our prosperity." To these ends, Canadian governments must "build constructive rapport with their Washington counterparts" (ibid., 334–5) and fund the military "to the point that Canadians can again have an impact commensurate with their aspirations and pretensions" (ibid., 23). Through such arguments, this brand of *neoconservative realism* has emerged as a key interpretation of the world order and Canadian foreign policy – one in which a "global war" on "Islamic extremists" is being fought in the "national interest."

Another branch of realism challenges these contentions. In his seminal work on the new "security state," Patrick Lennox (2007, 2009) demonstrates how Canada has been forced to internalize Washington's security and military doctrines. The host of constitutional, bureaucratic, defensive, and border infrastructural changes that Canada has implemented post-9/11 are not a "direct reaction to the objective threat of terrorism" (2007, 1018), but have been driven by concerns of either "economic isolation or American intervention" (ibid., 1033); in effect, "[b]ecause of its subordinate position in the North American hierarchy, Canada was compelled to take on the new security state form as defined and specified by its superordinate partner, the United States" (ibid., 1018). According to this line of *structural specialization* realism, then, Canada's sovereignty has been diminished, not strengthened, by new forms of continental integration.

A third stream of Canadian foreign policy analysis – often described as "critical international relations theory" – has developed in response to liberalism and realism. Influenced by postmodern methods of discourse analysis, this approach focuses on the social construction of liberal and realist theories. In particular, it deconstructs these theories as ideational forms of elite domination, or as linguistic tools of social power relations (see Beier and Wylie 2010). For example, Mark Neufeld (2007, 100) views the Middle Power project of classical liberalism as an ideological tool, designed to enforce hegemony on the home front as the Canadian state pursued a strategy of capitalist expansion abroad. Given Canada's alignment in the Cold War, he argues, "the regulative ideal of 'middle power' was framed in terms of dominant class interests and in tune with a hegemonic world global order." In other words, Canada's Middle Power strategy was complicit with hegemonic strategies for class domination both in Canada and around the world.

For scholars in the critical tradition, the human security agenda of contemporary liberalism serves the same political functions. According to Ann Denholm Crosby (2007, 270), Canada's "discourse and practice of human security can be understood as an informal conditioning framework for the pursuit of neo-liberal economic interests and processes in that human security is about security *within the context* of global market forces and the on-going efforts by the state to enforce them." Indeed, as Pratt (2007, 375) submits, the human security agenda is "totally compatible with the government's central preoccupation with fiscal constraint, with trade promotion, and with the accomplishment of a neo-liberal international economic order." As a result, a link must be drawn between the core propositions of liberal theory and the vested interests of dominant class forces in Canada.

A similar link exists between social power structures and realist theories of Canadian foreign policy. As Pratt (1983/84, 115) explains, realist notions of "national security" and the "national interest" are highly problematic because *antagonistic social classes* constitute capitalist economies. By disavowing the social relations of capitalism, realism functions as a form of ideological regulation, serving those who command power in the state and market. In effect, this theory abstracts the state from the social relations of capitalism, and thus shelters the foreign policy elite from any implication in class exploitation at home and abroad. As Crosby (2010, 36) elaborates: "Embedded in this world view are ... theoretical assumptions about the exogenously given nature of states and markets, and corresponding understandings of self-interest, competitiveness, and aggressive individualism as *a priori* characteristics of human nature. Resisting this worldview involves resisting the universalizing assumptions of these dominant theoretical perspectives in International Relations theory."

As part of this resistance, Sherene Razack (2004, 2008) argues that, in a white settler-state such as Canada, understandings of "self-interest, competitiveness and aggressive individualism" intersect with racialized and gendered notions of "the nation." In her view, the national security agenda is a discursive tool for constructing new forms of racialized and male-based power. The "global war on terror," for example, depends upon and works through a casting out of Muslims from the culture of the "nation" and, indeed, "humanity." The systematic torture and killing of Muslims in the "global war on terror," in fact, is a mechanism for western armies to reaffirm their sense of white supremacy and masculine power. With this in mind, the implication of Canadian forces in the detention and torture of Afghan prisoners is an example of the social violence that attends the "global war on terror" (Hunt and Rygiel 2006; Razack 2013; Sontag 2004; Williams 2006).

For critical theories of Canadian foreign policy, then, realism tends to obfuscate the class, race, and gender hierarchies of the state. As a discursive tool of power, it works by binding the nation in common cause against state-defined enemies; submerging dynamics of class, race, and gender in Canadian foreign policy practices; and justifying new patterns of neoliberal restructuring, continental integration, and counter-insurgency warfare (see Beier and Wylie 2010). In the process, it serves dominant social interests.

Through such arguments, the critical approach to Canadian foreign policy debunks and debases the mainstream theories. The limitation of the critical perspective, however, is the absence of any alternative theory of Canadian foreign policy. It deconstructs the mainstream theories and shows how they function in concrete case studies, but it has yet to explain *why* Canadian foreign policy operates in the way it does. The problem here is that the critical perspective often remains trapped in a discourse game, and therefore does not reconstruct or retheorize the logic of Canadian state power. For this reason, one must go beyond the framework of international relations theory and consider the political economy of Canadian foreign policy.

Canadian Political Economy

The fundamental insight of the Canadian political economy tradition is that no aspect of state activity or policy-making can be understood in abstraction from the intersecting forms of political and economic power in Canadian society and the wider world system. As a result, the foreign policies of the state must be viewed in relation to the patterns of accumulation and capitalist class formation at both the domestic and global levels. Indeed, Canadian foreign policy is an expression of the dialectical interface between global and national structures of economic and political power.

In the Canadian context, two theories of political economy have dominated debates on these issues: the theory of Canadian *dependence* associated with left-nationalist politics, and the theory of Canadian *imperialism* derived from Marxism. Although these theories have different understandings of Canadian political economy, both are organized around four key issues: the structure of production and labour in the Canadian economy; the patterns of trade and investment through which Canada engages with the world market; the social composition of the capitalist class or corporate elite; and the institutional form of the state and the corresponding logic of Canadian foreign policy. Here, I review these theories as part of defining a new research program.

The left-nationalist stream of political economy developed in the 1960s and 1970s during the height of US dominance in the Cold War system. The primary goal of this "New Canadian Political Economy" (NCPE) was to theorize the perceived dependence of Canada on US capital and export markets. Building on the staples theories of Harold Innis, William Mackintosh, and Donald Creighton, the NCPE located the roots of Canada's economic dependence in the resources sector. Given the role of mining, fishing, agriculture, and forestry in the national economy, Canada was said to be a "hybrid or 'incomplete' form of capitalism, which might be called advanced resource capitalism" (Drache 1977, 16). With the "underdevelopment" of the industrial sector and the "overdevelopment" of the resources and financial sectors, the Canadian political economy was said to be characterized by low productivity, technological dependence, and a staples-based export structure (Williams 1994). In the post-war context, US firms became entrenched in the manufacturing sector, triggering outflows of dividends, royalties, and rents (Watkins 1968). As Kari Levitt (1970, 26, 142) argued, the impact of US foreign direct investment was a "silent surrender" of national unity and political autonomy – an "internal balkanization of Canada and its piecemeal absorption into the US imperial system." The transformation of Canada into a resources provider within a continental system run by US capital thus engendered a commensurate weakening of the Canadian state and economy. Through the "new mercantilism" of the "American empire," Canada became a "colonial economy ... the world's richest underdeveloped country" (ibid., 15, 25).

The starting point of the NCPE, then, was that Canada had developed a form of continental resource capitalism that was dominated by staples industries and US firms. As a result, the Canadian ruling class was a financial-commercial elite whose interests lay in selling resources to foreign investors and financing their investments (Naylor 1972). Through a network study of interlocking directorates in the post-war period, Wallace Clement (1975, 6) argued that the Canadian corporate elite functioned in an "unequal alliance" with American capital as part of a continental class structure. In a follow-up study (Clement 1977, 179), he suggested that interlocking directorates flowed "mainly from Canadian finance to US manufacturing and from US manufacturing to Canadian finance – from strength to strength." As a result, Canada failed to develop an independent coalescence of industrial and financial capital – the hallmark of capitalist class formation in other advanced economies. Instead, "the financial-industrial axis [was] continental for Canada but national within the United States" (ibid.). For this reason, "it would not be correct to view Canadian capitalists as imperialist in their own right" (ibid., 131).[12] On the contrary, the capitalist class was merely "a sales agent of Canada's resources," and the Canadian state was "neither colonial nor imperial, but controlled by American corporations as seniors and Canadian financiers as juniors – a dependent capitalist state in the American empire" (R. Laxer 1973, 7–9).

This understanding of the state informed the NCPE's understanding of Canadian foreign policy. According to Leo Panitch (1977, 100), the expansion of US capital into Canada created "the economic basis for a new colonial relationship with the American empire which, through a policy of 'quiet diplomacy,' 'special-status,' and an 'ear in Washington,' resemble[d] very closely the neo-colonial relationship offered to Canada at the turn of the century by the British in the form of an 'Imperial Cabinet'." For Jim Laxer (1973, 127), this "special status" meant that Canada played a "sub-imperial" role alongside US foreign policy – it was not an independent imperialist power, but a subordinate ally of the United States. In the view of Melissa Clark-Jones (1987, 125, 181), "the 'little brother' position of Canadian military roles on the coattails of American foreign policy [was] an important corollary of a continental resource strategy." In fact, as a "junior partner" to US foreign policy, the Canadian state served a number of "go-between roles for US technology, capital, and ideology in the international context." Where "American embassies were viewed with suspicion, Canadian embassies maintained an aura of neutrality sufficient to gain access to information that they then passed on to the Americans." For John Warnock (1970), the military policy of Canada in NATO and the North American

Aerospace Defense Command, including support for US nuclear strategy, was a logical outcome of resource dependence.

For the NCPE, then, the Canadian-US foreign policy alliance was rooted in an unbalanced structure of production, class formation, and state autonomy. The key arguments of dependency theory were that the Canadian economy was a resources depot for US imperialism, that the corporate elite was a comprador class of commodity sellers and coupon clippers, and that the Canadian state served the interests of US capital in both the national economy and the world market. For these reasons, Canada's foreign policy was guided by a logic of dependence in its national economy and class structure. It was a sub-imperial policy of economic, political, and military subordination – a policy that could be resisted only by a left-nationalist project of "independence through socialism and socialism through independence" (R. Laxer 1973, 7–9, 24).

There were many points of strength in the left-nationalist perspective. One was a conceptual focus on intersecting forms of political and economic power – on the ways in which economic transformations were absorbed and reinforced by the institutions and policies of the state. Another strength was a focus on the particular regional patterns of economic development and class and state formation in North America. As the NCPE demonstrated, the Canadian state was closely bound to the economics of US capitalism on continental and global scales. Finally, the NCPE was notable for tracing the links between the structures of class power in the national economy and the foreign policies of the state, showing how Canada's external strategy was both a reflection and a catalyst of continental forms of economic integration.

The NCPE suffered, however, from several weaknesses. On a conceptual plane, it was limited by an empiricist tendency "to mistake the appearance of social reality for its essential relations and dynamics" (Carroll 1986, 23). The fundamental concern of dependency theory was not how capitalist class relations were reproduced in the context of the Canadian social formation, but how certain empirical variables such as "multinational corporations" or "foreign ownership" obstructed an ideal path of national development. It therefore displaced an abstract understanding of the laws of motion of capitalist production for a concrete focus on empirical phenomena. The particular attention given to the resources sector, for example, demonstrated the way in which dependency theory "appropriate[d] as real the superficial categories of capitalism and proceed[ed] to erect explanations that account[ed] for some [empirical] categories ... in terms of others" (ibid.). It thus defined the resources sector by the exchange of commodities in the market, rather than by the social relations of production through which such goods are produced. In the process, it recreated the "fetishism of commodities" that Karl Marx described as the core method of bourgeois economics (McNally 1981).

Although some versions of dependency theory overcame the problem of empiricism (Laxer 1989; Panitch 1981), the bulk of scholarship remained locked in such a framework, and thus was unable to explain the trajectory of Canadian economic development. For example, by failing to understand the mining and energy sectors as advanced forms of industrial production, the NCPE offered a mistaken perception of Canada as a resource colony.[13] For this reason, it also failed to perceive the linkages between industry and finance in the Canadian corporate network (Carroll 1986).

The second limitation of dependency theory was methodological – in particular, the emphasis given to the Canadian-US relationship. It is, of course, vitally important to analyse Canadian capitalism in the context of regional forms of economic development and class formation. In doing so, the NCPE offered a much stronger theorization of the Canadian state than the realist or liberal perspectives, which were often bereft of any theory of political economy.[14] At the same time, the dependency theory viewed the Canadian-US relationship without reference to global patterns of production, trade, and investment, and thus could see only a one-sided dependence of Canada on the United States. As a result, it was unable to theorize Canada's role beyond the North American realm, except as a tool of US power. In the process, it ignored the formal autonomy of the Canadian state and the independent interests of Canadian capital beyond the North American bloc. Although Canada was indeed a Cold War ally of the United States, it was so for distinct class interests, which cannot be captured by one-sided notions of dependency. To avoid these problems, the relationship between the two countries must be placed in the context of global patterns of economic and political power (Klassen 2009; Moore and Wells 1975; Williams 1988).

These critiques of the NCPE were developed in the 1970s and 1980s by a second stream of political economy in Canada – that of Marxism. By reconstructing the Marxist theory of capitalism, this perspective sought to demonstrate that Canada was an *imperialist state*. To this end, it revealed the balanced structure of finance, manufacturing, and oil and gas production in Canada, and the repatriation of key sectors of capital from the 1970s onward. In this context, the Canadian corporate elite became organized as a national bloc of *finance capital* – as an interlocking network of industrial and financial firms from all regions of the country (Carroll 1986). On this foundation, the Canadian capitalist class began a process of *internationalization*, first into the United States through the free trade agreements and later into Europe, Asia, and many developing countries. For this reason, Canada gained an elevated status in the institutions of global governance, including the UN, the Group-of-7, and the international trade bodies. In the words of Philip Resnick (1990, 187, 200), Canada moved from a position on the "semi-periphery" to a spot on the "perimeter of the core." Canada lacked the military power to enter the top echelon of the world system, but had achieved a "core-like power economically," and thus could not be described as dependent. For William Carroll (1986, 195–7), Canada's leading corporations were involved in a "cross-penetration of capital" on a global scale and thus participated in a "collective imperialism" of advanced capitalist states.

Through such concepts and propositions, the Marxist tradition developed a new perspective on Canadian state power. Yet it largely failed to scrutinize Canadian *foreign policy*. It theorized Canada as an advanced capitalist country with a globalized bloc of finance capital, but said next to nothing about Canada's diplomatic and military role in the world economy and nation-state system. Through notions of "collective imperialism" and the "cross-penetration of capital," it laid the foundation for a new theory of Canadian statecraft abroad, yet none was forthcoming. Even now, the Marxist tradition has yet to produce an academic study of Canada's economic, diplomatic, and military role in global politics. Recent studies of the capitalist class (Brownlee 2005; Carroll and Klassen 2010; Klassen and Carroll 2011), and of Canadian direct investment abroad (Burgess 2000; Gordon 2013; Kellogg 2013) provide a basis for such a study, but the implications of this research have not been spelled out in systematic form.[15] Indeed, with the exception of one volume on Canada's role in Afghanistan (Klassen and Albo 2013), the Marxist tradition continues to cede the field of foreign policy analysis to realism, liberalism, postmodernism, and dependency theory. My goal in this study, then, is to address this gap in the literature and to link a theory of Canadian capitalism to a theory of Canadian foreign policy. To this end, I highlight the way in which capital accumulation, class formation, and state restructuring intersect in the production of a new Canadian imperialism.

The Method and Structure of the Book

From the foregoing analysis, it is now possible to outline the method and structure of this book. As noted, its temporal frame is roughly the past two decades of neoliberal globalization, with a special focus on the political economy of Canadian foreign policy in the "global war on terror." The method of presentation, however, begins at a more abstract level of analysis – that is, with a general theory of capitalism as a mode of production with inherent tendencies to internationalization, uneven development, and military conflict. In this context, international relations between states are characterized by *imperialism* – that is, by the economic exploitation and military domination of weak states by the capitalist class projects of strong states.

To build this analysis, the book is organized into four parts. Part I deals with questions of theory and method; it delineates the book's key concepts and situates them in the context of the current dynamics of international political economy. In particular, I develop a theory of *capitalist imperialism* as an international process of economic exploitation and political domination.

To this end, Chapter 1 examines the meaning of empire and imperialism in realist, liberal, and Marxist theories of international relations. For realists, imperialism is a political project of building vast colonial empires or of destabilizing the current balance of power in the nation-state system. For liberals, imperialism is the policy thrust of liberal-democratic states to impose institutions on the world market or to stabilize the crises of governance in the postcolonial world. I argue, however, that both of these theories have limited notions of empire or imperialism. The common problem is their failure to highlight the social relations of capitalism as the fundamental source of economic inequality and political conflict in the global order. Indeed, both theories are based on a formal separation of politics and economics, and thus fail to trace the social connectivity of states and markets in the capitalist world system. By obfuscating the social relations of empire, the two theories preclude analysis for ideology and fall "too close to the fire" of extant power structures (Hoffman 1977, 59).

As an alternative to realism and liberalism, I revive the Marxist theory of imperialism. By appropriating Marx's theory of capitalism, I assess three stages of the Marxist research program: the classical theories of imperialism by Lenin, Bukharin, Hilferding, and Luxemburg; the welter of post-war writings on dependency theory and informal empire; and more recent debates on a "new imperialism" of transnational finance and US global primacy. By reviewing the strengths and weaknesses of Marxist theory, I offer a conceptual framework for the book. I argue that the Empire of Capital is a transnational process of economic exploitation and political domination. The key insight is the location of these dynamics in the social relations of capitalism.

With this in mind, Part II describes the evolution of US grand strategy since the Second World War, as well as Canada's role in continental structures of economic and political power. To begin, in Chapter 2, I explain US grand strategy as one of *hegemonic liberalism* – a dual-track strategy of expanding global capitalism and US global primacy. I show how this strategy is rooted in a particular structure of accumulation, class formation, and state construction in the global political economy. I demonstrate, specifically, how this strategy was advanced in the two decades after the Cold War. By mapping the economic, diplomatic, and military means of US global power, I set a framework for understanding Canada's role in North America and the wider world system.

Chapter 3, entitled "Continental Neoliberalism and the Canadian Corporate Elite," examines this role in greater detail. First, I explain the project of continental neoliberalism as a "spatial fix" to the economic crisis of the 1970s. Second, I reveal the critical role of corporate-led policy groups in framing and directing the free trade agenda. Third, I demonstrate how continental integration paved the way for the internationalization of capital on a broader scale and for the decomposition of working-class power in the domestic political economy. Finally, I show how popular forces in North America have responded to the strategy of continental neoliberalism with a corresponding project of *contentious transnationalism* – that is, with a multiscale protest movement. For this reason, the story of deep integration in North America has to be read through the lens of a geographical materialism – one that links class and state power at multiple scales of an emerging regional bloc.

With this framework established, in Part III, I address current issues of political economy and class formation in Canada, and study the links between Canada and the world economy as well as the recomposition of the Canadian corporate elite. Chapter 4, entitled "The Internationalization of Canadian Capital," examines the structural transformation of the Canadian economy during the period of neoliberalism. I demonstrate how an *internationalization of capital* occurred in Canada, and how the Canadian economy became entwined with global circuits of production and exchange. In mapping the new articulation between

Canada and the world economy, I reveal the vested interests of Canadian corporate elites in transnational neoliberalism.

In Chapter 5, I offer the key link between the internationalization of Canadian capital and the reorganization of the state as an institution of empire. I present, in particular, a sociological mapping of the Canadian corporate elite as a *transnational bloc of capital*. Through a study of interlocking directorates among leading corporations in Canada and around the world, I reveal the globalized set of firms that increasingly dominates the Canadian corporate network. More specifically, I show the declining presence of US capital in the Canadian corporate network and the diversification of corporate ties to Europe and Asia. The importance of this research is twofold. First, it demonstrates that the Canadian capitalist class cannot be understood through old notions of dependency or compradorization; second, it indicates a recomposition of the corporate elite around globalizing interests.

Against this backdrop, in Part IV, I examine the restructuring of the state in line with new modalities of capital accumulation and class formation. I contend that the qualitative transformation of the foreign policy apparatus is a structural effect of the internationalization of capital and the coalescence of a new power bloc in the Canadian political economy.

Following the methods of Nicos Poulantzas (1978a,b), in Chapter 6, I examine three key issues: first, the mobilization of a new power bloc in the Canadian social formation – that is, a new constellation of political forces with a vested interest in continental neoliberalism and transnational warfare; second, the articulation of a new grand strategy of neoliberal market enforcement, continental securitization, cooperative specialization with US global primacy, and disciplinary militarism towards the Third World; and, finally, the building of a state apparatus – or a machinery of government – for a class-based project of *armoured neoliberalism*. The upshot of this research is that the new foreign policy agenda is not simply an outcome of government preferences or bureaucratic initiatives, but a hegemonic response to the internationalization of capital and the recomposition of the corporate power bloc.

In the final chapter, I look at the two most important projects of Canadian foreign policy since 2001: the interventions in Afghanistan and Haiti. Whereas realist and liberal theories tend to view these interventions through the optics of the "global war on terror" or the "responsibility to protect," I show how these missions were in fact linked to a class-based effort at *joining empire*. As such, they were the primary means of testing the new grand strategy of the state and power bloc, a strategy of neoliberal market enforcement, stratified multilateralism, cooperative specialization with US global primacy, and disciplinary militarism towards the Third World.

In the end, the common thread that weaves through the book is that Canadian foreign policy is an avatar for complex transformations in the political economy and class structure of Canada. *The key link between the internationalization of the Canadian economy and the reorganization of the state as a military power in the new imperialism is the recomposition of Canada's capitalist class as a globalizing bloc of corporate power.* This new social class is the agency through which economic interests are absorbed by the state and externalized in the form of diplomatic and military strategies. For these reasons, the new Canadian foreign policy cannot be viewed in isolation from the changing dynamics of production, class formation, and state restructuring on both national and global scales. When these variables are mapped in dialectical interplay, the new Canadian foreign policy appears as neither a realist search for national security nor a liberal effort at the promotion of democracy or the protection of human rights. On the contrary, the new foreign policy is the external strategy of a capitalist class whose fundamental social power derives from global modes of economic exploitation and political domination. For this reason, the concept of empire, or imperialism, best explains Canada's role in the world economy and nation-state system today.

PART I

Theory and Method

1 Understanding Empire: Theories of International Political Economy

[F]or interpretative schools seem always to originate in social antagonisms.

Charles A. Beard (1913, 4)

Introduction: The New Imperialism

Over the past decade, the language of empire and imperialism has returned with a vengeance to world politics. The attacks of 9/11, and the US response to them, made empire and imperialism, as John Hobson ([1902] 1972, xvii) once put it, the words on "everybody's lips." These terms have shaped many perceptions of US global power, and given meaning to a variety of political projects, both in favour of and against, US statecraft abroad.

The "global war on terror" led by George W. Bush sparked this new discourse of empire. The strategies and tactics of the "global war on terror" were quickly associated with new forms of imperialism, including the aggressive use of military force, the disavowal of international laws and treaties, and the building of hundreds of military bases around the world. These interrelated elements of US national security strategy were endorsed by a wide array of commentators and analysts, who promoted a new imperial undertaking: winning the "global war on terror" and remaking the world in liberal democratic and free market directions (see, for example, Coyne 2008; Foote et al. 2004; Schramm 2010).

As a leading advocate of the new American empire, conservative historian Niall Ferguson (2003) framed the matter clearly: "Capitalism and democracy," he wrote, "are not naturally occurring, but require strong institutional foundations of law and order. The proper role of an imperial America is to establish these institutions where they are lacking, if necessary ... by military force."

Ferguson was not alone in making these claims for a new American empire. Writing as a Senior Fellow at the Council on Foreign Relations, Max Boot (2003) declared that "the greatest danger is that we won't use our power for fear of the 'I' word – imperialism." In his view, the American empire should embrace the label: "We're going to be called an empire whatever we do. We might as well be a successful [one]." Writing in *Foreign Affairs*, Sebastian Mallaby (2002) concurred. "The logic of neoimperialism," he averred, "is too compelling for the Bush administration to resist." The key issue, as he put it, "is not whether the United States will seek to fill the void created by the demise of European empires but whether it will acknowledge that this is what it is doing."

Michael Ignatieff (2003), then professor of Human Rights at Harvard University, argued similarly. "The 21st century [American] imperium," he explained, "is a new invention in the annals of political science, an *empire lite*, a global hegemony whose grace notes are free markets, human rights and democracy, enforced by the most awesome military power the world has ever known." Like those cited above, Ignatieff argued that "[t]he case for empire is that it has become ... the last hope for democracy and stability alike."

American historian John Lewis Gaddis embraced the same vision of a "lite" or "liberal" empire. Interviewed by the *New York Times*, he asked: "[W]hat kind of an empire do we have? A liberal empire? A responsible empire? I have no problem whatever with the proposition that the United States has an empire. The really important question is to look at the uses to which imperial power is put. And in this regard, it seems to me on balance American imperial power [is] a remarkable force for good, for democracy, for prosperity" (quoted in Gewan 2004).

The US strategy post-9/11 has thus been understood by its proponents as a dedicated project of empire – as a forceful undertaking by the most powerful state in the world to dispense and impose a certain type of order. For the new partisans of empire, the US alone possesses the means to stabilize the world and to extend the reach of liberal democracy and capitalism.

Despite the chorus for empire, Gaddis's question remains: "[W]hat kind of empire do we have?" With few exceptions, the new imperial project has been viewed as the *policy response* of the Bush administration to the perceived threats of terrorism, failed states, and weapons of mass destruction. In this line of reasoning, US foreign policy became imperialistic as the Bush administration sought to remake US national security strategy and the wider world order. As a result, the new imperialism was largely understood as a voluntary practice of the White House and its neoconservative backers.

Unconvinced by this analysis, *The Economist* (2003) raised a pertinent question: "So has a cabal taken over the foreign policy of the most powerful country in the world? Is a tiny group of ideologues using undue power to intervene in the internal affairs of other countries, create an empire, trash international law – and damn the consequences?" "Not really," came the answer. "American foreign policy has not been captured by a tiny, ideological clique that has imposed its narrow views on others. Rather, the neo-cons are part of a broader movement endorsed by the president, and espoused, to different degrees, by almost all the principals involved, [including] some Democrats, which is why it makes sense to think that a new foreign-policy establishment may be emerging."

Although this critique had the merit of examining the foreign policy establishment, it too failed to theorize or define the concept of empire or imperialism. The question thus remains: What defines imperialism, and how does it apply to US foreign policy? Is imperialism a policy choice of government actors or institutions, or does it express a logic or process in the contemporary world system? What are the forms through which imperialism operates, and how does it impact or structure the international political economy?

To answer these questions, in this chapter I examine the meaning of imperialism in the dominant paradigms of international political economy: realism, liberalism, and Marxism. The core contention is that realism and liberalism offer theories of empire that downplay or obscure the class relations of capitalism and, therefore, fail to analyse imperialism as a "law of motion" of the capitalist world system. Indeed, by ignoring the social relations of capitalism, these theories offer reified notions of power – both economic and political – in the current global order.

As an alternative, I develop the Marxist theory of imperialism as a *transnational relation of economic exploitation and political domination*. In this perspective, the capitalist world economy is an uneven structure of value production and class exploitation. The nation-state system condenses the hierarchies of the world market, and gives rise to the political aspects of imperialism, including military conflict, the balance of power, and the struggle for primacy. The specificity of capitalist imperialism is that it brings together the economic logic of value production and the political logic of the nation-state system. By mapping the social relations of these twin dynamics, I build a framework for understanding US grand strategy and Canadian foreign policy that reveals, specifically, the link between class and state power in the Empire of Capital.

States of Empire: Realism

The realist theory of international politics offers one perspective on imperialism. First developed in the years before and after the Second World War, realism presents a structural theory of international relations and the foreign policy interests of states. In the realist paradigm, states are the primary units of analysis, and the balance of power between them dictates the patterns of world order and the struggle for national security. These ideas are central to the classical realism of the 1930s to the 1960s, and to the various strands of neorealism of the 1970s to the present.

Writing around the Second World War, Hans Morgenthau, E.H. Carr, Robert Tucker, and Nicholas Spykman synthesized the first realist theories. For these thinkers, the liberal idealism of US policy-makers before the war had left the country unprepared for the conflict that ensued, and had to be expunged from state practices and international relations theory. With this in mind, they sought to foster an empirical science of world order. In particular, they aimed to ground the study of international politics in realistic or power-based concepts as opposed to idealistic or normative ones.

In the United States, Morgenthau's *Politics Among Nations* (1948) emerged as the seminal text of classical realism. In it, Morgenthau outlined the "six fundamental principles" of international relations – that states are the primary agents of world politics; that states operate according to laws found in human nature; that states are fully autonomous institutions; that states are unitary, rational actors vis-à-vis the nation-state system; that state policies are empty of moral calculations; and that all states seek power as a fundamental interest. Morgenthau argued that, because states are locked in a permanent competition for power, they must prepare for "organized violence in the form of war" ([1948] 1985, 52). In this perspective, the *balance of power* among states is crucial as it drives competition between them and shapes their strategies and tactics.

From this standpoint, Morgenthau derived a particular theory of imperialism as "a policy that aims at the overthrow of the status quo, at a reversal of the power relations between two or more nations" (ibid., 59). Imperialism works through military conflict, economic exploitation, and cultural penetration. However, "war does not pay," and "capitalists as a group ... [are not] enthusiastic supporters of imperialistic policies." As a result, imperialism is better understood as a strategy of adjusting the extant balance of power among states by those seeking "domination" in global, continental, or localized theatres (ibid., 65, 66). It is, simply, a political effort to rebalance the nation-state system in radical ways.

These ideas were emblematic of classical realism and its theory of empire. At the time of their development, they fit exceptionally well with the politics of the Cold War. In particular, they served to castigate the Soviet Union as the one imperial state, and to justify the military build up of US global power as a necessary riposte (see, for example, Morgenthau 1964). To buttress this agenda, realism took for granted the unique separation of politics and economics under capitalism, gave primacy to the former, and thus fashioned a theory of empire that seemed to match the international actions of the Soviet Union, but not those of the United States and its allies. As such, it proved useful to US power; it rationalized the strategy of containment, and sheltered the foreign policy elite from any imbrication with capitalist class relations.

When US power was stressed by the global revolutions of the 1960s and 1970s, however, realism was forced to adapt and reinvent itself, resulting in *neorealism*. The key innovation of neorealism was to purge the normative concepts of the classical paradigm – in particular, its subjective notions of human nature and power. Beyond this, it sought to reposition US strategy in a time of global crisis by replacing "reductionist theories," which "concentrate causes at the individual or national level," in favour of a "systemic theory," which attributes causes at "the international [scale]" (Waltz 1979, 18). The international scale is constituted, according to Kenneth Waltz, by the system of nation-states. The nation-state system is one of anarchy in the sense that no sovereign power exists to secure or protect the interests of individual states. As a result, states must rely upon "self-help" as a permanent "principle of action" (ibid. 102–4). In this context, the balance of power becomes paramount to state policy and survival. As Waltz (ibid., 117) put it: "If there is any distinctively political theory of international politics, balance-of-power theory is it."

Like the classical theories, neorealism offered a "state-centric approach" – that is, a "statist image of foreign policy" (Krasner 1978, 5). The state was theorized as both "an autonomous entity" and as "the principle actor in the international system" (Gilpin 1981, 16–17). The state was assumed to be a unitary, rational actor in pursuing the "national interest," which Stephen Krasner (1978, 12) defined as "the goals that are sought by the state." To achieve these goals, the state must "overcome domestic resistance" and deploy "instruments of control ... over groups within its own society" (ibid., 11). The key objective, in this perspective, is not to seek absolute gains with other states (because anarchy inhibits cooperation), but to "prevent others from achieving advances in their relative capacities" (Grieco 1988, 498). In neorealism, then, the balance of power innervates the nation-state system and guides the national interests of individual states.

In developing these concepts and propositions, neorealism extinguished the notion of empire save as an exception to the balance-of-power principle.[1] In place of imperialism, neorealism found *hegemony*. A hegemonic state, according to Robert Gilpin (1981, 29), is so powerful that it "controls or dominates the lesser states in the system." More than this, its presence is critical to the existence and survival of a liberal world order (Kindleberger 1973). As Krasner argued: "The most common proposition [among neorealists] is that hegemonic distributions of power lead to stable, open economic regimes because it is in the interest of a hegemonic state to pursue such a policy and because the hegemon has the resources to provide the collective goods needed to make such a system function effectively" (quoted in Ashley 1984, 246).

With this conceptual turn, the political aim of neorealism was achieved. America's global power was defined as hegemonic, not imperialistic, and was said to serve collective goods to other nation-states. Economic factors were banished from the theory of international relations, and the logic of US foreign policy was deemed benevolent and defensive. At the heart of neorealism, then, was a political strategy to reassert US power at a time of system-wide crisis and transition.[2] The intimate connection between this political aim on the one hand, and the concepts of neorealism on the other, gives proof to Stanley Hoffman's (1977, 59) accusation that international relations theory is "too close to the fire" of US foreign policy.

The Limits of Neorealism

The major strength of neorealism is the attention it gives to conflict and rivalry in international politics. As a form of statism, however, neorealism elides and obscures other factors of world order. The key theoretical issue is that it takes for granted the separation of politics and economics under capitalist social relations and reifies the state as a unitary, self-directing agent (Wendt 1987).[3] For this reason, the state-centricity of neorealism is narrow, artificial, and limited. Having no explicit theory of its micro-level concept, neorealism degrades the state as a site of political action. Indeed, with no allowance for politics beyond the structure of the nation-state system and its military balance, neorealism constitutes an *ideological defence of state power in regard to international relations and domestic politics*.[4]

As a theory of knowledge and action, neorealism is also problematic, particularly by incorporating a Weberian theory of states and their instrumental rationality. In neorealism, states are rational actors whose interests and calculations give form and content to world order and national security. Missing from this model, however, is any theory of instrumental rationality as something unique to capitalism (Wood 1995, chaps. 4, 5). Neorealism takes for granted the competitive dynamic of the nation-state system without examining the social, historical, and political roots of this dynamism. As a result, it can accept or practise only methods of thinking that valorize relative gains vis-à-vis other states defined as enemies or competitors (Ashley 1984, 244).[5]

Neorealism also adopts a rigid structuralism, and thus denies "process" and "practice" as key dynamics of international political economy. The nation-state system is given as a permanent structure of world order, and is assumed to dictate the interests and policies of states, understood as "like units" (Hobson 1998, 294). This view ignores, however, the social forms through which states operate, and the differentiation of states in time and space.[6]

In this regard, the key problem of neorealism is that it lives within the political forms of capitalism; it is troubled by "taking a form of thought derived from a particular phase of history (and thus from a particular structure of social relations) and assuming it to be universally valid" (Cox 1981, 133). As a result, it imbibes the formal sovereignty and centralized violence of the capitalist state, and cannot envision or allow any logic of social or political transformation to occur. It accepts without question the forms of the state and the patterns of world order that appear with capitalism.[7]

For a paradigm focused on power, neorealism also fails to examine the multiple ways through which power is exercised in world politics. In embracing a structural-functionalist theory of the state and a technicist conception of power – that is, power as an accumulation of material technologies, especially weapons – neorealism is unable to map the relations of class, race, and gender that constitute the international political economy as an unequal and oppressive structure. In their seminal text on postcolonial theory,[8] Geeta Chowdhry and Sheila Nair (2004, 1–2) argue that "conventional [international relations theory] obscures the racialized, gendered, and class bases of power." It "naturalizes these hierarchies and thus reproduces the status quo."

Markets of Empire: Neoliberalism

The neoliberal theory of international politics offers a second interpretation of imperialism. This perspective is rooted in the liberal understanding of states and markets. In the genealogy of liberalism, two very different theories of empire or imperialism emerge. The first is an economic critique of mercantilism and colonialism as inefficient methods of state intervention in the market. The second is a political defence of empire as a means by which individual rights, private property, and democracy might be globalized. This divergence reflects a real contradiction in the capitalist mode of production. As capitalism builds a world economy, it divides the spaces of production into nation-states of equal sovereignty. It creates a world market of production and exchange, but also a system of territorial states. The result is a structural contradiction between the economic trend of integration in the world market and the political trend of fragmentation in the nation-state system. This contradiction in the global political economy spawns tensions within liberalism as a theory of empire. It encourages, on the one hand, an embrace of global capitalism as the ultimate space of human freedom, and, on the other, an acceptance of empire as a means by which to stabilize the class relations of capitalism. The contradiction of liberalism, then, is that it incorporates two different theories of empire: the first as an impediment to, and the second as a guarantor of, the world market.

The liberal theory of empire developed in radically different ways in the centuries after John Locke linked a theory of colonization to capitalist development (Arneil 1994). For example, between 1776 and 1830, liberal theories of capitalism were unequivocal in opposing empire. For Adam Smith, the "discovery of America, and that of a passage to the East Indies by the Cape of Good Hope, [were] the two greatest and most important events recorded in the history of mankind." Despite its benefits, however, colonization rested on "savage injustice" towards non-Europeans, though such misfortunes "seem to have arisen rather from accident than from anything in the nature of those events themselves" ([1776] 1994, 476, 676). More than this, colonialism distorted the economic gains that attended the market. As Smith argued, the mercantile trading system was organized in support of monopolies and their merchant owners. As a result, it led to higher prices and profits in the mercantile sector and to lower employment and wages in the broader economy. It discouraged the specialization of production, the improvement of land, and the most efficient allocation of capital (ibid., 481–8, 660–2). As an alternative, Smith offered two solutions: emancipation of the colonies or parliamentary union. Free trade, he insisted, should apply to both (Winch 1965, 14–15).

David Ricardo also opposed the colonial system, and offered a new model of free trade, arguing that, under empire, "there will be a worse distribution of the general capital and industry, and, therefore, less will be produced" ([1817] 1963, 201). His vision was that of "perfectly free commerce" between states as a means of achieving "the universal good of the whole" (ibid., 70–1).

As Donald Winch (1965, 1) points out, the liberal theory of imperialism underwent a drastic change – "from skepticism to enthusiasm" – in the 1830s. In the context of the Colonial Reform Movement of Edward Wakefield, the leading philosophers of liberalism came to embrace the British Empire. For instance, after flirting with anti-imperialism in the 1790s, Jeremy Bentham came to support Wakefield's campaign for "systematic colonialism." John Stuart Mill concurred with the economic claims of Wakefield and Bentham, and added a moral injunction: colonialism, he argued, is "a step, as far as it goes, towards universal peace and general friendly co-operation among nations" (Winch 1965, 157). In his perception, the world is divided between "civilized nations and barbarians." The former "cannot help having barbarous neighbours" and so "finds itself obliged to conquer them, or to assert so much authority over them" (Mill 1859).

Across the texts of classical liberalism, then, a diversity of perspectives on empire appeared. For Smith and Ricardo, the structures of empire blocked and distorted the markets through which human development occurred. In their view, free trade should supplant the mercantile system, which only served monopoly interests. Free trade, in their estimation, served absolute gains, and thus precluded the need for empire. By way of contrast, Locke, Bentham, and Mill saw the importance of empire for expanding capitalism and "improving" the lot of "barbarous nations." These different views of empire span the history of liberal ideology and still shape debates on the topic.

In the aftermath of 9/11, for example, prominent liberal economist Deepak Lal (2004a, 37) argued that "[e]mpires have unfairly gotten a bad name, not least in US domestic politics. This is particularly unfortunate, as the world needs an American pax to provide both global peace and prosperity." With this in mind, Lal emphasizes three benefits of imperialism. First, it provides a "transnational legal system created for the protection of property rights, particularly those of foreigners." Second, it has the power to "quell ethnic conflicts" that are inimical to trade and investment. And third, it fosters a "liberal international economic order" and thus invites "mutual gains from trade" (ibid., 5, 10, 15; 2004b, 205).

The liberal theory of *comparative cost advantage* lies at the core of such arguments (see Hanieh 2006). The basic proposition is that every nation stands to gain from trade to the extent that it exports commodities that can be produced comparatively more efficiently at home, in exchange for commodities that can be produced comparatively more efficiently abroad. In this framework, it is comparative, not absolute, costs of production that should determine output and exchange. As a corollary, the model asserts that the terms of trade between nations will adjust automatically to balance the value of imports and exports, with no departure from full employment. In the process, free trade will equalize each nation's productive capacities.

In the neoclassical version of this theory – often described as the Heckscher-Ohlin model (Ohlin 1933) – free trade also encourages the specialization of production on the assumption that full employment is maintained before and after trade liberalization. To the extent that countries specialize in exporting goods in which they hold a comparative *factor* advantage in terms of capital, land, or labour, the benefits of trade will be propitious to all parties involved. Using a quantity theory of money, this theory avers that trade imbalances between countries will be cancelled out by corresponding movements of money or gold, which effect the relative prices of commodities in ways that point towards specialization and equilibrium. To make these claims, the modern theory of comparative advantage makes several further assumptions, including full capacity, full employment, perfect information, perfect competition, and equal productive functions. It concludes that countries with a comparative advantage in labour-intensive goods should specialize in exporting such items, and countries with a comparative advantage in capital-intensive goods should specialize in exporting those items.

Armed with this model of international trade, Lal (2004b, 210) builds his case for a new American empire as "the Pax necessary for globalization." In doing so, he develops a *market-based theory of empire*, endorsing the latter to the extent that it bolsters the former. In neoliberal theory, this economic case for empire is supplemented by a political case – namely, that imperial states are necessary for protecting private property, individual rights, and democratic state forms.

This perspective gained currency in the wake of the Cold War and the perceived "end of history" (Fukuyama 1992), and is premised on two key arguments. First, the world is divided into liberal and non-liberal states, with the former assumed to be democratic and peaceful and the latter assumed to be non-democratic and violent. Liberal states, in this view, are peaceful by virtue of being democracies that protect and promote individual rights. Such states, according to Michael Doyle (1986, 1162–3), "are capable of achieving peace among themselves because they exercise democratic caution and are capable of appreciating the international rights of foreign republics." These republics, however, "remain in a state of war with non republics. Liberal republics see themselves as threatened by aggression from non republics that are not constrained by representation."[9] For this reason, liberal states must be ready "to protect and promote – sometimes forcibly – democracy, private property, and the rights of individuals overseas against non republics, which, because they do not authentically represent the rights of individuals, have *no rights to noninterference*." The result is a "cosmopolitan" or "human rights" imperialism in which individual rights take precedence over state sovereignty (Doyle 1999; Held and McGrew 2003; Isaac 2002). In practice, advocates of this theory urge the liberal states of the West to intervene in the "rogue" or "failed" states of the non-liberal zone (Chesterman, Ignatieff, and Thakur 2005; Cooper 2002; Thürer 1999). In fact, the recent interventions in Serbia, Afghanistan, Iraq, Haiti, and Libya have been justified in such terms, giving power to neoliberal theory.

The Limits of Neoliberalism

The strength of neoliberal theory is the attention it gives to the economics of the world market and to the politics of the state and the state system. Neoliberalism offers a flawed theory of empire, however, as it fails to grasp the class relations of capitalism. The root cause of this failure is the theory of markets and states in the neoliberal model.

Regarding international trade, three problems are evident. First, the concepts and propositions of comparative cost theory are disconnected from real world trade. For one thing, the main agents of international exchange are profit-seeking corporations, not nations engaged in barter (Shaikh 2007, 52). For another, the theory fails to account for *competitive advantages* such as increasing returns to scale, information asymmetries, and first-mover advantages, among others (Porter 1990). The underlying problem is that, by using a hypothetical deductive method of abstraction, comparative cost theory ignores the test of empirical verification (Fine and Milonakis 2008).

Second, and as a consequence, the model fails to explain the history of capitalist development. As economic historian Ha-Joon Chang (2007) has noted, free trade has rarely, if ever, been a mechanism for capitalist "take off." In fact, virtually all of today's advanced capitalist countries relied upon interventionist measures such as tariffs and subsidies to protect and promote domestic industries, especially at their "infant" stage. Furthermore, such interventions were relaxed only after relative real capacities were established for competitive trade relations. For these reasons, the neoliberal insistence on free trade and *laissez-faire* industrial policies is tantamount to "kicking away the ladder" for Third World development (Chang 2002).

Third, and most important, the neoliberal model fails to account for real wage and productivity differentials as bases for *absolute cost advantages* in world exchange. Put in this frame of reference (Shaikh 1979/80, 2005, 2007; Milberg 1994), free trade will benefit countries to the extent that their domestic corporations obtain lower unit costs of production relative to those of competitors in other countries. As a result, countries with lower real costs of production will register trade surpluses, while countries with higher real costs of production will register trade deficits. In this context, the terms of trade will not adjust towards balance unless the relative real costs of production do. The more likely scenario is that countries with a trade surplus will be able to lower interest rates, expand domestic investment, and export profit-seeking capital in direct or portfolio forms – and that the opposite will occur in countries with a trade deficit. In the process, a division of labour will emerge between countries with advanced technologies and high wages, and countries with backward technologies and low wages. In such conditions, capital flows will cover, but not eliminate, trade imbalances, and might also crowd out production, increase unemployment, and spark financial crises (Jenkins 1987; Shaikh 1979/80, 2007; Singh 2007). By ignoring these tendencies of real competition, the comparative cost model obfuscates the economic hierarchies of the current world order (Chang 2007; Shaikh 2005, 2007).

Neoliberalism does the same as a political theory of empire. It is premised, after all, on a glaring contradiction between the model of the market as a realm of universal freedom and equality, and the reality of global capitalism as a system of class exploitation and uneven development.[10] To escape this contradiction, neoliberalism turns to empire – that is, to the unequal use of economic, political, and military power to salvage the interests of capital. It posits a moral value to the new imperialism, and defines war and empire as *policy choices* of liberal states rather than as systematic features of capitalism. In the process, it ignores or excuses the repeated violations of liberal norms and laws by western military forces in "failed" or "rogue" states – for example, the torture of prisoners, killing of civilians, and bombing of public infrastructure.[11]

The neoliberal case for empire, then, substitutes moral discourse for critical insight. In doing so, it incorporates a number of contradictions. First, it defends capitalism as a system of equal market exchanges, yet calls for unequal state powers to manage and secure this system. Second, it calls for military action in defence of human rights and democracy, but ignores the violation of these principles in waging war and imposing markets. For these reasons, neoliberalism does not provide a comprehensive theory of world order, but a functional paradigm for *capitalist class interests* and their articulation with empire.

Classes of Empire: Marxism

In the social sciences, Marxism offers the third interpretation of imperialism. The key insight of this perspective is that a focus on *social relations* can overcome the state/market binary in realist and liberal theories. Indeed, in Marxism, the social relations of capitalism are the source of class exploitation, uneven development, and inter-state conflict in the global political economy.

Marx's Critique of Capitalism

To understand the Marxist view of imperialism, it is necessary to grasp the critical theory of capitalism that Karl Marx developed. This theory is based on a dialectical method of abstraction and on a materialist ontology of history. In particular, Marx believed that human beings build their economic, political, and cultural worlds through productive social relations in concrete time and space, or through what he called *modes of production*. He developed this approach to social science most rigorously in his most important book, *Capital*.

Capital begins not with predetermined concepts, but with the "elementary form" of appearance of the capitalist mode of production – that is, with the commodity (Marx [1867] 1990, 125). Like the classical political economists, Marx distinguishes between the use value and the exchange value of a commodity. The former is determined by the materiality of the use value in question, while the latter is determined by the amount of labour that goes into producing it. What is measured in exchange, though, is not the quantity of concrete labour that goes into producing a commodity, but the quantity of abstract labour that can be indexed or compared to the concrete labour embodied in other use values. The exchange of commodities is therefore regulated by the socially necessary or average labour required to fashion any particular good or service, what Marx calls "the law of value."

As Marx demonstrates, the role of money can be traced to the relations between use value and exchange value, and between concrete labour and abstract labour. As the universal measure of value, money is the means by which concrete labours are rendered abstract and hence socially equivalent to one another. In this context, money functions as a means of payment in exchange and as a measure of socially necessary labour time. As a material incarnation of abstract labour, money can be accumulated as an end in itself or as a social form of power. For this reason, the circulation of capital can be depicted in the formula, $M - C - M'$, where money, M, is exchanged for commodity, C, for the purpose of accumulating more money, M'.

For Marx, the expansion of value under capitalism occurs not through exchange, but through production, P – the process by which concrete labour power, LP, is applied to means of production, MP, to manufacture new commodities, C'. As a result, the circuit of capital can be expanded as follows:

$$M - C \; (MP + LP) \ldots P \ldots C' - M' \ldots$$

Through the circuit of capital, Marx reveals the spring of surplus value: the application of concrete labour time in production. In the sphere of production, the "living" labour of workers is combined with the "dead" labour of means of production to generate new commodities that embody higher values. If the new value produced exceeds the value of labour power (that is, of wages), a profit will be earned if buyers are found for the new commodities. The critical insight is that the accumulation of capital takes place through the *exploitation of labour power* in production.[12] As a result, capital is not a "thing" like money or commodities, but a *social relation*. It is the relation between the buyers and sellers of labour power, or between the capitalist class, which owns the means of production, and the working class, which has nothing to sell but its capacity to work for wages.[13]

From his theory of value, Marx explains other tendencies of capitalism. First, he demonstrates how the whip of competition drives firms to invest in labour-saving technologies, thus increasing the productivity of labour and cheapening the value of goods for which workers must be paid wages to consume. In technical terms, Marx shows that surplus value can be expanded "relatively" through investments in means of production that reduce the quantity of abstract labour in commodities, and "absolutely" by extending the length of the working day so that more time is dedicated to unpaid labour for profit. As a result, the capitalist labour process is always beset by class struggles over wages and working conditions, and over the use of technology to displace and deskill workers.[14]

The whip of competition also shapes the forms through which capital is accumulated. Although the reinvestment of surplus value allows capital to "concentrate" in new productive capacities, the welding together of masses of capital through joint-stock companies or violent annexations allows for the "centralization" of capital in fewer and fewer hands. The drive for surplus value thus leads to expanded forms of production, to monopolistic forms of distribution, and to polarized class relations.

As Marx points out, the *financialization* of capital is related to these built-in tendencies of production. In particular, the financial system is necessary to overcome limits or barriers to accumulation. It combines and lends money so that firms can invest in new machines and equipment, workers can purchase large-scale consumer items, states can build costly infrastructure projects, and companies can purchase one another. In these ways, the financial sector becomes the "general manager of money capital" (Marx [1894] 1993, 528).

At the same time, the financial sector is unable to contain the crises of capitalism. As Marx demonstrates, the same dynamics that enable the accumulation of capital also undermine the long-term health of the system. The key dynamic here is the *rate of profit* – the ratio of profit to capital invested in a given cycle of accumulation.[15] To win greater market share, capitalists invest in ever-larger masses of constant capital (machines, plants, tools, and so on) vis-à-vis variable capital (that is, labour power). As the technical composition of capital increases, the production of value is truncated and the rate of profit sinks, producing crisis.

According to Marx, the *internationalization of capital* is one countertendency to a falling rate of profit, and one further expression of the self-expansion of value. As Marx ([1939] 1973, 415) put it, capital is motivated by a "general tendency to drive beyond every barrier to production," including borders of nation-states. Indeed, "[i]f capital is sent abroad, this is not because it absolutely could not be employed at home. It is rather because it can be employed abroad at a higher rate of profit" (Marx [1894] 1993, 364–5). What Marx called the "world market" is the end result of this tendency to expand the space of production. For this reason, "the tendency to create the world market is directly given in the concept of capital itself" (Marx [1939] 1973, 408).

The world market, however, does not resolve, but compounds the crisis tendencies of capitalism. Indeed, while the internationalization of capital might increase the average rate of profit, it also "transfers the contradictions [of capitalism] to a wider sphere and gives them greater latitude" (Marx [1885] 1992, 544). "The world market crises," then, "have to be understood as the real condensation and violent solution of all contradictions of bourgeois economy" (Marx, quoted in Winternitz 1949).

The internationalization of capital, therefore, has a dual character immanent in it. On the one hand, it is the pioneer of development, the revolutionary force that "compels all nations, on pain of extinction, to adopt the bourgeois mode of production" (Marx and Engels [1848] 1985, 84). On the other hand, capitalism expands across the world economy through "extirpation, enslavement, and entombment," and in the process, heralds "the form of transition towards a new mode of production" – namely, communism (Marx [1894] 1993, 572).[16] For Marx, it is through the political agency of the proletariat – the majority class within capitalism – that communism will emerge. In the process, the private ownership of production will be replaced by a collectivized system of economic relations.

In sum, Marx reveals how the social relations of production generate the internal laws of capitalism. Though Marx never modelled the world economy, and hardly theorized the global role of the state,[17] his method inspired the Marxist theories of imperialism of the twentieth and early twenty-first centuries. Developed in three key stages, these theories focus on the Great Power conflicts of classical imperialism, on the informal empire of post-war reconstruction, and on the "new imperialism" of global finance and US primacy in the post–Cold War period.

Marxist Theories of Imperialism

The immediate followers of Marx used the term *imperialism* to describe the phase of capitalism that existed between 1870 and 1919. During this period, international relations were based upon competitive rivalries between nation-states and national blocs of capital. This was the period in which monopoly firms in Europe, Japan, and the United States engaged in a fierce struggle for world markets – a struggle that culminated in new patterns of colonialism and the First World War (Anievas 2012; Hobsbawm 1987; Kennedy 1989).

In this context, Vladimir Lenin, Nikolai Bukharin, Rudolf Hilferding, and Rosa Luxemburg developed their seminal theories of imperialism, which were based on four propositions. First, imperialism was the outcome of monopoly capitalism – of the concentration and centralization of capital in the advanced economies in the late 1800s. Second, the merger of industrial and banking capital was the most important feature of monopoly capitalism, creating what Hilferding ([1910] 1981, 21) called *finance capital*, the economic agent of imperialism. Third, in the context of monopoly, finance capital was forced to look abroad for investment outlets (Lenin [1917] 1982, 60). Finally, the export of capital drove the colonial process of classical imperialism, especially for investing surplus profits and advancing capitalism globally (Lenin [1917] 1982; Luxemburg [1914] 2003).

For these reasons, the classical theorists argued that unique laws of motion define the world order of capitalism. As Bukharin (1917, 62) recognized, tendencies of *internationalization* and *nationalization* occur simultaneously in the capitalist world economy. On the one hand, the global expansion of capital leads to an "interdependence of countries" (ibid., 39). On the other hand, finance capital creates a fusion of economic and political power in the form of "state capitalist trusts," and thereby generates a nationalization of capital (ibid., 52–62). In this context, economic rivalries between national blocs of capital are translated into political rivalries between states. As Bukharin argued, the capitalist world system is a battleground on which "state capitalist trusts" compete and wage war. For this reason, economic rivalries are "only partial sorties, they are only a sort of testing the ground." In time, they must be "solved by the interrelation of 'real force,' *i.e.*, by the force of arms" (ibid., 87).

Through these concepts and propositions, the classical theorists were able to explain the political forms of competition in the world market and the economic logic of inter-state conflict and warfare (Anievas 2012; Fischer 1967; Kennedy 1989). They also erred, however, in several ways. To begin, Lenin's argument that colonies were needed as spaces for investment is contradicted by his own data, which show that the bulk of foreign direct investment occurred among the advanced capitalist countries. Similarly, Bukharin's theory of "state capitalist trusts" was relevant only to a few countries and ignored the structural tendency for a separation of class and state power under capitalism (Brewer 1990, 109–35).

Probably the weakest part of their theories, though, was the argument that colonialism is necessary for capitalist development. The expansion of finance capital at the time through territorial gains gave Lenin ([1917] 1982, 84) a strong foundation for saying that imperialism is "capitalism at that stage of development at which ... the division of all territories of the globe among the biggest capitalist powers has been completed." But important changes in the world economy after the Second World War were to render this theory of imperialism increasingly anachronistic.

Indeed, thirty years of war, depression, and revolution destroyed the capacity of European states to dominate world politics. After 1945, the European empires were gradually dismantled, and a more integrated world economy took shape under US direction (see Chapter 2). Out of this context emerged a new form of imperialism, an *informal empire* that defied the classical theories. As a result, new debates on the post-war imperium moved to the fore of Marxist theory.

For example, across the Third World, radical activists and academics developed a theory of *dependence* to explain the structural inequalities of the capitalist world system and to guide alternative policies of economic, political, and social development (Nkrumah 1965; Prashad 2007). As a founder of this theory, Raúl Prebisch (1950, 1959) argued that global capitalism was a division of labour between high-tech manu-facturing nations at the centre and low-tech staples-producing nations at the periphery. Given the gap in labour productivity between the two zones, the periphery was bound to experience declining terms of trade, balance-of-payments crises, increasing debt burdens, high lev-els of foreign ownership, and declining real wages. The result was a dependent structure of economic relations between the industrialized and the non-industrialized worlds. As an alternative, Prebisch argued, the periphery must break its ties with the world market and practise import-substitution industrialization. In this respect, dependency the-ory was based less on Marxism than on a liberal theory of supply-side gaps in technology (Brenner 1977; Weeks 1981).[18]

With this in mind, US-based scholars sought to reposition depen-dency theory in a neo-Marxist framework.[19] In their models of the "world system," global capital exploits the resources and labour supplies of the periphery, value is transferred to the core through unequal exchange, ruling classes of the periphery are complicit in the disaccumulation of capital, and genuine development is possible only through delinking from the world economy. At the time, these theories seemed to explain the patterned hierarchies of the capitalist world system, but they tended to ignore the diversity of states in the global order, the manifold paths of development in the periphery, the unique class struggles of individual countries, and the problematic nationalism of disengaged autarky (Brenner 1977; Laclau 1971; Leys 1977). As such, they were too simplistic as theories of international political economy.

During the same period, Marxists also addressed the new modes of informal empire that the United States was pioneering. In place of the formal empires of classical imperialism, the United States advanced what Harry Magdoff (1969, 2003) called "imperialism without colonies." Under the leadership of Washington, this new structure of empire was premised on the economic power of US capi-tal. Through means of foreign direct investment, US capital estab-lished itself as the dominant class faction in Europe and, to a lesser extent, in Asia. In the process, inter-imperialist rivalries were tran-scended, and US leadership was established at the core of global capitalism (Poulantzas 1978a).

This particular stage of empire, however, was short lived. As the post-war boom came to an end in the late 1960s, new contradictions emerged in the global political economy. On the economic front, the reconstruction of western Europe and Japan undercut US competitiveness in world markets and, between 1968 and 1973, sparked declining rates of profit in the Group-of-7 industrialized states (Brenner 1998, 2006a). At the same time, a number of political factors, including working-class struggles in core states and nationalist movements in peripheral ones, amplified the economic crisis (Armstrong, Glyn, and Harrison 1991). A combination of factors, then, undermined the structures of post-war capitalism. In response, states experimented with two key forms of crisis resolution.

First, a spatial fix was sought through the *internationalization of capital* (Harvey 1990; Jenkins 1987; Palloix 1977). New forms of international trade and investment allowed capital to overcome national systems of production and distribution. Multinational corporations emerged as the dominant actors of the world economy, and oversaw the concentration of financial resources during this period. The end result was an integrated world economy – a new stage of internationalization in the circuits of capital.

Second, *states* themselves were transformed in order to manage the globalization process (Helleiner 1995; Panitch 1994). The decentralization of economic activity required the centralized support of states – of the American state, in particular. Richard Nixon's ending of the dollar standard and the subsequent push by the United States for capital account liberalization across the core cleared important obstacles to the globalization process (Panitch and Gindin 2005a). The "internationalization of the state" (Cox 1987) also occurred through a new constitutionalism of global governance, including new trade and investment agreements. In the Third World, states were disciplined through the structural adjustment policies of the World Bank and the International Monetary Fund, both of which advanced a free market program. The drive towards globalization was predicated, therefore, on the systematic use of state power.

In this context, Marxists engaged in a third stage of research on imperialism. Since the 1990s, four key theories of the "new imperialism" have been produced. The first stresses the role of US state power in making global capitalism (Gowan 1999; Panitch and Gindin 2005a,b). In this model, the new imperialism is an *American empire*. Under US political leadership, the world economy is constituted by liberalized flows of trade and investment and by the synergy of Wall Street and the US Federal Reserve. Through the "Dollar-Wall Street Regime," US capital dominates global finance, and the US state manages the global commons through an empire of bases and regional command structures. Although this model highlights the critical role of US power in making global capitalism, it fails to see imperialism as a general tendency of capitalism, involving other states and class factions in transnational modes of economic exploitation and political domination.

The second model telescopes the new competition in the world economy and the likelihood of inter-imperialist warfare (Arrighi 2005; Callinicos 2001, 2002; Harvey 2003). In this framework, the key contradiction of the world system is between the economic logic of capital accumulation and the political logic of the nation-state system. Although the accumulation of capital is now global, surplus value is realized at different rates in competing nation-states. As a result, the world economy turns on national patterns of competition and sparks geopolitical conflicts. In making these arguments, writers in this tradition offer an updated version of the classical theory, but fail to grasp the new features of global capitalism – particularly the new modes of interdependence in the world economy and the primary power of Washington.

If the second theory highlights competition as the nub of world order, a third emphasizes cooperation in global affairs (Bromley 2006). Building on Karl Kautsky's ([1914] 1970) notion of "ultra-imperialism," this model focuses on the economic, political, and military collaboration of core states, especially with respect to maintaining world trade and policing the Third World. In this stream of analysis, the key contradiction of global capitalism is between the dominant core and the dominated periphery. Although such a division persists, the neo-Kautskyian model fails to account for rivalries among the advanced capitalist states and for the leading role of Washington globally. It also ignores the variety of states in the periphery, and the more nuanced hierarchy of power in today's world system.

The final perspective places even greater stress on international cooperation (Gill 2003; Hardt and Negri 2000; Robinson 2004). In this stream of Marxism, new forms of economic integration have established a global system of capitalism in which transnational classes and transnational state apparatuses are emerging. In the process, the economic and political rivalries of classical imperialism are giving way to transnational modes of class and state power. Although this model highlights the dramatic increase of cross-border trade and investment during the period of neoliberalism, it is based on a fetishism of exchange, and thus ignores the differential forms of exploitation across spaces of global capitalism. For this reason, it is unable to capture the ongoing conflicts of space and territory in the world system today.

In sum, over the past decade, the Marxist tradition has produced four models of the new imperialism. At best, these theories offer an interactive, and multiscale, model of production, exploitation, and class and state formation in the world market and geopolitical system. They often focus, however, on only one tendency of global capitalism, and ignore the multiple, and contradictory, tendencies at work.

What framework, then, is applicable to mapping Canada's global role?

The Empire of Capital: A Framework for Analysis

To reposition the theory of imperialism, it helps to focus on the following points. First, the spring of empire must be located in the spatial dynamics of capitalism. As Marx revealed, the capitalist mode of production is driven by an inner tendency to "tear down every spatial barrier to intercourse, i.e. to exchange, and [to] conquer the whole earth for its market" (Marx [1939] 1973, 539). As a result, it exhibits an infinite process of spatial expansion, what I term the *internationalization of capital*.

The second point is that the internationalization of capital occurs in contradictory ways. On the one hand, it creates a world economy under the law of value and common class relations – it generates a global system of production and complex forms of economic interdependence. On the other hand, the world market is based on absolute cost competition, and thus *transfers value* to the most efficient units of capital in the most competitive zones of production. In this context, movements of money capital tend to compound trade imbalances and to concentrate financial resources in leading productive spaces (Shaikh 1979/80). For these reasons, the capitalist world economy is governed by a law of *combined and uneven development* (Desai 2013; Rosenberg 1996; Trotsky [1932] 1961).

The Marxist theory of imperialism is based on this law. The Empire of Capital is not premised on territorial conquest, and cannot be reduced to the policy preference of a state or government actor. It is, rather, the unique world order that springs immanently from the laws of motion of the capitalist system – especially the tendencies to internationalization and combined and uneven development. It is the process "whereby an international division of labour is created through the extension of the conditions of capitalist accumulation on a world scale" (Gulalp 1986, 139, quoted in Kiely 2010, 86). Although capitalism engenders an integrated world economy, it develops unevenly across spaces of production, and "does not necessarily exclude the possibility of ... causing underdevelopment" (ibid.). The capitalist form of imperialism, then, is bound up with the uneven and unequal ways in which the world economy develops in time and space.

The Marxist theory of the state – and of the nation-state system – must be viewed in relation to these abstract tendencies of the capitalist world market. The social relations of capitalism give rise to a new state structure or political form of class rule. In particular, the "privatization" of exploitation under the capitalist mode of production creates a new possibility for "economics" and "politics" to be separated and for a "relatively autonomous" state to emerge (Wood 1995). However, although the capitalist state is formally independent of the exploitation process, it is structurally dependent on both the accumulation of capital and the exploitation of labour.[20] For this reason, the state tends to manage and regulate the accumulation process on capital's terms.

It follows that the international state system is inextricable from the class relations of capitalism. In Marxism, the nation-state system is reproduced as a structure through the uneven development of the capitalist world economy. In fact, the quantitative expansion of the nation-state system coincides with the qualitative expansion of capitalist competition and the requisite need to secure private property, organize production, and manage exploitation on a global scale (Wood 2005). As a result, the nation-state system has been incorporated into, or subsumed by, the laws of motion of capitalism; it mediates the competition between national blocs of capital and reproduces capitalist class relations on a system-wide level (Pozo-Martin 2007).

The international system of geopolitics must be viewed in this context. The internationalization of capital spawns multiple tendencies in the nation-state system. On the one hand, it generates new modes of interdependence between states and a geopolitical interest in cooperation and alignment. In this context, a "collective imperialism" of the advanced capitalist countries can emerge to manage the world economy and the hierarchy of states. In the process, these states might engage in joint methods of disciplinary militarism towards the periphery, especially to the end of securing private property and punishing states or political movements that trouble global capitalism (Wood 2005). On the other hand, the very process of internationalization increases competition between capitals of different nation-states, and thus generates an opposite tendency towards Great Power rivalry. Inter-imperialist warfare is the ultimate end of this tendency, and expresses the latent contradiction between the internationalization of capital and the national system of states (Callinicos 2009; Harvey 2003). The fundamental point is that the capitalist mode of production creates twin dynamics of rivalry and interdependence in the nation-state system (Albo 2004).

The predominance of any one tendency, however, depends upon the *concrete forms of class and state formation in real time and space*. In a unipolar world, the internationalization of capital is concentrated within the borders of a single nation-state, which can manage the world economy as a political and military hegemon. In this kind of system, secondary states will be dependent on the economic, political, and military resources of the hegemon, and forced to cooperate with it in specialized ways or to balance against it through tariff wars, alliance formations, and military conflicts. The likelihood of either strategy will be determined, however, by the concrete patterns of accumulation and class formation within and between the states in question. The same logic applies to a multipolar system in which the world economy is partitioned into regional concentrations of economic, political, and military power. Regional blocs might compete through the internationalization of capital, but cooperate in the regulation of the world market if the class power of each bloc is not so great as to warrant a struggle for hegemony. Again, the basic logic will be determined by the concrete spatialization of value flows, class structures, and state formations in real time.

The final point is that, in such a system of international political economy, *social conflict and anti-imperialist resistance* will be integral vectors of world politics. The reason for this is that the Empire of Capital is premised on social relations of economic exploitation and political domination. In this context, a range of contentious politics will be generated: workers will contest their exploitation in global production chains; peasants and indigenous people will fight displacement from their land; poor nations will contest the political, economic, and military encroachments of rich ones; and so on. The key point is that the social relations of global capitalism form a crucible for anti-imperialist struggles of workers, oppressed nations, and other subaltern agents (Kiely 2010; McNally 2006; Panitch and Leys 2000; Young 2009).

The Marxist theory of imperialism thus can be summarized in three hypotheses. First, the world market is constituted by a constantly shifting hierarchy of productive spaces and class relations. Second, geopolitical strategies will tend to reflect concrete spatializations of value flows, state structures, and capitalist class interests within and between states. Third, a range of resistance is bound to contest the social relations of political domination and economic exploitation in the capitalist world system.

With this in mind, the research program of Marxism should be to *track or map the value flows, class structures, and state strategies that intersect in the reproduction of combined and uneven development – and that catalyse contentious resistance to the Empire of Capital.* For the case of present-day Canada, this means examining the new foreign policy agenda as (1) a political expression of the internationalization of capital; and (2) the reorganization of the state as an institutionalization of capitalist class relations at national, continental, and international scales.

To set the context for this analysis, Chapter 2 maps the political economy of US grand strategy.

PART II

American Power and Continental Integration

2 Hegemonic Liberalism: The Political Economy of US Primacy

Introduction: The Unipolar Moment

Since the end of the Cold War, the United States has led the international political economy as an uncontested superpower. The demise of the Soviet Union and the collapse of various forms of Third World nationalism allowed the United States to operate as a de facto hegemon. For the Canadian state, the imperative to work closely with the economic, political, and military structures of US global power thus became even stronger.

In this context, it became common to speak of a "unipolar moment" in world politics. This term was coined by American journalist Charles Krauthammer (1990/91, 23), who argued that "[t]he most striking feature of the post-Cold War world is its unipolarity." For Krauthammer, the United States alone possessed the means to secure markets and democracy globally, and therefore was right to pursue a strategy of global preeminence.

Throughout the 1990s, analysts from across the spectrum of international relations theory agreed with this basic assessment of world order and US power. For commentators in both realist and liberal circles (Ikenberry 2006; Wohlforth 1999), the world order of the 1990s was based on US dominance of political, economic, and military affairs. As the primary agent of the international political economy, the United States was responsible for expanding markets, promoting democracy, and maintaining security. To these goals, it was argued, a strategy of primacy was necessary and justified (Brzezinski 1997; Huntington 1993; Kagan 2014).

In the United States, several critiques have been levelled at this strategy. For critics such as Christopher Layne (2006b) and John Mearsheimer (2014), two realities act against the primacy strategy: the counterbalancing of rival states, and the wars of the past two decades. If both these factors erode US dominance, the unipolar moment is bound to wane. As G. John Ikenberry (2002, 58) has warned, "the neoimperial grand strategy poses a wider problem for the maintenance of American unipolar power. It steps into the old trap of imperial states: self-encirclement." More than this, as Nuno Monteiro (2011/12, 12) notes, it "creates significant conflict-producing mechanisms that are likely to involve the unipole itself" in self-defeating measures, including endless wars and failed occupations, as occurred in Afghanistan and Iraq.

In this chapter, I argue that, despite the veracity of such critiques, they fall short of explaining US global primacy and the grand strategy motivating it. In particular, they fail to explain the structural dynamics of US foreign policy. By remaining within the framework of realism and liberalism, these critiques can grasp the primacy strategy only as a mistaken policy choice of the American state and its foreign policy establishment. Following the method of Marxism, I map an alternative thesis – namely, that US global primacy is an expression of the power of US capitalism. In particular, it is an outcome of the patterns of accumulation, class formation, and state construction that attend the internationalization of US capital. As such, it is a strategy that accords with the class interests of US policy-makers and the power bloc in which they operate.

With this in mind, I will demonstrate that, since the Second World War, the United States has pursued a policy of *hegemonic liberalism* – a strategy to expand capitalism on a global scale and to embed US primacy in worldwide structures of economic, political, and military power. The United States has established a hub-and-spokes system of international security in which US primacy is globally paramount. In the process, secondary powers have been incorporated into US-led structures of multilateral governance, and have largely aligned their economic, diplomatic, and military strategies accordingly. In this context, a US-led *Empire of Capital* has supplanted the classical system of imperialism (Wood 2005).

States of the periphery, however, have experienced the Empire of Capital in different ways. It has generated new forms of class inequality and uneven development, and thus has called forth new modalities of *anticapitalist and anti-imperialist resistance*. In response, the United

States and its subdominant allies have embraced a policy of *disciplinary militarism* – of coercively repressing any social or political movements that challenge the rights of capital. The American empire, therefore, has been associated with escalating forms of military violence, especially in the periphery. In the process, it has followed the logic of hegemonic liberalism.

More recently, though, new dynamics have tested US grand strategy. First, the globalization of capital has generated new centres of production, finance, and trade in the world economy, and thus eroded US dominance in this register of empire. The rise of China, in particular, is a sign of how the internationalization of capital has created new sites of accumulation, class formation, and state power in the capitalist world system.

Second, it is evident that US militarism has reached an apogee in terms of dictating outcomes and securing dominance for the US state in world politics. Although the US military "commands the commons" of the sea, sky, and space (Posen 2003), the limits of US militarism are increasingly apparent. The failed occupations of Iraq and Afghanistan, for example, have created a context in which other states and non-state actors have begun to challenge US pre-eminence in the Middle East, Central Asia, eastern Europe, and beyond. As a result, it is unclear if the US strategy of disciplinary militarism will sustain other measures of US global primacy. In this context, the further expansion of US militarism might trigger the conflicts and rivalries of classical imperialism.

To develop these arguments, I have organized this chapter into four sections. The first examines the policy of "multinational liberalism" that US elites developed during the Second World War. The second analyses the implementation of US grand strategy in the post-war period. The third looks at the global crisis of the 1970s and at the reconstitution of US primacy through the political economy of neoliberalism. In the final section, I consider the strategies and tactics of US foreign policy in the post–Cold War period. By examining these issues, I offer a framework for mapping Canada's role in the US-led structure of empire. The core argument is that the US strategy of primacy has been rooted in dynamics of production, accumulation, and class and state formation in the capitalist world system. The key theoretical point is that the internationalization of capital has buttressed US foreign policy in pre-eminent ways, at least until recently.[1] As a result, the "unipolar moment" has been an effect of US imperialism and its dominant class relations. For a secondary state such as Canada, the global power of the American empire has shaped the nature of its economic, political, and military strategy.

Planning Empire: The Power Bloc and Hegemonic Liberalism

From the very beginning of the Second World War, the political and economic leaders of the United States were co-involved in planning the post-war order. On 1 September 1939, the day that Germany invaded Poland, US President Franklin Delano Roosevelt announced that a special session of Congress would be called to amend the Neutrality Act to allow arms shipments to the United Kingdom and France. In the process, "[he] decided to support the Allied war effort from the very onset" (Hearden 2002, 13). Eleven days later, the Council on Foreign Relations struck key planning groups to assist the State Department. Within the State Department itself, Secretary Cordell Hull established several planning bodies on peace, reconstruction, and trade (Aaronson 1991; Shoup and Minter 2004). These planning boards were constituted by leading figures of US business and politics, and formed a new power bloc that was dedicated to "multinational liberalism." In particular, it brought together the "Wilsonian liberals" of the State Department and the leading agents of "capital-intensive industries, investment banks, and internationally oriented commercial banks" in the United States (Ferguson 1984, 46–7; Rupert 1995, 57; see also Kolko 1969, 17; Leffler 1992, 14). According to Patrick Hearden (2002, xii), these "architects of globalism" in the foreign policy establishment were responsible for the US strategy that ensued.

The United States joined the war out of several concerns. First, it feared that the rimlands of Eurasia would fall under Japanese and German domination, thus precluding US access to continental markets and resources. In particular, the United States feared that a German victory over the USSR would create a rival pole of political, economic, and military power (Leffler 2013, 66–7). In this context, Roosevelt worried about "losing the entire European market" (see Hearden 2002, 24). Second, US planners feared that a long war in Europe would catalyse communist parties, stoke revolution, and limit the scope of capitalism (Kolko 1968, 31–42). Finally, US leaders feared that a British victory over Germany would extend mercantile trading practices in the post-war period. For US planners, such practices were a cause of the Great Depression and the Second World War, and had to be replaced by a liberal trading system (ibid., 243–4).

On the surface, the vision of US planners was one of *liberal internationalism*. Their assessment of the inter-war period led them to believe that, if geopolitical conflict was to be avoided in the future, trade blocs, spheres of influence, and protectionist rivalries had to be replaced by an "open door" system of free trade and multilateral governance. To this end, they envisioned the creation of new institutions to regulate and manage the world economy. In particular, they hoped to embed global finance and trade in a political order of multinational liberalism. At the same time, US planners assumed that the United States would be the foremost power of the post-war order, that new institutions would depend upon and reproduce US leadership, and that the United States was right to seek global primacy. As a result, the United States pursued a policy of *hegemonic liberalism*.

In various planning documents, this strategy was spelled out in concrete terms. In the planning memoranda offered to Roosevelt, an "integrated policy" was articulated "to achieve military and economic supremacy for the United States within the non-German world."[2] In this vision, the United States was to dominate the "Grand Area" of the western hemisphere, the British Empire, and Asia. In establishing the Grand Area, the United States would take steps towards creating a "world economy," and achieve the "elbow room" necessary to maintain trade surpluses, access raw materials, and secure investment outlets.[3] To these ends, the United States would assume "world responsibility," according to Isaiah Bowman, then director of the Council on Foreign Relations (Shoup and Minter 2004, 163).

At the end of the war, the United States found itself in possession of the means to implement this policy. On the political terrain, the United States was either occupying or exerting power over the industrial centres of the world economy, including western Europe, Britain, Japan, and the United States itself. It also held a monopoly on the atomic bomb, had the world's largest air force and navy, and operated hundreds of overseas bases. In these respects, the United States exercised what the State Department called "preponderant power" (Leffler 1992, 2, 18–19).

On the economic front, the United States had widened the base of accumulation that had made it the leading space of global capitalism. For example, by June 1945, capital assets in the United States were 65 per cent greater than in 1939. Over the same period, US exports increased by a factor of four. More strikingly, US gross national product (GNP) in 1945 accounted for half of world GNP. At the same time, the United States commanded two-thirds of world gold reserves, three-quarters of world fixed capital investments, half of world manufacturing capacity, one-third of world manufacturing exports, and half of world shipping business. The US economy was three times greater than the Soviet economy, and five times the British economy. By 1948, the United States was consuming approximately half of the world's production of copper, lead, zinc, and steel (Armstrong, Glyn, and Harrison 1991, 151; Brenner 2006a, 52–3; Lundestad 1986, 264; Kolko and Kolko 1972, 20, 624–5; Magdoff 1969).

As a result, the United States was critically dependent on foreign sources of raw materials. According to Paul Hoffman, the administrator of Marshall Plan aid, "our own dynamic economy has made us dependent on the outside world for many critical raw materials" (Kolko 1969, 50). Strategic minerals such as iron ore, bauxite, copper, lead, zinc, mica, tungsten, columbium, nickel, chromium, and cobalt were all sourced from foreign countries – in particular, from developing ones. In fact, in 1950, the US International Development Advisory Board reported that "it is to these countries that we must look for the bulk of any possible increase in [resource] supplies. The loss of any of these materials, through aggression, would be the equivalent of a grave military setback" (Magdoff 1969, 51).

For this reason, US planners recognized that open trade had to be a key desideratum of US grand strategy (Williams 2009). From this recognition flowed a new diplomatic and military strategy, one geared towards the world system as a whole. In the words of then US Army chief, George C. Marshall, "[i]t no longer appears practical to continue what we once conceived as hemispheric defense as a satisfactory basis for our security. We are now concerned with the peace of the entire world" (Layne 2006a, 41–2).

Although US strategy called for new institutions to embed the world market in liberal norms, it was expected to benefit the United States first and foremost.[4] In a top-secret memorandum, the State Department's George Kennan (1948) explained:

> we have about 50% of the world's wealth but only 6.3% of its population. This disparity is particularly great as between ourselves and the peoples of Asia. Our real task in the coming period is to devise a pattern of relationships which will permit us to maintain this position of disparity without positive detriment to our national security. To do so, we will have to dispense with all sentimentality and day-dreaming; and our attention will have to be concentrated everywhere on our immediate national objectives.

We need not deceive ourselves that we can afford today the luxury of altruism and world-benefaction.

US strategy, then, was not simply to reconstruct global capitalism through an "embedded liberalism" (Ruggie 1982, 36), but to expand US dominance in all registers of global power. For many US policy-makers, these two objectives were complimentary and mutually rein-forcing. As Joyce and Gabriel Kolko explain (1972, 2), "[e]ssentially, the United States' aim was to restructure the world so that American busi-ness could trade, operate, and profit without restrictions everywhere." However, "American business could operate only in a world composed of politically reliable and stable capitalist nations, and with free access to essential raw materials. Such a universal order precluded the Left from power and necessitated conservative, and ultimately subservi-ent, political control throughout the globe." For this reason, the United States "internationalized" domestic class struggles in countries around the world, as it tried to make the world safe for capitalism (ibid., 30). The result was new patterns of economic, political, and military inter-vention in the decades that followed.

The political forms of US grand strategy thus flowed from the eco-nomic dynamics of US capitalism. As such, they were tailored to the needs of US imperialism at multiple scales and in each region of the world. It is important to recognize, though, that the concrete practice of US grand strategy failed to achieve the vision of multinational liberal-ism. On the contrary, it reproduced the contradictions of capitalism on a world-wide scale, generated mass resistance, and demanded escalating forms of militarism to secure private property and US global primacy.

Securing the Grand Area: US Strategy in Practice

After the war, the grand strategy of US imperialism was put into prac-tice at multiple scales of political, economic, and geographic reality. At the political apex of US strategy was a plan for "collective security" through the United Nations, founded at the San Francisco Confer-ence in 1945. The UN Charter, based upon key submissions from the United States, embodied tenets of liberalism such as the right to self-determination, the sovereign equality of states, and collective security. At the same time, a Security Council of permanent members, granted the right to veto resolutions, striated the UN. As a result, the UN incor-porated the material hierarchies of the world economy and nation-state system. More specifically, it served to manage the tension between liberalism and empire in US grand strategy. In particular, it established an international security organization "without taking away the independence of the United States in any shape, manner or form," as Roosevelt put it (Hearden 2002, 172; see also Kolko 1968, 267–9, 457–8).

The United States pursued a similar policy of hegemonic liberalism for the world market. Through the Bretton Woods Agreement (1944), the International Monetary Fund (IMF) was created as a stabilization fund for balance-of-payments crises, and the International Bank for Reconstruction and Development (the World Bank) was established to guarantee private loans for long-term development projects. By creating a stable international monetary system, one in which the dollar was pegged to gold at $35 an ounce, the Bretton Woods Agreement was designed to overcome the dollar gap in global payments and to revive world trade, especially with Europe. To these ends, the Articles of Agreement allowed for capital controls, which also aided post-war reconstruction and full-employment policies (Eichengreen 2008, 228). Although the United States compromised on the issue of capital controls for other countries, it secured the means to dominate the voting mechanisms of the Fund and the Bank, both of which were based in Washington (Kolko 1968, 257). Through the dollar-gold peg, US primacy was also expanded by allowing the United States to run current account deficits and to earn seigniorage by exploiting the difference between the value of dollars and the cost of producing them.

For Eric Helleiner (1996, 4), the result was "a decidedly *non*liberal financial order." As Leo Panitch and Sam Gindin point out, however, the compromise with liberalism was less important than the power of the United States in organizing global capitalism. Indeed, "it was the intervention of the American state in shaping the pattern of European reconstruction which – far more than the 'repression' of finance via Bretton Woods, or the deployment of Keynesianism as a policy technique – made the postwar golden age of capitalist growth possible" (Panitch and Gindin 2005a, 51). As a result, the United States obtained what Susan Strange (1994, 25) calls "structural power" in the international political economy. In nearly every region of the world, US primacy was evident as it tried to shape the post-war order.

Towards Canada, for example, US strategy was to foster economic integration and military collaboration to enable US power at home and abroad. This strategy was spelled out in a confidential 1951 State Department policy on Canada that called for "economic and military interdependence" and for the "free flow" of "North American resources," including "critical defense materials" (Stewart 1992, 188). As Gordon Stewart (ibid., 201) observes, "American policymakers were never challenged [in the post-war period] by the Canadian question; their goals were achieved with a minimum of effort and with a considerable degree of support from their Canadian counterparts."[5]

Likewise, in western Europe, the fundamental strategy was to integrate Germany into a regional bloc under US dominance. The key fear was that, in a Europe without America, regional powers "would be strongly tempted to adopt a neutralist position" vis-à-vis the Soviet Union, as the US National Security Council put it (United States 1953b). To prevent such neutralism, Secretary of State Dean Acheson (1952) argued for the creation of a "well-knit larger grouping of Atlantic states within which [a] new [European] grouping can develop, thus ensuring unity of purpose of [the] entire group and precluding [the] possibility of [Europe's] becoming [a] third force or opposing force." In line with this concern, the United States spurned offers from the Soviet Union for the reunification of Germany, and took actions that led directly to the bifurcation of that country (Hearden 2002, 256; Kolko and Kolko 1972, 357; Layne 2006a, 64–7; Leffler 1992, 513). In 1949, the North Atlantic Treaty Organization (NATO) was founded for similar reasons, especially to "keep the Americans in, the Russians out, and the Germans down," as Lord Ismay, the first secretary general of NATO, explained (Reynolds 1994, 13).

US strategy in western Europe was motivated by two further concerns: the future of the British Empire, and the challenge of the post-war left. With regard to the first, the United States was determined to crack the Empire so that a liberal trading system could be established, and so that US firms could access global markets (Steil 2013, 3). To these ends, the United States demanded economic concessions from Downing Street on the Atlantic Charter (1941), Lend Lease (1942), Bretton Woods (1944), the balance-of-payments crisis (1945), and the Marshall Plan (1947). Regarding the second concern, the United States feared the radical edge of partisan movements in Italy and France, and used covert action to marginalize communist parties in these and other countries. The rise of the post-war left was also a factor in NATO's origins. According to US Senator Arthur Vandenberg, a key player in NATO's founding, the alliance would function "chiefly for the *practical* purpose of assuring adequate defense against internal subversion" (Kolko and Kolko 1972, 499).[6]

In eastern Europe, US policy was dictated by the Cold War – in particular, by the strategy of containing and destroying Soviet power. Although many analysts (Acheson 1969; Kennan 1947; Schlesinger 1967) tried to portray the Cold War as a defining feature of world order after 1945, the conflict with the Soviet Union was more of a regional flashpoint in a global system of capitalist imperialism. The Cold War was indeed an "inter-systemic conflict" (Kiely 2010, 128), and at times did assume global dimensions (Westad 2007), but as Geir Lundestad (1986, 263) explains, "the American expansion was really more striking than the Soviet one. Only the United States became a global power ... While America's influence could be felt in most corners of the world, with only a few exceptions the Soviet Union counted for little outside its border areas, however vast these border areas. The American expansion went so deep and affected so many different parts of the world that it can be said to have resulted in an American empire." Indeed, as Layne (2006a, 3) argues, "Washington's ambitions were not driven by the cold war but transcended it. The cold war was superimposed on an existing hegemonic grand strategy that the United States would have pursued – or at least attempted to pursue – even if there had been no rivalry with the Soviet Union."

Internal planning documents support such analyses. As US National Security Council (NSC) Directive 68 (United States 1950) put it, "[o]ur overall policy at the present time may be described as one designed to foster a world environment in which the American system can survive and flourish." As such, it is "a policy which we would probably pursue even if there were no Soviet threat." To deal with this threat, however, NSC 68 called for a policy of "containment" to "foster the seeds of destruction within the Soviet system." It recognized that "[t]he United States now possesses the greatest military potential of any single nation in the world," yet it called for a fourfold increase in military spending to "take initiative" in the Cold War, to "check and roll back" the Soviet Union, and to avoid "a position of neutrality" on the part of Germany and Japan. In addition, it called for "the necessity for just suppression" of democratic freedoms at home, because "[a] free society is vulnerable in that it is easy for people to lapse into excesses – the excesses of a permanently open mind." Thus, through a "policy of calculated and gradual coercion," the United States hoped to re-impose capitalism in Russia and eastern Europe.

In Asia, the United States pursued a broadly similar policy – namely, the revival of Japanese capitalism in a regional zone of production and exchange secured by US militarism. After the Chinese Revolution (1949), the United States began to promote Japan as a manufacturing power in Asia, linked to regional resource chains. As US President Dwight Eisenhower put it, "[o]ne of Japan's greatest opportunities for increased trade lies in a free and developing Southeast Asia ... The great need in one country is for raw materials, in the other country for manufactured goods. The two regions complement each other markedly" (Magdoff 1969, 53).

In Korea, the United States enforced the division of the country at the end of the Second World War, ignored the People's Republic that had emerged in the course of the liberation struggle, organized elections that were widely boycotted, imposed the right-wing presidency of Syngman Rhee, opposed land reform, blocked the expropriation of Japanese property, and repressed strikes by students, peasants, and workers – all before the war began in 1950. During the war itself, the United States and its allies inflicted mass destruction on civilian populations on both sides of the 38th parallel, leading to the deaths of several million people (Cumings 2011). Despite the armistice of 1953, the United States refused to negotiate a peace treaty, causing the division that remains to this day.[7] The internationalization of the Korean class struggle was an outcome of US grand strategy in the post-war period, and was a precursor to the war in Vietnam, which also pit the United States against a revolutionary movement that could not be defeated by foreign intervention (Kolko 1994).

The war in Korea was an expression of US strategy towards the Third World as a whole. Although the United States envisaged decolonization as a step towards an open world economy,[8] the liberation movements of the Third World were viewed as a threat to capitalism in Europe, Japan, and the United States itself. As a result, the United States embraced an "eclectic strategy" of supporting gradual decolonization in some regions, and recolonization in others by the British and the French (Kolko 1988, 11). In 1948, the US Central Intelligence Agency (CIA) captured the problem for US policy-makers: "[the] shift of the dependent areas from the orbit of the colonial powers not only weakens the probable European allies of the US but deprives the US itself of assured access to vital bases and raw materials." The main threat was "economic nationalism in the 'underdeveloped' countries." Indeed, the problem was that "[t]he aim of this economic nationalism is to attain greater economic self-sufficiency through development of a diversified economy, usually by industrialization. It has led the underdeveloped countries to favor tariffs, import restrictions, and other trade barriers to protect their Infant Industries," thus blocking the reach of US corporate power (United States 1948).

US policy in the periphery, then, was constituted by an "ambivalent tension" (Kolko 1988, 19). On the one hand, it offered a liberal promise of decolonization and self-determination; on the other, it embraced an imperialistic practice of exploitation and repression, including the recolonization of key countries by European powers. In 1958, Douglas Dillon, the Assistant Secretary of State for Economic Affairs, summarized the contradictions of US strategy: "We do not want to prevent change in the less developed areas, but neither can accept the prospect of its evolving along lines which could throw Asia and Africa open to the unrestrained play of revolutionary enthusiasms and national ambition. We want to help new governments attain their reasonable goals" (Dillon 1958).

In the Middle East, the contradictions of US grand strategy were plainly evident. Between September 1939 and December 1941, US policy-makers concluded that the future security of US capitalism relied upon the development and protection of foreign oil supplies. The broad strategy was to conserve domestic reserves, develop extraterritorial sources, safeguard and expand US claims to foreign deposits, and to use such claims to expand US global dominance (Hearden 2002, 119, 128). As an expression of this strategy, US Navy Secretary James Forrestal wrote that "[t]he prestige and hence influence of the United States is in part related to the wealth of the Government and its nation in terms of oil resources, foreign as well as domestic. It is assumed, therefore, that the bargaining power of the United States in international conferences involving vital materials like oil and such problems as aviation, shipping, island bases, and international security agreements relating to the disposition of armed forces and facilities, will depend in some degree upon the retention by the United States of such oil resources" (Layne 2006a, 46).

Out of such calculations, the Middle East became critical to US grand strategy. In this region, the contradictions of hegemonic liberalism ran through US foreign policies. On the one hand, the United States signed the Anglo-American Petroleum Agreement (1944), which guaranteed that "petroleum supplies should be made available to all countries in a non-discriminatory manner" (see Hearden 2002, 129). In 1945, the United States also recognized the independence of Syria and Lebanon, and shipped Lend Lease to Egypt as part of the move to sideline British influence.

On the other hand, the United States planned to seize control of key oil deposits. According to NSC 5428 (United States 1954), "United States policy is to keep the sources of oil in the Middle East in American hands." However, "[c]urrent conditions and trends in the Near East are inimical to Western interests [because] ... [t]he nations of the Near East are determined to assert their independence and are suspicious of outside interest in their affairs." As a result, "[i]t is in U.S. interests to help guide the social and economic pressures for revolutionary change into channels leading to healthy economic growth while maintaining and improving political stability." To this end, "[a]n increase in military training and strength in the Near East would help to induce internal stability and political orientation towards the West."

With this in mind, Saudi Arabia and Iran were integrated into the US structure of empire. In 1943, Saudi Arabia was offered Lend Lease to secure existing and future oil contracts. The reason for doing so, as Secretary Hull explained, was that "the oil of Saudi Arabia constitutes one of the world's greatest prizes, and that it is extremely shortsighted to take any step which would tend to discredit the American interest therein" (Hearden 2002, 124). Two years later, the State Department described the oil reserves of Saudi Arabia as "a stupendous source of strategic power, and one of the greatest material prizes in world history" (United States 1945, 45).

For US policy-makers, Iran was a second key front in the battle for global primacy. In October 1946, the Joint Chiefs of Staff insisted that, "as a source of supply Iran is an area of major strategic interest to the United States." In particular, "the area offers opportunities to conduct delaying operations and/or operations to protect United States-controlled oil resources in Saudi Arabia" (Stokes and Raphael 2010, 84). Three years earlier, the State Department warned that "vigilance may be needed to prevent [Iranian oil] from falling into exclusive British use after the war" (Hearden 2002, 133). To claim this oil, the United States abrogated the US-British "Red Line" agreement of 1928, seized control of oil fields in Iran and Iraq, and in 1953 installed Mohammed Reza Pahlavi as shah of Iran by way of a coup against a democratic government.[9] In the wake of the Eisenhower Doctrine (1957), arms and aid flowed to Iran, as well as to other states in the US-led alliance system.

In Latin America, the US employed a similar strategy. According to US Secretary of War Harry Stimson, "I think that it's not asking too much to have our little region over here which never has bothered anybody." In the words of his assistant, John J. McCloy, "we ought to have our cake and eat it too ... we ought to be free to operate under this regional arrangement in South America, at the same time intervene promptly in Europe; we oughtn't to give away either asset" (Ambrose 1988, 62). For the United States, the particular goal in Latin America was to maintain and extend the hemispheric structure of dependence that had been established even before the Second World War. Indeed, US corporations had implanted deep circuits of production and trade in the region, which accounted for one-fifth of total US exports and one-third of total US imports. US corporations were also earning double the rate of profit in Latin America that they were in the United States itself (Kolko 1988, 97).

US strategy emerged from these vested interests. In 1953, the NSC delineated the goals of US policy as "[a]dequate production in Latin America and access by the United States to, raw materials essential to U.S. security; [t]he ultimate standardization of Latin American military organization, training, doctrine and equipment along U.S. lines ... [and] [e]ncouraging Latin American governments to recognize that the bulk of the capital required for their economic development can best be supplied by private enterprise and that their own self-interest requires the creation of a climate which will attract private investment." In the same directive, however, the NSC warned that "there is a trend in Latin America toward nationalist regimes maintained in large part by appeals to the masses of the population. Concurrently, there is an increasing popular demand for immediate improvement in the low living standards of the masses, with the result that most Latin American governments are under intense domestic political pressures to increase production and to diversify their economies." Against such popular demands, the NSC argued that it was "essential to arrest the drift in the area toward radical and nationalistic regimes" (United States 1953a).

In 1954, the CIA followed through with a military coup in Guatemala, where the democratic government of Jacobo Arbenz had legalized unions and launched a program of land reform, literacy improvement, and nationalization of hydro and shipping industries (Cullather 1994). According to Charles R. Burrows of the US State Department's Bureau of Inter-American Affairs, the problem was that "Guatemala has become an increasing threat to the stability of Honduras and El Salvador. Its agrarian reform is a powerful propaganda weapon; its broad social program of aiding the workers and peasants in a victorious struggle against the upper classes and large foreign enterprises has a strong appeal to the populations of Central American neighbors where similar conditions prevail" (Stokes 2005, 26). To address these threats, the US backed a forty-year military dictatorship that terrorized the "masses of the population" with repression, disappearances, and mass killings. After the Cuban Revolution (1959), the Guatemalan model was applied to Brazil, Uruguay, Bolivia, Chile, and Argentina, where the United States backed military dictatorships and counterinsurgency wars against "workers and peasants" (Chomsky and Herman 1979; Stokes 2005).

In the post-war era, then, the United States pursued a policy of hegemonic liberalism. In particular, it sought to globalize the capitalist mode of production and to embed US primacy in the nation-state system. This was done in two ways. First, the United States incorporated the second-tier states into US-led structures of economic, political, and military governance. In the process, it established a hub-and-spokes system of global power in which US dominance was paramount. Second, the United States deployed escalating forms of militarism to contain or roll back any threats to capital in the periphery. By instigating coups, supporting dictators, training militaries, selling arms, building bases, and waging wars, the United States developed new techniques of empire to repress any resistance to capitalism. Through this vicious circle, the Empire of Capital was constituted and contested.

Neoliberalism and US Primacy

In the late 1960s, the contradictions of the post-war order reached fruition. At the scale of world politics, US primacy was thoroughly discredited by the wars in Indochina and by US support for dictatorships in Latin America, the Middle East, and Africa. At the same time, the world economy of the Bretton Woods system began to unravel. As Japan and West Germany rebuilt their economies through export-led development strategies, firms from these countries began to seize market share from US corporations in the world economy. As a result, the obverse side of German and Japanese reconstruction was a "tendential decline of US manufacturing competitiveness, [a] tendential rise of US external deficits, and [a] tendential decline of the US currency. Implied was the declining capacity of the US market to absorb its allies' and rivals' goods and thus to serve as the 'motor of last resort' of their economies. The very processes by which the German and Japanese economies achieved rapid growth during the post-war boom tended to destroy the foundations" of US global dominance (Brenner 2006a, 5). Indeed, by

1966, the United States was running balance-of-payments deficits with Japan and West Germany, and by 1971 was running trade deficits with the world as a whole (ibid., 125). The core problem was that the world economy was wracked by a crisis of overproduction and overcapacity, causing declining rates of profit, investment, and employment. In fact, "[b]etween 1968 and 1973 the profit rate for the advanced capitalist countries as a whole fell in the business and manufacturing sectors by one-fifth. By 1973 the profit rate in business and manufacturing had fallen from its previous peak in each major bloc by about one-third. The fall began in Europe in 1960, in the United States in the mid-1960s, and in Japan in 1970" (Armstrong, Glyn, and Harrison 1991, 182–3).

In these conditions, the United States faced mounting trade deficits, shrinking gold reserves, and runs on the dollar in European financial markets. With dollar liabilities exceeding gold reserves by a factor of twenty, the value of the greenback and the political power of US primacy, were called into question. At this critical juncture, the United States looked for new means of reconstituting global capitalism, and with it, US hegemony. In pursuit of these goals, the political economy of neoliberalism emerged.

To begin, in 1971, US President Richard Nixon suspended dollar convertibility, and imposed a 10 per cent surcharge on imports. In the process, the United States terminated the Bretton Woods Agreement on currency pegs. In the same year, the Group-of-Ten Smithsonian Agreement imposed a dollar devaluation of 7.89 per cent, and a revaluation of German marks and Japanese yen by 13.5 and 16.88 per cent, respectively. Through such measures, the United States established a new international monetary system based on floating exchange rates unlinked to gold or to any other commodity basis. In this context, the dollar became the universal equivalent – the measure of global value and the means of facilitating global trade. For countries that relied upon exports to the United States, the dollar became a primary source of global income, and thus was accumulated in reserves. Of critical importance, the United States refused to cooperate in any regime to govern global finance (Helleiner 1996). For example, in 1973, the United States rejected discussions of the Group-of-Twenty to use IMF special drawing rights as a principal reserve asset. After the oil price shocks imposed by the Organization of the Petroleum Exporting Countries, the United States also refused to participate in any regime to manage petrodollar flows. Instead, Wall Street issued massive new loans to developing countries, setting the stage for crisis a decade later.

A new structure of empire thus emerged in the international political economy. Through new modes of *financialization*, the United States reconstituted the world market and the nation-state system under its global leadership. In particular, the United States used the global financial system to re-engineer capitalism and to bolster US primacy. Indeed, by imposing a credit money system, it established Wall Street as the centre of global finance, and absorbed dollars circulating in world markets. In the process, the dollar was salvaged as world money, capital controls were degraded in rival states, and the United States gained the means to run trade and government deficits. By importing global savings, the United States also financed new military expenditures and new research and development projects. Most important, the new financial hegemony induced a "competitive deregulation dynamic" in the world economy, and thus enhanced the internationalization of US capital (Helleiner 1995, 316; Seabrooke 2001, 97–8, 106). Through the "Dollar-Wall Street Regime" that emerged, the United States launched a program of neoliberal capitalism (Gowan 1999).

The 1979 Stabilization Program introduced by US Federal Reserve chair Paul Volcker was critical in this regard. By hiking the rate of interest, the "Volcker Shock" imposed a recession that destroyed the power of labour and the stock of unproductive capital in the US economy. It also attracted global savings to Wall Street, bankrupted the Third World, and cleared the ground for a new phase of accumulation, both locally and globally. Indeed, from the trough of 1982, the rate of profit in the United States began to rise, paving the way for US growth in the 1990s and 2000s (Duménil and Lévy 2004). As a result, "[t]he reconstitution of empire ... began at home" (Panitch and Gindin 2005a, 59).

The remaking of the American empire also brought to the fore in the domestic political economy a new power bloc of globalizing bankers and transnational industrial firms that superseded the New Deal bloc of embedded liberals (Helleiner 1996, 120). At the macro level, this new bloc was constituted by the Dollar-Wall Street Regime and by the financialization of US capitalism. At the micro level, it was constituted by new structures of corporate ownership and management, which emphasized shareholder value, lean production, and mergers and acquisitions on a global scale. The result was that the rising rate of profit was not translated into new patterns of investment, employment, and rising real wages for workers. On the contrary, profits were seized by a financial system that rewarded upper management and disciplined workers through downsizing, offshoring, speed-up, unemployment, and stagnant real wages. For these reasons, "average rates of growth of output, capital stock (investment), labour productivity, and real wages for the years 1973 to the present have been one-third to one-half of those for the years 1950-73, while the average unemployment rate has been more than double" (Brenner 2006a, 4). The political economy of neoliberalism, then, has been one of relative economic stagnation and polarizing class relations (Duménil and Lévy 2004; Piketty and Saez 2007).

In the periphery, the crisis was resolved in more acute ways. First, the debt crisis of the 1980s was used to break the model of import-substitution industrialization that most Third World countries practised in the post-war period. In particular, the IMF and the World Bank were used to restructure the economies of the periphery in ways commensurate with neoliberalism and US primacy objectives. Indeed, rather than reducing debt levels, the structural adjustment policies of the IMF were designed to liberalize trade and investment, and to discipline social spending. In the process, overall debt levels rose across the period of neoliberalism.[10]

Second, new modalities of disciplinary militarism were used against popular and revolutionary movements. In Latin America, the United States backed military coups in Chile (1973) and Argentina (1986), and outsourced the repression of the *Frente Sandinista de Liberación Nacional* in Nicaragua and the *Frente Farabundo Martí para la Liberación Nacional* in El Salvador (Chomsky 1985; LaFeber 1993). These conflicts were a crucible for the neoconservatives in Washington who would later staff the George W. Bush administration (Grandin 2006). In Afghanistan, the United States supported the *mujahideen* insurgency against the communist government and the occupying Soviet military forces. In the Middle East, the Carter Doctrine was announced in the wake of the Iranian Revolution (1979), establishing Rapid Deployment Forces *cum* US Central Command in the Gulf. In 1982, the United States allowed Israel to attack the Palestine Liberation Organization in Lebanon, and across the decade financed both sides of the Iran-Iraq war. In Africa, Ronald Reagan backed the apartheid regime in South Africa, labelled the African National Congress a terrorist organization, and defended South Africa's intervention in Angola. Through these "savage wars by proxy" (Tirman 2011, chap. 6), the United States tried to defeat or degrade the opposition to its empire that emerged in the 1970s and 1980s.

Through the political economy of neoliberalism, then, a new structure of empire was produced. The economics of the Dollar-Wall Street Regime preserved the United States as the critical nexus of global capitalism, and allowed for an external strategy of primacy. In the aftermath of the Cold War, this strategy was extended in radically new ways.

Full-Spectrum Dominance: US Strategy since 1990

As the Soviet Union crumbled, US elites saw new opportunities to expand the policy of hegemonic liberalism. Facing no peer competitor, the United States set out to realize the fundamental goals of its foreign policy: the globalization of capitalism as a mode of production, and preponderant power for the United States itself. As in the post-war period, the first objective relied upon the second; the class relations of global capitalism were too unstable to exist without disciplinary militarism. Since 1990, US foreign policy has worked through this dynamic of economic and political expansion. It has sought to maintain the United States as the pre-eminent state of global capitalism in light of new forms of economic competition and political resistance in the world order.

Consider, first, the *National Security Strategy* (United States 1990) of President George H.W. Bush (1988–92). As the world's only "global power," it argued, "our goals and interests remain constant." In particular, the United States should pursue "a free and open international economic system" and "the flourishing of democracy." To these ends, the United States holds a "vital interest to prevent any hostile power or group of powers from dominating the Eurasian land mass." As in the past, the United States will continue to challenge "threats to U.S. interests that [can]not be laid at the Kremlin's door."

Two years later, in its *Defence Planning Guidance*, the US Defense Department (United States 1992) encouraged the Bush administration to ensure that the United States remained "the world's preeminent power" and "only superpower." To this end, US strategy must focus "on precluding the emergence of any potential future global competitor." Towards Europe, this meant preserving "NATO as the primary instrument of Western defense and security, as well as the channel for U.S. influence and participation in European security affairs." In Asia, the strategy called for "maintain[ing] our status as a military power of the first magnitude." Likewise, in the Middle East, "our overall objective is to remain the predominant outside power in the region and [to] preserve U.S. and Western access to the region's oil."

Guided by such objectives, the Bush administration engaged in several military conflicts. It invaded Panama to oust Manuel Noriega, bombed Iraq to liberate Kuwait and to protect regional oil interests, and oversaw German reunification under US auspices. From the experience of Operation Desert Storm, US Defense Secretary Richard Cheney drew the lesson that "[w]e must be prepared to act decisively in the Middle East/Persian Gulf region ... if our vital interests are threatened anew." Indeed, the United States "must maintain a level of forward military presence adequate to reassure our friends and deter aggressors and present a credible crisis response capability" (Stokes and Raphael 2010, 92–3). To these ends, Bush signed, in May 1991, a presidential finding on regime change in Iraq. In such ways, the Bush administration changed the pretexts, but "[preserved] the essential continuity of U.S. policy across the historical divide of 1989" (Bacevich 2002, 71).

Under the Clinton administration (1992–2000), the US policy of hegemonic liberalism was synthesized and expanded. In public statements, the United States was defined as "the indispensable nation" that can "see further into the future than other nations," as Secretary of State Madeleine Albright (1998) put it. Throughout the 1990s, the United States pursued what National Security Assistant Anthony Lake (1993) called a strategy of "enlargement" with respect to "democracy and market economics." According to Lake (1994), the key targets of enlargement were the "backlash states" that "assault the basic values of the international community and quarantine themselves from the global trend of freedom and openness." To support this project, the *Quadrennial Defence Review* (United States 1997, vol. 8) described the purpose of the US military as one of "sustain[ing] American global leadership" and of "securing uninhibited access to key markets, energy supplies and strategic resources." According to Defense Secretary William Cohen (United States 1999), the United States was "a global power with worldwide interests," and must "retain the capability to act unilaterally when necessary," and to "execute the full spectrum of military operations." As the Joint Chiefs of Staff (United States 2000, 6) explained, the new military policy was one of "full spectrum dominance – the ability of US forces, operating unilaterally or in combination with multinational and interagency partners, to defeat any adversary and control any situation across the full range of military operations."

In practice, Bill Clinton's foreign policy agenda was focused heavily on economic concerns. In the White House, Clinton established the National Economic Council chaired by Robert Rubin. From the work of this council, Clinton signed more than three hundred trade deals, and oversaw the implementation of the North American Free Trade

Agreement and the World Trade Organization. As Barry Posen (2003, 41) points out, however, Clinton's foreign policy agenda "also depended heavily on military power." For example, the Clinton administration worked to keep Germany in NATO, to expand NATO into eastern Europe, and to fortify the US military presence in the Gulf. In addition, Clinton endorsed ballistic missile defence and rejected the Ottawa Treaty on land mines. In the Middle East, he embraced a strategy of "dual containment" of Iraq and Iran "to protect the United States' vital interest in the region – uninterrupted, secure U.S./Allied access to Gulf oil" (United States Central Command 1995). To these ends, Clinton signed the Iraq Liberation Act in 1998, and enforced the UN sanctions program through several bombing campaigns. In South America, his government launched Plan Colombia "to destroy any threat to US hegemony" and "to stabilize Washington's allies in the region" (Stokes 2002, 74). In eastern Europe, the United States covertly lifted an arms embargo on Bosnia, supplied the Croat army before Operation Storm in Krajina, and exacerbated the conflict in Kosovo by waging unilateral war on Serbia (Chomsky 2003, chap. 3). During the same period, the United States deployed Special Forces to Somalia, ignored the genocide in Rwanda, and launched cruise missiles at a pharmaceutical plant in Sudan in response to embassy bombings in Kenya and Tanzania. Out of the Nye Report (United States 1995), the United States committed 100,000 troops to Asia as part of maintaining a hub-and-spokes system of regional security. In such ways, Clinton advanced the policy of hegemonic liberalism.

Against this backdrop, the foreign policy agenda of George W. Bush (2000–08) was hardly novel; rather, it merely intensified the structural tendencies of US foreign policy. As a result, "Bush was acting firmly within the programmatic and strategic consensus of the American capitalist class since 1990," if not earlier (Gowan 2003, 48; see also de Graaf and van Apeldoorn 2010). At the same time, the Bush administration was forced to engage new dynamics in the world economy and nation-state system. First, the 9/11 strikes on the Pentagon and the World Trade Center were direct ripostes to US grand strategies in the Middle East – in particular, to US support for Israel and the pro-western Arab regimes (Mohamedou 2006). In response, the Bush administration invaded Afghanistan and Iraq as opening salvos of a "global war on terror," the purpose of which was to reassert US primacy across Eurasia (Brzezinski 1997, 2009; Hanieh 2013).

Second, the United States began to face new competitive challenges in the world economy, particularly from China. Although much of China's economic development was predicated on foreign direct investments by US-based transnational corporations and on the re-investment of dollar savings in US Treasury bonds (Hart-Landsberg 2011), indigenous patterns of production, finance, and investment were beginning to erode US economic leadership (Arrighi 2009; Black 2011). China's development as an independent pole of accumulation was apparent in the rising share of Chinese-owned exporting firms and in the global expansion of Chinese capital itself, often in direct competition with North American and European corporations (*Financial Times* 2012; Rotberg 2008; cf. Nolan 2012). On this foundation, the Chinese state began a military modernization program to secure its national territory and to limit or degrade US primacy in Asia (Fravel 2008). In this context, the Bush administration was inclined to assert Washington's military powers more aggressively, especially with regard to energy supplies in the Middle East and Central Asia (Hanieh 2013). What came to be known as the Bush Doctrine was based on such considerations.

For example, Bush's *National Security Strategy* (United States 2002b, preface) declared that the United States "will actively work to bring the hope of democracy, development, free markets, and free trade to every corner of the world." To this end, it articulated a program "to dissuade potential adversaries from pursuing a military build-up in hopes of surpassing, or equaling, the power of the United States" (ibid., 30). It also justified preventative war, and called for "organizing coalitions" to fight the "war on terrorism" (ibid., 25). In addition, it supported NATO expansion in eastern Europe as well as ballistic missile defence as both a defensive and an offensive tool of nuclear war.

To implement this strategy, the *Quadrennial Defence Review* (United States 2001, 26) called for a "basing system that provides greater flexibility for U.S. forces in critical areas of the world, placing emphasis on additional bases and stations beyond Western Europe and Northeast Asia." Furthermore, in the *Strategic Master Plan* of the US Air Force Space Command (United States 2002a, foreword), the Bush administration sought "to fully exploit space, to not only maintain our current military advantage, but also to enable ... asymmetric advantage through a capabilities-based air and space force." In particular, the strategy was "to deny the advantages of space to our adversaries" and "to transform space power to provide our Nation with diverse options to globally apply force in, from, and through space with modern ICBMs, offensive counterspace, and new conventional prompt global strike capabilities." In the 2001 *Nuclear Posture Review*, the Bush administration "ordered the Pentagon to draft contingency plans for the use of nuclear weapons against at least seven countries, naming not only Russia and the 'axis of evil' – Iraq, Iran, and North Korea – but also China, Libya, and Syria" (Arkin 2002). The key point here was that the United States would use nuclear weapons against states that do not possess them.

In practice, the Bush administration was consistent with doctrine. In response to 9/11, it invaded Afghanistan in the first battle of the "global war on terror." From this position, it also waged unilateral war on Iraq in 2003. If both of these wars had not become quagmires for the US military, plans were in place to invade Iran, Syria, Libya, and North Korea as well (Clark 2003, 130). More radically, the Bush administration approved the detention, rendition, and torture of terrorist suspects in a global network of secret prisons and concentration camps. It also withdrew from the Anti-Ballistic Missile Treaty, and violated the Non-Proliferation Treaty (NPT) in supporting India's nuclear program. Under the Bush presidency, military spending increased to roughly half of world defence outlays, and the United States expanded the "National Surveillance State" at home through the Authorization of the Use of Military Force Act (2001), the Patriot Act (2001), the Protect America Act (2007), the FISA (Foreign Intelligence Surveillance Act) Amendments Act (2008), and the Military Commissions Acts (2006, 2009) (Balkin 2008). As part of this, the National Security Agency received new funding for extending a global communications surveillance capacity – one that supports US military forces in combat, gleans information about military technologies, monitors regional conflicts, carries out industrial espionage, and gathers political and diplomatic information in "virtually every country" (MacAskill and Ball 2013).

Thus, while the Bush administration developed certain tactics of US foreign policy, it was acting with the logic of US grand strategy since the Second World War. As such, it sought to expand global capitalism through the economic, political, and military dominance of Washington. However, the evident failure of this project – as symbolized by the 2008 financial crisis and the military debacles in Afghanistan and Iraq – has raised questions of a relative US decline or, indeed, of a "post-American world" (Zakaria 2012; see also Layne 2012; cf. Beckley 2011/12).

In this context, Barack Obama was elected in 2008 on a platform to re-establish US primacy on more strategic foundations. With the backing of corporate, financial, and military elites, the Obama administration has sought "to find a more effective response to the continuing contradictions of and challenges to US power while continuing to be committed to the goal of US primacy" (de Graaf and van Apeldoorn 2010).

For instance, at the level of doctrine, the Obama administration has articulated a *National Security Strategy* (United States 2010b) to "underwrite global security" and to renew the domestic economy as "the wellspring of American power." To these ends, this document outlines a "whole of government approach," combining defence, homeland security, private sector engagement, diplomacy, development, strategic communications, and intelligence. In a tactical shift, it calls for "comprehensive engagement" with traditional allies and multilateral institutions as part of "renewing American leadership." It insists, however, that the US military "continues to underpin our national security and global leadership, and when we use it appropriately, our security and leadership is reinforced." In a similar vein, the Joint Forces Command (United States 2010a, 22) argues that "one large 'export' that the United States provides to the world [is] the armed force that underpins the open and accessible global system of trade and travel that we know as 'globalization.' At a cost of 600 billion dollars a year, US Joint Forces around the world provide safety and security for the major exporters to access and use the global commons for trade and commerce." According to President Obama's *Nuclear Posture Review* (United States 2010c, viii), "the United States will not use or threaten to use nuclear weapons against non-nuclear weapons states that are party to the NPT and in compliance with their nuclear non-proliferation obligations." In other words, "there remains a narrow range of contingencies in which U.S. nuclear weapons may still play a role in deterring a conventional or [chemical or biological weapons] attack against the United States or its allies and partners. The United States is therefore not prepared at the present time to adopt a universal policy that deterring nuclear attack is the sole purpose of nuclear weapons."

In the wake of Iraq and Afghanistan, the Obama administration began to develop unconventional warfare and Special Forces doctrines. According to the US Army *Special Forces Unconventional Warfare* manual (United States 2010g, 1), the aim of unconventional warfare is "to enable a resistance movement or insurgency to coerce, disrupt, or overthrow a government or occupying power by operation through or with an underground, auxiliary, and guerrilla force in a denied area." "For the foreseeable future," it contends, "U.S. forces will predominantly engage in irregular warfare operations" – in particular, by enabling or supporting guerrilla movements and insurgencies against enemy governments (ibid., iv, 1).

At the level of practice, the Obama administration has escalated the policy of hegemonic liberalism in numerous ways. In Afghanistan, it expanded the counterinsurgency war against the Taliban, with devastating consequences for civilians (Klassen 2013). As part of "overseas contingency operations," it expanded the use of Special Forces and drones in Pakistan, Yemen, and Somalia (Scahill 2013). In Iraq, it sought to maintain a permanent military presence before the government of Nouri al-Maliki demanded a full withdrawal. Through his first term, Obama failed to close the prison at Guantánamo Bay, refused to pursue torture prosecutions of CIA agents, extended the jail policy of Bagram Airbase in Afghanistan that denies *habeus corpus*, and expanded the scope of foreign and domestic signals intelligence. In response to the Arab Spring, the United States recognized a military coup against the democratic government of Egypt, exploited a UN resolution to oust Libya's Moammar Gadhafi, and increased ties with the absolutist states of Saudi Arabia, Qatar, and Bahrain. Towards Iran, the United States imposed sanctions unilaterally and multilaterally, built up a military force in the Gulf, and carried out cyber attacks in alliance with Israel, before falling back on selective engagement with nuclear negotiations. In Syria, the CIA was deployed to support a proxy war against the government of Bashar al-Assad, in ways consistent with US Army unconventional warfare doctrines (Chivers and Schmitt 2013). In Ukraine, the White House backed the 2014 *putsch* of neofascist, oligarchic, and anti-Russian forces.[11]

Most important, Obama announced a military pivot to Asia for the purpose of holding regional dominance. Designed to block China's rise as a regional hegemon or future peer-competitor, the pivot anticipates enhanced military ties with Australia, Thailand, Vietnam, Taiwan, the Philippines, Japan, South Korea, Indonesia, Singapore, Malaysia, and Mongolia. As Secretary of State Hillary Clinton (2011) revealed, this "strategic turn to the [Pacific] fits logically into our overall global effort to secure and sustain America's global leadership." To supplement this military agenda, the Obama administration has pursued a new trade deal called the Trans-Pacific Strategic Economic Partnership Agreement. In this effort to impose a hub-and-spokes system in Asia, the United States is creating a powder keg that could be ignited by several flash points.

Across the past two decades, then, successive US governments have pursued a project of hegemonic liberalism. This has involved, on the one hand, the global expansion of US military power, and, on the other, the internationalization of capital through the Dollar-Wall Street Regime. Although each administration has emphasized certain regions or tactics over others, the common project is to widen the scope of capitalism and US political dominance. To these ends, the state and power bloc have dedicated US strategy at home and abroad.

With this in mind, in Chapter 3 I examine Canada's role in the North American bloc during the period of neoliberalism. I look, in particular, at the class dynamics of deep integration in the continental realm. In the process, I reveal the social forces of Canada's alignment with US global primacy.

3 Continental Neoliberalism and the Canadian Corporate Elite

For more than two decades, the foreign economic policy of the Canadian state has been driven by a strategy of *continental neoliberalism* (Carroll 1990, 1993).[1] This strategy has encompassed a twofold attempt at reorganizing the Canadian economy within regional structures of accumulation and restructuring the state along neoliberal or free market lines. This strategy was first pursued through the Canadian-American Free Trade Agreement (CAFTA) of 1988, and then advanced through the North American Free Trade Agreement (NAFTA) of 1994. Through these agreements, Canadian governments embedded the national economy in a continental system of production and exchange, and established an external constitution for rationalizing the state in ways commensurate with neoliberal principles.

The results, of course, have been nothing less than revolutionary in terms of remaking the economic space of the continent. The NAFTA region is currently home to more than 450 million people, who produce more than US$17 trillion annually in goods and services. The NAFTA trading bloc is the largest in the world, and now accounts for more than US$1 trillion of yearly trade – three times the level of 1994, when NAFTA came into effect. The creation of a continental trading zone has also encouraged new flows of foreign direct investment (FDI) by multinational corporations seeking to exploit the markets, resources, and labour supplies of the region. Indeed, FDI flows have increased among the NAFTA partners and between the NAFTA bloc and the wider world economy.

For Canada, the pursuit of continental neoliberalism has transformed the national economy and employment structure in fundamental ways. By 2008, one in five jobs was linked to trade within the NAFTA zone, which accounted for $381.3 billion of Canada's merchandise exports and $245.1 billion of its merchandise imports. In the same year, Canada held $314.6 billion in FDI stocks in the other two NAFTA countries, and was liable for $292.9 billion in FDI stocks held by corporations based in the United States and Mexico. Through such modes of economic integration, the Canadian state has been incorporated into a continental economy in which north-south ties increasingly predominate over east-west ones. For this reason, the project of continental neoliberalism has been highly contested in Canada, both inside and outside Parliament and by a wide array of political and economic forces.

The same contestation has appeared in the social sciences, wherein two main theoretical viewpoints have emerged. The first is the neoliberal theory of comparative cost advantage. The central axiom of this theory is that free trade will effect relative price movements to balance accounts between nations with no departure from full employment; as a result, gains from trade are propitious to all nations that participate in the free exchange of commodities. In the more refined theory of comparative factor advantage, each nation is said to benefit from trade to the extent that it specializes in exporting those commodities that it can produce relatively most efficiently. In effect, nations will gain by specializing in the export of commodities whose factors of production are present in relative abundance, giving those products a comparative cost advantage in world markets. The end result of trade liberalization, then, is a world economy of specialized production for export, leading to economic convergence among nations and a general rise in global welfare.

In the Canadian context, it was precisely this theory of neoliberal trade convergence that guided the project of continental integration (Canada 1985). Proponents of neoliberalism (Harris and Cox 1983) sought to demonstrate that free trade with the United States would discipline the national economy and thereby trigger productivity gains, industrial specialization, and economies of scale for Canadian firms in a regional trading zone. Advocates of free trade predicted that Canada would also receive new inflows of FDI, leading to an upgrade of the manufacturing sector into more competitive lines of value-added production for export. In the process, the country would experience a net growth of gross domestic product (GDP) and overall employment, allowing governments at both the federal and provincial levels to maintain robust welfare and social programs.

As Jim Stanford (2006a) reveals, these prognoses were based on certain assumptions in the neoliberal models of equilibrium trade. These assumptions included full employment of factors of production, uniform factor pricing, perfect information, constant income shares, capital controls, balanced trade, and no barriers to entry – none of which existed in the real-world economics of North America. As a result, the models of free trade theory could not foresee the limits and pitfalls of continental neoliberalism. Although Canada has developed new forms of trade and investment integration with the United States and Mexico, it has not reaped the gains in productivity, employment, and GDP growth that neoliberal theory projected (Jackson 2007; D. Robinson 2007; Seccareccia 2007). It has also not experienced the expected qualitative leap in value-added production for export, but instead has become more dependent on sales of resources to the US economy. For such reasons, Stanford (2006a, 181) argues that the neoliberal models have been "one-sided and misleading."

In making this critique, Stanford clears the way for a second key theory of continental integration: the dependency theory of left-nationalist political economy. Inspired by the Latin American dependency theories of the 1960s and 1970s, this framework examines Canada as an economic, political, and military dependency of the American empire (Levitt [1970] 2002). The core argument is that Canada's economic development has been stymied by a branch-plant economy in which foreign capital is dominant in the industrial sectors and Canadian capital is limited to the resources and financial sectors. With a dependent economic structure and a comprador capitalist class (Clement 1977), the Canadian state has been impelled to service both the economic interests of US capital on a regional scale and the political-military interests of US imperialism on a global scale (Clark-Jones 1987). With this understanding of the Canadian-US relationship, the free trade agenda has been perceived as the logical outcome of the continental structure of economic dependence. As Leo Panitch (1994, 78) puts it, "the free trade treaty of 1988 was designed not to inaugurate but rather to constitutionalize, formalize and extend Canada's dependence on the US."

If, as Stanford argues, the neoliberal models are weakened by a hypothetical-deductive method of abstraction, the dependency theory is notable for grounding itself in the real structures of economic and political power in the continental social formation. Despite this strength, dependency theory is limited by three key problems (Carroll 1986). First, it tends to focus on the Canadian-US relationship at the expense of examining Canada's wider role in the world economy and nation-state system. Second, it tends to emphasize the categories of nationalism – and the politics of national independence – at the expense of analysing the structural logic of capitalism and its fundamental social relations. Finally, it employs an empiricist understanding of the "circuits of capital," and thus cannot understand the resources sectors – for example, oil, gas, and mining – as advanced forms of industrial production. For these reasons, dependency theory offers a one-sided view of the Canadian political economy and of political contestation under the banner of national independence or sovereignty (see Hurtig 2003).

To address these problems, in this chapter I develop a Marxist understanding of continental neoliberalism. This perspective is informed by the Marxist theory of capitalism as a generalized system of commodity production for profit, and according to which the capitalist class, which owns and controls the means of production, earns profit or surplus value through the exploitation of labour power in the productive process (Marx [1867] 1990). The accumulation of capital proceeds through twin dynamics of concentration and centralization (Shaikh 1983), and creates a corresponding imperative for international expansion (Jenkins 1987). In this perspective, the internationalization of capital is a spatial fix to the contradictions of production – in particular, to the forms of class struggle and overinvestment that dampen the rate of profit (see Chapter 1). The immanent drive towards the internationalization of capital is thus produced by the internal crises of capitalism.

To develop this theory for the case of Canada, I trace the mobilization of the capitalist class around a project of continental neoliberalism from the 1980s to the present, and demonstrate how the Canadian corporate elite has pursued an escalating strategy of North American integration as a spatial fix to crises of production. On this foundation, I also explain the new modes of popular protest to the free trade agenda, and consider, specifically, the new forms of national and transnational resistance to continental neoliberalism.

For conceptual purposes, the narrative is centred around three key terms: David Harvey's (1990) "spatial fix," William Domhoff's (2006) "corporate community," and Jeffrey Ayres's (2004) "contentious transnationalism." According to Harvey, one pathway out of an economic crisis is for capital to seek new spaces in which to organize labour power and means of production on a more profitable basis. By reorganizing the world economy through new forms of cross-border trade and investment, capital can engineer a spatial fix so that profits may rise. As I demonstrate in this chapter, the project of North American integration can be viewed as such a method of crisis resolution within new spaces of production.

To engineer this spatial fix, however, the corporate community has had to self-organize. For Domhoff, a corporate community is formed through the interlocking directorships that exist between large corporations as well as through the policy organizations that are funded and directed by the same corporate interests. These vehicles of economic and political cohesion give the corporate community the means to advance a common class interest to the state. With this in mind, sociologists have mapped "the overlapping memberships of governance boards in the fields of corporate business, policy-formation and the state," as a way of documenting the social organization and political action of corporate elites (Carroll and Shaw 2001, 203).

During the period of neoliberalism, the mobilization of the corporate community through intersectoral policy groups has been critically important as a means of achieving political hegemony. As the network of directorship interlocks has become sparser in line with new corporate governance reforms,[2] intersectoral policy groups have emerged as key sites of class formation and political activism for capitalist class factions. In Canada, "business associations along with the associated networks, coalitions and lobbies have proven the most powerful societal force in practice when setting the broad agenda for North America's political economy" (Clarkson 2008, 180). Indeed, policy groups such as the Business Council on National Issues (BCNI) and the Canadian Chamber of Commerce have played vital roles in advancing the strategy of continental neoliberalism in conjunction with key state agencies and counterparts abroad.

As a capitalist class strategy, however, the project of integrating the North American bloc has produced new forms of "contentious politics" on both national and transnational scales (Ayres and Macdonald 2009, 7). The project of continental neoliberalism has radically transformed the economic structure and political landscape of the region to the benefit of capital and to the detriment of labour and more marginalized social strata. Denied any role in the negotiating process, working-class and popular forces have mobilized against the integration agenda on multiple occasions, using local, national, and transnational modes of protest. To date, these mobilizations have yet to impede or arrest the free trade agenda. But as "deep integration" proceeds, it is worth exploring the extent to which a strategy of "contentious transnationalism" (Ayres 2004) might reverse or reform the project of continental neoliberalism.

In short, this chapter examines the ways in which the corporate community of Canada pursued an escalating strategy of continental neoliberalism as a spatial fix to the crises of capitalism. It shows, as well, how this strategy has provoked a contentious opposition to the internationalization of capital in the North American bloc.

To map the history of this process, I have organized the chapter into four sections. In the first, I analyse the economic crisis of the 1970s and the mobilization of the BCNI around a free trade strategy. I also examine the unique popular protests that met the CAFTA negotiations. In the second section, I address the corporate activism around NAFTA in the early 1990s. I also consider the new types of cross-border protest that emerged in response to the NAFTA accord. In the third section, I examine the "deep integration" strategy of the Canadian corporate elite in the post-9/11 period. I look, in particular, at the role of the Canadian Council of Chief Executives (CCCE) in advancing the Security and Prosperity Partnership (SPP). In the final section, I consider more recent developments in continental integration, particularly the 2011 Border Declaration on Perimeter Security and Economic Competitiveness. In examining these issues, I link the project of "deep integration" to the social relations of capitalism, and appraise what this project has meant for the balance of class forces in Canada and beyond. More than this, I reveal the dedicated efforts of corporate elites to embed themselves in a continental economy as a first step towards internationalization on a broader scale.

From Crisis to Neoliberalism: The BCNI and CAFTA

In the aftermath of the Second World War, a "permeable" type of Fordism characterized the political economy of Canada. According to Jane Jenson (1989), this "regime of accumulation" differed from both the social democratic welfare states of Europe and the liberal variant of Fordism in the United States by its combination of three important features. First, the state recognized union rights and collective bargaining in the private sector without incorporating working-class organizations into public planning mechanisms. Labour relations were managed at a distance by the state, which endorsed a private sector system of production and distribution.

Second, because the state did not organize the capital/labour compromise, welfare state programs were more limited than in Europe. In this context, the primary intervention of the federal government was in supporting the social program spending of the provinces through cost-sharing arrangements and in funding national infrastructure programs such as the TransCanada Highway and the St. Lawrence Seaway.

Third, the Canadian economy was embedded in a regional structure of accumulation. The Fordist complex of "mass production for mass consumption" was organized around the export of resources to the US market in exchange for imports of manufactured goods and FDI. The permeable nature of this accumulation strategy meant that Keynesian techniques of demand-side management were less effective in Canada, and that the Canadian state and corporate elite were highly dependent on the political economy of US capitalism. Nevertheless, the strategy was effective at building a diverse national economy, with value-added capacities, advanced infrastructure, and modest social programs, all of which supported the accumulation of capital and rising living standards. That the Canadian economy expanded at an average annual rate of more than 5 per cent in the three decades after the Second World War was a sign of the success of permeable Fordism as a mode of accumulation.

This post-war strategy reached a limit in the late 1960s, however, when the world economy experienced a crisis of profitability (Brenner 2006a). The crisis registered in Canada in several ways. First, after a quick recovery in the early 1970s, the rate of profit began a sharp descent from 1974 to 1982 (see Figure 1; and McCormack 2014). The result was a decade of economic stagnation, characterized by low rates of investment and GDP growth, and high rates of unemployment. Second, the crisis was compounded by high rates of inflation, which accompanied the oil shocks of 1973. In this context, Canadian workers increasingly went on strike to maintain their wages and living standards. In 1976, "a record one and a half million strikers marched in more than a thousand picket lines and stopped production for 11.6 million person days. Three out of ten strikes in the 1970s were wildcats, [and] Italy was allegedly the only country in the Western World to match Canada in terms of militancy. The country was witnessing a *full-scale mass revolt*" (Heron 1996, 94, emphasis added). Third, in the aftermath of Bretton Woods, the value of the Canadian dollar increased against the US dollar, from a pegged rate of 92.5 cents in 1970 to above par in 1974. In this context, the current account deficit increased, the merchandise balance slipped into deficit, and Canada experienced new forms of capital flight.

For all of these reasons, the 1970s was a decade of *systemic crisis* for the Canadian state and capitalist class. Facing the turbulence of falling profits, striking workers, rising prices, and trading deficits, Canada abandoned the strategy of permeable Fordism and began to explore

Figure 1. The Rate of Profit in Canada, 1961–2010

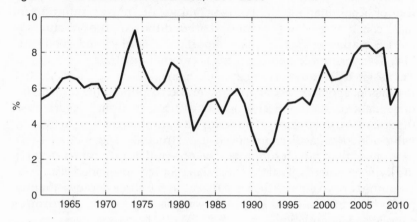

Source: Author's calculations, from Statistics Canada, CANSIM II database, table 0310002; and table 3800016.

new methods by which to escape the crisis. For the Liberal government of Pierre Trudeau, the first task was to halt inflation through wage and price controls and collective bargaining restrictions (Panitch and Swartz 1993). A new industrial policy was also imposed to increase domestic ownership in the mining, energy, and manufacturing sectors. The most important elements of this "Third National Policy" were the Foreign Investment Review Agency (created in 1973) and the National Energy Program (1980). By screening foreign investment and nationalizing the energy industry, the Trudeau government sought to lead a "resource-driven restructuring of the industrial sector" (Brodie and Jenson 1988, 27, quoted in McBride 2005, 38).

In alliance with many provincial governments, the capitalist class rejected this strategy of "continental nationalism" (Niosi 1985b). For the former, the strategy was an affront to their constitutional rights over resources development. For the latter, the strategy conflicted with the political interests of the private sector, which feared the growing autonomy of the state and its "interventionist, centralist and nationalistic" agenda (Pratt 1982, 27, quoted in McBride 2005, 38).

Moreover, since the early 1970s, the leading factions of the capitalist class had derived a different set of economic interests that were not reflected in Trudeau's strategies. Five transformations in the political economy of Canada were critical in this regard. First, from a peak in 1971, foreign ownership began a steep descent as US capital fled in light of the crisis. Second, as Canadian firms took control over key sectors of the economy, they increased the patterns of concentration and centralization. As a result, by 1978, "the 17 largest enterprises controlled 63.6 per cent of the assets of the *Financial Post's* largest Canadian corporations. By 1987, 74.5 per cent of the assets of the 186 largest Canadian non-financial corporations were controlled by just 17 dominant enterprises" (Richardson 1992, 311–2). Third, on this foundation, the Canadian corporate network was reconstituted, with directorship interlocks taking the form of a national bloc of "finance capital" (Carroll 1989). Fourth, Canadian capital expanded abroad through cross-border investments and multinational forms of production. Canadian finance invested deeply in the Caribbean and Latin America (Kaufman 1984), and Canada's leading industrial firms purchased assets around the world (Niosi 1985a). Finally, much of this expansion took the form of continental integration; as Jorge Niosi (1985b, 63) reveals, "Canadian enterprise [had become] increasingly continental both in terms of its market orientation and in terms of investment patterns."

The crisis of the 1970s produced, therefore, a new structure of accumulation and capitalist class formation in Canada. Canadian capital regained control over key sectors of the economy, engineered new forms of concentration and centralization, and expanded internationally, especially within the North American bloc. As a case in point, between 1981 and 1990, Canadian direct investment stocks in the United States grew by an annual average of 12 per cent, and doubled between 1981 and 1985. More broadly, Canadian firms were increasingly active in the world market of export production. For example, by the early 1980s, 40 per cent of firms represented by the Canadian Manufacturers' Association were involved in export production, up from 15 per cent in the early 1970s (Clarkson 2008, 173). From 1980 to 1991, the share of domestic manufacturing output that went towards exports also increased from 23 to 43 per cent (BCNI 1993).

Thus, by the early 1980s, a gap was growing between the national policies of the state and the economic patterns of internationalization in the Canadian political economy. In this context, the corporate elite became increasingly concerned with the growing autonomy of the Trudeau government, which was ever less attuned to the class-wide interests of Canadian capital (Clarkson 2002, 26). To secure these interests, the corporate elite self-organized to re-exert power in and over the state (Langille

1987, 46–7). The goal was not just to discipline the Trudeau government, but also to advance a new regime of accumulation in Canada and a new framework for the internationalization of capital on national, regional, and global scales. This project, which came to fruition through CAFTA, is best described as *continental neoliberalism*.

It is important to recognize the leading role of the BCNI (established in 1976) in directing this project. Modelled on the US Business Roundtable, the BCNI was formed, in the words of long-time president Thomas d'Aquino, because "major business leaders wanted to be able to move quickly on issues and address them at the highest level" (Langille 1987, 53–4). The intention was not simply to respond to government initiatives, but also to shape those initiatives in the first place to advance the class-wide interests of capital. Indeed, through the BCNI, the corporate community found a means of developing a common class consciousness and a program for action.

In the early 1980s, as the economy entered a new stage of crisis,[3] the BCNI went on the offensive. In particular, it began to campaign for a comprehensive trade pact with the United States. For the BCNI, "free trade" was the panacea to the crisis – it would secure export markets, protect investments in both countries, and put downward pressure on wages in Canada. In a key speech for the BCNI, d'Aquino (1987) argued that free trade was necessary to overcome protectionism in the US Congress, to attract FDI to Canada as an emerging base for US imports, to provide a "model" for liberalization on a global scale, to "magnify Canada's ability to compete in the global marketplace," and to "encourage larger, lower-cost production in our factories," leading to productivity gains, specialization, and economies of scale within a regional trading zone. For the BCNI, then, the free trade agenda was the keystone of a broader strategy of continental neoliberalism, which itself was viewed as a step towards the internationalization of capital on a wider scale. The fundamental goal was to reorganize class relations in Canada and to restore the rate of profit through the spatial fix that a trade agreement would effect.

To these ends, the BCNI began a major mobilization for free trade. After reaching an internal consensus in 1982, it began to lobby other business policy groups in Canada as well as the US government and private sector. It made key submissions to the Macdonald Royal Commission (Canada 1985), and by 1984 had enlisted the support of Progressive Conservative Prime Minister Brian Mulroney. In March 1985, seventeen members of the BCNI travelled to Washington for three days of meetings with US corporate elites and cabinet members, and earned the Business Round-table's endorsement of free trade.[4] In the same month, at the "Shamrock Summit" in Quebec City, Mulroney and US President Ronald Reagan announced the beginning of negotiations for a preferential trading agreement. These negotiations were highly secretive and closed except to members of the corporate elite, who were present in Canada's advisory committees (Clarkson 2008, 176).[5] For its part, the BCNI formed the Canadian Alliance for Jobs and Opportunities (CAJO) to shape the outcome of the "free trade election" of 1988.[6] In the two years leading up to the election, the CAJO spent roughly $18 million on pro–free trade advertising, or more than that spent by all political parties combined (Richardson 1992, 322). In these ways, the BCNI played a critical role in shaping the political discourse of the country, the policy framework of the federal government, and the outcome of the election, which gave the Progressive Conservative Party another majority government.

CAFTA came into effect on 1 January 1989. As a preferential trading agreement, it reduced tariffs on key products over a ten-year period, enshrined the principal of "national treatment" of foreign-produced goods and services, and established new investor protections and dispute settlement mechanisms. It did not, however, eliminate the right of US governments to impose antidumping and countervailing duties, and thus represented a more modest achievement than the Canadian government had sought.

Opposition to the agreement was widespread in Canada, and included a broad coalition of unions, church groups, women's organizations, environmental campaigners, provincial governments, and the opposition parties in Ottawa, representing a majority of Canadian voters.[7] In 1987, the opposition formed the Pro-Canada Network, which later changed its name to the Action Canada Network in light of protests from Quebec. The opposition argued that free trade would damage the manufacturing and cultural sectors of the Canadian economy as well as the universal social programs of the state. To its own strategic detriment, the opposition in English Canada framed the debate in terms of national sovereignty and independence, and thus blocked the possibility of forging deep alliances with activists in Quebec, who were uninterested in defending a strong federal state (Brunelle and Dugas 2009, 63–4). In addition, the New Democratic Party – Canada's social democratic party – largely ignored the movement against CAFTA and in the 1988 election merely offered a "contentless populism" (McBride 2005, 66). The same was true of the wider opposition, which framed the battle in terms of nationalism over class. As Leo Panitch (1994, 80) notes, "it must be admitted that this coalition, and much less the opposition parties, never really made clear what their alternative really was. The experience with the 1980–84 Liberal Government showed that a policy for more economic independence and social justice could not rely on the cooperation of business. Yet the anti-free trade coalition [was] afraid to spell out the conclusion that the alternative had to involve fundamental challenges to capital's power and radically democratizing the state."

For all these reasons, the opposition failed to build an effective counterpower to CAFTA and the leading factions of capital behind it. Part of the problem was a failure to recognize the multinational character of the Canadian state and the pitfalls of left-nationalism as a political framework for action. Part of the problem, as well, was a reluctance to analyse CAFTA in terms of the internationalization of capital and to build a program that addressed this reality. Although various socialist groups offered such a program, they did not participate in the mainstream movement, and thus exerted no influence on the 1988 election campaign. It should be noted as well that the movement against CAFTA was based overwhelmingly in Canada, rather than in the United States, and few ties were established to opposition forces across the border.

With the failure of the movement, however, new modes of transnational opposition were set to emerge as part of the protests against NAFTA in the early 1990s.

NAFTA and the Internationalization of Capital

The passing of the Canadian-American Free Trade Agreement marked a key turning point for Canadian capitalism. With the framework of continental integration in place, the structural logic of the Canadian economy was set to change. After the recession of 1990–92, the rate of profit began a steep ascent that would last for a decade and a half, from 2.5 per cent in 1992 to 8.4 per cent in 2006. By 2007, corporate profits reached a historic record of $203.2 billion, or more than 13 per cent of GDP (Baragar and Seccareccia 2008, 68–9).[8] This radical rise in corporate profits was based, in part, on the rationalization of production that free trade encouraged.

According to John Baldwin and Guy Gellatly (2007, 25–6), the Canadian manufacturing sector experienced a rapid rate of turnover in the decade after 1988, with 40 per cent of factories in 1997 representing new outlays of productive investment. Conversely, approximately

47 per cent of factories in 1987 were no longer operative a decade later. Although foreign firms exhibited a stronger tendency to expand via mergers and acquisitions, domestic firms were three times more likely to engage in greenfield investment, and thus generated a new pattern of industrial expansion under Canadian control. As the free trade opposition had argued, however, this process of rationalization cost the economy a net loss of 276,000 jobs between 1989 and 1997 (Scott, Salas, and Campbell 2001). Although CAFTA alone cannot be blamed for these losses, it was a critical part of the restructuring agenda, and had the effect of reconstituting class relations in the country.

The North American Free Trade Agreement of 1994 compounded or intensified all of these dynamics, and further entrenched the power of capital in Canada. The agenda for a new agreement was first discussed in a 1990 phone conversation between the BCNI's d'Aquino and Claudio Gonzales, a prominent Mexican businessman and a key member of the Club of 30, a highly secretive association of large-scale capitalists in Mexico. According to d'Aquino,[9] Gonzales and the Club wanted to extend CAFTA to Mexico, to create a continental zone of trade, production, and finance. In particular, the Mexican group sought expertise in negotiating a free trade agreement with the United States. After hosting the Club of 30 in Toronto for meetings on these issues, d'Aquino placed a call to Prime Minister Mulroney, who then consulted with US President George H.W. Bush. After the United States and Mexico began discussions on a formal treaty, the Canadian state – under the guidance of the BCNI – moved to be included. The key trade-off for Canada was the commitment of military forces to Operation Desert Storm in 1991 (Drohan 1991). With this commitment, negotiations for another trade agreement became trilateral in scope.

After fourteen months of negotiations, a trilateral trade deal was announced on 12 August 1992, and then signed on 17 December. NAFTA was the most comprehensive trade deal of the time, and soon served as a model for other multilateral agreements on trade and investment liberalization. The agreement included the phased elimination of tariffs on all manufactured goods; the removal of quotas, government procurement, state trade enterprise and general systems of preference; the free trade of agricultural products between the United States and Mexico within fifteen years; the principle of trade in services, finance, insurance, transportation, telecommunications, and government services; a dispute settlement mechanism with strong enforcement; investor protections via Trade-Related Investment Measures; and intellectual property rights through Trade-Related Investment Protections.

Most notoriously, Chapter 11 of the agreement gave corporations from NAFTA-zone countries the right to sue governments in the event of losing profits from "unfair" barriers to trade and investment. Article 1902 allowed for countervailing duties and antidumping laws, and the agreement imposed strong limits on nationalization and expropriation. As a result, many critics argue that NAFTA did not so much establish rules for trade disputes as empower corporations to defend their profits against all state encroachments. For Canada, NAFTA also imposed a new regime on the energy sector, including national treatment for member-state corporations; the principle of "proportional sharing" to safeguard current export levels to the United States; the end of preferential pricing for Canadian consumers and businesses; and the elimination of export taxes, impact assessments, and export licences.

For all of these reasons, NAFTA reflected the hierarchies of the North American bloc; it incorporated the *asymmetry of power* between the United States and the other two member states (Cameron and Tomlin 2000, 15, 229). In the words of Stephen Clarkson (2002, 41–2), NAFTA "reconstituted American hegemony in the form of an economic rule book that establishes an unevenly liberalized market and a set of supra-constitutional constraints on the policy-making options of both Canada and Mexico." As such, the agreement helped to "construct" a continental platform for US power in North America and, indeed, in the world (Clarkson and Mildenberger 2011, 22–3). At the same time, it embodied the structural contradiction between capital and labour, and between *capitalism* and the environment. Although it included side agreements on labour rights and environmental cooperation, these "were largely consultative mechanisms ... with limited means of enforcement" (Hufbauer and Schott 2005, 7).

The BCNI fully endorsed this new framework for continental neoliberalism. In a key submission to the Senate Standing Committee on Foreign Affairs, the BCNI (1993) argued that the "liberalization of global trade and investment regimes on a multilateral basis must remain at the core of Canada's foreign economic policy." To this end, NAFTA would not only expand CAFTA, but also "improve Canada's ability to compete in the global marketplace ... forge stronger trading links with other Latin American countries, ... [open] the Mexican market for Canadian goods, services and investments on an equal basis with the United States, ... forestall the emergence of a 'hub-and-spoke' trading system, ... [and pave] the way for any Canadian involvement in broader trade liberalization arrangements that may evolve in the Western hemisphere." For the BCNI, then, NAFTA was a critical framework for the internationalization of capital on national, regional, and global scales. It provided a spatial fix for the concentration and centralization of capital at new levels of the world market.

In pursuit of these goals, the BCNI played an important role in mobilizing the continent's governments and corporate communities. In 1990, for instance, it helped establish a sister organization in Mexico, the *Coordinación de Organismos Empresariales de Comercio Exterior*, which helped initiate the early negotiations. Through a variety of lobbying measures, the BCNI also convinced the Liberal government of Jean Chrétien to endorse NAFTA after the 1993 election. In fact, the BCNI put "blood, sweat, and tears" into this lobbying effort.[10] The Liberal platform had called for a renegotiation of NAFTA, but this promise was broken soon after taking office. The implementation of NAFTA thus demonstrated the multiscale capacities of the Canadian corporate elite in advancing continental neoliberalism.

As a transparent strategy of capital, NAFTA provoked a wide array of political contestation. The negotiations of the early 1990s generated a wave of protest in all three countries, including new forms of transnational collaboration between opposition currents (Ayres and Macdonald 2009, 10). In Canada, Common Frontiers, a broad coalition of unions, environmental groups, churches, and women's organizations, led the movement in civil society. Common Frontiers engaged in a mix of national and transnational activities, and tried to build a regional campaign of working-class and social movements against the trade accord. In Quebec, the opposition was led by the Coalition on Trilateral Negotiations, which changed its name to the Network on Continental Integration in 1995 upon deciding to focus on the upcoming Free Trade Agreement of the Americas (Brunelle and Dugas 2009, 69). Around NAFTA itself, however:

[t]here was a substantial increase in cross-border activity between Canadian, US, and Mexican groups leading up to and during the negotiations for NAFTA. There was increased experimentation at the margins of the national protest repertoire even before NAFTA came into effect. In an attempt to rally their national publics against the accord, citizen groups in the three member countries shared information and plotted strategy leading to the emergence of cross-border and cross-sectoral cooperative strategizing. Canadian groups played a leadership role by sharing their experiences of networking against [CAFTA] with their US and Mexican counterparts. Regular cross-border exchanges and conferences between

various organizations began as early as 1990, when discussions over a possible continental accord became more serious. Consultations on free trade and its impact were held in Canada, the US, and Mexico and along the US-Mexico border. While many of these actions were short-lived, narrowly focused campaigns critiquing the possible sectoral implications of NAFTA, long-term strategic relationships also emerged. These relationships provided the building blocks for more sustained forms of contentious North American civic activity. (Ayres 2004, 104–5)

This wide-ranging opposition failed to stop the agreement, but it did establish a new tradition of transnational organizing, which would later re-emerge in the mass struggles against the Multilateral Agreement on Investment (1997), the World Trade Organization (1999), and the Summit of the Americas (2001). For the left in Canada, this experience of cross-border protest was transformative: instead of framing the "threat" (and the movement) in terms of nationalism, it began to comprehend the free trade agenda in the language of capital and class, while recognizing the national asymmetries between the United States and Canada on the one hand, and Mexico on the other. The result was a more class-conscious and internationalist movement that avoided the pitfalls of national chauvinism (Coburn 2011).

If the opposition failed in the end, what did NAFTA accomplish? The relative value of Canadian exports continued to escalate, from 25.7 per cent of GDP in 1989 to 45.5 per cent in 2000, while the value of imports soared from 25.7 per cent to 40.3 per cent of GDP over the same period. Furthermore, between 1992 and 2002, manufacturing output and employment grew rapidly – the former by 47.6 per cent, the latter by 21.5 per cent. In this context, the share of manufacturing output dedicated to exports jumped from roughly 33 per cent in 1988 to 53 per cent in 2007 (Jackson 2007, 213–6). Over the same period, Canadian direct investment in the United States and Mexico increased so much so that Canada became a net exporter of FDI. To some extent, then, NAFTA supported the expanded reproduction of capital in Canada.

Yet NAFTA also produced several contradictions in the Canadian political economy. For one thing, Canada's trade balance became more reliant on macroeconomic conditions in the United States and on low-dollar monetary policies at home (Seccareccia 2007). Canada's export power also became more reliant on low-wage manufacturing production, as unit labour costs were forced down by US competition and the threat of capital flight (Ayres 2004, 115). In this context, the unionization of Canada's workforce dropped from 39.5 per cent in 1988 to 30.7 per cent in 2005, a clear sign of the decomposition of labour power in the context of continental neoliberalism (D. Robinson 2007, 273). Finally, the productivity gap between Canada and the United States continued to increase, and Canada failed to receive a surge of manufacturing FDI. With this in mind, Stanford argues that, "[w]hat is obvious ... is that the most important *qualitative* shifts that were supposed to be motivated by trade liberalization have clearly not occurred" (2006a, 154).

What has occurred, though, is a spatial transformation of production, accumulation, and class formation in the Canadian political economy (see Chapter 4). NAFTA sparked an *internationalization of Canadian capital on national, regional, and global scales*. It has allowed, for example, the Canadian economy to overcome trade deficits with Europe, Asia, and many developing regions by securing even greater trade surpluses with the United States. It also has allowed Canadian firms to reap economies of scale in a regional trading zone as a precursor to expansion abroad in other continents. Furthermore, NAFTA has entrenched the rights of capital to do business wherever and however it likes, and induced a downward movement of wages and working conditions in Canada. It also has allowed Canadian capital to hire seasonal Mexican labour power, especially for low-wage, non-unionized agricultural work. Through this new regime of accumulation, then, the Canadian economy has become increasingly internationalized, with economic linkages spanning the continent and, indeed, the globe. In fact, recent studies indicate that Corporate Canada has not been "hollowed out" by free trade so much as reconstituted around transnational business interests (Carroll and Klassen 2010).

As a critical framework for all of these changes, NAFTA can be viewed, therefore, as an external constitution for the internationalization of capital on multiple scales. It is a framework for imposing disciplinary neoliberalism on working classes and marginalized groups across the continent.

From 9/11 to "Deep Integration": The Class Politics of the SPP and the NACC

The attacks of 11 September 2001 triggered a third conjuncture in the political economy of continental neoliberalism: a new phase of "deep integration" for Canada within a "Fortress North America" (Barlow 2005; Grinspun and Shamsie 2007). The closing of the border on 9/11 and the new agenda of "homeland security" in the United States placed limits on the continental system through which Canadian capital operated. Fearing such impediments, Canada's corporate elite looked to embed the continental project in a new security architecture. Through a host of ad hoc coalitions and permanent lobby groups, this project became one of deep integration with US power structures as a necessary trade-off for unfettered access to continental markets.

Between 2001 and 2005, for example, the Coalition for Secure and Trade-Efficient Borders – "one of the largest business coalitions formed in Canadian history" (CSTB 2005, 1) – published a number of recommendations on trade and security policies for North America and the wider world system, many of which were incorporated into the US-Canada Smart Border Declaration and 30-Point Action Plan of December 2001. Likewise, in 2003, the Public Policy Forum (2003) – a think tank comprised of leading members of the Canadian corporate community – delivered a key report to the incoming Liberal government of Paul Martin on the urgent need for closer ties with the United States in matters of continental trade and international security. Over the same period, the C.D. Howe Institute repeatedly called for a new "grand bargain" with the United States in terms of regional integration (Dobson 2002a,b). In these studies, a new strategy for deep integration emerged: in exchange for economic access to the US market, the Canadian state should collaborate in the "global war on terror" at all scales of concern – national, regional, and international.

As in the past, the BCNI-turned-Canadian Council of Chief Executives (CCCE) articulated this strategy most clearly.[11] Between 2001 and 2008, the primary project of the CCCE was the Security and Prosperity Initiative, a comprehensive policy package on border security, continental integration, free trade, and national defence. This initiative consisted of four key proposals. First, Canada and the United States should rethink border security by shifting the focus from the internal to the external border of North America. By focusing on external points of entry, the two countries might protect the continent from outside security threats and maintain the free flow of goods across their internal border, which should function as a "shared checkpoint within an integrated economic space" (CCCE 2003, 4). Second, Canada and the United States should maximize economic efficiencies by harmonizing their regulatory regimes with respect to trade, investment, foreign ownership, health, safety, and the environment to match the economic integration that already exists. Third, the two countries should sign a "resource security pact," which would operate according to the principles of open access and free trade. In this way, the United States would achieve guaranteed access to Canada's oil and natural gas supplies, while Canada would gain exemption from US antidumping laws and countervailing duties. Finally, Canada should rebuild and restructure its military since, for too long, it has been "a free rider on American coattails and a toothless advocate of soft power" (CCCE 2004, 17). In the new security environment, Canada should "contribute more effectively to the global war on terror," and build "a credible capacity … to respond meaningfully and rapidly to crises anywhere in the world" (CCCE 2003, 5; CCCE Defense and Security). These four recommendations were designed, in short, to consolidate the economic position of the Canadian corporate elite in the North American bloc and the political-military capacities of Canada as a secondary power on the global stage. As such, they formed the key political strategy of Canada's corporate elites: a strategy of neoliberal market enforcement, continental security alignment, and disciplinary militarism.

As in the earlier campaigns of the BCNI, the CCCE lobbied key business associations and governments of the three NAFTA countries. By 2005, it had earned the support of the US-based Council on Foreign Relations and the Mexican-based *Consejo Mexicano de Asuntos Internacionales*. In a joint report (Council on Foreign Relations 2005), these groups presented a comprehensive plan to "Build North America." The plan called for a common external tariff and outer security perimeter, a North American border pass with biometric information, a unified border action plan, the coordination of law enforcement and the sharing of intelligence, and a common economic space in which capital and commodities would move freely.

In March 2005, at the regional summit in Waco, Texas, the governments of the three countries agreed to launch a Security and Prosperity Partnership (SPP), thus formalizing the CCCE's Security and Prosperity Initiative. As an integral aspect of this initiative, the North American Competitiveness Council (NACC) was formed in March 2006. The NACC was an official business adjunct to SPP, consisting of ten corporate executives from each country. On 13 June 2006, Canadian Prime Minister Stephen Harper announced the names of the ten Canadian representatives on the NACC, five of whom were members of the CCCE – the other five subsequently joined the CCCE.

The formation of the NACC was important in two respects. First, it was an expression of the internationalization of capital in the continent.

Figure 2. The NACC's Circle of Capital, 2007

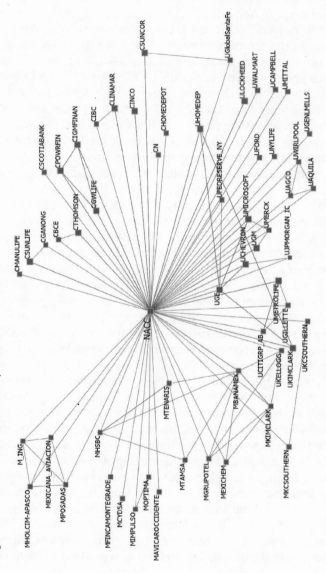

Note: Canadian firms begin with a "C," US firms with a "U," and Mexican firms with an "M"; the author thanks William K. Carroll for providing this figure.

Viewed through a sociogram of corporate directors and their interlocks (Figure 2), the NACC appears as a condensation of capitalist class power in the regional setting. In Figure 2, five important features stand out:

1. In the case of interlocks involving US and Canadian firms, the majority exist within the national groupings themselves, suggesting a meeting of relatively equal national corporate communities.
2. No interlocks exist between Canadian and Mexican firms, reflecting the relative absence of economic ties between the two countries.
3. US firms share interlocks with Canadian and Mexican firms involved in the NACC, and thus appear as corporate anchors or mediators of a regional planning body.
4. Few interlocks exist within the Mexican complement of firms, indicating a relative absence of national corporate ties, in contrast to those within the US and Canadian complements.
5. At the level of individual directors, the firms of the Mexican complement show a tendency of *interiorizing* US- (and European-) based corporate connections, as an indication of their dependence on foreign-based capital. Related to this, Mexican members of financial institutions tend to link to foreign-controlled firms, while Canadian and US members are linked to financial firms under domestic control.

In these ways, the NACC was a symbol of regional class formation in the context of unequal power relations in the North American zone. It was an expression of the uneven development of capitalism, and of capitalist class formation, in the continental bloc.

At the same time, NACC was a sign of effective mobilization by the continental corporate community. As an advisory body to the SPP, the NACC represented a vehicle for shaping, directing, and influencing the further alignment of US, Canadian, and Mexican public policies. In the process, it served as an organizational nexus for class and state formation on the continent, in the same manner as the European Roundtable on Business works towards the European Council (Carroll and Sapinski 2011; van Apeldoorn 2002). The relationship between the NACC and the SPP, however, was more personal, and more productive, to corporate interests. Held in the same location, meetings of the NACC were used to devise proposals that were then submitted to summits of the SPP. As Teresa Healy (2007) documents, many of these proposals were incorporated directly into SPP agreements and declarations.

For example, in February 2007, the NACC issued a report (NACC 2007) with fifty-one recommendations for "enhancing North America's competitive position in the world economy." These recommendations included improving "the secure flow of goods and people within North America," cutting "red tape" in government-business relations in North America, and ensuring a "secure supply of imported energy" to the United States (ibid., 1). In the final leaders' statements of the Summit held in Montebello, Quebec, in August 2007, these recommendations were included in the agreements on intellectual property, cooperative regulations, and energy science and technology. Although the NACC was unable to secure every policy it submitted to the SPP over the course of its existence, it pushed forward a new stage of continental neoliberalism, one in which the state-capital nexus was aligned ever more closely. In the process, the democratic structures of each country were constrained and marginalized, as the corporate sector alone was given access to summits on "security" and "prosperity." As Healy (2007, iii) argues, "democratic participation has become so discredited in the eyes of the elite that government leaders are now taking their direction openly and explicitly from a group of unelected corporate leaders. The CEO 'prosperity' agenda is presented and justified through a 'security' discourse. The CEOs go to great lengths to show how the two agendas can be mutually reinforcing. In the view of the NACC, security doesn't *trump* trade. Rather, trade can *grow* security."

In this context, the SPP invited a wave of protest in all three North American countries. Building on the cross-border networks that were formed against NAFTA, the protests took aim at the summit meetings of the SPP and the NACC. On 19 August 2007, for example, thousands of protestors gathered on Parliament Hill in Ottawa to register dissent with the SPP and the Montebello Summit. At the site of the Summit, several thousand protestors were corralled into police-mandated "protest pens," and the Sûreté du Québec used *agents provocateurs* to justify the use of pepper spray, tear gas, and rubber bullets on protestors approaching the site (Healy 2012, 158). In April 2008, further protests met the Leaders Summit in New Orleans, and faced similar modes of police intervention. On 9 August 2009, protests also took place against the Leaders Summit in Guadalajara, Mexico. Despite a massive security operation, protestors demanded a renegotiation of NAFTA with full public involvement, and criticized Canada for imposing visa restrictions on Mexican tourists while supporting contentious mining projects in Mexico. Involving members of trade unions, church groups, student councils, environmental agencies, immigrant organizations, and peasant associations, the protests in all three countries were a product of the undemocratic manner in which the SPP was organized. For demonstrators, the response of security personnel in all three countries showed the class-based nature of continental neoliberalism and the growing embrace of "technocratic authoritarianism" by North America's governments and corporate communities (Carroll 2009b, 3660). With this in mind, Healy's (2007, 31) assessment of the SPP is vital to understanding this recent phase of continental neoliberalism:

> Posing as democrats, the CEOs come to these meetings as civil society organizations advising government. Yet they continue to discredit public participation and undermine the democratic wishes of the people. They provoke in the name of security, and for the benefit of profits. They sustain markets freed by technologies of fear. They assert the ever-present twin threats of war and off-shoring. They ally themselves with political leaders who push government past the bounds of legality into a secretive territory, in which the use of surveillance and intimidation to quell dissent is normalized. This is a territory fraught with human rights abuses, attacks on sovereignty and communities. This is the territory of the new North America in which corporate rights and military power are enshrined.

Beyond the Borders: Future Directions of Continental Integration

In 2009, as the global economic crisis was deepening, the SPP's ambitious agenda was terminated by the new administration of US President Barack Obama. Fearing the comprehensive thrust of the SPP in a time of crisis, and concerned with the optics of "security" in the wake of the George W. Bush administration, the White House announced that the SPP was "no longer an active initiative" (Dobbin 2009). The mobilization of conservative and far-right political forces against the SPP was perhaps another factor in the Obama administration's decision (Ayres and Macdonald 2012a, 348). On the Mexican side, the new government of Felipe Calderón was also wary of the SPP in the context of deep concerns about narco-trafficking and drug-related violence. For Stephen Harper, the SPP was far too ambitious in light of domestic conflicts in Parliament and growing protests in the streets. At the time, Harper wished for a smaller, more focused agenda for continental integration, and to this end, continued to meet with the

Canadian complement of the NACC for two years after the SPP was formally abandoned.[12]

Beyond these problems at a national level, the SPP failed because it "had been designed as an executive-branch-only, closed-door process" (Bow 2012, 75), and because of its "complete lack of democratic practice" (Healy 2012, 163). In this context, the "ad hoc, technocratic, and decentralized nature of the SPP working groups made it difficult for them to carry out the functions assigned to them of outreach and consultation with a wide range of stakeholders" (Ayres and Macdonald 2012a, 346). As a case in point, proponents of the SPP were unable to build a hegemonic or consensual culture of regional identification in North America, one that would be accepted and embraced by a wide array of civil society actors in the United States, Canada, and Mexico. Indeed, "[i]f successful region-building projects are based on a process of gradual identification of all participating states as 'us' and identification of outsiders as 'them,' the architects of North American regionalism ... failed woefully" (Ayres and Macdonald 2012b, 18). The SPP fell apart, then, for several reasons, including "the basic ideological incompatibility between regionalists' proposals and the Obama administration's sense of its problems and priorities; the 'distraction' of the three leaders by other kinds of policy and political challenges; and the shifting momentum between societal players, with the business community apparently discouraged and disinterested, and the unions and civil society organizations confident and engaged" (Bow 2012, 71).

In the wake of the SPP, new debates have emerged on the future of North American integration. For Emily Gilbert (2012, 200), the end of the SPP "marks a general waning of enthusiasm for regional initiatives, especially on the part of the United States." In this context, Randall Germain (2012, 34) argues that regionalism in North America will become "even more hollowed out than at present, and importantly, it will be accompanied by a reassertion of American influence via the steady increase of informal economic integration among Canada, Mexico, and the United States." In a similar vein, Stephanie Golob (2012) anticipates a future of "double-bilateralism" in North America, with the United States at the centre of a hub-and-spokes system.

As Jeffrey Ayres and Laura Macdonald (2012a, 336) observe, however, "the failure of the SPP initiative by no means suggests the basic neoliberal framework of security and prosperity via militarism and free trade has been eliminated from the regional agenda." In fact, despite the failure of the SPP, the integration of North America, particularly of

US-Canadian relations, has proceeded in new ways. The key change has been a move away from the grand vision of the SPP towards what d'Aquino calls "aggressive incrementalism" – a determined, yet slower, process of deep integration, with less obvious input from corporate actors (Healy 2012, 150).

In February 2011, for example, Canada and the United States moved forward with a new project of continental neoliberalism in the form of the Beyond the Borders Declaration (Obama and Harper 2011). The Declaration incorporated the political substance of the SPP, but in a bilateral, and more piecemeal, manner. It was also unhinged from any corporate advisory body such as the NACC, thus giving it a less controversial, and more low-key, profile.

Similar to the SPP, the Declaration called for Canada and the United States to "pursue a perimeter approach to security, working together within, at, and away from the borders of our two countries to enhance our security and accelerate the legitimate flow of people, goods, and services." In line with the notion of perimeter security, it also called on the two states to "develop the next generation of integrated cross-border law enforcement operations that leverage cross-designated officers and resources to jointly identify, assess, and interdict persons and organizations involved in transnational crime." To these ends, it established the Beyond the Border Working Group (BBWG), composed of representatives from the relevant departments of each state. Since 2011, the BBWG has focused on core issues such as early threat assessment, trade facilitation, economic growth, cyber security, intellectual property, and integrated cross-border law enforcement.

Although the Canadian corporate community has not been involved directly in the BBWG, it has offered guidance and support for the ongoing project of continental neoliberalism. On 25 March 2011, the Canadian Manufacturers & Exporters, the US National Association of Manufacturers, and the Mexican Confederation of Industrial Chambers issued a joint letter to the governments of North America requesting a coordinated strategy to "improve the capability of North American manufacturing to attract investment, strengthen our ability to compete in both domestic and overseas markets, and reduce market-distorting foreign trade practices."[13] In May 2011, the CCCE (2011) also voiced support for the Beyond the Borders Declaration. In a submission to the BBWG, the CCCE endorsed the "perimeter security and competitiveness action plan." On matters of common security, it recommended "[e]xpanding bi-national border enforcement efforts" and "a comprehensive, well-tested bilateral border contingency plan ... [with] joint infrastructure protection for pipelines and electricity grid systems as well as contingencies for regional or isolated border incidents." Likewise, regarding regulatory harmonization, it "strongly welcomed the Leaders' statement on the need for closer regulatory cooperation and the creation of the United States-Canada Regulatory Cooperation Council." Finally, on energy and environmental policy collaboration, it argued that "Canada can be an important partner in improving continental energy security," and that the two states should "expand the supply of all forms of energy" through "market-driven energy policies."

Formed in 2005, the North American Forum is one further vehicle through which the political, economic, and military establishments of the continent are pursuing integration. Involving members of the corporate community, the defence lobby, and the political elite of the United States, Canada, and Mexico, the North American Forum is a key site of concept-formation for the deep integration of energy, security, immigration, regulatory, and trade policies. Although it is formally unconnected to the BBWG or to any other trilateral process, it is "the only game in town" involving all three countries in new discussions on regional integration.[14] The low profile of both the North American Forum and the BBWG augers well for such a project. Unassociated with large summit meetings or comprehensive policy packages, these modules for a new stage of deep integration have yet to generate a contentious parry by transnational social movements.

Conclusion

Building on the extant relations of permeable Fordism, the project of North American integration since the 1980s has been driven by a capitalist class strategy of spatial restructuring. Led and directed by the corporate community, this strategy has been used to hike the rate of profit in a regional zone of production and exchange. As such, it has reconstituted the social relations of capitalism in Canada and across North America.

One finding of this chapter is that the Canadian corporate elite has played a vital role in activating continental neoliberalism. Through intersectoral policy groups such as the BCNI/CCCE, the Canadian capitalist class has been able to discipline the state in favour of a neoliberal policy course, especially with respect to "free trade" in North America. For the corporate elite of Canada, both CAFTA and NAFTA were capstones of a neoliberal architecture; they reorganized the class relations of Canadian capitalism, established economies of scale in a regional trading zone, and laid the foundation for global expansion. They also constrained the activist state in a "new constitutionalism" for neoliberal governance (Gill 1995).

In this context, descriptions of deep integration as a corporate-led "sell-out" seem one-sided and misplaced. Rather, continental neoliberalism is a *hegemonic class strategy* for the accumulation of capital and the discipline of labour in a continental trading zone. As such, it is a mechanism for the concentration and centralization of capital in new spaces of production and accumulation.

Since September 2001, a comprehensive security program has embellished the economic agenda of continental neoliberalism. Embodied in the SPP and the BBWG, the security agenda is designed to consolidate the North American space as an integrated zone of production, and to protect the continent from a host of security threats. These threats are not limited to foreign-based terrorism, but also include domestic social movements of environmental, labour, indigenous, and immigrant activists, from whom the class-based space of the continent needs protecting. As a framework for defending this realm, the new security agenda is inextricable from the class relations of neoliberalism on the continent and, indeed, around the world. In this respect, the building of Fortress North America has global implications in accordance with the internationalization of capital.

For students of Canadian politics, it is vital to recognize that the new security agenda is not simply a policy preference of certain governments in Ottawa – one that can be changed or transformed with ease by a different executive office. On the contrary, it is about fundamentally transforming the state as an *institution of class rule* in a field of continental social relations. In particular, it is about building a "strong state" that can defend private property in national, regional, and world markets against claims of popular and democratic forces. As Andrew Gamble (1988, 236) explains, "the strong state that is needed so that this economy may remain free is a state able to conduct effective surveillance and policing of the unemployed and the poor, able to confront and defeat any union challenge, [and] able to contain any upsurge of terrorism or public disorder."

For social movements in North America, the pace and scale of deep integration should induce sober senses. Even before 9/11, the cross-border movements of contentious resistance "had little or no impact on the strategy of market liberalization at a macro-economic level" (Brunelle and Dugas 2009, 58). Under new conditions of technocratic authoritarianism, these movements will confront a more implacable structure of class and state power on the continent. In this context, the politics of contentious transnationalism could become vital to the circulation, and further development, of movements for social justice. Although the "mass base of popular sector forces ... remain national in character," and although the nation-state remains "the most productive site for social and political contestation" (Ayres 2004, 118–19), cross-border movements can still shape the strategies and tactics of opposition forces, as the spread of Occupy Wall Street in 2011 testifies. In this context, as Ayres (2004, 119) notes, "[t]he key question is how to rekindle and build national strategies that are not competitive with, but are in fact compatible with, the continuation of limited projects of more focused contentious transnationalism." In these ways, the power of capital in driving continental neoliberalism might yet be challenged by a counterpower of working-class and popular forces.

PART III

Canadian Capital and Transnational Neoliberalism

4 The Internationalization of Canadian Capital

Over the past three decades, the Canadian economy has been restructured in two important ways. First, as discussed in the previous chapter, it has been rescaled through a capitalist class project of continental neoliberalism. Second, as I discuss in this chapter, it has been enmeshed in a wider process of *transnational neoliberalism* – in a broader structure of "transnational circulating capital" (Overbeek and van der Pijl 1993, 15). By connecting the Canadian economy to global circuits of production and exchange, the Canadian state has sought to maintain itself as a competitive space of accumulation and to support the expansion of Canadian firms across the world economy.

To these ends, successive Canadian governments have worked to construct a new framework for global capitalism. In the early 1990s, as part of the Uruguay Round of the General Agreement on Tariffs and Trade (GATT), the Canadian state helped to establish the World Trade Organization (WTO) (Froese 2010, 1, 24). In the same decade, Canada also advanced trade liberalization in the Asia-Pacific region – in particular, through the Asia-Pacific Economic Cooperation (APEC) forum. Within the Organisation for Economic Co-operation and Development (OECD), the Canadian state also pursued, in the late 1990s, the Multilateral Agreement on Investment (Coleman and Porter 2003, 256). In 2001, Canada hosted the Summit of the Americas in Quebec City, as part of the negotiations for a Free Trade Agreement of the Americas (FTAA). Less ambitiously, yet more productively, Canada signed a host of bilateral trade and investment agreements with countries such as Chile, Colombia, Costa Rica, Honduras, Israel, Jordan, Panama, and Peru. Through these different tools of foreign economic policy, the Canadian state has helped to advance what Stephen Gill

(1995, 412) calls a "new constitutionalism" for transnational neoliberalism.[1] In doing so, it has had the backing of the national corporate community.

For example, the Business Council on National Issues (BCNI) was heavily involved in domestic and international negotiations around the WTO. In particular, the BCNI attended GATT planning meetings in Geneva, submitted proposals to Canadian governments in Ottawa, and issued several reports on the merits of building a multilateral trading institution.[2] Throughout the 1990s, the BCNI was also present in forums related to APEC. For instance, during the 1997 APEC Summit in Vancouver, the BCNI hosted the first Chief Executive Officers' Summit of the Asia-Pacific region. Dubbed as a "private-sector counterpart to the APEC Leaders' Meeting," the Summit brought together more than two hundred business leaders from Asia and North America to discuss trade and investment liberalization (BCNI 1997). The BCNI also played an active role in shaping the FTAA – in particular, by attending the first Summit of the Americas in Miami as well as other planning meetings in the hemisphere.[3] Although the FTAA was exposed to public attention only in 1997, the Canadian Chamber of Commerce, the Canadian Council on International Issues, and the BCNI were discussing the agreement with the Department of Foreign Affairs and International Trade as early as 1993 (Barlow 2000). In these ways, the Canadian corporate elite has played an active role in shaping the strategy of transnational neoliberalism.

Along the way, popular forces at home and abroad have contested this strategy. At the APEC Summit in Vancouver, for instance, thousands of protestors faced off against quasi-police-state tactics, including protest pens, pre-emptive arrests, and pepper spray attacks on peaceful demonstrators. In late November 1999, many activists in Canada's social movements converged in Seattle to protest the WTO meetings being held there. In April 2001, the "antiglobalization movement" in Canada erupted against the Summit of the Americas in Quebec City, which was fenced off for visiting heads of state and leading corporate executives from the hemisphere. There, too, demonstrators were arrested en masse and attacked with rubber bullets, tear gas, and pepper spray by security forces. In protesting these institutions of transnational neoliberalism, the global justice movement positioned itself as a critical pole of extraparliamentary activism in Canada. In alliance with social movements from around the world, it sought to contest the one-sided approach to global integration by the Canadian state and corporate elite.

Despite such efforts by Canada's social movements, the strategy of transnational neoliberalism was advanced and consolidated. Through the new institutions of global capitalism, the Canadian state has built an external framework for sweeping transformations of the national economy and class structure. In particular, it has encouraged an *internationalization of capital* in Canada. Through new patterns of commodity trade and financial investment, the Canadian economy has been effectively globalized. This globalization, however, has not simply increased the quantitative ties of *value appropriation* between Canada and the world market, but also has established new, qualitative ties of *labour exploitation* across borders. Through these diverse patterns of transnational neoliberalism, the Canadian corporate elite has derived new means of accumulating capital in national, continental, and international markets. In the process, it has emerged as a leading faction of transnational corporate power (Klassen 2009; Klassen and Carroll 2011).

The goal of this chapter is to map the internationalization of capital in Canada. I start from the recognition that the internationalization of capital is an abstract tendency of the capitalist mode of production – one that drives towards an integrated system of finance, trade, and production on a global scale. As Christian Palloix (1977, 20) argued, the internationalization of capital is "defined by the fact that the process of converting the functional 'money' form [of capital] into the commodity form and into the productive form (and vice versa) can no longer be fully realized inside of a single capitalist social formation. In effect, the central element in this process of transformation, the commodity, is no longer produced in one nation. It is no longer limited in this way. *The commodity, or rather the commodity-group, can only be conceptualized, produced, and realized at the level of the world market.* This tendency is becoming more and more pronounced." Indeed, during the period of neoliberalism, the relationship between the "national" and the "international" has been transformed in dialectical ways, as both of these scales have been progressively intertwined. In these circumstances, "[t]he internationalization of capital and the workings of the internal national economy are not antagonistic, not two alternative realities, but are two phenomena which constantly mirror each other, amplifying each other in their own historic development because they are both shaped and moulded by capital" (ibid., 23).

Figure 3. The Internationalization of Capital: A Two-Scale Diagram of Value Flows

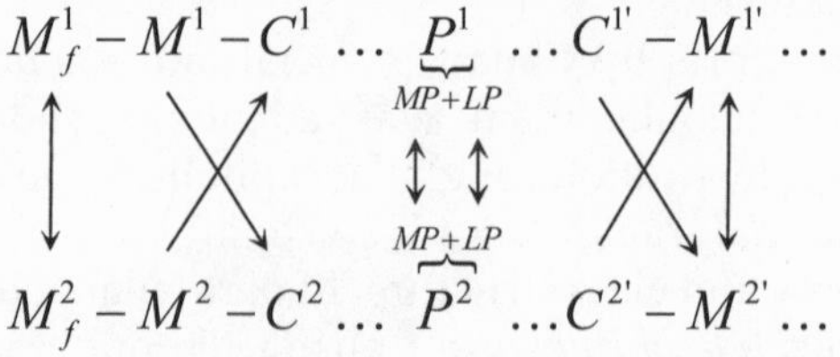

$$M_f^1 - M^1 - C^1 \ldots \underbrace{P^1}_{MP+LP} \ldots C^{1'} - M^{1'} \ldots$$

$$M_f^2 - M^2 - C^2 \ldots \underbrace{P^2}_{MP+LP} \ldots C^{2'} - M^{2'} \ldots$$

As a diagram of this process, Figure 3 depicts the value forms through which the internationalization of capital occurs. In this figure, the circuits of capital in two nation-states are intertwined through cross-border movements of money capital (M), commodity capital (C), and productive capital (P). As these movements of capital become increasingly pronounced, value is conceptualized, produced, and realized at a worldwide scale, and national circuits of capital are increasingly meshed with global ones. Over the past three decades, the world economy has been restructured in precisely such ways.

To map this process in Canada, I develop a "circuits-of-capital" approach.[4] In particular, I examine the internationalization of capital within the money, productive, and commodity circuits of accumulation. This approach is derived from Karl Marx's decomposition of value flows in *Capital* ([1867] 1990, vol. 2). Using dialectical methods, Marx reveals how the self-expansion of value occurs through different social forms in the circuit of capital, including the money form, the productive form, and the commodity form. Each of these forms is associated with a particular circuit through which value is objectified, as well as with a corresponding fraction[5] of capitalist class power (see Table 1). For example, the circuit of money capital involves the investment of money by *finance capitalists* to claim a profit of enterprise or interest. Likewise, the circuit of productive capital involves the purchase of means of production and labour power by *industrial capitalists* for the purpose of producing and selling new commodities with a higher value. Finally, the circuit of commodity capital involves the buying and selling of commodities by *commercial capitalists*, with the aim of seizing a share of total profit. Through these separate, yet connected, circuits of capital, the production, exchange, and distribution of value occurs under capitalism.

The key point for this chapter is that the internationalization of capital can be mapped through these integrated circuits. In fact, each circuit is associated with particular forms or pathways of internationalization

Table 1. The Circuits of Capital

Circuit	Value Form	Class Fraction
Productive circuit	$P(MP+L) - C' - M' - C' - P'$	Industrial capital
Commodity circuit	$C' - M' - C'$	Commercial capital
Money circuit	$M - C - P(MP+L) - C' - M'$	Finance capital

Table 2. Value Forms of Internationalization, Categorized by Circuits and Measures

Circuits of Capital	Value Form	Empirical Measures
Productive circuit	$LP + MP$	Labour flows
		Production chains
Commodity circuit	$C^{1'} - M^{2'}$	Exports
	$C^{2'} - M^{1'}$	Imports
Money circuit	$M^1 - C^2$	Direct investments
	$M^1_f - M^2_f$	Portfolio investments
	$M^{2'} - M^{1'}$	Profit repatriation

(see Table 2). For example, the internationalization of productive capital occurs through migrant labour flows and cross-border production chains, creating an internationalization of production. Likewise, the globalization of commodity capital occurs through imports and exports of goods and services, creating a world market of exchange. Finally, the internationalization of money capital occurs through direct investments, portfolio investments, and profit flows, creating an internationalization of finance. Through these concrete pathways, the circuits of capital at different scales of the world economy are entwined and co-mingled.

Three important points flow from this analysis. First, the neoliberal period is demarcated by the globalization of productive capital alongside the globalization of money and commodity capital (Palloix 1977; Robinson 2004).[6] As a consequence, the most advanced spaces of capital now command or incorporate these articulated circuits of value, and the most competitive units of capital are now engaged in both the exploitation of labour and the appropriation of value on a global scale (Carroll 2010; Hart-Landsberg 2013). With this in mind, the project of locating Canada in the world economy should pay attention to globalizing links of finance, production, and exchange in Canada and around the world (Klassen 2009; Klassen and Carroll 2011). In particular, it needs to determine the extent to which the Canadian capitalist class operates across the circuits of capital, both at home and abroad (Clement 1975, 1977; Carroll 1986, 2010).

The second point is that *transfers of value* are embedded in global flows of capital, creating combined and uneven forms of economic development (Desai 2013).[7] The transfer of value occurs through unequal exchange, royalty and profit streams, interest payments on debt, and cross-border movements of labour power – that is, migration (Carchedi 1991, 2001; Cooney 2004; Emmanuel 1972; Hanieh 2009; Mandel 1983; Shaikh 1979/80; Shaikh and Tonak 1994). Put in this frame of reference, the capitalist world economy is structured by *imperialism* – that is, by the concentration and centralization of value in unequal ways between states and their national blocs of capital. It follows that a state is *imperialist* to the extent that its leading corporations command and appropriate value on a global scale. By way of contrast, a state is *dependent* to the extent that it is dominated by, or drained of, global value flows. If, as in the case of Canada, both tendencies are present, the balance between them must be considered.

The final point is that new modes of *contentious resistance* are inextricable from the internationalization process. Indeed, as the circuits of capital have globalized, new patterns of working-class and even anticapitalist opposition have emerged. This is evident in the productive circuit in the form of strikes and protests in export-processing zones and of social movements of migrant workers; in the financial circuit in the form of anti-austerity and Third World debt campaigns; and in the commodity circuit in the form of consumer boycotts and retail labour strife. The internationalization of mining and energy capital has also triggered new "resource conflicts" (Klare 2002; UNEP 2009), as well as new patterns of collective resistance by indigenous people, rural communities, and environmental activists (Blackwood and Stewart 2012; Gordon and Webber 2008). In mapping the reach of Canadian corporate power, then, it is vital to recognize the social relations of exploitation and expropriation that inhere to capitalism and that prompt new modalities of social contestation at home and abroad.

With this in mind, and to map the economic foundations of Canada's new imperialism, I have divided the chapter into three sections. The first locates the Canadian economy in the global hierarchy of states. Using comparative data on gross domestic product (GDP) and value added by sector, I demonstrate that Canada is a secondary power in the capitalist world system. In the second section, I map the internationalization of capital in Canada. In particular, I demonstrate the integration of Canadian capital with transnational modes of production, finance, and exchange. By using a circuits-of-capital approach, I reveal how Canadian firms participate in global forms of exploitation and appropriation, and how Canada is linked to a particular structure of spatial relations in the capitalist world economy. The key finding is that the North American economic space fits into a wider pattern of economic relations for the Canadian capitalist class. As such, the latter plays a definite role in the economics of imperialism. In light of these findings, the final section examines the contradictions of Canada's role in transnational neoliberalism – contradictions that have prompted new types of contentious resistance to Canadian capital at home and abroad.

Locating Canada in World Accumulation

Over the past several decades, Canada's role in global capitalism has been a flashpoint of contention in critical political economy. In these debates, two paradigms have sought to locate the Canadian state in world accumulation. The first is the dependency theory of left-nationalist political economy. This theory argues that the Canadian economy is characterized by a resources-based structure of production, a branch-plant manufacturing sector, high levels of foreign ownership and staples exports, and negative net flows of dividends, royalties, and interest payments. Although Canada is a rich country, this perspective argues, it is dominated by foreign capital, and thus positioned as a dependency in the capitalist world system (Drache 1977; Levitt 1970; Williams 1994).

The second theory, rooted in certain streams of Marxism, views Canada in a different light. It argues that the Canadian economy is constituted by balanced forms of industrial production, declining patterns of foreign ownership, a diversified export structure, and growing outflows of direct investment capital. Taken together, these dynamics make the Canadian state a leading space of world accumulation. For advocates of this position (Burgess 2000; Kellogg 2005), Canada is an imperialist power no different than the United States, France, and the United Kingdom. Against this "classical" theory of Canadian imperialism, others have argued, more cautiously, that Canada is best viewed "as a lesser region within the centre of the international political economy" (Williams 1988, 130).

With this debate in mind, how should Canada be located in world accumulation? The most appropriate starting point is Canada's overall standing in terms of world economic activity. Typically, this is measured by a country's GDP – the value of all final goods and services produced in a nation in a given year. There are many ways to calculate a country's GDP, but the most common include nominal GDP, purchasing power parity (PPP) GDP, and GDP per capita derived from PPP calculations.[8] According to the International Monetary Fund (IMF), Canada in 2011 ranked near the top of the world economy in all three measures. Although Canada's position in each measure has descended recently, it is still the tenth largest when measured by nominal GDP, the fourteenth largest when measured by PPP GDP, and the twelfth largest when measured by GDP per capita PPP.[9] These measures indicate that, despite its relatively small population, Canada is one of the richest and most productive countries in the world. It is not a leading economy of global capitalism on the scale of the United States or China, but located in a secondary tier of advanced capitalist states that includes France, Germany, Japan, Spain, and the United Kingdom. Thus, although Canada has experienced a relative slide in terms of hosting global value, it is a highly advanced economy of world significance and has not experienced a disaccumulation of capital. As a result, when comparing national wealth, Canada must be ranked as a secondary power in the top tier of states.

Canada's industrial structure provides another measure of economic development. This structure has been a central focus of left-nationalist political economy, which, for more than four decades, has argued that Canada needs a national industrial strategy to shift the economy away from staples and towards high-value-added production. According to this analysis, such a policy would reposition the Canadian economy as a competitive space of global capitalism, and raise the standard of living in the country. To assess these claims, one needs to compare Canada's economic structure with that of other industrialized countries.

To start, it is commonly understood that the economic structures of advanced capitalist countries were radically transformed during the period after the Second World War (Rowthorn and Ramaswamy 1997; Singh 1977). High rates of profit in productive circuits of capital allowed for new investments in financial and commercial circuits of capital, which soon came to dominate national industrial structures. In the terms of liberal political economy, the goods-producing sectors were supplemented by the services-producing sectors, both public and private. This trend has continued in the period of transnational neoliberalism, as the geographic dispersal of low-end manufacturing to countries on the periphery has been mirrored by a geographic concentration of finance, management, research and development, business services, advertising, and high-end production in the core capitalist states (Gereffi 2005; Linden, Kraemer, and Dedrick 2007; Sassen 2005; cf. Gerrefi, Humphrey, and Sturgeon 2005). In these states, the circuits of financial and commercial capital typically account for the greatest shares of GDP, generally followed by manufacturing, mining, transportation, utilities, and agriculture, forestry, fishing, and hunting.

All of these trends are evident in the Canadian economy today. Far from demonstrating a lopsided staples economy, or one biased against services, manufacturing, and heavy industry, the breakdown of Canada's GDP is consistent with general trends in the advanced capitalist world. As Table 3 demonstrates, in 2011, services-producing industries accounted for 71.6 per cent of Canada's GDP, while goods-producing industries accounted for 28.8 per cent. Overall, finance and insurance accounted for the greatest share of GDP (20.9 per cent), followed by manufacturing (12.8 per cent). Within the goods-producing sector itself, the manufacturing share represented 44.4 per cent of the total, followed by construction (20.9 per cent), mining and energy (15.7 per cent), utilities (9.3 per cent), and agriculture, forestry, fishing, and hunting (7.9 per cent). Although Canada's manufacturing sector has experienced recession since 2005, it still accounts for the largest share of productive capital in the national economy, and has grown in absolute terms since 2002. Over this period, the strongest rate of growth occurred in the mining and energy sectors, which experienced a compound annual growth rate of 4.5 per cent. As key pillars of the productive circuit of capital, these sectors have been vital for maintaining output and profitability in a period of heightened competition in global manufacturing.[10]

Canada's industrial structure, as measured by GDP per industry, thus reveals both a general and a particular pattern of development. On the one hand, unique circuits of productive capital, especially in mining and energy, are constituent of Canadian capitalism. On the other hand, these circuits coexist with – in fact, are dwarfed by – many other forms of value production and exchange in the Canadian economy. For this reason, there is no basis for one-sided theories of Canada as a low-end staples or peripheral economy. On the contrary, Canada's economy is structured around circuits of commerce, finance, and production that are typical of advanced capitalist countries.

Table 3. Canada's GDP by Industry, 2011

Sector	Total (constant 2002 $ millions)	Share of GDP (%)	Compound Annual Growth Rate, 2002–11 (%)
All industries	1,266,578	100.0	1.9
Goods-producing industries	365,036	28.8	0.6
Agriculture, forestry, fishing, and hunting	29,093	2.3	2.5
Mining, oil, and gas	57,443	4.5	4.5
Manufacturing	162,072	12.8	2.4
Construction	76,514	6.0	3.2
Utilities	34,058	2.7	1.8
Services-producing industries	906,458	71.6	2.6
Transportation and warehousing	59,743	4.7	2.0
Information and culture	45,907	3.6	2.1
Wholesale trade	71,034	5.6	2.8
Retail trade	76,832	6.1	3.1
Finance, insurance, renting, leasing, and management of companies and enterprises	264,270	20.9	3.0
Professional, scientific, and technical services	61,566	4.9	2.7
Administrative and support, waste management, and remediation	30,752	2.4	2.4
Public administration	76,374	6.0	2.4
Educational services	63,150	5.0	2.3
Health care and social assistance	84,485	6.7	2.4
Arts, entertainment, and recreation	11,227	0.9	0.9
Accommodation and food services	27,341	2.1	0.8
Other services	33,093	2.6	2.2

Source: Statistics Canada, CANSIM II database, table 3790017; and table 3790020.

Table 4. Gross Value Added by Sector, G7 Countries

	United States	United Kingdom	Japan	Italy	Germany	France	Canada
				(%)			
Agriculture	1.2	0.7	1.2	1.9	0.8	1.8	1.9
Total industry	16.2	15.6	21.9	19.3	23.9	12.5	24.9
Manufacturing	13.1	11.4	19.5	16.7	20.9	10.7	11.9
Wholesale and retail trade	18.2	20.5	23.9	22.1	17.4	19.2	20.5
Financial services	33.5	33.5	16.9	28.3	30.8	34.1	25.7
Other services	27.1	23.1	30.6	22.1	23.8	27.0	19.9

Source: Derived from OECD, *OECD.Stat Extracts*, available online at http://stats.oecd.org/, using the most recent available data.

Notes: Gross value added is defined as output minus intermediate consumption. It also equals the sum of employee compensation, net operating surplus, net mixed income, depreciation of capital assets and other taxes less other subsidies on production. The growth rates shown here refer to volume estimates of gross value added. Agriculture includes hunting, fishing, and forestry. Industry includes energy, mining, and manufacturing, among other sectors. Financial services includes real estate and business activities.

For reasons of brevity, these numbers do not add up to 100.

Data for the United States, United Kingdom, Japan, Italy, and Germany are for 2010; for France, 2009; and for Canada, 2008.

Using the Group-of-7 (G7) major industrialized economies as benchmarks, Table 4 makes this point in comparative perspective. Derived from OECD data sets on gross value added,[11] it reveals that the distribution of value in Canada broadly matches that in the other G7 economies. For example, agriculture, which includes farming, hunting, forestry, and fishing, accounts for only 2.1 per cent of value added. On par with other G7 countries, the largest share of value added occurs in the financial sector (25.7 per cent), followed by industry (24.9 per cent). Manufacturing's share of value added in Canada exceeds that in France and the United Kingdom and just trails that in the United States. Although the share of value added accounted for by finance and other business services is below the G7 average in Canada, the share of value added by

industry, which includes manufacturing, mining, and energy complements, is above average. Like the other G7 countries, then, Canada has
a highly diversified economy, and shares with them broad similarities
in terms of value added by sector.

In sum, Canada's economy includes circuits of capital dominated by
finance and commerce, but it is supported by a large and diverse industrial base. Clearly, Canada is home to circuits of money, commercial, and
productive capital that give the national economy a secondary ranking
in world accumulation, and the analysis shows that theories of Canada
as a dependent or peripheral state are one-sided and misleading.

But how does Canada *fit into* transnational patterns of production,
finance, and exchange? In particular, how does the *internationalization
of capital* affect Canada's location in world accumulation? Is the Canadian state a dependency, or an imperialist power, in the nation-state
system? Using a circuits-of-capital approach, in the next section I map
the links between Canada and the world economy. I demonstrate that
the Canadian economy is increasingly bound with global modes of
exploitation and appropriation and that, through such circuits of capital, the state secures a secondary position on the chain of value added.

The Internationalization of Canadian Capital

The Circuit of Commodity Capital

Consider, first, the relationship between Canada and the world market –
the circuit of commodity capital in Marxist theory. During the period of
neoliberalism, Canada's integration with the world market has experienced both a quantitative and a qualitative transformation. As a secondary space of global capitalism, Canada has been at the forefront of world
trade expansion. Between 1971 and 2008, the nominal value of Canadian
exports increased from $18.4 billion to $488.7 billion, while the nominal
value of Canadian imports increased from $15.8 billion to $443.7 billion.
In 2010, after two years of global crisis, the nominal value of exports and
imports was $404.8 billion and $413.8 billion, respectively. As a result,
Canada ranked thirteenth in world export standings (2.54 per cent of
world exports) and eleventh in world import standings (2.54 per cent
of world imports) (UNCTAD 2012, 16–17). Although Canada's share of
world trade has declined since 1980, when it accounted for 3.32 per cent
of exports and 3.01 per cent of imports, it remains a power in world trade

Figure 4. Goods and Services Trade as a Share of GDP, Canada, 1970–2010

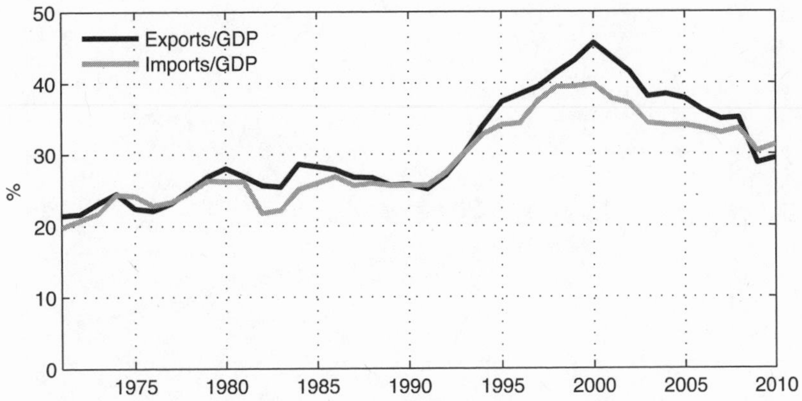

Source: Author's calculations, from Statistics Canada, CANSIM II database, table 3800027, V647592, V647609; and table 3800017, V646937.

similar to countries such as Belgium, France, the United Kingdom, Italy, the Netherlands, and South Korea. In fact, despite its relatively small population, Canada has one of the highest levels of trade per capita in the world, at more than $5,000 per person (Roy 2006, 1).

The importance of trade to the Canadian economy, however, is best measured by the ratio of trade to GDP. Between 1971 and 2000, the ratio of exports to GDP increased from 21.4 per cent to 45.6 per cent and the ratio of imports to GDP increased from 19.8 per cent to 39.8 per cent (see Figure 4). Similarly, total trade (exports plus imports) increased at a rate 50 per cent faster than nominal GDP from 1990 to 2008 (Canada 2011c, 92). As a result, exports accounted for 20 per cent of corporate income in 2004, up from 14 per cent in 1991 (Ghanem and Cross 2008, 3).

In the 1990s, this boom in the trade-to-GDP ratio was led by the manufacturing sector – in particular, by exports and imports of auto goods and merchandise. In the 2000s, this boom was dampened, or partially reversed, by the energy and mining expansion, which raised the value of the Canadian dollar and thus diminished foreign demand for manufactured exports (Stanford 2008). However, even though the trade-to-GDP ratio has fallen, the total value of Canada's exports and imports has continued to rise, and still equals more than 60 per cent of GDP. As a result, the circuit of commodity capital is still highly globalized.

Figure 5. Net Merchandise Trade by Product, Canada, 1970–2010

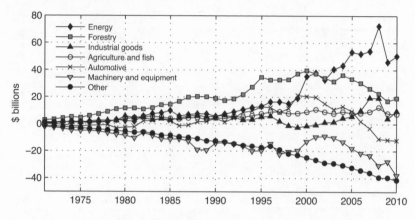

Source: Author's calculations, from Statistics Canada, CANSIM II database, table 3860006, V114277, V114278, V114279, V114280, V114281, V114282, V114283, V114331, V114332, V114333, V114334, V114335, V114336, V114337.

At the macro scale, Canada's exports and imports are concentrated in key sectors. In 2010, the greatest share of exports was in machinery and equipment (21.7 per cent), followed by energy products (21.6 per cent), industrial goods (21.4 per cent), and automotive merchandise (14.0 per cent). In the same year, imports were registered in broadly similar sectors, including machinery and equipment (27.5 per cent), industrial goods (21.0 per cent), automotive merchandise (16.6 per cent), and energy products (9.8 per cent).[12] On a sectoral basis, Canada has been locked in a particular structure of merchandise trade in which it runs systematic deficits in consumer goods and machinery and equipment, and systematic surpluses in energy, forestry, agriculture, fishing, industrial goods, and automotive products (see Figure 5). Although Canada exports large quantities of high-technology goods, it is increasingly dependent on energy, mining, and forestry exports to cover imports in the balance of payments. With the shift to dollar parity over the past decade, this tendency has become more pronounced, as manufacturing exports have declined in the wake of the "resources boom" (Stanford 2008).[13]

The internationalization of commodity capital is also evident at the micro scale. Here, Canadian firms increasingly are involved in export activity. For example, between 1997 and 2007, the number of firms engaged in merchandise exports grew by 11.5 per cent, and the value of their exports increased by 48.3 per cent, or $134 billion. As a result, by 2007, 45,260 Canadian enterprises were exporting roughly $414 billion of merchandise goods (Nadeau, Préfontaine, and Mei 2010a).

Canada's integration into global commodity circuits has also encouraged the specialization of production in leading export industries. For example, in sectors such as transportation equipment, chemicals, metals, wood and paper, and machinery and equipment, more than 50 per cent of output is now exported directly. In the oil and mining sectors, the output-to-export ratio reaches 80 per cent if one includes processing and refining (Ghanem and Cross 2008, 3–4). The manufacturing sector, in particular, is highly internationalized in the circuit of commodity exchange, as shown by the increase in the number of exporting manufacturing firms from 15,667 to 20,358 between 1993 and 2007. In 2007, this sector alone accounted for 44.9 per cent of the total number of exporting enterprises and for 58.8 per cent of the total value of merchandise exports. In second place was the wholesale trade sector, whose 10,104 exporting firms accounted for 22.3 per cent of all exporting firms, up from 7,079 in 1993. This sector also accounted for 12.8 per cent of the total value of exports. Between 1997 and 2007, the mining and energy sectors witnessed similar changes, with the number of exporting enterprises increasing by 25 per cent, from 408 to 510, while their share of exports increased from 4.1 per cent ($11.5 billion) to 8.6 per cent ($35.6 billion) (Nadeau, Préfontaine, and Mei 2010a). At this scale of analysis, then, it is evident that leading sectors of Canadian capital are increasingly engaged in export activities.

The same dynamics appear on the import side of the commodity circuit. Between 2002 and 2007, the number of enterprises that purchased imports rose from 137,592 to 168,142. During this period, the value of imports increased from $321.9 billion to $371.1 billion, a record high. In 2007, more than 35,000 wholesale traders and more 27,000 retail traders reported purchasing imports of $112.3 billion and $16.1 billion, respectively. Similarly, more than 27,000 manufacturing establishments and nearly 1,200 mining and energy establishments purchased imports worth $129.5 billion and $2.0 billion, respectively. Likewise, in the agriculture, forestry, fishing, and hunting sector, the total number of importing firms reached 8,634 in 2007, up from 4,283 in 2002 (Nadeau, Préfontaine, and Mei 2010b). In these measures of internationalization, then, there is an increasing trend towards purchases of imports.

But how does Canadian capital fit into *spatial flows* of global exchange? In other words, what is the *geography of internationalization* in the commodity circuit of capital? In particular, with which countries does Canada trade, and how does this trade position the Canadian state in global capitalism? In 2010, Canada's trade was predominantly with other advanced economies, reflecting the general trend of trade among the major states in the world economy. Nearly 90 per cent of Canada's exports were destined to other advanced economies, with the United States accounting for 74.9 per cent of those exports, followed by the European Union and Japan at 8.6 per cent and 2.3 per cent, respectively. Exports to developing economies accounted for only 12.1 per cent of Canada's exports, with the majority (7.1 per cent) going to East, South, and Southeast Asia. Just 0.9 per cent and 3.1 per cent of exports went to Africa and the Americas, respectively (UNCTAD 2012, 59).

These spatial trends are also evident at the scale of the firm. In 2007, approximately 60 per cent of Canada's exporters relied solely on the United States for their international purchases. In the same year, more than 80 per cent of Canada's exporters sold goods to the United States, representing 79 per cent of the total value of exports, which indicates the close connection of Canadian exports to US demand (Nadeau, Préfontaine, and Mei 2010a). At the same time, however, the share of Canada's exporters relying exclusively on the US market has diminished since 2001, when it reached 71.8 per cent. Since then, Canadian firms have diversified their export markets. By 2007, Canadian firms that exported to the United States *and* to other economies accounted for 47.5 per cent of total domestic exports. As part of this shift, more than 40 per cent of Canada's exporters sold goods to non-US economies.

These data indicate that Canadian firms increasingly are engaged in export activity and that the geographic spread of foreign sales has increased beyond the United States. According to another study (Sui and Yu 2013, 520), "fewer Canadian exporters have needed to use the US market as their primary learning platform in order to expand into emerging markets." Furthermore, "there are a growing number of Canadian firms that violate the traditional sequential exporting pattern by exporting directly to emerging markets." These links between Canada and the world market demonstrate a real globalization of commodity capital – in other words, a growing focus on diversified export production on the part of Canadian corporations.

On the import side, several trends are worth highlighting. First, in 2010, nearly 70 per cent of Canada's imports came from other advanced economies, reflecting a common trend of global capitalism. Of these imports, 50.4 per cent were purchased from the United States, 11.9 per cent from Europe, and 3.3 per cent from Japan. Second, although Canada exports relatively little to developing economies, it imports

Figure 6. Canada's Trade Balance by Region, 1970–2010

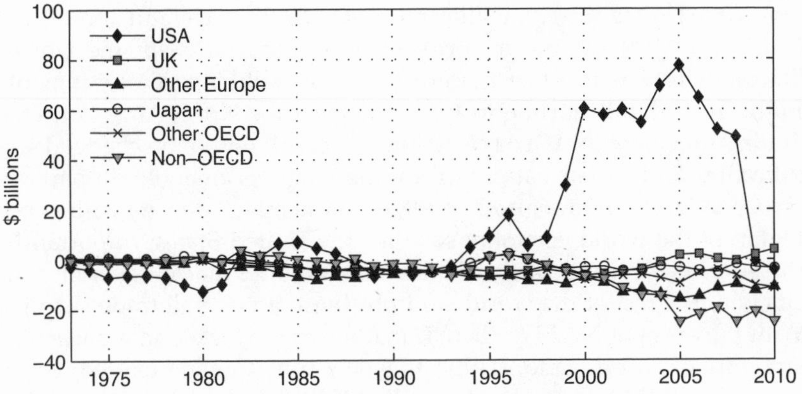

Source: Author's calculations, from Statistics Canada, CANSIM II database, table 3760001, V113803, V113876, V114020, V114092, V114164, V114236.

a much greater share from them: in 2010, 30.1 per cent of Canada's imports were from developing economies, of which 16.9 per cent were from East, South, and Southeast Asia, 9.5 per cent from the Americas, and 2.5 per cent from Africa (UNCTAD 2012, 71).

The diversification of Canadian imports also appears at the micro level. For example, in 2007, 135,325 Canadian firms – accounting for 80.5 per cent of total importing firms – imported goods from the United States, reflecting the high degree of trade between the two countries. However, the number of firms that imported goods exclusively from the United States (65,299) was surpassed by the number (70,026) that imported from both the United States and other countries. Of the 102,843 firms that purchased imports from non-US sources in 2007, 48,872 imported from the European Union, 18,488 from Japan, 14,755 from Mexico, 8,587 from South America, and 79,793 from other countries in Asia and Africa.

These data suggest that, although Canadian firms are highly engaged in commodity exchange within North America, they are increasingly broadening the scope of their imports from other sources, both advanced and developing. Indeed, as Statistics Canada points out, the 70,026 firms that imported from both the United States and other countries in 2007 accounted for $358.5 billion of Canada's imports that year, or 96.6 per cent of the total value of imports (Nadeau, Préfontaine, and Mei 2010b).

Figure 6 depicts the spatial pattern of trade through which the commodity circuit has been internationalized on a balance-of-payments basis. It demonstrates that, between 1973 and the early 1990s, Canada registered small current account surpluses and deficits with the United States, the United Kingdom, Europe, other OECD states, and non-OECD countries. Although the majority of trade occurred with the United States, there was no clear pattern to the overall balance of payments in this regard, but starting in 1994 – the year the North American Free Trade Agreement (NAFTA) came into effect – the situation changed significantly, and a clear pattern of trading relations emerged. In particular, Canada began to register small, but systematic, deficits with every region of the world economy save for the United States. Importantly, the surplus with the United States was so large that it covered deficits with the rest of the world, and produced an overall trade surplus. With the onset of NAFTA, then, Canada became locked in a particular structure of world trade. Within this structure, Canada tended to run deficits with Europe, Asia, Africa, the Middle East, and Latin America and the Caribbean, and surpluses with the United States. Furthermore, these surpluses were so great that they allowed Canadian companies to import what they needed from both the periphery and other advanced capitalist countries.

The NAFTA relationship, then, has been critical for the expanded reproduction of Canadian capital on a *global scale*. Through this relation, Canada has financed a deficit with the rest of the world, and, until recently, earned a surplus for either expanded reproduction at home or capital exports abroad.[14] The NAFTA zone thus has been the spatialized system through which Canadian firms have accumulated capital for growth and expansion in the world economy. In the process, it has secured for Canada a tier-two position on the chain of value added.

In sum, the evidence suggests that a complex process of internationalization has occurred in the commodity circuit of capital. On the one hand, Canada's trading patterns are highly *regionalized*, with the United States now accounting for nearly 75 per cent of Canadian exports and for more than 50 per cent of Canadian imports. This bilateral trading relation has grown at a rapid rate since 1989, and is now the largest in the world.

On the other hand, Canada is part of a *worldwide* trading system that binds together the advanced capitalist regions of North America, Europe, and developed Asia. With these regions, Canada tends to import and export the goods and services that are produced and consumed by advanced capitalist countries, and in the process, tends to earn a surplus in the current account of the balance of payments. Like other states in the core of global capitalism, Canada also imports a greater share from the periphery than it exports. The vast majority of these imports are the consumer goods – textiles and apparel, food, and low value-added manufactures – that account for Canada's trade deficit in this category (see Figure 5). Similarly, Canada imports from the periphery large quantities of raw materials that are processed for consumption in Canada or for export to other countries. From these trends of exchange at the global scale, the geographic distribution of Canadian trade is typical of an advanced capitalist country. Through such dynamics of internationalization, the Canadian economy has remained a secondary space of global capitalism.

The Circuit of Productive Capital

Alongside the globalization of commodity capital has been the globalization of productive capital as Canadian firms have increased their integration with international supply chains, which, in turn, has led to the internationalization of production itself. The use of foreign inputs in leading sectors of the Canadian economy is the best measure of this process. For example, in 2006, foreign goods accounted for only 11 per cent of total inputs, but for 36 per cent of inputs in oil refining, 20 per cent in chemicals and plastics, 23 per cent in metal manufacturing, 26 per cent in machinery and equipment, 43 per cent in transportation equipment, and 24 per cent in all other manufacturing industries (Ghanem and Cross 2008, 7). Because of this, the foreign content of Canadian exports has increased, rising from 23 per cent to 32 per cent between 1987 and 1999, before dropping to 27.3 per cent in 2004 as the Canadian dollar depreciated against the US dollar. More recently, as the Canadian dollar rose to parity with US currency, there were signs of increasing import intensity, though trends have yet to be analysed (Cross and Ghanem 2008, 8). According to the Conference Board of Canada (2007, 8), from the late 1980s to the mid-2000s, the domestic content of Canadian exports decreased from over 70 per cent to 65 per cent, reflecting the growing integration of Canadian capital with international supply chains and the qualitative transformation of the production process under neoliberal globalization.

Another measure of this transformation involves the share of intermediate imported inputs to production. Here, considerable growth is evident. For example, between 1961 and 2006, the share in total intermediate inputs nearly doubled, from 6.5 per cent to 11.5 per cent. In terms of manufactured intermediate inputs, the share of imported inputs increased from 24.1 per cent to 64.8 per cent, representing a key form of internationalization in the productive circuit (Canada 2011c, 94).

Although most offshore activities involve material goods for commodity production, offshoring of services has also increased – in fact, at a faster rate than the offshoring of material inputs: between 1961 and 2003, the offshoring of service inputs grew at an average annual rate of 11.9 per cent, as opposed to 8.8 per cent for material inputs. Imports of intermediate service inputs have also increased dramatically, from less than 7 per cent in the early 1960s to a peak of 21.3 per cent in 1998 (Baldwin and Gu 2008; Canada 2011c, 94). In these ways, the services sector has incorporated new patterns of globalization in its operational processes.

It is vital to recognize that the NAFTA relationship accounts for most of these changes in production. The extent to which the circuit of productive capital has been *continentalized* is indicated by the fact that 70 per cent of Canadian-US trade occurs in similar industries and that the majority of Canadian imports from the United States are semi-finished inputs to production (Conference Board of Canada 2007, 10–11).[15] At the same time, however, Canadian firms increasingly are buying industrial goods and means of production from other countries. As a case in point, approximately 50 per cent of all imported machinery and equipment now comes from sources other than the United States and Japan, with China, Mexico, and Europe accounting for most of the remainder (Roy 2006, 5–6). As Canada's second-largest trading partner, China, in particular, has become an important source of means of production, now accounting for 10 per cent of Canadian imports, the majority of which are machines and equipment (Wyman 2007, 10). So, although the United States remains the primary trading partner of the Canadian state, the growth in trade between Canada and China represents an important diversification of economic relations (Cross and Ghanem 2008; Wyman 2007). In fact, it creates a new geography of production, wherein Canada exports raw materials and industrial goods to China in exchange for low-cost means of production, which are then used to produce manufactured exports (along with energy and mining products) for the US economy. This structured pattern of economic relations signifies a new stage in the internationalization of capital (Klassen 2009; Souare and Wang 2009).

Canada's position in world value-added chains also can be observed at the sectoral scale of analysis. In the auto sector, for example, Canada is home to more than 1,300 firms, which employ approximately 130,000 workers, and have annual revenues of $71 billion and annual exports of more than $53 billion. As a consequence, Canada is the eleventh-largest site of auto production in the world, producing a wide array of light and heavy-duty vehicles and a broad range of parts, components, and systems. The domestic auto industry is structured around the foreign direct investments of major US and Japanese firms. From their bases of operations in Canada, these firms produce primarily for the US market, but also for Canadian domestic consumption. Concentrated in southern Ontario, the auto sector is constituted by cross-border production chains that, for the most part, are centrally managed in the United States. In fact, "in many respects, the southern Ontario automotive components industry can be viewed as part of a larger Lower Great Lakes trans-border automotive manufacturing cluster centred on Detroit" (Rutherford and Holmes 2007, 206–7). Within this cross-border system, approximately 85 per cent of Canadian vehicle production and 60 per cent of parts production is exported to the United States. Through these integrated circuits of capital, the Canadian auto sector is geared towards serving transnational corporate interests, especially US ones. As such, it represents a form of dependent production in Canada.

Although it lacks an Original Equipment Manufacturer (OEM), however, Canada has developed a globally competitive parts industry in and around the assembly operations of US and Japanese firms. Canadian component companies, including Magna International, Linamar, and Woodbridge, employ nearly 79,000 workers and export roughly $20 billion worth of parts and components on an annual basis (Macaluso 2012; Van Alphen 2011). As Canada's leading parts producer, Magna International has even been internationalized in important ways. For instance, three years after purchasing a majority shareholding in Steyr-Daimler-Puch AG in 1998, it founded Magna Steyr as an Austria-based subsidiary to design and assemble vehicles for OEMs such as Audi, BMW, Fiat, Peugeot, and Mercedes-Benz. In such ways, Canadian capital has positioned itself at home and abroad in a supplementary role to OEMs in the auto sector. In the process, it has enmeshed itself in new forms of internationalization in the productive circuit, albeit in a secondary role to transnational corporate interests. At the same time, evidence suggests that, in Canada's auto sector, "power imbalances between [transnational corporations] and cluster-based suppliers ... are growing. These power asymmetries stem from the ... OEMs['] control of the key assembly and retailing segments of the value chain and their immense accumulated financial assets. Over the last several years, the growing imperative to stem financial losses and reverse declining share values has caused the OEMs to reassert and exercise their power over suppliers" (Rutherford and Holmes 2008, 520). In this context, the Canadian parts sector has been forced to rationalize production through "leaner" methods of employment and remuneration.

Canada's defence sector is also integrated with global production networks, and relies upon foreign sales for approximately half of total industry revenues (Berthiaume 2014). Since the Second World War, two trends have characterized the defence industrial base: "[t]he first is closer cooperation with, and integration into, the U.S. defence industry and market; the second is the shift away from the domestic production of major platforms towards a concentration on subsystems and components" (Edgar and Haglund 1995, 62). In other words, the Canadian defence industry has become both integrated into, and specialized within, US-led procurement systems. Through more than fifty bilateral production agreements, Canada and the United States have established a North American defence industrial base, centred first and foremost on US military requirements. In this continental system of production, Canadian capital operates as a subsystem or component supplier to the Pentagon and to US prime contractors and their subsidiaries in Canada (ibid., 64). As a result, foreign ownership of Canada's defence production system is estimated to exceed 60 per cent, and the United States accounts for approximately 80 per cent of Canadian defence exports, including key parts and components for fighter jets, attack helicopters, bombers, heavy artillery systems, guns, combat vehicles, missile guidance controls, and advanced electronics and aerospace subsystems (COAT 2011; Edgar and Haglund 1995, 76).

Canadian defence exporters are highly specialized in US-led production systems, but they have also developed a broader export capacity to niche markets of allied states (Berthiaume 2014). For example, between 2003 and 2006, Canadian-based defence industries exported more than $7.3 billion worth of military equipment to eighty-eight countries (Sanders 2009, 22). Likewise, between 2007 and 2009, these industries exported approximately $1.4 billion of military goods and technology, the majority of which ($737 million, or 52 per cent) was purchased by member states of the North Atlantic Treaty Organization. Given more rein by the Conservative government of Stephen Harper, Canadian military exporters sold more than $12 billion of weapons and ammunition in 2012 alone (Berthiaume 2013a). Beyond the United States, the leading buyers of Canadian military products are, typically, the United Kingdom, Australia, Italy, France, Germany, Norway, New Zealand, Malaysia, Israel, South Korea, and Saudi Arabia (Canada 2011b). To some extent, then, the Canadian defence industry has developed into a specialized producer for the global military purchases of allied states. In doing so, it has supported the globalization of production and exchange in Canada and beyond.

The internationalization of production is evident not only in terms of *material* but also in new flows of cross-border *human* labour power – that is, migration. During the period of neoliberalism, Canada has experienced new dynamics of emigration and immigration. On the one hand, Canada has seen an escalating drain of emigrants to the United States over the past three decades, registering a net loss of 76,712, 133,691, and 154,160 over the periods 1980–89, 1990–99, and 2000–09, respectively.[16] On the other hand, overall net immigration to Canada has increased steadily throughout the period of neoliberalism, from a trough of 22,839 in 1978 to 228,335 in 2010.[17] Interestingly, beginning in the early 1980s, an inverse relationship has developed in Canada's policies for landed immigrants. In the permanent resident category, economic immigrants accounted for 66 per cent of landed immigrants in 2010, up from 36 per cent in 1986. Over the same period, family class immigrants dropped from 42.7 per cent to 21.5 per cent, and refugees dropped from 19.3 per cent to 8.8 per cent (Canada 2011a, 4–5). In the category of economic immigrants, the vast majority of permanent residents are now skilled workers (ibid., 7). In 2010, 51.5 per cent of economic immigrants were accepted from the Asia-Pacific region, 23.9 per cent from Africa and the Middle East, 16.4 per cent from Europe (including the United Kingdom), 6.5 per cent from South and Central America, and 1.8 per cent from the United States. Thus, the evidence suggests that, over the past several decades, Canada's immigration policy has been economized in *imperialist* ways – in particular, by importing skilled workers from developing regions of Asia, the Middle East, and Africa.

Canada's recent immigration policy has also been characterized by a great increase in the number of temporary foreign workers permitted to enter, who now exceed the number of permanent resident economic immigrants landed each year. In 2000, for example, 136,282 permanent

Figure 7. Economic Immigration by Category, Canada, 1985–2011

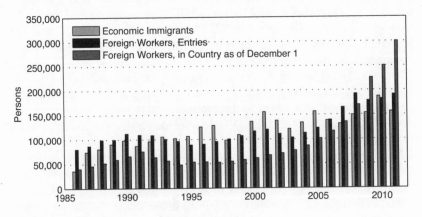

Source: Author's calculations, from Canada (2011a).

resident economic immigrants were landed, while 61,290 temporary foreign workers were given permission to enter (see Figure 7). By 2011, the number of temporary foreign workers reached 300,111, compared with 156,077 permanent resident economic immigrants.

Thus, not only has Canadian immigration policy become more economized; it has also become more exploitative, since temporary foreign workers, who are denied the rights and benefits of citizenship, have become the leading source of economic migration. Indeed, evidence suggests that Canada's labour market is distinctively exploitative of recent immigrants. Using data from Statistics Canada's 2008 Labour Force Survey, Jason Gilmore (2009) demonstrates that "immigrant employees from most periods of landing and occupational groups [have] hourly wage rates which [are] below those of their Canadian-born counterparts." In fact, the share of immigrants earning below $10 per hour was nearly twice the rate of Canadian-born workers. According to Gilmore, "[t]he gap was wider for employees with university degrees. When comparing immigrants aged 25 to 54 with university degrees with their Canadian-born counterparts, there was a $5 hourly-wage gap in 2008 ($25.32 vs. $30.33)." Compounding this problem, recent immigrants also have a "lower share of union coverage, higher shares of involuntary part-time work, higher shares of temporary jobs, [and] lower shares of employer-sponsored pension plans and life insurance coverage compared with the Canadian born." These statistics on labour market inequalities between immigrants and non-immigrants are another sign of what Grace-Edward Galabuzi (2006) describes as Canada's growing "economic apartheid" (see also Block and Galabuzi 2011).

In this context, it is vital to consider the extent to which the internationalization of production has effected a broader polarization of class relations in Canada. According to the OECD (2012a), between 1990 and 2006, the labour share of national income in Canada dropped by five percentage points to 60.3 per cent. At the same time, the share of the top 1 per cent of income earners increased by 20 per cent. If this top complement of income earners is excluded from calculations, the declining share of labour income is much higher, suggesting a strong polarization of productive class relations. Interestingly, the OECD notes that the rise of income inequality has been greater in Canada than in other advanced economies, and cites "globalization and [information and communications technology]-driven technological change" as the main reasons. Although such factors are "important drivers of overall economic growth," they have simultaneously fostered new inequalities of class in production. The result, for Canadian capital, as we have seen in Chapter 3, has been a rising rate of profit.

In sum, during the period of neoliberalism, the productive circuit of capital in Canada has witnessed new forms of internationalization. The key measures of this process include the increased use of foreign inputs in production and the increased foreign content of Canadian exports. At the sectoral level, Canada exhibits a strong tendency towards deep integration with continental value chains, especially in the automotive and defence sectors. Although foreign capital dominates these cross-border circuits, Canadian firms have established themselves as second-tier suppliers with a global reach of their own. As such, they have not been sidelined by escalating patterns of foreign ownership and control, which, in fact, have declined in most sectors of Canadian capitalism (see the Appendix).

The productive circuit has also been transformed by new patterns of emigration and immigration. Although Canada continues to register a "brain drain" to the United States, it is running a more significant "brain surplus" from the rest of the world. In the process, Canada is expropriating the value of international labour power in the form of economic migration. Importantly, in this regard, Canada's immigration policy has been largely economized to take advantage of both high- and low-skilled labour imports from developing countries. As a result, the circuit of productive capital shows evidence of racialized and imperialistic exploitation, as recent immigrants

Figure 8. Ratio of Direct Outward and Inward Investment to GDP, Canada, 1960–2010

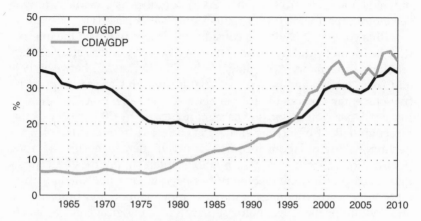

Source: Author's calculations, from Statistics Canada, CANSIM II database, table 3800017, V646937; table 3760037, V235396; and table 3760037, V235412.

are paid lower wages and have fewer benefits and protections (Sharma 2006). Canada's creeping economic apartheid, however, is part of a broader transformation of class relations under neoliberalism. Indeed, as the productive circuit has been internationalized, the labour share of income has dropped significantly, while the rate of profit for capital has increased dramatically. In these ways, the internationalization of production rests on new class relations in Canada and around the world.

The Circuit of Money Capital

The internationalization of Canadian capital is evident, lastly, in the money circuit. This circuit involves the investment relations through which Canada articulates to the world economy. It is constituted through direct and portfolio investments, and through cross-border flows of profit.

The evidence on foreign direct investment (FDI) demonstrates that Canadian firms have been central to the internationalization of capital. In fact, there has been an explosion of Canadian direct investment abroad during the period of neoliberalism, with the stock of such investment skyrocketing from $6.8 billion to $616.6 billion between 1971 and 2010. As a result, by 2009, the foreign asset base of Canadian capital reached 40.6 per cent of Canada's GDP, up from 7.0 per cent in 1971 (see Figure 8).

Figure 9. Canada's Net Foreign Direct Investment Position, 1926–2010

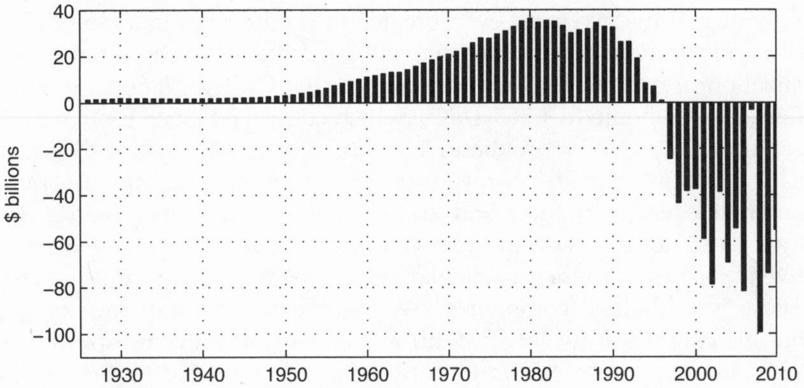

Source: Author's calculations, from Statistics Canada, CANSIM II database, table 3760037, V235412, V235396.

At an ever-increasing rate, then, Canadian firms have expanded control of production and accumulation in the world economy.

Canada also receives a large quantity of FDI. As Figure 9 reveals, for most of the twentieth century, Canada imported more direct investment capital than it exported. As a result, foreign firms had greater claims on production and value flows in Canada than did Canadian firms on production and value flows abroad. For example, between 1926 and the early 1980s, Canada experienced annual net increases of FDI, meaning that foreign firms increased their rate of investment in Canada more quickly than did Canadian firms elsewhere. Over the past several decades, Canada has continued to attract large amounts of FDI: between 1971 and 2010, the stock of FDI increased from $28.9 billion to $561.6 billion, and the ratio of FDI to GDP increased from 29.5 per cent to 34.6 per cent (see Figure 8), numbers that influence the perception that Canada is dominated by foreign capital.

Interestingly, however, as Figure 9 shows, over the past decade and a half, Canada has moved from being a net importer of direct investment capital to a net exporter. This turning point in Canada's international investment position occurred in 1996, and the trend has increased strongly since then. Importantly, this shift resulted not from a decline in the absolute amount or rate of FDI in Canada, but from the greater and more rapid increase of Canadian direct investment abroad. In other words, transnational corporations (TNCs) – companies with operations in three or more states – still invest in the Canadian economy, but now Canadian firms invest an even greater sum in foreign markets. Canadian corporations, then, have actively participated in the internationalization of capital. Indeed, according to the United Nations, in 2010 Canada was home to 1,565 TNCs, which controlled 6,508 foreign subsidiaries, employed more than 1.1 million workers abroad, and earned $462.2 billion in overseas revenues.[18] Some of these companies rank among the leaders in their field: according to one study (Scoffield 2006), Canada is home to seventy-two companies that rank among the top five in the world in their particular sector, up from thirty-three in 1985. These "world-class" companies have become not only more numerous, but also significantly larger, with average annual revenues today of $3.7 billion, up from $2.0 billion two decades ago (ibid.). These companies, then, have made Canada one of several command-and-control centres of global capitalism.

Indeed, according to the *Forbes Global 2000* – a listing of the world's top 2,000 firms by assets, revenues, profits, and market capitalization – in 2012 Canada ranked fifth in terms of the number of firms on the list, behind the United States, Japan, the United Kingdom, and China, and higher than countries such as France, Germany, Italy, Spain, India, and Brazil, whose populations far outnumber Canada's. What is most impressive about the *Forbes* list, however, is the diversity of sectors in which Canadian TNCs operate. Representing Canada are firms in banking, finance, insurance, oil and gas, telecommunications, transportation, food, utilities, industrial materials, mining, business services, retailing, media, high technology, consumer durables, aerospace, engineering, chemicals, and defence (see *Forbes* 2012). In other words, Canadian firms from across the circuit of capital compete on a worldwide scale.

The sectoral distribution of Canadian direct investment abroad is depicted in Figure 10. In 2010, finance and insurance led the way, accounting for 51.8 per cent of the total, followed by energy and metallic minerals (23.5 per cent), services and retailing (9.7 per cent), manufacturing ("other," 9.6 per cent), machinery and equipment (3.6 per cent), and wood and paper (1.7 per cent). The trends indicate that, during the period of neoliberalism, a financialization of Canadian direct investment abroad has occurred, as well as an international expansion of mining and energy firms. However, although Canadian TNCs are specialized in these particular circuits of capital, they are also embedded in other circuits, including retailing, services, and manufacturing. In these

Figure 10. Canadian Direct Investment Abroad, by Sector, 1980–2010

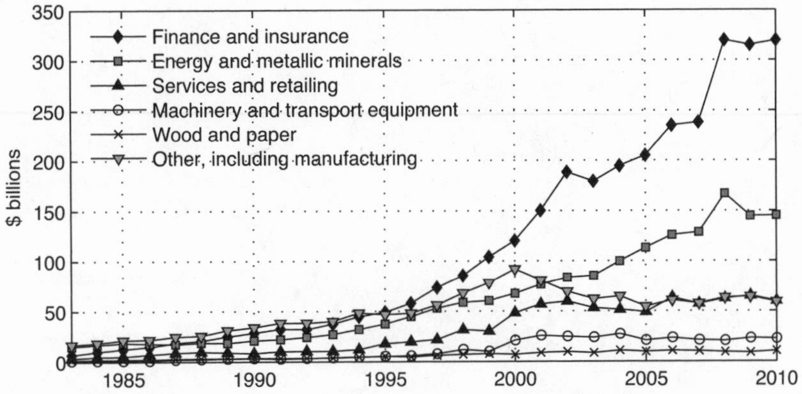

Source: Author's calculations, from Statistics Canada, CANSIM II database, table 3760038, V235581, V235582, V235583, V235585, V235586, V235587, V235584.

ways, Canadian capital is invested in diverse shares of production and exchange in the world economy. In the process, Canada has become one of the leading sources of FDI capital, accounting for 3.17 per cent of world outward direct investment stock in 2011 and ranking tenth behind the United States, the United Kingdom, Switzerland, the Netherlands, Japan, Germany, France, China, and Belgium. Like most of these states, Canada also has a lower share of inward FDI, meaning that Canada has greater claims on production abroad than do foreigners on production in Canada. At the same time, Canada continues to attract direct investment imports, and in 2011 accounted for 2.91 per cent of world inward direct investment stock, ranking tenth behind the United States, the United Kingdom, China, France, Belgium, Germany, Hong Kong, Brazil, and Spain. Furthermore, between 2001 and 2011, Canada received $400.4 billion in direct investment flows, positioning it seventh in the world behind China, Hong Kong, France, Germany, the United Kingdom, and the United States.[19]

As Figure 11 shows, in 2011 FDI stocks in Canada were concentrated in three key sectors – energy and mining (34.4 per cent), finance (24.6 per cent), and manufacturing (21.2 per cent) – followed by machinery and equipment (9.2 per cent), services and retailing (9.1 per cent), and wood and paper (1.6 per cent). Between 2005 and 2011, however, net flows

Figure 11. Foreign Direct Investment in Canada, by Sector, 1980–2010

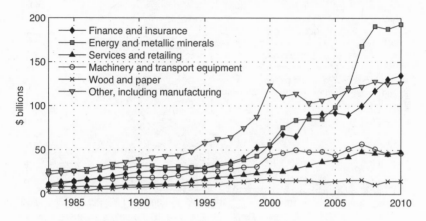

Source: Author's calculations, from Statistics Canada, CANSIM II database, table 3760038, V235599, V235601, V235597, V235602, V235598, V235600.

of FDI were overwhelmingly concentrated in the energy and metallic minerals sector (58.9 per cent), followed far behind by the manufacturing sector (18.0 per cent), the financial sector (11.0 per cent), services and retailing (7.6 per cent), and machinery and equipment (3.4 per cent).[20] The current trend of inward investment, therefore, is focused on energy and mining assets in the productive circuit of capital. This surge of direct investment in the resources side of the productive circuit pushed up the value of the Canadian dollar between 2009 and 2012, and diminished the global competitiveness of Canadian manufacturing, although this trend was partially reversed through 2013. The recent reduction of Canadian manufacturing exports to the United States and the onset of merchandise trade deficits in the balance of payments are partially related to these new trends in the circuits of money and productive capital. In these ways, the internationalization process has generated new contradictions in Canada's political economy, especially between different sections of industrial capital.

The financialization of the money circuit is evident as well in new flows of portfolio investment in bonds, stocks, and money market instruments. As in the case of FDI, portfolio investment has increased sharply as a share of GDP in Canada during the period of neoliberalism. For example, between 1971 and 2010, the ratio of portfolio investment to GDP leaped from 33.9 per cent to 68.3 per cent, turning Canada into a second-tier market for global finance. In fact, commanding 3.74 per cent of total world market capitalization, Canada in 2011 ranked sixth in the world behind the United States, Japan, the United Kingdom, China, and Hong Kong (Bespoke Investment Group 2012). Focused largely on resources industries in the productive circuit, the Toronto Stock Exchange is particularly important for transnational mining capital, listing 56 per cent of the world's public mining companies and trading more than $50 billion of mining company shares in 2013.[21] Through such money flows, Canada's political economy has become tightly linked to global circuits of finance capital in key industrial sectors. On this note, it is important to highlight that, although Canada imports more portfolio investment than it exports, the outward movement of portfolio investment has increased dramatically in recent decades. Indeed, from 1971 to 2010, the ratio of portfolio investment abroad to GDP at home increased from 3.1 per cent to 24.3 per cent, marking an exteriorization of finance capital in Canada. In this context, Canada became, at year-end 2013, a *creditor nation*, with Canadian investors owning a greater value of direct investments, stocks, and currency reserves abroad than do foreign investors in Canada (McKenna and Blackwell 2014).

The internationalization of Canadian money capital is apparent in two further ways: by the spatial relations of direct investment and by flows of profit across borders. Consider, first, the geographic ties of FDI and Canadian direct investment abroad. In 2010, the United States accounted for the largest stock of FDI in Canada at 54.5 per cent, followed by Europe (30.5 per cent), Asia (11.1 per cent), South and Central America (2.6 per cent), and Africa (0.2 per cent) (see Figure 12). The evidence suggests, then, that Canada attracts investment from core regions of the world economy, not from the periphery. A somewhat similar trend is evident in Canada's outward investment relations. As Figure 13 demonstrates, Canadian direct investment abroad is concentrated in the United States at 40.5 per cent, followed by Europe (25.5 per cent), various offshore financial centres ("other") (19.2 per cent), Asia (8.9 per cent), South and Central America (5.4 per cent), and Africa (0.5 per cent).[22] Thus, just as Canada tends to attract FDI from other advanced economies, it also exports capital to these same spaces of accumulation. As an advanced capitalist country, though, it also exports a large *quantity* of direct investment capital to non-OECD countries, which, in 2010, held $169.3 billion of stocks of Canadian direct investment abroad, primarily in finance, insurance, energy, mining, and manufacturing.[23]

Figure 12. Foreign Direct Investment in Canada, by Region, 1985–2010

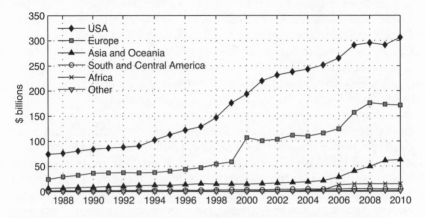

Source: Author's calculations, from Statistics Canada, CANSIM II database, table
3760051, V7117859, V7117879, V7117901, V7117993, V7117880, V7117946.

Figure 13. Canadian Direct Investment Abroad, by Region, 1985–2010

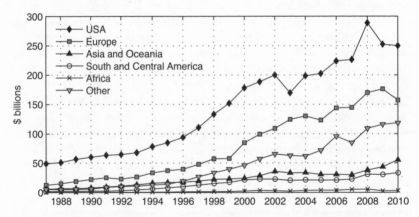

Source: Author's calculations, from Statistics Canada, CANSIM II database, table
3760051, V7117682, V7117702, V7117724, V7117816, V7117703, V7117769.

From these investments in circuits of production, finance, and
exchange on a global scale, Canadian capital has been able to earn,
and import, growing levels of profit from the world economy. As one
measure of this relationship, the ratio of foreign to domestic profits
for Canadian-owned businesses has increased dramatically in recent

Figure 14. The Foreign-to-Domestic Ratio of Canadian Corporate Profits, 1960–2010

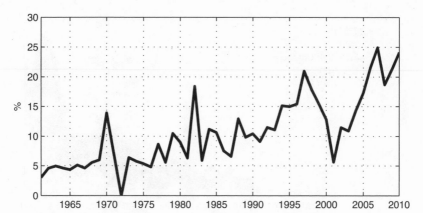

Note: Data on direct investment income receipts include only the profits repatriated to Canada. Likewise, the data on direct investment income payments do not account for reinvested earnings by foreign corporations in Canada. Nevertheless, Figure 14 approximates the growing ratio of foreign to domestic profit for Canadian corporations.

Source: Author's calculations, from Statistics Canada, CANSIM II database, table 3800016, V646928; table 3760012, V112586; and table 3760012, V112555.

decades. In 1976, the ratio of FDI income receipts to domestically controlled before-taxes profit was 4.8 per cent; by 2007, it had increased to 24.9 per cent (see Figure 14), indicating that the profits of Canadian enterprises have become more dependent on circuits of global value.

The internationalization of Canadian capital is evident, lastly, in the geographic source of investment income receipts. By this measure of internationalization in the money circuit of capital, a bimodal distribution of investment income receipts by state or region has emerged. As Figure 15 reveals, in 2010, 36.2 per cent of investment income receipts originated in the United States, 23.9 per cent in the United Kingdom and Europe, 1.0 per cent in Japan, 10.0 per cent in other OECD countries, and 35.3 per cent *in all other countries*, primarily in the periphery. Thus, although Canada's foreign investment relations are focused on the advanced capitalist world, especially on the United States and Europe, they tend to earn roughly one-third of global investment income from non-OECD countries. It is important to highlight, moreover, that the numbers reach into the hundreds of billions of dollars. For example, between 2004 and 2010, total investment income earned from

Figure 15. Canadian Foreign Investment Income, by Region, 1960–2010

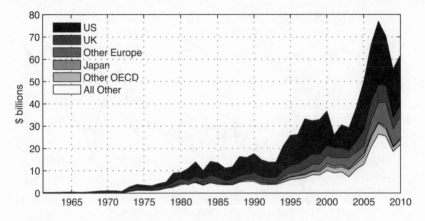

Note: Includes direct and portfolio investment income.

Source: Author's calculations, from Statistics Canada, CANSIM II database, table 3760001, V113780, V113853, V113997, V114069, V114141, V114213.

non-OECD sources was $136.6 billion, representing a massive transfer of value to Canada. From these numbers, it is apparent that Canadian capital is engaged in escalating forms of global exploitation and appropriation, especially in poor countries.

To summarize, then, Canada's political economy connects to the world market through four relations of money capital. First, Canada has a unique bilateral investment relationship with the United States, one that binds together the two economies in important ways. Although US firms invest more in Canada than Canadian firms do in the United States, the latter have narrowed the investment gap and become competitive investors inside the NAFTA zone. Their US competitors, in other words, have not marginalized them; instead, except in key sectors, Canadian and US firms tend to invest as equals in the continental economic space. This regional investment relationship is centrally important to the expanded reproduction of Canadian capital, and reinforces the secondary status of Canadian imperialism.

Second, the investments of Canadian TNCs extend beyond the NAFTA zone. Canadian firms invest in many states and regions, and are active players in the internationalization of capital. As a result, the growth and expansion of Canadian capital is now connected to the production and circulation of value on a global scale. In other words, Canadian TNCs have a global investment strategy – their base of accumulation is not limited to the NAFTA zone, but extends across the worldwide circuits of capital. This expansion supports the growth of transnational corporate power in Canada, and gives the Canadian capitalist class an independent interest in the world market. It has also given the national economy a net creditor status, as Canadian ownership of assets abroad now exceeds foreign-owned liabilities in Canada.

Third, Canadian direct investment abroad is located overwhelmingly in the core regions of North America, Europe, and developed Asia. Interestingly, although Canada imports more capital from the United States than vice versa, it exports more to Europe and Asia than it receives in return. The United States, then, is the only country among the imperial core with which Canada runs an investment surplus. In all other cases, Canada exports more than it imports, meaning that Canadian capital has greater claims on value production abroad than do foreign firms in Canada. In response to US competition, then, Canadian firms have increased investment in both the United States and other leading markets.

Finally, like other leading states, Canada runs a massive investment deficit with countries lower down the value-added chain. Although only a small portion of Canadian direct investment abroad is sent to Africa, Asia, and South and Central America, this amount is not at all reciprocated by inward FDI from these regions. Canada's investment relationship with the periphery, then, is characterized by a structural imbalance. In fact, Canadian capital plays a dominant role in many Third World countries, from where it earns large-scale profits for expanded reproduction. In these ways, Canadian capital is externalized in global forms of exploitation and appropriation.

Conclusion: A Contentious Transnationalism

This chapter has demonstrated that, during the period of neoliberalism, a structural transformation of Canadian capitalism has occurred. In particular, Canada's political economy has been internationalized across the circuits of productive, commercial, and financial capital. In the process, Canadian capital has become more engaged in transnational forms of exploitation and appropriation, and established flows of value that have positioned the state as a secondary power in the chain of imperialism. Although the Canadian economy incorporates dependent circuits of capital in several key sectors, the internationalization process has been characterized by two-way flows of value in which Canadian

TNCs increasingly, if not more importantly, are present. As such, Canadian corporations have benefited from transfers of value in the world economy, and thus have participated in the exploitation of labour and the appropriation of value on a global scale.

For these reasons, the Canadian state must be located as a secondary imperialist power in world accumulation. It is tightly bound with the political economy of US capitalism, but also linked to wider circuits of capital in the world economy. In fact, the evidence suggests that the NAFTA zone has been the *spatial lynchpin* of a transnational process of expansion. Indeed, through NAFTA, Canada has overcome trade deficits with other regions of the world economy, and Canadian corporations have placed foreign direct investments as a first step towards full-throttled transnationalization. As a result, Canada's role in the NAFTA bloc is best analysed from the standpoint of the world economy as a whole. In other words, it must be theorized in terms of global flows of value.

Although the internationalization of capital has tended to strengthen the role of Canadian TNCs in global exploitation and appropriation, it has also generated several contradictions in Canada's political economy, especially between different fractions of productive capital. For Canadian capital, these contradictions have included, at times, a rising currency value caused by energy and mineral exports and new inflows of FDI, resulting in declining exports of manufactured goods and other processed merchandise products. Canadian capital has also suffered from a declining rate of productivity growth caused by the reorganization of production under transnational management strategies and the shift towards energy and mining production, which typically involves lower scales of fixed capital investment (Stanford 2008).

For workers employed in the transnational relations of Canadian capital, however, the contradictions are of a different order altogether. Although the process of transnational neoliberalism has generally augmented the power of capital, it has disorganized and decomposed the power of labour. As Canada has become more entwined with transnational circuits of capital, downward pressures on income have generated new dynamics of class exploitation in two key respects. First, the share of labour income in Canada's GDP has shrunk dramatically as the ratio of profit to GDP has increased.[24] Second, Canadian immigration policy has been used increasingly to transform labour markets in racialized and imperialistic ways. Thus, the internationalization of capital in Canada is premised on new social structures of class exploitation that intersect with new patterns of racism in Canada's political economy.

Canada's role in the world market has also been marked by transnational modes of exploitation and appropriation. Through a mix of investment practices, Canadian capital has staked claims on global forms of value production and exchange, especially in finance, mining, and energy. For critics (Deneault and Sacher 2012), it is in the mining sector that the implication of Canadian capital in transnational modes of exploitation and appropriation is most evident, and perhaps, alarming. Indeed, with more than three thousand projects in over one hundred countries, Canadian mining capital has been associated with human rights abuses, land confiscation, bribes and corruption, political repression, labour exploitation, gendered violence, and ecological destruction. In the process, it has often stoked contentious resistance on the part of workers, indigenous peoples, and poor communities in peripheral states (Blackwood and Stewart 2012). This new resistance is a concrete example of global justice in action, and points toward a different type of globalization – that of people over profit.

In the Colombian city of Bucaramanga, for instance, tens of thousands of people have marched against the exploration activities of Vancouver-based Eco Oro Minerals (Arango 2013). In Chile, Barrick Gold's Pascua-Lama project has been targeted for serious environmental violations (*Reuters* 2013). Barrick Gold's Porgera mine in Papua New Guinea has also been the site of human rights abuses, including gang rapes by private security forces (Human Rights Watch 2011). In 2013, a state of emergency was declared in Kyrgyzstan, where Toronto-based Centerra Gold was confronted by protests and riots (*Associated Press* 2013). Likewise, in 2012, the government of Bolivia expropriated the silver and indium mine of Canada's South American Silver after indigenous people called for nationalization of the project (*Agence France-Presse* 2012). In cases like this, popular movements have arisen to confront what David Harvey (2003) calls "accumulation by dispossession" – an integral aspect of the "new imperialism."

The key point of this chapter, though, is that the internationalization of capital has created a structural change in the political economy of Canadian capitalism. In particular, it has invested the Canadian capitalist class in global forms of exploitation and appropriation and in the political project of transnational neoliberalism. As the next chapter reveals, these changes in the structure of accumulation have sparked a commensurate shift in the structure of the Canadian corporate elite. Indeed, from the economics of transnational neoliberalism, a new agent of capitalist class power has emerged.

5 Transnational Class Formation: Globalization and the Canadian Corporate Network

WITH WILLIAM K. CARROLL[1]

The issue of transnational class formation has figured centrally in recent debates on globalization and the world economy. These debates revolve around the question of whether or not new patterns of cross-border trade and investment have established global circuits of capital out of which a transnational capitalist class has emerged. For Stephen Hymer (1979, 262), who first observed this trend in the 1970s, "an international capitalist class is emerging whose interests lie in the world economy as a whole." At the time, Hymer noticed "a strong tendency for the most powerful segments of the capitalist class ... to see their future in the further growth of the world market rather than its curtailment."

With recent trends in economic globalization, many researchers have pushed this theory in new directions. For Michael Hardt and Antonio Negri (2000), globalization has created a new form of *empire* – a world economy so interconnected that it overcomes rivalries between states and national blocs of capital: "What used to be conflict or competition among several imperialist powers has in important respects been replaced by the idea of a single power that overdetermines them all, structures them in a unitary way, and treats them under one common notion of right that is decidedly postcolonial and postimperialist" (2000, 9). In a similar vein, Jerry Harris (2005, 329) argues that "[t]he major dialectic in the present period is the contradiction between the descending form of capitalism organized around the nation-state system and an arising form of accumulation organized in the transnational world order." For this reason, Stephen Gill (2003, 59) views globalization as the political project of a "transnational historic bloc." According to Leslie Sklair (2001), it is leading "corporate executives, globalizing bureaucrats and politicians, globalizing professionals, and consumerist elites," who produce and represent this new class agency.

William Robinson (2004) provides perhaps the most systematic version of this theory. In his view, the current period is defined by an epochal shift away from a world economy to a global economy, or from a period in which capitalism was organized nationally and integrated through trade in commodities, to a period in which capitalist production itself is organized globally. New forms of foreign direct investment (FDI), outsourcing, and subcontracting have unified the world into "a single mode of production" and brought about "the integration of different countries and regions into a new global economy" (ibid., 15). According to Robinson, a transnational capitalist class has formed in and around these newly globalized circuits of capital. This class, moreover, is *the dominant, or hegemonic, fraction of capital on a world scale*" (ibid., 21). It manages global production chains and incorporates multiple class agents and formerly national groupings into a new power bloc whose material interests and class unity are located in transnational processes. The transnational capitalist class is the most dynamic class force in the world economy, and the competitive logic it triggers forces local and national capitalists to become more globally integrated as well. The result has been the formation of a new transnational power bloc that integrates multiple levels of capital, and is organized through global patterns of production and accumulation instead of through national ones. For Robinson (ibid., 87), this new power bloc has established a transnational state apparatus, which includes "transformed and externally integrated national states, together with the supranational economic and political forums," such as the International Monetary Fund, the World Bank, the World Trade Organization, and the United Nations. The transnational state institutionalizes "the new class relation between global capital and global labor," and "forge[s] together a new global capitalist historic bloc" (ibid., 88).

As one of the more lucid and theoretically grounded versions of the transnational hypothesis, Robinson's work has generated much debate (Bello 2006; Desai 2007; Moore 2002; van der Pijl 2005). For detractors, Robinson's theory has three limitations. First, in terms of methodology, it tends to use fixed categories and positive reasoning, and therefore lacks appreciation of dialectical tendencies. Second, it overstates the extent to which globalization has equalized value production and exchange across spaces of the world market. Although capital now circulates on a global scale, the world economy is characterized by uneven productive capacities and systematic imbalances between states and regions, which compete for investments, export markets, and profits.

Third, the transnational hypothesis tends to mistake the global circulation of capital for the microeconomic integration of capitalist classes. Related to this, it has yet to map a network of cross-border corporate elite connections, which might offer the best empirical evidence of transnational class formation. If such a class *is* driving the globalization agenda, it should appear, or take concrete shape, in directorship interlocks between transnational corporations (TNCs), for it is precisely at the site of corporate ownership and oversight that capitalist class power emerges and gains political, social, and cultural traction (Brownlee 2005; Carroll 2004; Scott 1997).

In this chapter, we take up the notion of transnational class formation in Canada. We examine the extent to which globalization is transforming the national corporate community and creating a transnational capitalist class in the form of cross-border interlocking directorates among leading firms in Canada and the world economy. Canada is a particularly interesting case for the study of how transnational capitalist class formation intersects with the reproduction (and possible decline) of national corporate communities. For more than three decades, the issue of transnational corporate interlocking has been a mainstay of political economy research in Canada (Carroll 2008). In the 1970s, Tom Naylor (1972) and Wallace Clement (1975, 1977) argued that US multinationals had fragmented the corporate network in Canada and established a "continental" structure of corporate power, headquartered in the United States yet supported domestically by a "comprador" elite. More recently, Leo Panitch and Sam Gindin (2004, 2005a) have used this understanding of "interior" class formation under US hegemony to construct a theory of globalization and American empire. This conceptualization of the Canadian corporate elite, however, has often lacked empirical evidence. In the 1980s, the network analysis of Jack Richardson (1982, 1988) and William Carroll (1986) revealed a national bloc of "finance capital" – an integrated network of industrial and financial firms in Canada, independent of US imperialism and expanding autonomously into world markets. In a more recent study of directorship interlocks, Carroll (2004, 81, 85) finds that, by 1996, "*the entire transnational sector [in Canada] was highly integrated*," that Canadian transnational firms were interlocked with subtransnationals, and that finance capital "radiate[s] from Canada in a way that *has not* disorganized the national network, but has *embedded* it more extensively in a circuitry of global accumulation." In other words, Carroll documents a globalization of Canadian finance capital, rather than a process of comprador or transnational class formation.

Over the past decade, the Canadian economy has maintained a high degree of integration with world markets. Among the Group-of-7 major industrialized countries, Canada ranks second in terms of both the ratio of trade to gross domestic product (GDP) and the ratio of FDI to GDP, and fourth in terms of the United Nations Conference on Trade and Development's (UNCTAD) index of "transnationality."[2] Since the mid-1990s, Canada has also become a net exporter of capital, as the post-war trend of inward direct investment flows (mostly from US firms) has been superseded by outward direct investments by Canadian corporations (Burgess 2000; Kentor 2005, 271; Klassen 2009). As we saw in Chapter 4, Canada is now home to more than 1,500 TNCs, which control approximately 6,500 foreign affiliates. Canada is also home to seventy-two "world class" corporations, which rank among the top five in their line of business globally. According to *Forbes*, Canada ranks fifth among countries with corporations listed among the top 2,000 worldwide. Although Canada is highly integrated with the United States through the North American Free Trade Agreement, Canadian firms are increasingly engaged in a wider process of internationalization, especially through FDI in Europe and Latin America.

These basic indicators of economic globalization make Canada a prime candidate for the investigation of transnational class formation. With a highly advanced and globalized economic structure, Canada should exhibit new forms of corporate organization, including directorship interlocks between national and transnational firms, as is evident in similar countries, such as the Netherlands (Heemskerk 2007). A key question is whether the Canadian corporate community is becoming "disarticulated" (Scott 1997) as companies based in Canada become more transnational in their investment, ownership, and directorate interlocks.

The purpose of this chapter is twofold: to update the study of class formation in Canada's political economy, and to highlight the consolidation of a transnational bloc of corporate power in Canada, with independent interests in the world economy and the new imperialism.

We theorize the process of class formation by means of two concepts: William Domhoff's (2006) "corporate community," and Leslie Sklair's (2001) "transnational practice." According to Domhoff, large corporations and corporate directors are drawn together through interlocking directorships to form a corporate community – a more or less cohesive elite with common goals and shared understandings. The corporate community is a root metaphor for charting capitalist class formation at its higher reaches. In Domhoff's conception, the community is integrated not only through corporate board interlocks, but also through the participation of corporate directors on policy-planning boards and other elite vehicles for building consensus; this chapter, however, restricts itself to corporate interlocks.

Sklair (2001), in theorizing the transnational capitalist class, defines transnational practices as those "that cross state boundaries but do not necessarily originate with state agencies or actors" (Sklair and Robbins 2002, 82). For any given corporation, three such practices are particularly relevant. First, there are the firm's foreign direct investments – that is, its outward reach, via ownership of subsidiaries, into various other countries, which represent an *exteriorization* of its corporate power beyond the domestic scene. Second is the inward reach of a foreign corporate interest via major shareholding in the firm – that is, foreign control of the company – which represents an *interiorization* of foreign corporate power into the domestic scene. The third practice is directorate interlocking between the firm and large corporations domiciled in other countries – that is, *transnational interlocking*.

Although all three practices contribute to transnational class formation, the first and the second carry quite different implications for the meaning of the third. For a company *exteriorizing* its corporate power through outward investment, transnational interlocks improve the business scan that facilitates effective decision-making beyond familiar locales (Useem 1984). Alternatively, a firm controlled by a foreign-based parent might share directors with the parent, enabling the latter to oversee its operations, as was the case in the mid-1970s network of European and US corporations studied by Meindert Fennema and Huibert Schijf (1985). As Jeff Kentor (2005, 282) suggests, "ownership of a foreign subsidiary transfers some amount of power from the host country to the TNC," with board interlocks providing a conduit of that power. A familiar example is Chrysler Group LLC, the reborn version of a firm first established by Walter Chrysler in 1925 and controlled in the United States until it merged with German-based Daimler in 1998, at which time its domicile moved to Germany, although US-based capitalists' continued to be represented in top management and on the supervisory board (Neubauer, Steger, and Radler 2000). Daimler eventually cashed out its US investment to private equity firm Cerberus and severed its ties with Chrysler. In 2009, in the wake of the global financial crisis and on the verge of bankruptcy, Chrysler was bailed out by US and Canadian governments and a significant stake was acquired by Fiat of Italy, which currently appoints three of nine directors as well as the chief executive officer.

These microeconomic scenarios bear upon the fate of national corporate communities and their location within the world system. For a corporate community whose leading companies fall under foreign control, rising incidences of transnational interlocking might indicate a "hollowing out" (Arthurs 2000) – a compositional shift towards an "interior bourgeoisie" that represents, on the domestic scene, the corporate power of foreign-based interests (Poulantzas 1978a, 72). As the accumulation base for the national corporate community shrinks, transnational interlocks reinforce a dynamic of compradorization (Clement 1977) that further erodes that national corporate community's competitive position within the world system. The result can be a "harvest of lengthening dependency," which Kari Levitt (1970, 116) predicted for Canada in the wake of the post-war expansion of US corporate capital.

Alternatively, a corporate community that expands into other countries and establishes transnational board interlocks develops its base of accumulation beyond the domestic market, and exteriorizes the reach of its corporate power.

In reality, both these tendencies are present in any national locale. The key empirical issue in assessing the impact of globalization on a corporate community is the extent to which one or the other predominates. An additional consideration is how transnational practices of exteriorization, interiorization, and directorate interlocking articulate with the domestic corporate network – the centre of gravity of a national corporate community. Schematically, several combinations of tendencies in the corporate community's accumulation base and in its board interlocks are possible, five of which are delineated in Table 5. Scenario A, which might be deemed a null hypothesis, represents a national corporate community unaffected by the transnational practices we have discussed. Scenario B shows a corporate community exteriorizing its accumulation base and establishing transnational interlocks while maintaining a strong national network. Scenario C depicts the same expansion of foreign investment and of transnational interlocks, in step with the atrophy of the national network. In scenario D, transnationalization takes an interiorizing form, shrinking the corporate community's accumulation base and eroding its national network, as proliferating transnational interlocks trace the power of foreign parents over domestic subsidiaries. In scenario E, the corporate community expands its accumulation base and its connections abroad even as foreign interests penetrate and the national network declines. This is the scenario of transnationalization and national disarticulation predicted

Table 5. Scenarios of Transnationalization for National Corporate Communities

	Accumulation Base		Corporate Network	
Scenario	Exteriorization	Interiorization	Transnational Interlocking	National Interlocking
A				+
B		+	+	+
C		+	+	−
D	+		+	−
E	+	+	+	−
F	+	+	+	+

by John Scott (1997) and Robinson (2004). Finally, in scenario F, all three transnational practices occur, yet the national network remains a robust source of cohesion for the corporate community.

Below, we analyse recent tendencies in Canada, in view of these scenarios, and draw conclusions about the social composition of the corporate elite in the recent period of neoliberal globalization.

Methodology

To represent the national corporate community, we use Carroll's (2004) data for year-end 1996 as a starting point and replicate his methods for defining and analysing the corporate network in 2006. Over this ten-year period, we examine the changing composition and interlock network of a "C250" set of firms headquartered in Canada, consisting of the two hundred largest non-financial corporations (ranked by total revenue) and the fifty largest financial institutions (ranked by total assets).[3] To track relations between Canada's corporate community and the world's largest non-Canadian corporations, we examine the boards of a "G500" set of firms, representing the five hundred largest companies globally, consisting of the four hundred largest non-financials (ranked by revenue) and the one hundred largest financials (ranked by assets).[4] We explain how we operationalize our variables as we introduce successive phases of the analysis.

The Scope of Transnationalization in Canada

We first report on changes to the accumulation base for leading Canadian firms, as evident in three measures: the *degree of transnationality* in the C250, the *geographic spread* of C250 subsidiaries,[5] and the *country of*

Table 6. Transnationality of C250 Corporations

Transnationality	Number of Firms		Mean Revenues (current $ billions)	
	1996	2006	1996	2006
Nationally bound	112	115	2.35	3.41
Continental	38	40	2.34	4.01
Near transnational	48	36	3.42	6.42
Transnational	50	56	5.77	10.03
Total	248	247	3.25	5.45

control (Canadian controlled versus foreign controlled) of C250 firms.[6] The first two of these are measures of exteriorization: the outward reach of corporate power from Canada. The third is an indicator of interiorization: the inward reach of corporate power into Canada, via FDI. To operationalize exteriorization, we follow Jorge Niosi's (1985a) typology of transnationality and distinguish four categories: (1) TNCs, incorporated in Canada and holding subsidiaries in four other countries (the most exteriorized firms); (2) near-TNCs, owning subsidiaries in fewer than four countries, including at least one country other than the United States; (3) continentalized firms, operating subsidiaries only in the United States; and (4) nationally bound firms, having no foreign subsidiaries.[7]

As Table 6 shows, in the decade following 1996, we find an increase in the number of fully fledged Canadian TNCs, but a decrease in the complement of near-transnationals. There is no general tendency for C250 firms to become more "transnationalized"; rather, to some extent, *the C250 becomes more polarized*: by 2007 it contains a larger complement of TNCs, but also a larger complement of nationally bound or continentally oriented firms. This polarization in transnationality has occurred in conjunction with a polarization in firm size within the C250. Typically, it is only very large firms that become TNCs, as they outgrow their home market, and this is certainly the case in Canada. In 1996, Canadian TNCs had revenues on average twice as large as those of nationally bound C250 firms. In the decade under study, TNCs and near-TNCs grew much more quickly than other C250 firms, so that, by 2006, the four categories of transnationality accounted for 14.4 per cent of the variance in revenue, compared with 10.0 per cent in 1996.[8] We therefore find evidence of different rates of accumulation between faster-growing TNCs and slower-growing, nationally bound firms in the C250.

Table 7. Number of C250 Foreign Subsidiaries, Categorized by Host Region

Domicile of Subsidiary	1996	2006	% Change
United States	1,013	884	−12.7
Europe	771	1,138	+47.6
Latin America	230	152	−33.9
Asia Pacific	240	270	+12.5
Africa	26	15	−42.3
Total	2,280	2,459	+7.9

Another basic indicator of transnationalization is the total number of foreign subsidiaries owned by C250 companies. Although this value dipped slightly over the decade under study (from 2,523 to 2,509), closer inspection shows the overall shift to be attributable to a sharp decrease in foreign subsidiary listings in known tax havens (from 243 subsidiaries in 1996 to 50 in 2006). The significance of this decrease is unknown; however, such subsidiaries typically are more strategic devices for sheltering income than they are sites for accumulating capital through production, circulation, and finance. Leaving aside the tax havens, the intercontinental spread of C250 foreign subsidiaries is shown in Table 7. Across the decade, the number of (non-tax-haven) foreign subsidiaries of C250 firms grew by approximately 8 per cent, as Europe displaced the United States as the main host region. Canadian foreign subsidiaries also proliferated in the Asia-Pacific region, but their numbers diminished in Latin America and Africa.

Although, on average, each corporation in the C250 owns ten foreign subsidiaries, the distribution of ownership is highly skewed. Overwhelmingly, ownership of foreign subsidiaries is concentrated among the Canadian transnationals: our database shows that, in 1996, 79.9 per cent of all C250 foreign subsidiaries were owned by the fifty Canadian TNCs; in 2006, fifty-six TNCs owned 84.7 per cent of all C250 foreign subsidiaries. Among foreign subsidiaries domiciled outside the United States, the concentration of transnational investment was even more pronounced. Canadian TNCs owned 92.0 per cent of such firms in 1996 and 93.7 per cent in 2006. Moreover, subtransnationals active in FDI tended to restrict their investments to subsidiaries in the United States or the United Kingdom. Broadly, the pattern is for Canadian TNCs to own subsidiaries in the United States and the United Kingdom, plus several other countries, often in Europe but also in Latin America and

Table 8. Transnationality and National Locus of Control

Country of Control	National		Continental		Near TNCs		TNCs		Total	
	1996	2006	1996	2006	1996	2006	1996	2006	1996	2006
Canada	54.5	67.0	89.5	87.5	72.5	86.1	94.0	91.1	71.4	78.5
United States	27.7	13.0	5.3	5.0	14.6	13.9	6.0	3.6	17.3	9.7
Europe	10.7	14.8	2.6	7.5	4.2			1.8	6.0	8.5
Asia-Pacific	7.1	5.2				8.4		1.8	4.8	2.8
Other			2.6					1.8	0.4	0.4
Total (%)	100	100	100	100	100	100	100	100	100	100
Total (number)	112	115	38	40	48	36	50	56	248	247

the Asia-Pacific zone. Subtransnationals that own foreign subsidiaries typically are restricted to direct investments in the United States and secondarily in the United Kingdom. These countries, culturally similar to anglophone Canada and, in the case of the United States, spatially proximate, might serve as staging grounds for further transnationalization by Canadian corporations.

As Table 8 demonstrates, there is an important inverse relationship between exteriorization and interiorization – that is, between a firm's degree of transnationality and whether it is controlled by foreign interests.[9] Almost all Canadian TNCs are controlled domestically, and the slight rise in foreign control of TNCs (from 6.0 per cent to 8.9 per cent) coincides with a decline in US control. At the other end of the continuum, foreign control is most prevalent among nationally bound companies – that is, firms that have not exteriorized their accumulation bases – one-third of which were foreign controlled in 2006. Overall, most C250 firms are controlled by Canadian interests (whether capitalists, the state, or, in a few cases, cooperatives), and this trend strengthened over the decade, as the number of C250 firms controlled outside Canada dropped from 71 (28.5 per cent) to 53 (21.2 per cent). It is particularly among the near-TNCs and the nationally bound firms that foreign control dropped. For the latter, US control plummeted, but European control increased slightly. The relationship in Table 8 implies that, when we speak of Canadian transnationals, in nearly all cases we are speaking of very large, Canadian-controlled corporations, not of Canadian branch plants that act as "go-betweens" in managing the foreign investments of their parents (Clement 1977). In contrast, nationally bound firms are not only smaller; a good many are foreign-owned subsidiaries that interiorize foreign-based interests.

To summarize, our findings on the transnationality of C250 corporations, the geographic spread of their subsidiaries, and the locus of
national control indicate that key transformations have taken place in
the accumulation base of corporate Canada. First, we observe a *polarization* in the C250 between TNCs, which are leading sites of capital
accumulation, and non-TNCs, which are less dynamic in their rates of
growth. Second, we find evidence of a more diverse geographic spread
of subsidiary locations, as C250 firms have expanded rapidly beyond
North America into Europe, Asia, and other regions of the world economy. Finally, we note a decline of foreign control among the C250, a
transnational diversification of that control, and a tendency for foreign
control to be concentrated among nationally bound firms. These transformations indicate a complex process of transnationalization in the
accumulation base of the C250. Both interiorization and exteriorization
are evident, but they apply to different C250 firms, and the overall
trends favour externalization and a diversification of foreign domiciles – both
as destinations for Canadian direct investment and as loci of foreign
control.

Transnationality and Interlocking Directorates:
Changes in the Corporate Community

How do these changes in the accumulation base bear upon the network of interlocking directorates, and what are the implications for the
national corporate community? To answer these questions, we first need
to distinguish between two kinds of corporate interlocking. *National*
interlocking occurs when two companies based in the same country
share one or more directors; its effect is to help *bond* corporate directors
into a national corporate community. In an entirely introverted corporate community (scenario A in Table 5), all ties would bond members to
each other. *Transnational* interlocking occurs when two firms domiciled
in different countries share one or more directors, thus *bridging* across
national borders (Carroll 2010). A major shift from national to transnational interlocking could disarticulate the relatively introverted corporate communities that were a legacy of twentieth-century organized
capitalism (Scott 1997), as in scenarios C, D, and E in Table 5.
Recent scholarship has established an uneven shift towards transnational interlocking among the world's largest corporations (Carroll
2009a; Kentor and Jang 2004). However, the increase in transnational
interlocking has not supplanted national corporate networks, and

much of the growth in transnational interlocking reflects the consolidation of a pan-European corporate community (Carroll 2009a). It is well to note also that the decade between 1996 and 2006 marked widespread adoption of US-style corporate governance practices, which tended to decrease the size of corporate boards and the extent of directorate interlocking in pursuit of efficiencies that enhance shareholder value and consolidate both operational and strategic control in parent head offices (Carroll 2010).

In the case of Canada, Carroll (2004) finds that, between 1976 and 1996, the transnationalization of Canadian corporations did not lead to a weakening of the elite network. In both years, TNCs were the most central firms in the network and their boards were densely interlocked with the directorates of Canadian-controlled sub-TNCs. The tendency was for the network to become "centred more around a core of transnational banks and corporations, controlled by capitalists based in Canada" (ibid., 85), matching our scenario B and pointing up "the resilience of the national factor in elite organization" (ibid., 209). More recently, Carroll and Klassen (2010) have discovered for 2006 the reproduction of a national corporate community, against the tendency towards "hollowing out" associated with FDI and cross-border mergers and acquisitions.

What, then, are the most recent developments in the network of directorship interlocks, both within Canada and between Canada and the world economy? How did the dialectic of accumulation and class formation materialize over the decade between 1996 and 2006? Is a transnational capitalist class in the making?

Figure 16 charts levels of interlocking (mean degree) – both national (top panel) and transnational (bottom) – in 1996 and 2006 for C250 corporations, grouped by transnationality. The top panel confirms a continuing decline after 1996 in the degree of national interlocking – that is, the number of other C250 firms with which a company shared one or more directors. Over all subcategories of C250 firms, the mean national degree of interlocking fell from 8.9 to 4.6; in other words, the number of other C250 corporations with which a company shared one or more directors decreased by nearly half. Comparing the top and bottom panels, the vast difference in the degrees of national and transnational interlocking across all categories of transnationality indicates that the corporate network remained nationally centred over the decade. Over all subcategories, the mean transnational degree of interlocking – the number of non-Canadian G500 corporations with which a company

Figure 16. The Mean Degree of National and Transnational Interlocking for Categories of Transnationality in the C250 Firms, 1996 and 2006

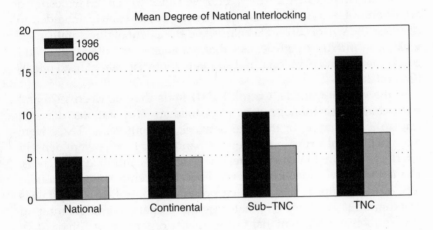

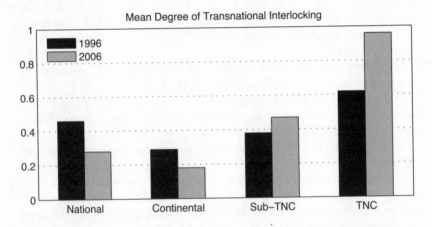

shared one or more directors – remained constant, at 0.45. This apparent stasis, however, belies a definite polarization as *TNCs became more
engaged in transnational interlocking, while nationally bound and continentally invested firms became less engaged in transnational interlocking.* In
1996, the four categories of transnationality in Figure 16 accounted for
a trivial 0.5 per cent of the variance in the transnational degree of interlocking; a decade later, the same between-group differences accounted

for 7.0 per cent of the variance. Still, by 2006 Canadian TNCs continued to show the highest mean degree of interlocking with C250 firms, and the between-group differences in the national degree were sharper than in the transnational degree.[10] These findings suggest that Canadian TNCs, nearly all of which are domestically controlled, continue to match our scenario B: transnationalized in their investments and interlocks, they remain extensively networked with other Canadian corporations.

How does the phenomenon of interiorization figure in the network? Overall, as Figure 17 shows, foreign-controlled firms began the decade substantially less interlocked with other C250 corporations, at a mean national degree of 5.0, than did Canadian-controlled companies, at 10.4. Although the grand mean for all C250 companies fell from 8.9 to 4.6 over the decade, US-controlled companies in particular withdrew from the network of national interlocks after 1996. The four categories of country of control in Figure 17 account for 8.1 per cent of the variance in the national degree of interlocking in 1996 and 9.9 per cent in 2006 – the increase indicating a sharpening of the tendency for companies controlled in Canada to bond with other C250 corporations.[11]

We saw in Table 8 that foreign control of C250 firms decreased between 1996 and 2006, but that it persisted to some degree among firms lacking any foreign subsidiaries (matching the classic "branch plant" pattern of corporate control and management; see Levitt 1970); indeed, such nationally bound firms accounted for nearly three-quarters of all foreign-controlled C250 companies in both years. As shown in Figure 18, which focuses only on the nationally bound subgroup, the mean degree of national interlocking for Canadian-controlled firms fell only mildly after 1996, while for (nationally bound) firms under foreign control, it plummeted. Thus, in the same decade that Canadian TNCs increased their participation in the transnational network, foreign-controlled branch plants became more detached from the national network. In effect, over the decade from 1996 to 2006, the network became more "Canadian" (less interiorized) in its national, bonding aspect, yet more linked into the global corporate elite (more exteriorized), particularly through Canadian TNCs that are controlled domestically.[12]

Although Figure 16 shows that Canadian TNCs tended to interlock extensively with C250 companies, this does not tell us whether their interlocks led simply to other TNCs – potentially constituting a transnationalized network disarticulated from the rest of the Canadian

Figure 17. The Mean Degree of National and Transnational Interlocking for Categories of C250 Firms, by Country of Control, 1996 and 2006

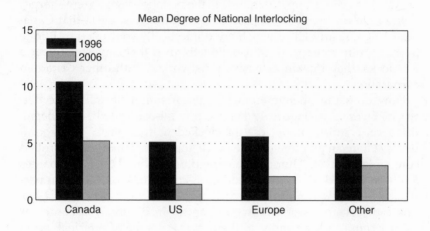

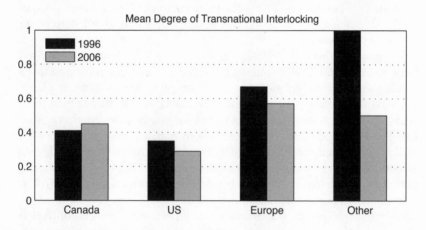

corporate community – or to the full range of large Canadian firms. By charting the *density* of interlocking within and between segments of the network, we can appraise these scenarios. Density – the number of actual interlocks divided by the maximum possible number of interlocks; that is, if all pairs of firms were directly linked – indicates the probability that a pair of companies is interlocked. In 1996, the overall density for the C250 was 0.0721; in 2006, it was 0.0374.

Figure 18. The Mean Degree of National Interlocking for Categories of Nationally Bound Companies, by Country of Control, 1996 and 2006

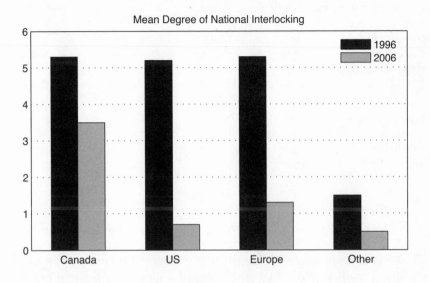

Using these as benchmarks, we see in Table 9 that, in both years, the network was centralized around the TNCs, which interlocked extensively with each other (particularly in 1996) and less extensively with near-TNCs and continental firms. In sharp contrast, nationally bound firms (comprising nearly half of the C250) rarely interlocked with each other, and after 1996, did not share directors to any appreciable extent with the more transnationalized companies. In this sense, the national network not only became sparser over the decade, *it became primarily a configuration of the boards of corporations whose investments extend beyond Canadian territory.*

As for transnational, bridging interlocks, these also increasingly became the province of TNCs. Whereas in 1996 there was no tendency for transnationality in direct investments to be associated with transnational interlocking,[13] our database shows that, by 2006, transnationality explained 7.0 per cent of the variance in the transnational degree of interlocking. Among the thirty corporations that ranked as TNCs in both 1996 and 2006, the growth in transnational interlocking was particularly notable. Already in 1996, the mean degree of transnational interlocking for these firms, at 0.73, was nearly double the grand mean.

Table 9. Sectoral Densities within and between Categories of Transnationality

	National	Continental	Near-TNC	TNC
	1996			
Nationally bound	0.013	0.025	0.027	0.036
Continental	0.025	0.047	0.039	0.066
Near-TNC	0.027	0.039	0.045	0.079
TNC	0.036	0.066	0.079	0.134
	2006			
Nationally bound	0.008	0.012	0.016	0.012
Continental	0.012	0.015	0.025	0.034
Near-TNC	0.016	0.025	0.027	0.040
TNC	0.012	0.034	0.040	0.056

By 2006, at 1.33, it was triple the grand mean – that is, the long-standing TNCs had three times the number of transnational interlocks as did C250 corporations overall. It is particularly among the well-established, top-tier Canadian TNCs that transnational interlocking became fairly common after the mid-1990s.

Instead of comparing the *positions of firms* within the network, another way of mapping the relationship between transnational investment and transnational interlocking is to examine the *distribution of the interlocks* across categories of transnationality. *How much* of the interlocking between C250 firms and non-Canadian G500 firms involved Canadian TNCs, in comparison with, say, nationally bound companies? In 1996, there was a total of 111 interlocks between C250 firms and non-Canadian G500 firms; in 2006, the total number of transnational interlocks was 110. As Figure 19 shows, in 1996, thirty-one transnational interlocks were carried by Canadian TNCs, comprising slightly more than a quarter of the total. A decade on, nearly half of all transnational interlocks linked G500 boards with the boards of Canada's fifty-six major TNCs.[14] Besides the increasing role of Canadian TNCs in transnational interlocking, the other major shift evident in Figure 19 is the sharp drop in transnational interlocks that involved, on the Canadian side of the relationship, firms with operations only in Canada. In effect, over the decade, *transnational interlocking became much less dispersed among many firms bound within Canada, and more concentrated within a*

Figure 19. Transnational Interlocks Classified by Transnationality, 1996 and 2006

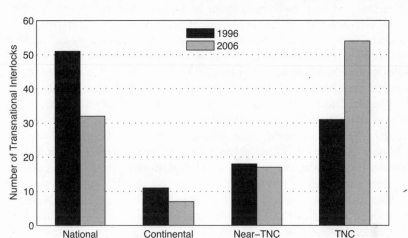

relatively compact group of TNCs, even as the TNCs continued to claim a constant proportion of the bonding ties that knit together a national corporate community.

Recalling our earlier analysis, which showed relatively high rates of foreign control among nationally bound corporations and flagging rates of participation in the national network by nationally bound firms under foreign control (Figure 18), it is worthwhile to unpack the nationally bound category further, but now on the issue of participation in the transnational network. When we do so, we find that, in 1996, most of the transnational interlocks carried by nationally bound firms directly reflected interiorizing, transnational parent-subsidiary relations. Of the fifty-one transnational interlocks carried by nationally bound firms, thirty-five were carried by foreign-controlled companies, mostly connecting them back to their parents.[15] By 2006, as we have seen, nationally bound firms played a more circumscribed role in transnational interlocking, carrying a total of thirty-two such ties. Again, there was a tendency for these interlocks to be part and parcel of interiorizing relations: eighteen of the thirty-two involved Canadian subsidiaries of foreign-based transnationals.[16] These interlocks were generated through parent-subsidiary relations that reached into the Canadian economic space.

The bimodal distribution of transnational interlocks across the four categories of transnationalization in Figure 19 reflects the double-sided character of corporate organization in an era of extensive multi-national cross-penetration of investment among developed capitalist economies. The two categories that account for most transnational interlocks reflect complementary insertions into global capitalism. Comparing 1996 with 2006, we find a shift from transnational inter-locking of the *interiorizing* sort to transnational interlocking of the *exteriorizing* sort. In the interiorizing mode, as explained earlier, board interlocks extend from foreign parents to Canadian subsid-iaries, expressing a penetration of corporate power from without. Across the decade, the number of transnational interlocks involving foreign-controlled C250 firms decreased by nearly half. The decline of such interlocks reflects both the decreasing complement of foreign-controlled firms in the C250 and the waning tendency for foreign-controlled branch plants to maintain directoral ties to their parents – in part due to a transformation of the organizational structures of TNCs (Carroll and Klassen 2010).

In contrast, exteriorizing transnational interlocking occurs as Canadian TNCs (controlled mostly by Canadian interests) share direc-tors with large corporations based elsewhere. Here, transnational interlocks have a quite different meaning. In 1996, fourteen TNCs in the C250 had thirty-one transnational interlocks. By 2006, twenty-two TNCs carried fifty-four such interlocks (see Figure 19). In percentage terms, the shift from interiorizing to exteriorizing interlocks was sub-stantial. In 1996, 31.5 per cent of all transnational interlocks were of the interiorizing type (involving foreign-controlled firms). By 2006, that proportion had fallen to 16.4 per cent. In 1996, 27.9 per cent of transna-tional interlocks were carried by Canadian TNCs; by 2006, 49.1 per cent were. This is evidence that the transnational elite network follows in the grooves of transnational investments and expansion – with effects going in both directions but trending recently in the direction of expan-sion from Canada.

There is thus a relationship between the transnationalization of capi-tal and transnational interlocking – in both directions, inward and out-ward. The bidirectional relationship points to a process of capitalist cross-penetration. But for large Canadian firms, the outward dynamic of Canadian-based internationalization has recently been dominant, and the inward-moving relationship has been decreasingly US-centred and increasingly multinational in ownership.

Figure 20. Interlocks among Canadian TNCs and non-Canadian G500 Firms, 1996

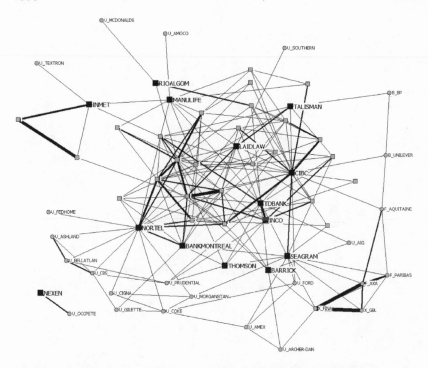

Key: Black squares: Canadian TNCs with transnational interlocks; grey squares: Canadian TNCs without transnational interlocks; grey circles: non-Canadian G500 members. Line thickness indicates the number of directors shared by a pair of firms. The leading character of each node label identifies each G500 company's domicile: "B" = Britain; "F" = France; "U" = United States; "X" = Belgium.

Figures 20 and 21 provide a visual representation of the exteriorizing interlocks that link Canadian TNCs to large corporations domiciled in other countries. The sociograms represent the social space at the seam between the Canadian national network and the global network, at two moments in time. Figure 20 shows the network of sixty-five firms in 1996, made up of forty Canadian TNCs (shown as squares) that interlocked either with other Canadian TNCs or with non-Canadian members of our G500 (the latter shown as circles). The latter category numbers twenty-five, including eighteen US-based firms and seven

Figure 21. Interlocks among Canadian TNCs and non-Canadian G500 Firms, 2006

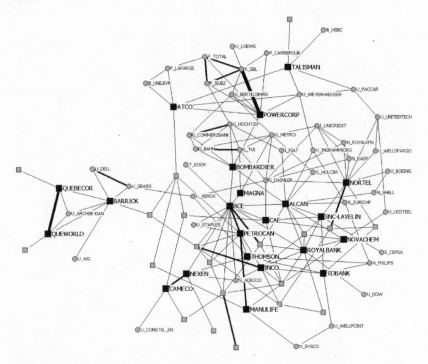

Key: Black squares: Canadian TNCs with transnational interlocks; grey squares: Canadian TNCs without transnational interlocks; grey circles: non-Canadian G500 members. Line thickness indicates the number of directors shared by a pair of firms. The leading character of each node label identifies each G500 company's domicile: "B" = Britain; "E" = Spain; "F" = France; "G" = Germany; "I" = Italy; "N" = Netherlands; "S" = Switzerland; "T" = Turkey; "U" = United States; "X" = Belgium.

firms based in Europe. The fourteen Canadian TNCs with interlocks extending beyond the national border are shown as large black squares labelled with an abbreviation of the corporation's name; non-Canadian G500 members are also labelled, enabling one to trace all the interlocks that embed Canadian TNCs in the global corporate network. The leading character of each node label identifies the company's domicile. Line thickness indicates the number of directors shared by a pair of firms. The same graphical conventions apply to Figure 21, which shows, at year-end 2006, forty-two Canadian TNCs and the forty-three non-Canadian G500 companies that interlocked with twenty-two of the Canadian TNCs. In both years, two of the Canadian TNCs in the network were foreign controlled.[17]

Because these sociograms were constructed using a spring-embedding algorithm, the relative distances between the points in each diagram approximate the distances in the actual network of corporations. At 1996, the network was clearly centred around forty Canadian TNCs, which entirely occupied the core of the space and were extensively interconnected. Large corporations domiciled outside Canada surrounded this core, with eleven of the eighteen US-based firms forming a single component to the south, and with all seven European firms also forming a connected component to the east; five French and Belgian companies (linked mainly to Montreal-based Seagram) shared multiple directors.

By 2006, the network was far less compactly centred upon Canadian TNCs: among the Canadian TNCs, density fell from 0.1872 to 0.0929. Moreover, companies based in Europe outnumbered the eighteen US-based firms that interlocked with the Canadian TNCs; indeed, firms of varying domiciles intermingled in a more diffuse social space. The change is neatly summarized by considering the largest set of firms whose members each had k or more ties to each other – the $k$core (Seidman 1983). In 1996, we find at the centre a five-core of twenty-eight firms, each interlocked with five or more other members of the five-core – all of them domiciled in Canada. By 2006, the largest $k$core was a four-core of eighteen firms. Not only was the $k$core greatly diminished in size; its members were also less profusely interlocked, and four of them – Daimler, UniCredit, Royal KPN, and EADS – were Europe based, with Daimler playing an integrative role through its interlocks with Nortel, CAE, and the three other European companies. There was, at this seam between the Canadian network and the global network, not only a weakening in the centrality of Canadian TNCs, but a definite shift towards a European presence. Comparing the two sociograms, between 1996 and 2006 the total number of interlocks involving US-based firms dropped from fifty-two to forty-two, while the number involving European companies rose from twenty-nine to eighty-nine.

In both years, ties connecting Canadian TNCs and G500 firms domiciled elsewhere were "thin" (carried by single directors), which is indicative not of control relations but of informal alignments that facilitate business scan (Useem 1984), and help to build a transnational corporate community (Carroll 2010). With one important exception, "thick" ties, carried by multiple interlocked directors and often indicative of deeper capital relations (Carroll and Sapinski 2011), remained within national borders. The noteworthy exception, in 2006, linked Montreal-based Power Corporation with Brussels-based Groupe Bruxelles Lambert via four shared directors. This transnational interlock represents a key nexus for what Carroll (2009a) describes as the only transnational financial empire of significance among the world's five hundred leading corporations: an alliance of the Desmarais family of Montreal and the Frère family of Brussels, which controls a number of major corporations in Canada and Europe.[18]

To summarize, the data on directorship interlocks reveals that, over the past decade, a significant recomposition of the Canadian corporate community took place. This recomposition appears both within the C250 and between the firms of the C250 and the G500. The evidence demonstrates a less dense, yet relatively stable national network of directorship ties among C250 firms, which interlock with each other at a greater scale than with G500 firms. Over the period, Canadian-based transnationals came to play a more central role in the national network, while nationally bound firms were relegated to its margins or detached from it entirely. The evidence also reveals that directors of foreign-controlled firms became significantly less connected to the national network and that, by 2006, such interlocks represented a more diverse complement of cross-border ties, as ties with European subsidiaries increased vis-à-vis US ones. The implications of this finding are that the corporate network in Canada is largely dominated by nationally owned firms – in particular, by leading TNCs under Canadian ownership – and that a more geographically diverse (less "continental") network is emerging. Finally, the data indicate a growing set of directorship interlocks between Canadian-owned TNCs and the largest foreign-based firms in the world. These interlocks demonstrate primarily an exteriorization of corporate power, and thus exhibit a new process of transnational class formation by Canadian firms as they expand operations beyond the United States into Europe and other regions of the world economy.

Conclusion

Complex transformations have taken place in the Canadian corporate network during the past decade of neoliberal globalization – transformations that shed light on new forms of transnationality in the corporate power bloc. On the one hand, there has been growing polarization within the two hundred largest Canadian non-financial corporations and the fifty largest Canadian financial institutions – the C250 – marked by the absolute decline and relative stagnation of nationally bound firms and the rapid growth and international expansion of TNCs and near-TNCs. The evidence indicates a progressive concentration of capital within the TNCs of the C250, and a marked tendency for these firms to interlock more with each other than with subtransnational firms. Within the C250, foreign control, although increasingly marginal, emanates almost entirely from North America, western Europe, and Japan (the Triad), and is most extensive among those with no foreign subsidiaries of their own – classic branch plants. Some of these firms are involved in transnational interlocking of the interiorizing sort, but they rarely participate in the Canadian corporate network. Instead, the national network is carried mostly by Canadian-owned firms, particularly TNCs and near-TNCs. For this reason, we concur with Robinson's (2004) assessment of TNCs as leading agents of capital accumulation, but note the persistence of a "national corporate community" in Canada (Scott 1997) and the bifurcation of this community into TNCs and non-TNCs.

In addition, we observe a more transnational scope of investment by Canadian firms, which increasingly hold subsidiaries in the Triad – most importantly in the United States and Europe. In this sense, Canadian firms in the C250 operate not as continental "compradors" but as active members of an "Atlantic ruling class" with transnational reach into both developed and developing countries (van der Pijl 1997). Over the decade, as the number of large Canadian TNCs grew, the national network became more focused upon them and their transnational interlocking expanded considerably, effecting a relative shift from interiorizing to exteriorizing interlocks.

As a result, the interface between capital accumulation and class formation broadly matches our scenario F, with several specifications. First, transnational interlocking became weighted more towards the exteriorization of Canadian-based capitalist interests and less towards the interiorization of foreign-based corporate power. Second, exteriorizing and interiorizing practices took in a widening range of foreign domiciles. Third, the national network became increasingly centred on the same Canadian TNCs that participate heavily in the transnational network. In short, globalizing firms became increasingly dominant in the national network, and increasingly integrated with the transnational network of corporate power. Subtransnationals, particularly firms whose investments are restricted to the home market, came to participate less in the national network, whose own centre of gravity is increasingly transnational. The reasons for the growing marginality of nationally bound firms are not immediately apparent. It might be that, in an era of corporate governance practices favouring "leaner, meaner" boards and fewer directorships per director, diminishing opportunities for interlocking are promoting a clustering of elite affiliations among the big, transnational players that shuts out many of the subtransnationals, thereby amplifying the network's core-periphery structure.

One trend worth highlighting is the elevated presence of Canadian TNCs in Europe and the increased presence of European TNCs, through their subsidiaries, in Canada. As we have demonstrated, *the elite network of directorship interlocks follows these trends in capital accumulation –* in particular, through greater network connections between European and Canadian firms. In this regard, it is worth speculating that current moves towards a Canada-European Union free trade agreement stem from new patterns of direct investment and corporate interlocking between these economies.

Regardless, in the case of Canada, we have observed an emerging relationship between the transnationalization of capital and transnational interlocking – in both directions, inward and outward. The two-way relationship signals a process of *capitalist cross-penetration*, as TNCs based in Canada and around the world place investments in each other's national domains while also exporting capital to developing countries (Carroll and Klassen 2010, 23; Portes and Walton 1981, 142). For Canadian TNCs, however, the outward dynamic of internationalization has recently been dominant, while the inward dynamic is decreasingly US-centred and increasingly multinational in scope. The trend is *dialectical*: Canadian TNCs have reinforced a national network of corporate power and simultaneously interlocked with foreign-based TNCs both inside and outside Canada, in the grooves formed by transnational investment. The trajectory of Canada's corporate community exemplifies Saskia Sassen's (2007, 1) maxim: "the global partly inhabits and partly arises out of the national." Sassen goes on to note that the global/national nexus troubles two core propositions in modern social science: (1) that the nation-state is the container of political, economic, and social processes; and (2) that the global and the national are two mutually exclusive entities. This case study of Canada underlines the importance, in an era of global capitalism, of analysing the national and the transnational as mutually constitutive elements in processes of class formation. Further comparative research could consider the conditions under which interiorizing and exteriorizing processes come to predominate at specific national sites in the world system, and the ramifications for corporate communities at national and transnational levels.

In conclusion, we have found definite relationships between investment and interlocking that shape the social space of national corporate communities and the global corporate elite. Corporations with a transnational accumulation base tend to participate in transnational interlocking. Successful capital accumulation and corporate interlocking appear as mutually reinforcing processes, as transnational firms increasingly network in their "home" domiciles and with others emanating from the Triad. Although national corporate communities have not been transcended, they are increasingly inhabited by transnational firms, which articulate with other TNCs on a global scale. These corporations constitute the leading edge of capital accumulation and, through their dense network of cross-border investments and interlocking directorates, form the rudiments of a transnational capitalist class.

As the next chapter demonstrates, the development of this new social class in Canada has had a critical impact on the state and its role in the US-led Empire of Capital.

PART IV

The Canadian State and Foreign Policy

6 Armoured Neoliberalism: The Power Bloc and the New Imperial State

The transformation of the state during the period of neoliberalism has been a key issue of debate in the social sciences. The globalization of the world economy through new patterns of trade, investment, and production has challenged, or upended, the national systems of governance that regulated post-war economies. In this context, new concerns have arisen regarding the balance of power between states and markets, and between politics and economics. In particular, new debates have emerged around the question of the changing form and function of the state in light of globalizing processes.

In the early stages of these debates, the primary focus was on the power of states to manage or discipline transnational capital flows (Ohmae 1990; Teeple 2000; cf. Helleiner 1996; Hirst and Thompson 1999; Weiss 2000). These debates were premised on a conceptual binary between states and markets, and assumed that the expansion of the latter truncated the power of the former, and vice-versa. The limits of this institutionalist approach to political economy was the evident strengthening of the state in certain realms of governance and the persistence – even spread – of the nation-state system during the period of neoliberalism. To overcome these problems, institutionalist theory turned to focus on the "competitive state" of neoliberal capitalism and on the rescaling of sovereignty – both upward and downward – in light of new corporate networks and technological innovations (Castells 2000; Cerny 2005; Hall and Soskice 2001). In making this turn, institutionalist theory embraced a politics of "progressive competitiveness" – the notion that new training policies can bring about high-skill, high-wage industrial restructuring in leading export sectors. The theory failed to recognize, however, that "this export-oriented strategy, too, has become incorporated in the pressures producing competitive austerity throughout the world economy and converged with neo-liberalism" (Albo 1994, 168).

With this in mind, scholars in the Marxist tradition emphasized that the globalization of capitalism was not undermining the state as a territorial or administrative unit, but transforming it as an integral moment of neoliberal class relations (Panitch 1994; Robinson 2004; Wood 1999). In this perspective, states are the authors of globalization and the unifying agents of transnational corporate power. The strength of this perspective was that it maintained a general critique of capitalism – and of the state and state-system – vis-à-vis the institutionalist focus on "varieties" of corporate structures and governance networks (Albo 2005; Fast 2005).

In the aftermath of 9/11, social science focused again on the remaking of the state at the national and international scales. In particular, it was impelled to address the armouring of the state at home and abroad as part of the "global war on terror." In this context, new theories emerged of the "national security state" (Balkin 2008; Gill 2005; Ripsman and Paul 2010), and the "new imperial state" (Colás and Saull 2006; Ikenberry 2006; Panitch 2000). For the most part, these theories concentrate on the American state and its role in the global political economy. Indeed, these theories are concerned overwhelmingly with the political, diplomatic, and military means by which the United States manages a global empire of liberalizing markets and governing structures. These theories also engage the creeping authoritarianism of the American state, as it has built a national security apparatus for the "global war on terror." The contribution of historical materialism to these debates has been a focus on new forms of militarism and securitization that attend the internationalization of capital. In particular, it has sought to link a theory of globalization and transnational class formation to contemporary patterns of state power and military violence. In the process, it offers an updated theory of *imperialism* to account for current dynamics of class and state power at different scales of the world economy and nation-state system (Anievas 2010; Callinicos 2009; Harvey 2003; Kiely 2010).

In Canada, debates on the state have tracked and mirrored general trends in the social sciences. In the 1990s, the primary concern was with the relative sovereignty of the state in the face of globalization and continental neoliberalism. For example, in the field of Canadian political economy (Clement and Vosko 2003; Clement and Williams 1989; Shields and McBride 1997), the neoliberal agenda often has been perceived as a process of political subordination to US power in North America. In this framework, the continental ties of trade and investment are balanced in favour of US corporate interests, and are eclipsing the autonomy of the state in matters of social, economic, cultural, and environmental policy.

In the aftermath of 9/11, issues of sovereignty and independence were raised anew in the Canadian social sciences. As successive governments in Ottawa pledged to support the "global war on terror," and embraced a sweeping set of policy reforms as part of building a national security apparatus, new debates emerged on the restructuring of the state and on Canada's global role. In the framework of dependency theory (Grinspun and Shamsie 2007), the transformation of the state post-9/11 was a logical outcome of continental neoliberalism. The building of a national security state at home and the turn to militarism abroad were thus viewed as a culmination of Canada's economic subordination to "Fortress North America" (Hurtig 2006; McQuaig 2007). The limitation of this approach, however, has been a one-sided focus on the interiorization of US corporate power in the Canadian political economy, to the detriment of understanding the exteriorization of Canadian capital in transnational patterns of exploitation and accumulation. For this reason, the dependency theory of the national security state, and of the new foreign policy agenda, has failed to grasp the domestic forces of empire in the Canadian political economy.

Realist theories of Canadian foreign policy are affected by similar shortcomings. In this paradigm, the shift in the form and function of the Canadian state was a response to external stimuli in the balance of power or security environment. For example, Elinor Sloan (2005) views the national security state as a positive reflex to a "terrorist era." In her perspective, the threat of terrorism is a defining, or constitutive, feature of world order, and Canadian governments have acted rationally in defending the nation against such omnipresent challenges.

Other realists, however, have questioned this approach. Patrick Lennox (2007), for instance, contests the notion that Canadian governments responded to genuine security threats in building a national security state after 9/11, arguing instead that an asymmetry of power between Canada and the United States drove the institutional and policy reforms of this period. Although Lennox captures the way in which the ideas and practices of *securitization* were internalized by different Canadian governments, he fails to account for social forces in the making of public policies and governance structures. As a result, his mapping of the national security state abstracts from the social relations of capitalism, both at home and abroad. In particular, it ignores the role of Canadian capital in global forms of exploitation and appropriation and the role of the state in serving Canadian corporate interests.

To address these gaps in the extant debates, this chapter maps and examines the *social relations of Canadian state power since 2001*, with a particular focus on the national security and foreign policy agenda of the "global war on terror." I start from the premise that, during the period of neoliberalism, an internationalization of capital has occurred in the political economy of Canada (see Chapter 4). In particular, the circuits of money, productive, and commodity capital have been globalized at national, regional, and international scales. As a result, the economics of Canadian capitalism have become increasingly bound with transnational patterns of exploitation and accumulation. In this context, a new structure of transnational class power has evolved in the Canadian corporate network, which increasingly ties the leading firms of Canada to the leading firms in the world economy, as discussed in Chapter 5. In the process, the Canadian capitalist class has developed a vested interest in transnational neoliberalism. For this reason, it has endorsed, or worked to build, a new structure of national governance to extend and replicate the class relations of empire on a global scale. The changing form and function of the state, then, is a product of the internationalization of capital and the reconstitution of the power bloc around globalizing corporate interests.

To develop this argument, I have divided the chapter into four sections. In the first, I outline a materialist theory of the state and its role in imperialism. I delineate a framework for understanding the new imperial state as a concentration of globalizing class forces. In the second section, I examine the new "power bloc" that emerged in Canada's political economy in the wake of 9/11 – a new constellation of social and political forces that have extolled a strategy of empire for Canadian foreign policy. In the third section, I look at how the state absorbed, synthesized, and externalized this strategy in the decade that followed. I show how successive governments have developed a new grand strategy of *neoliberal market enforcement, continental securitization, stratified multilateralism, and disciplinary militarism*. Codified in key planning documents, these principles have guided the transformation of the state in foreign and domestic contexts. To map this transformation, the final section looks at the institutional restructuring of the state at national and international scales. I show how the building of a national security state at home and the shifting thrust of foreign policies abroad are two sides of a new imperial project for the state and power bloc. The key argument is that the transformation of the Canadian state since 2001 is a structural effect of the internationalization of capital and the recomposition of the power bloc around globalizing corporate interests. As such, the armouring of the state as part of the "global war on terror" is linked to a capitalist class project of *joining empire* – of making the state an economic, political, and military power in the US-led system of transnational neoliberalism.

Imperialism and the State: The Social Content of Power

A key theoretical insight of historical materialism is that the state is an organization of social power relations. It is not a disembodied institution that acts by itself vis-à-vis the global balance of power, nor is it an inert structure that is simply put to use by external agents in civil society. On the contrary, the state is a crystallization of capitalist social relations. It emerges as a structure from the social relations of production, and it congeals these relations – and their contradictions – in the basic structures and apparatuses of ruling. It is a terrain of political agency – indeed, of active class formation – and its institutions and policies are a manifestation, and a balance sheet, of social power relations. As a result, the inner content of state power is always, and irreducibly, social (Cox 1981).

With this in mind, the study of the state must be grounded in a mapping of capitalist class relations. Indeed, the starting point for analysis must be the social relations of exploitation between the capitalist class, which owns and controls the means of production, and the working class, which sells its ability to work for wages. The specificity of this relationship is that it allows for the production of surplus value in an "economic" sphere that is formally distant from the "political" sphere. In other words, it involves an exploitation of labour power without direct intervention by the state (Wood 1995). In this context, the state is defined by what Nicos Poulantzas (1978a,b) called a *relative autonomy* from capital. It sets a framework for the production and distribution of value, but does not intervene directly in the process of value production and exploitation. As a result, it tends to function in ways that accord with the *class power* of capital.

This understanding of the state is vital to a theory of politics and governance. As Poulantzas (1978b, 190) observed, the capitalist state is an institution through which "hegemonic class leadership" is developed, enforced, and extended. As such, it "does not *directly* represent the dominant classes' economic interests, but their *political interests*," including the protection of private property, the general management of accumulation, and the long-term reproduction of capitalist social relations. In this model, the state is a crucial – indeed, a paramount – vehicle of capitalist class formation. In fact, it is only through the state that capitalist class power is unified, exercised, and managed. For this to occur, the capitalist class must forge and direct a *power bloc* within and beyond the state. For Poulantzas (ibid., 234, 239), the power bloc is "the particular participation of several classes and class fractions in political domination." It is anchored and guided by a "hegemonic fraction" of capital, but also incorporates a constellation of social, political, and economic forces that buttresses the governing process. By consolidating such forces in a common political project, the power bloc engenders hegemonic class unity, both inside and outside the state.

It is vital to recognize the material, as well as the ideological, forms through which the power bloc is consolidated. The material force of unity is a common class interest in exploitation and accumulation. However, to overcome problems of market competition and intra-class conflict and to ground the power bloc more deeply in civil society, ideational forms of unity are also required. As Andrew Gamble (1988, 208, 241) explains, a hegemonic project of class domination requires a "politics of support" as much as it necessitates a "politics of power." To foster such support, the power bloc must recruit, train, and mobilize what Antonio Gramsci (1971, 134–5) called *organic intellectuals* – "one or more strata of intellectuals which give it homogeneity and an awareness of its own function not only in the economic but also in the social and political fields." For Gramsci (ibid., 145), organic intellectuals are "the dominant group's 'deputies' exercising the subaltern functions of social hegemony and political government." They give political direction to the hegemonic fraction of capital, and create discourses through which other social groupings are integrated into the state and governing process.

The scope and influence of the power bloc, however, is always troubled and contested. Just as the social relations of production give rise to capitalist forms of class domination in civil society, so too do they generate class struggles of those who work, or try to work, for wages. As Poulantzas (1978b, 45) recognized, these contradictions in the social relations of production are transposed into the organs of the state in two key respects. First, the legislative field is a terrain upon which competing power blocs of capital and labour vie for political sovereignty. In each social formation, the policies of the state will thereby reflect the balance of power in civil society. Second, the administrative apparatus will always incorporate the class conflicts of capitalism. Indeed, the state will be constituted by a contradictory network of institutions that reflect the patterns of class conflict in any particular social formation. The key point is that, as an active terrain of conflict between contending social classes, and as an institutional resumé of the balance of class forces, the state will never resolve, let alone transcend, the contradictions of capitalism. It will, instead, reproduce these contradictions in its policies, structures, and apparatuses of ruling.[1] In this context, the political hegemony of the power bloc will be constantly contested, both inside and outside the state.

With this in mind, how should the *new imperial state* be understood and analysed? To begin, it should be located in the patterns of transnational production and accumulation that define neoliberalism. In this way, the new imperial state can be viewed as the political form of neoliberal class relations. It can be conceptualized, in other words, as a political condensate of transnational patterns of exploitation and appropriation, and of capital's need to advance and secure private property on a global scale – and to discipline any opposition to this agenda at home or abroad. Indeed, as the circuits of capital have materialized in global spaces of production, the state itself has been tuned in line with transnational value flows (Cox 1987; Piccioto 1991; Wissin and Brand 2011). As a result, it seeks to manage, or to superintend, the class relations of global capitalism (Panitch and Gindin 2005b).

In this context, a transnational capitalist class has come to anchor and direct the new imperial power bloc (Carroll 2010; Murray 2014; Robinson 2004).[2] As a constellation of social forces, this bloc includes the most advanced factions of capital, as well as a mix of political parties, think tanks, lobby groups, business forums, security and defence agencies, and organic intellectuals that support the project of transnational neoliberalism and US global primacy (Gill 1991; Staples 2007). Through the conquest of the state, this new power bloc has sought to globalize the circuits of capital. Since 9/11, it has augmented this economic agenda with a new security and military agenda. It has pursued what I call *armoured neoliberalism*: a fusion of the economic logic of global exploitation with the political logic of disciplinary militarism.

To this end, the administration of the state has been restructured and recalibrated. For example, at the national level, institutions of social welfare have been marginalized or restructured in service of transnational neoliberalism (Peck 2001; Pierson 2001; Teeple 2000). At the same time, institutions of the state involved in trade and finance have been empowered in terms of their access to government officials and monetary resources (Cox 1987; Tsoukalas 1999). Most importantly, the state has been repositioned around security and defence apparatuses – in particular, those involved with the surveillance and discipline of any perceived threats to capital (C. Bell 2006; Boukalas 2014; Gill 2005). With this in mind, one can define the new imperial state as a *centralized structure of capitalist class hegemony*, one that links an authoritarian structure of security in the national setting to an expansive military and diplomatic structure in the global setting, with the goal of institutionalizing capitalist class power at home and abroad.

To achieve hegemony, however, the power bloc must bridge the state with civil society in a common project of national and international security. In the wake of 9/11, the power bloc has constructed a discourse or ideology of *securitization* to justify the centralization of state power, the diversion of resources to national security agencies, and the projection of disciplinary militarism abroad. In this context, the "global war on terrorism" emerged as a critical praxis of dominant class interests at the national and international scales. As a doctrine of totalizing warfare that is spatially infinite, temporally permanent, and operationally flexible, it offered a new ideology for the Empire of Capital, under US global dominance.

To advance this project, the new imperial state has promoted, or sought to inculcate, a culture of militarism in civil society. As Karl Liebknecht (1917, 90–1, 39) observed in the context of the First World War, "[m]ilitarism ... appears in the first place *in the army itself*, then as a system reaching *beyond the army and embracing all of society* in a net of militaristic and semi-militaristic institutions." The political point of militarism, though, is "not only [to] serve for defence and attack against the foreign enemy; it has a second [purpose] ... that of protecting the existing state of society" – in other words, capitalism. In the present conjuncture, the same system of militarism is germane to the new imperial state. For example, the "global war on terror" is infused with the culture of militarism, which glorifies hierarchy, violence, and discipline. By promoting this ethos, the state seeks to rationalize the purchase of new weapons systems and the centralization of governance, and to bind the nation against state-defined enemies at home and abroad. In this context, a new culture of racism, xenophobia, and national chauvinism has been nurtured as a means of fortifying the state and power bloc (McKay and Swift 2012; Razack 2008).

Despite this, the new imperial state is fraught with contradictions. For example, while projecting a national interest in war and militarism, it redistributes wealth to upper factions of capital (Duménil and Lévy 2004; Piketty and Saez 2007). Similarly, while wrapping itself in the banner of freedom and democracy, it constitutes a vast machinery of discipline and surveillance (C. Bell 2006; Gill 2005). Likewise, while waging war ostensibly for human rights and development, it compounds social inequalities, environmental degradation, and human rights abuses, including torture and attacks on civilians (Klassen and Albo 2013; Tirman 2011). Thus, while the new imperial state works in the service of globalizing class forces, it reproduces within itself the ideological and material contradictions of transnational neoliberalism, and thereby generates *anti-imperialist resistance* in a multitude of forms (Kiely 2010; McNally 2006; Panitch and Leys 2000). With this in mind, the task of a critical social science is to map the social relations of empire, which might give rise to a democratic counterhegemony of antiracist, working-class politics.

In sum, from a Marxist standpoint, the new imperial state is a political agent of globalizing class relations. Its fundamental purpose is to secure the conditions for exploitation and appropriation by the hegemonic faction of capital within it. To this end, it builds a national security apparatus at home, and deploys military and security agencies abroad. To build hegemony for such a project, it attempts to foster a militaristic nationalism in civil society. Yet, however successful it is in building a social basis for empire, it cannot repress or mollify the crisis tendencies of capitalism, and thus invites new movements of anti-imperialist resistance. In these ways, the new imperial state incorporates the inequalities, and the imbalances, of global capitalism.

The Politics of Support: The Power Bloc and the New Imperial Strategy

In the aftermath of 9/11, two structural pressures confronted the Canadian state. The first involved the closing of the US-Canadian border and the subsequent enforcement of new security measures at all border crossings. With the border accounting for nearly $2 billion of trade per day at the time, the Canadian state faced an economic crisis of epic proportions if it failed to allay US security concerns. The onset of recession in 2002, and the related turn to protectionism in the US Congress, further threatened the continental system through which Canadian capital operates.

The second pressure involved the "global war on terrorism" invoked by US President George W. Bush in his speech to Congress of 20 September 2001. To the American public, Bush (2001) declared that "[o]ur war on terror begins with al-Qaeda, but it does not end there. It will not end until every terrorist group of global reach has been found, stopped and defeated." As a result, "Americans should not expect one battle, but a lengthy campaign unlike any other we have ever seen." To the rest of the world, Bush warned that "[e]very nation in every region now has a decision to make: Either you are with us or you are with the terrorists. From this day forward, any nation that continues to harbor or support terrorism will be regarded by the United States as a hostile regime."

For the Canadian state, these two external forces were portentously ominous. At the time, several US newspapers were reporting that members of al-Qaeda had entered the country through Canada. The Canadian government was further worried by the fact that Bush, in his speech to Congress, failed to thank Canada for its support on 9/11. Although the 9/11 Commission later dispelled the rumour of al-Qaeda's transit through Canada, the idea that the northern border was porous to terrorism led the United States to shift military units to Canadian border crossings on 2 December 2001, and to impose new strictures on trade and tourism. In this context, the Canadian state was forced to respond quickly to the "global war on terror" at national, continental, and international scales.

As much as the United States was the source of these new structural pressures, *domestic social forces* played a critical role in fashioning a new paradigm for Canadian public policy at home and abroad. In the wake of 9/11, the corporate community worked decisively to anchor a new power bloc of economic, political, and military forces that was itself linked to similar networks of power in the United States and other advanced capitalist countries. This new power bloc brought together globalizing corporate interests, neoliberal think tanks, national security and defence lobby structures, business-minded politicians and parties, and a plexus of academic institutions and analysts. Together, this constellation of social forces developed a new grand strategy for the state, one that supported the economic project of transnational neoliberalism and the political project of US primacy and the "global war on terror." Through this new grand strategy, an *imperial power bloc* was formed in Canada.

It is vital to recognize the leadership role of the corporate community in devising and directing the new grand strategy. On 3 October 2001, more than fifty-five business associations and individual companies in Canada formed the Coalition for Secure and Trade-Efficient Borders to assist the federal government with border and security issues. Self-described as "one of the largest business coalitions formed in Canadian history," the Coalition (CSTB 2001) "represent[ed] the vast majority of business activity in Canada," and its members were based in all sectors of the national economy.

On 1 November 2001, the Coalition issued a letter (ibid.) to Prime Minister Jean Chrétien advising him to recognize that "security and trade are linked." In this context, the Canadian government was asked to "take immediate action to present a comprehensive and integrated solution to security and borders." For the Coalition, "[s]uch a strategy would not only provide a level of confidence to Canadians, but it would also allow Canada to demonstrate leadership on this issue to our American neighbours." To these ends, the Coalition advocated "an approach that would ease Canada-U.S. border crossings by increasing Canada's ability to guarantee security at other points of entry." In this perspective, the Canadian government should rethink border security in terms of "three lines" of defence, including offshore interception, perimeter entries into North America, and the Canadian-US border itself. By committing to this approach, the Coalition argued, the Canadian state would be able to secure and extend the continental system of trade, production, and investment. Through meetings with cabinet ministers, Members of Parliament, and federal officials, as well as with US government officials and their diplomatic agents in Canada, the Coalition was able to shape and direct the security arrangements that ensued, particularly the 2001 Smart Border Declaration.

Beyond this ad hoc response to 9/11, the corporate community in Canada began to mobilize for longer-term influence on foreign and domestic policies, especially those related to continental linkages. For corporate leaders in Canada, the time was ripe for redefining the US-Canadian relationship. As a representative of the Canadian Manufacturers & Exporters put it at the time, "Canada cannot take its economic and political relationship with the United States for granted. We have to be smart about assessing the economic and social impacts of policy decisions in light of our unequal dependence on the American economy. We have to be focused, and we have to be proactive in defining the future of that relationship" (Canada 2002a, 8). The Canadian Chamber of Commerce concurred with this call for decisive action on continental integration. As one spokesperson argued,

the reality is that integration is not going away, so whatever decisions we make, we must make them quickly or the opportunity to actually make a choice will pass us by. Canada has the ability to control the evolution of our relationship [with the United States], primarily because it's one that matters more to us than to them ... The question we are faced with is whether we are going to make incremental changes to take what comes and to adjust to the changing global circumstance as they are forced upon us, or whether we are going to approach this with bold vision and strong leadership. The Chamber believes we can't let the future happen by default ... Canada must be in the driver's seat, not the passenger seat. (Ibid., 25)

To this end, Canada's leading business think tanks began to envision a new grand strategy for US-Canada relations – and for Canada's role in the world more broadly. According to Wendy Dobson, who authored a major study for the C.D. Howe Institute (Dobson 2002a), the 9/11 attacks "opened a window of opportunity for a great leap forward in managing the bilateral relationship" (2002b). In her perspective, "[a] Big Idea is needed to wrap what we want and need – customs-union-like and common-market-like arrangements to get at the obstacles remaining after NAFTA [the North American Free Trade Agreement] – in exchange for what a wide swath of U.S. political interests wants: joint continental defence, closely aligned immigration policies toward third-country migrants, border security, and energy security" (ibid.). To effect this bargain, Dobson (2002a, 1, 27) outlined "a joint strategy for achieving a common goal of North American physical and economic security." Through such a strategy, the United States would achieve a new degree of political security in exchange for "reduce[d] obstacles to the freer flow of goods, services, capital, technology, and people within the North American economic space."

In 2003, the Public Policy Forum, another major think tank of corporate Canada, raised similar concerns and proposals in an open letter to the incoming government of Liberal Prime Minister Paul Martin. According to the Forum (2003), "we have a vital strategic interest in our relationship with the United States, yet we have allowed that relationship to deteriorate in recent years. More generally, we have never developed an agreed strategy for identifying and pursuing our interests in the world." To address the widespread concern that "Canada's status or influence has diminished," the Forum called for the government to "undertake an immediate, comprehensive review of our international policy [strategies], one that will integrate the main policy and program instruments at our disposal – defence, development, diplomacy and now, demographics." In particular, the Forum urged the government to "define a defence and international security strategy guided by our national interests," and to "develop a credible military capability in the areas where we know we can contribute," especially "nation-building." For this purpose, it advocated "increased spending on our armed forces."

As in the past, the Canadian Council of Chief Executives (CCCE) served as a hegemonic vehicle for synthesizing, and advancing, the corporate approach to the "global war on terror" and US primacy objectives.[3] On 25 September 2001, the Council's president, Thomas d'Aquino, delivered a speech to the House of Commons Standing Committee on Finance in which he exhorted a new approach to trade and security. Embracing the Bush agenda, d'Aquino (2001) argued that "there will be no neutrals" in "the global war that was unleashed by the attacks of September 11." In his view, "Canada faces real and pressing demands for action" because "we may be unable to ensure an open southern border unless we are able to convince our American allies of the integrity of our external perimeter." To do this, he suggested new public spending on security and defence, and a "strategy of distinct advantage" to "position [Canada] inside the American tent." In this way, he contended, Canada would stand to gain "uninhibited access to the United States market."

Over the next several years, the CCCE packaged these ideas into a comprehensive strategy for the state and power bloc. Under the banner of a "Security and Prosperity Initiative," this strategy embodied the economic and political interests of corporate capital in Canada, and it consisted of four key proposals. First, the United States and Canada should rethink border security by shifting the focus from the internal border of North America to the continent as a whole. In focusing on perimeter security, the two countries could protect the continent from external threats and maintain the free flow of goods and people across their mutual border, which should function as a "shared checkpoint within an integrated economic space" (CCCE 2003, 4).

Second, the regulatory regimes of both countries should be harmonized to maximize economic efficiencies. In this vision, regulations on trade, investment, foreign ownership, health and safety, and the environment should be harmonized to match the economic integration that already exists. Doing so would improve customs processing, reduce costs and redundancies, and facilitate the movement of goods and skilled labour across the border. To enhance North American competitiveness, the Council also recommended a common external tariff for the continent as a whole (CCCE 2004, 8).

Third, Canada and the United States should sign a "resource security pact," which would operate according to the principles of open access and free trade (d'Aquino 2003, 9). In particular, Canada should offer the United States energy security in exchange for free trade in other resources, including forestry, mineral, and agricultural products. Through this pact, the United States would achieve guaranteed access to Canada's oil and natural gas supplies, while Canada would gain exemption from US antidumping laws and countervailing duties (CCCE 2004, 12).

Finally, the Canadian Forces should be rebuilt and restructured for the "global war on terrorism." For too long, the Council argued, Canada has been "a free rider on American coattails and a toothless advocate of soft power" (CCCE 2003, 5). In the new security context, Canada must "contribute more effectively to the global war on terror," and build "a credible capacity ... to respond meaningfully and rapidly to crises anywhere in the world" (ibid.; CCCE n.d.). This kind of "[g]lobal reach continues to be in Canada's strategic interests and will preserve our ability to have influence on the world stage and to project force abroad" (CCCE 2004, 17). To do this, the Canadian military must be "fully interoperable with allied forces," and trained in "asymmetric warfare" – that is, in the types of combat that occur in places such as Iraq and Afghanistan (ibid., 14–15). In addition, Canada should renew the North American Aerospace Defense Command (NORAD) agreement, and support ballistic missile defence (CCCE 2003, 10).

The Council hoped these four proposals would consolidate both the economic position of the Canadian state in the North American bloc and the political-military capacities of a secondary power in the US-led Empire of Capital. In these regards, the Security and Prosperity Initiative was a hegemonic effort to gain unfettered access to the US market in exchange for deep integration of the two countries' economic, security, and military policies. Through such a bargain, the Council contended, the Canadian state would be able to secure the interests of capital at national, regional, and international scales.

If the corporate community played a primary role in the new power bloc, the *defence lobby* played a secondary, or supporting, one. Indeed, the growing interest of the corporate sector in security and defence matters gave the military establishment a new degree of credibility and influence in the state and policy field. In the Canadian context, the defence lobby includes a wide number of "defence associations, retired military officers, university-based military and strategic studies programs, foreign policy institutes, defence industry associations, and hawkish parliamentarians" (Staples 2007, 162). Many of these actors have been funded by the Department of National Defence (DND) or by Canada's leading military hardware producers. Through various conferences, publications, research institutes, and media campaigns, they have played a key role in shaping public perceptions of security and defence issues (Chase 2008; Gabriel and Macdonald 2004). Since 9/11, in particular, they have been able to shape and influence Canada's new foreign policy agenda, especially the focus on military spending, terrorism, continental security, missile defence, and counterinsurgency.

The lead organization, perhaps, through which the new military agenda has been advanced is the Conference of Defence Associations (CDA). Financed in part by the DND, the CDA is the most established and influential military advocacy group in Canada, and represents more than fifty defence associations from all regions of the country. With a board of directors that condenses the state-corporate-military nexus in Canada, it organizes conferences around security and defence issues, lobbies for military spending increases, publishes papers on defence strategy, and funds sympathetic research on university campuses. Since 9/11, the CDA has worked to influence the rebuilding and retraining of the Canadian Forces, with an eye towards increasing defence spending and interoperability with US security platforms in North America and around the world.

For the CDA (2002, 5), 9/11 signalled a threat of *total instability* in global politics, a new security environment in which all aspects of world order – political, economic, cultural, and ecological – are subject to destabilization by terrorist groups, rogue states, insurgencies, and other nefarious actors. As the CDA (2004) put it, "[t]he harsh reality is that in today's world, no nation or individual is immune from instability. At home and abroad, Canadian citizens and companies are feeling the pressure." In this context, "the decline of the Canadian Forces is putting the entire nation at risk in terms of economic prosperity and well being, but especially in terms of loss of national sovereignty. This loss is evident with respect to Canada's relations with the United States, its ability to influence international affairs, and its ability to contribute to international peace and stability" (CDA 2002, 1).

To address such concerns, the CDA insisted that "Canadian domestic security is intrinsically linked to the security of North America which, in turn, is connected to the wider global security system." However, "Canada's most important defence relationship is with the United States," with which it must work closely to realize national, continental, and international security objectives. The enduring practice of "defence freeloading" on the United States, however, is a grave risk to Canadian sovereignty and security, and invites US unilateralism (ibid., xxi). To avoid these risks, the CDA demanded a rebuilding and transformation of the Canadian military to guarantee that present and future forces are "combat capable; flexible and adaptable; deployable and sustainable; and self-sufficient and interoperable" (CDA 2004). By reinvesting in the military and by supporting US security strategies, Canada would be able to augment its sovereignty and to reclaim its fading power and influence globally (CDA 2002, xxi). To these ends, the CDA, like the CCCE, called for the Canadian state to align with US security platforms in North America, especially NORAD and ballistic missile defence. For the CDA, then, the Canadian state faces a new structure of international *in*security, which can be contained only by a new strategy of disciplinary militarism and cooperative specialization with US security structures at national, continental, and international scales.

The defence lobby extends into other realms of civil society and policy formation. In the academic context, the Security and Defence Forum is a DND program that, until 2012, financed academic research with a hawkish bent. Military industry groups such as the Canadian Association of Defence and Security Industries and the Aerospace Industries Association of Canada also lobby the government for military contracts and for a more militaristic approach to foreign affairs and national defence (Staples 2007, 162–4). As part of these efforts, the Canadian Association of Defence and Security Industries organizes Canada's largest arms bazaar, CANSEC, in the Ottawa region on an annual basis.

In the broader policy field, think tanks such as the Canadian Defence and Foreign Affairs Institute, the Canadian International Council, the Atlantic Council, and the Macdonald-Laurier Institute for Public Policy have called for similar approaches to military and security issues. The Canadian Defence and Foreign Affairs Institute (CDFAI) perhaps has been the most important of these think tanks. With links to corporate, government, and academic resources, it has published numerous studies on national security and defence, including one sponsored by the CCCE (see Bercuson 2003). The starting point of this research is that "the rise of international terrorism combined with a growing 'failed state' phenomenon and the emergence of the United States as the only superpower has undermined long-held tenets of Canadian foreign policy," including peacekeeping, multilateralism, and Middle Power diplomacy. As a result, "Canada has slipped badly in international influence" (Stairs 2003, vii–viii).

To reverse this tendency, the CDFAI has argued for Canada to play "an active role in North American defence even as it is called upon by the [United States] to play a larger role in the war against terrorism abroad" (ibid., vii). To serve these roles, the CDFAI has recommended, first, that "Canada should restore its lost capabilities in world affairs by substantially increasing its now-gravely-eroded investment in all its foreign policy assets, including the Canadian Forces, the Foreign Service, and the development assistance establishment." Second, "Canada should put more emphasis ... on the protection and maintenance of Canadian *interests* than on the projection abroad of Canadian *values*" (ibid., 12, 14, emphasis added). Third, governments must recognize that "the only real imperative in Canadian foreign policy is Canada's relationship with the [United States]." Indeed, "[a]ll other Canadian international interests are far behind the importance of maintaining friendly and workable relations with the Americans." With this in mind, governments must acknowledge that "the general principles of 'quiet diplomacy' are as relevant today as they were during the cold war." Furthermore, "in promoting multilateral initiatives and institutions, Ottawa must be careful to demonstrate the relevance of multilateral solutions to American interests" (ibid., viii, 41, 19). Fourth, "[w]henever possible, Canada should take the lead in presenting concrete proposals for a more effective co-ordination of security measures undertaken on both sides of the border in such areas as the standards and procedures governing immigration, the identification of refugees, and customs inspection" (ibid., 23). Finally, "Canadian Forces doctrine, force structures, equipment, and the like should be re-oriented to serve the requirements of national and continental defence and operations in support of Canadian foreign policy, stressing (1) combat capability,

(2) deployability, (3) interoperability with US forces, [and] (4) jointness among the different commands of the Canadian Forces" (ibid., 36). In this domain, Canada "must identify the specific *specializations* it wishes to develop to complement or supplement United States [military] requirements" (Bercuson 2003, 7, emphasis added). In addition, governments must keep in mind that "interoperability with US military systems is a prerequisite for procurement decisions in the Canadian Forces" (Stairs 2003, 42).

With these recommendations, the CDFAI offers a new grand strategy to the Canadian state: a programmatic vision for Canada's engagement with US primacy objectives and the "global war on terrorism." At the heart of this strategy is an armoured approach to security and defence – one that seeks to position the Canadian state as a secondary power in the US-led Empire of Capital. As a result, the CDFAI's vision fits with that of other agents in the military-industrial complex.

In the wake of 9/11, then, a new power bloc emerged in the political economy of Canada. Combining the economic and political interests of the capitalist class and the defence lobby, it has developed a new grand strategy for the Canadian state. Distilled into five essential points, this new grand strategy includes:

1. *neoliberal market enforcement*, or the commitment to global exploitation and appropriation under the hegemonic direction of Canadian capital;
2. *continental securitization*, or the convergence of US and Canadian security policies as part of building a "Fortress North America" for unfettered accumulation;
3. *cooperative specialization with US primacy*,[4] or the search for niche functions within US-led security platforms, especially in North America but inclusive of forward-deployed structures, vehicles, and missions;
4. *stratified multilateralism*,[5] or support for international regimes and institutions to the extent that they enable transnational neoliberalism, US primacy, and capitalist class interests in Canada; and:
5. *disciplinary militarism*,[6] or armed intervention in "failed" or "rogue" states to neutralize any perceived threats to capital, with a focus on counterinsurgency, asymmetric warfare, and interoperability with US and other North Atlantic Treaty Organization (NATO) forces.

If these principles have formed the key desideratum of the new imperial power bloc, how has the Canadian state responded?

The Politics of Power: State Strategies since 2001

The events of 9/11 were a turning point not just for the capitalist class and defence lobby in Canada, but for the Canadian state as well. Under the Liberal governments of Jean Chrétien and Paul Martin, and the Conservative government of Stephen Harper, there has occurred a radical rethinking of security and defence issues inside the executive, legislative, and administrative organs of governance. In the context of the "global war on terrorism," Canadian governments have pursued a more class-conscious statecraft – one dedicated to neoliberal market enforcement, continental securitization, stratified multilateralism, cooperative specialization with US global primacy, and disciplinary militarism towards the Third World. As key strategy documents reveal,[7] Liberal and Conservative governments have worked to synthesize and advance the economic, political, and military demands of the new imperial power bloc.

Consider, first, the response to 9/11 by Chrétien's Liberal government. In the wake of the attacks, it responded with practical, yet decisive assistance to the United States and its plan for a "global war on terrorism." As part of these efforts, the Chrétien government helped to rescue 33,000 airline passengers who were forced to land in Canada on 9/11; initiated the declaration of war by NATO through Article 5 of the North Atlantic Treaty; and committed to other security and defence initiatives of the Group-of-8 (G8) and G20. In addition, it established an ad hoc Cabinet Committee on Public Security and Anti-Terrorism; increased funding for national security and defence by $7.7 billion in the December 2001 federal budget; participated in Operation Enduring Freedom in Afghanistan; and allowed the use of Canadian airspace and airports for flights associated with detentions and extraordinary renditions by the US Central Intelligence Agency.[8] Yet despite these contributions to the "global war on terrorism," the Chrétien government was loathe to articulate a comprehensive strategy for national, continental, and international security. As a result, it appeared to lack intent or direction, save for supporting the short-term security demands of the United States and the short-term economic interests of Canada.

During this period, the primary structure in the state that *did* consider matters of strategy was the House of Commons Standing Committee on Foreign Affairs and International Trade (SCFAIT). In the wake of 9/11, it published several key documents on continental integration. For example, in November 2001, it released *Towards a Secure and Trade-Efficient*

Border (Canada 2001, 3, 10), which warned that, "[w]ith so much of Canadian economic output destined for the large U.S. market, maintaining a trade-efficient border with our American neighbours has become more vital than ever before. Whether Canada will be able to continue as a key part of the North American integrated economic system hangs in the balance." To secure this part, the committee argued that "[i]t is important for Canada to make bold proposals to the United States on how to work together to make the border function considerably more effectively. It would be far better to work with the Americans to accommodate their security needs than to react to their unilateral decisions and/or attempt to undo a bad decision down the road." With this in mind, in 2002, the SCFAIT recommended a "Strategic North American Policy Direction for Canada." For the committee (Canada 2002b, 1.5), this strategy must "explicitly affirm North American relations as a top priority," and "address Canada's diminished international policy capabilities" – in particular, by refunding the Department of Foreign Affairs and International Trade (DFAIT) and the DND. Despite these legislative efforts, however, the articulation of a clear state strategy did not occur.

This was most evident around the war in Iraq. Although the new power bloc was firmly behind the US-led mobilization,[9] Chrétien announced in Parliament that Canada "would not participate" in the war "without a new resolution of the [United Nations] Security Council." At this level of politics, Chrétien seemed to respond positively to protests in the streets, to opposition in caucus, and to European concerns over multilateral governance and international law. Behind the scenes, however, his government offered multiple forms of covert or discreet support to the war effort. Indeed, according to a classified US embassy cable, "[w]hile for domestic political reasons ... [Canada] has decided not to join in a U.S. coalition ... they are also prepared to be as helpful as possible in the military margins" (Weston 2011). Thus, Canadian naval ships and surveillance aircraft were tasked with supporting the US mission in several capacities; more than one hundred Canadian military officials participated in exchange programs with the US military as the war was planned and executed; and the Canadian government agreed to lead a future NATO mission in Kabul, Afghanistan, as part of relieving US soldiers for deployment to the Gulf (Harvey 2004, 234–6; Stein and Lang 2007, 48–50). In these ways, the Chrétien government tried to balance public opposition to the war with a practical contribution to Operation Iraqi Freedom. In this context, US Ambassador Paul Cellucci (2003) could not help but notice that, "[i]ronically, Canadian naval vessels, aircraft and personnel ... will supply more support to this war in Iraq indirectly ... than most of those 46 countries that are fully supporting our efforts there."

Nevertheless, the power bloc viewed the coming to power of Liberal Prime Minister Paul Martin in 2004 as an opening to break with the contingencies, or contradictions, of Chrétien's rule (Dobbin 2003). As a sign of his commitment to a new global agenda, Martin made his first visit as prime minister to the DND; appointed veteran politician Frank McKenna as ambassador to the United States; selected Rick Hillier as Chief of Defence Staff; increased defence spending; and redeployed Canadian troops to Kandahar, Afghanistan. To make sense of these actions, the Liberal government produced two key strategy documents, the *National Security Policy* (NSP; Canada 2004) and the *International Policy Statement* (IPS; Canada 2005b).

As Canada's first national security strategy, the NSP set a new agenda for Canadian foreign policy. It conceptualized the notion of security mainly in terms of the "security of the state," and emphasized the "international nature of many of the threats affecting Canadians" (Canada 2004, 3). With these starting points, the NSP laid the groundwork for a new strategy of cooperative specialization with US foreign policy practices and disciplinary militarism towards the Third World. This strategy was evident in the call to support international efforts against terrorism, rogue states, and weapons of mass destruction. The NSP claimed that antiterrorism must become the "highest priority" for government officials, and outlined the type of security apparatus that Canada must build to defend itself against this perceived threat (ibid., 48).

The IPS (Canada 2005b) developed this agenda into systematic strategy. As a key initiative of Martin himself, the IPS outlined a grand strategy for the state, covering, in separate papers, four areas of international policy: defence, diplomacy, development, and commerce. It developed an integrated approach to global politics and economics, and articulated a new set of international strategies and tactics for the state. In doing so, it helped to externalize the international agenda of the new imperial power bloc. The section on commerce, for example, supported the global expansion of Canadian capital and the continental agenda of the Security and Prosperity Initiative. It reaffirmed the importance of the World Trade Organization, and revealed the variety of financial and diplomatic supports given to Canadian companies through Export Development Canada and the Canadian Commercial Corporation. In the process, it revealed the active role of the state in supporting both the worldwide expansion of capital and the main institutions of neoliberal globalization.

The IPS's sections on defence, diplomacy, and development (the 3Ds) outlined the political side of the new foreign policy agenda. They acknowledged Canada's "growing stake in international developments" and the need for a strategy "adapted to a globalized world" (Canada 2005b, "Diplomacy," 1). They called for new modes of alignment with US foreign policy and a new willingness to confront terrorism, failed states, and weapons of mass destruction in the Third World. To do these things, the IPS supported the CCCE's Security and Prosperity Initiative, as well as Canada's role in the G8 and NATO. It argued, specifically, that "influence ... with the US can be a major asset in the pursuit of our own objectives," and that "cooperation with the United States is therefore central to advancing Canada's regional and global interests" (Canada 2005b, "Overview," 5).

The centrepiece of the IPS, however, was the 3D strategy for defence, diplomacy, and development. The basic proposition of the 3D strategy was that DFAIT, the DND, and the Canadian International Development Agency (CIDA) would work together as part of joint missions in failed states and counterinsurgency wars. In countries such as Haiti or Afghanistan, for example, the Canadian foreign policy apparatus should train itself for a "three-block war" of fighting insurgents, engaging in diplomacy, and proving aid to civilians (Canada 2005b, "Defence," 8). Through such measures, the IPS envisioned a new apparatus of state for engaging the world economy and nation-state system under neoliberalism and US primacy.

During this period, the Senate Standing Committee on National Security and Defence published several reports with the same prognoses and prescriptions. In doing so, it played an important role in generating cross-party support for Canada's involvement in the "global war on terrorism." For instance, in several studies, the committee focused on the perceived threats of "Islamic Jihad," "failed states," and "extremists in the Bin Laden mould" (Canada 2002a, 23; 2006, 11, 17–18). The committee acknowledged other sources of global instability, including economic inequality and the environmental crisis, but focused primarily on the military and defence capabilities of the state. According to the committee, Canada should reinvest in the military as a form of "global insurance policy," abandon the image of a peacekeeping nation, "mount enough military strength to protect its own borders, assist in the protection of North America, and ... assist in defusing international instability" (Canada 2005c, 4). To these ends, the committee (Canada 2002a, 2005c, 2006) urged new funding and training for the Canadian Forces and an expanded role internationally for the Canadian Security Intelligence Service (CSIS). Through investments such as these, the committee believed, Canada would achieve greater independence in world affairs and more security from threats such as terrorism, failed states, and weapons of mass destruction. It argued that Canadian security was connected to international security and that Canada should act as a primary force in the "global war on terrorism." Like the Martin government, the Senate committee thus supported methods of continental securitization, cooperative specialization with US foreign policy, and disciplinary militarism towards the Third World.

Under the Martin government, the SCFAIT also played a key role in forging new global strategies. In particular, it began to promote an "emerging market strategy" for the internationalization of Canadian capital. For example, in *Elements of an Emerging Market Strategy* (Canada 2005a), the SCFAIT argued for the Canadian state to support new trade missions, bilateral trade and investment-protection treaties, and a "whole-of-government" approach to assisting Canadian corporate expansion in East Asia, South Asia, and Latin America. The Martin government thus sought to advance the economic, political, and military interests of the power bloc in Canada. It is true that it bent to popular pressure (Ferguson 2010, 246) in opposing the US project of ballistic missile defence, and thus invited vocal protests by the corporate sector and defence lobby (CCCE 2005). Beyond this one particular case, however, it made important advances in conceptualizing a new grand strategy for Canadian state power – one that, like the Chrétien government before it, revolved around an armoured, neoliberal agenda.

Since 2006, the Conservative government of Stephen Harper has pursued this agenda with even more tenacity. From the start, Harper pledged to amend relations with the United States and to pursue a strong national interest in world affairs. Across several planning documents, this pledge has been turned into systematic strategy. The *Canada First Defence Strategy* (CFDS) was the first such document. The CFDS was premised, first, on the notion that Canada faces new security threats from "global terrorism," "failed and failing states," "insurgencies," "Islamist militants," and "nuclear capable adversarial states" (Canada 2008a, 6); and, second, on the notion that "[a]s a trading nation in a highly globalized world, Canada's prosperity and security rely on stability abroad" (ibid., 8). To meet these challenges, the CFDS envisioned a "fully integrated, flexible, multi-role and combat-capable military," that would be "interoperable" with US forces. To build these capacities, the CFDS promised $490 billion in military spending over twenty years – in particular, to expand the number of Canadian Forces personnel from 62,000 to 100,000 and to acquire new weapons systems for both conventional and asymmetric warfare. Through such expenditures, the CFDS would support the defence industry in Canada, helping it to "become [a] more effective [player] in the supply chains of the world's primary defence equipment manufacturers" (ibid., 20). In these ways, the CFDS offered a "Strategic Investment Plan" to position the Canadian state as a secondary power in the US-led Empire of Capital.

In the same year, the Harper government released *Seizing Global Advantage: A Global Commerce Strategy for Securing Canada's Growth and Prosperity* (Canada 2008c). Working with the logic of transnational neoliberalism, the document outlined a strategy for advancing the internationalization of capital, primarily through bilateral trade and foreign investment protection agreements. With this strategy, the Harper government aimed to integrate the Canadian economy more closely with global circuits of capital, and to expand the reach of Canadian corporations.

To these ends, in 2013 the Harper government also released its *Global Markets Action Plan* (GMAC), according to which "all Government of Canada assets [will be] harnessed to support the pursuit of commercial success by Canadian companies and investors in key foreign markets" (Canada 2013, 6). Developed in close consultation with the CCCE and other corporate lobby groups, the GMAC is "squarely aligned to the needs of Canadian business" (ibid., 6). In fact, the GMAC "entrenches the concept of 'economic diplomacy' as the driving force behind the Government of Canada's activities through its international diplomatic network" (ibid., 11). As part of this, it envisions the "development of an extractive sector strategy to further the interests of Canadian companies abroad," the "launch of a defence procurement strategy with a clear export-oriented component," and the further "alignment among Export Development Canada, the Business Development Bank of Canada and the Canadian Commercial Corporation to ensure effective financing support for Canadian businesses in priority markets" (ibid., 12, 15). Through such means, the

GMAC aims to expand the reach of Canadian capital in both emerging and established economies.

To secure this class-based economic agenda, the Harper government has also released a document entitled *Building Resilience against Terrorism: Canada's Counter-Terrorism Strategy* (Canada 2012a). The Counter-Terrorism Strategy (CTS) outlines a state-led approach to "countering domestic and international terrorism in order to protect Canada, Canadians and Canadian interests" (ibid., 10). The CTS advances the logic of securitization in three critical ways. First, it proceeds from the notion that "[v]iolent Islamist extremism is the leading threat to Canada's national security" (ibid., 4). From this premise, the CTS frames the issue of terrorism as an act of religious-based aggression, lacking roots in politics and history and unrelated to western foreign policies in Muslim countries.[10] It also lumps together various strands of Islamist politics, and conflates different types of armed movements. Second, the CTS links political movements of "environmentalism and anti-capitalism" to "[d]omestic [i]ssue-based [e]xtremism" (ibid. 9). In particular, it warns of the threat these movements pose to "[c]ritical infrastructure includ[ing] energy, transportation and oil and gas assets" (ibid., 22). It thus embellishes the framework of antiterrorism to include working-class and environmental movements. Third, it broadens the scope of counterterrorism policy to include unspecified "Canadian interests," which must be secured through diplomatic, intelligence, and military efforts, primarily in "failed states" (ibid., 31). In these ways, the CTS provides an ideological program for the national and international security agenda of the Canadian state and power bloc.

Since 9/11, then, the strategy of the Canadian state has evolved in ways that increasingly match and support the economic and political interests of the capitalist class and defence lobby. Indeed, the evidence suggests that the internationalization of capital has created a base of accumulation upon which the power bloc and the state have outlined a new grand strategy. This strategy is dedicated to neoliberal market enforcement, continental securitization, stratified multilateralism, cooperative specialization with US primacy, and disciplinary militarism towards the Third World. Although some of these practices are not entirely new, they have been advanced qualitatively over the past two decades, especially since 9/11. In fact, as the final section demonstrates, these practices have guided the restructuring of the Canadian state as part of the new security and foreign policy agenda.

The New Imperial State

In the years since 9/11, the Canadian state has been transformed in line with the strategy documents analysed above. In the process, it has been infused with the logic of armoured neoliberalism in three key respects: (1) the deeper integration of US-Canadian relations in terms of policy harmonization, perimeter security, and economic convergence; (2) the centralization of the state around national security and defence apparatuses; and (3) the positioning of global exploitation and disciplinary militarism at the core of Canada's foreign policy directives. Taken together, these three developments form the basis of a *new imperial state* in Canada.

The Continental Architecture

Consider, first, the deep integration of the North American bloc since 9/11. The first moment of this process occurred on 12 December 2001, when the United States and Canada signed the Smart Border Declaration on trade and security. On 7 January 2002, a follow-up Action Plan for Creating a Secure and Smart Border was released, outlining a new regime of continental integration. According to the Action Plan, this would involve biometric identifiers, permanent resident cards, convergent refugee and asylum processes, coordination of visa policies, joint air passenger analysis units, compatible immigration databases, harmonized commercial processing, joint border facilities, customs data sharing, integrated intelligence operations, and common border enforcement teams, deportation policies, and antiterrorist laws and training.

Although the impetus for the Smart Border Declaration came from the structural pressures of the "global war on terrorism," its specifics were shaped directly by the power bloc and state in Canada, including the Coalition for Secure and Trade-Efficient Borders, the SCFAIT, the Borders Task Force of the Privy Council Office, and DFAIT. Through the efforts of these agencies, the Canadian state has secured a new regime of continentalism – one that supports the economic interests of Canadian capital and the security interests of the United States. Indeed, "it was Canadian ideas and Canadian language that formed the basis for Washington's first major policy initiative on homeland security after 9/11" (Carpentier 2007, 23).

On 5 December 2002, the Canadian and US governments also signed the Safe Third Country Agreement, stipulating that refugees must claim protection in whichever of the two countries in which they first arrive. By deeming the United States a "safe" country for asylum seekers, the agreement had the effect of blocking refugee claimants whose only point of access to Canada was through a US port of entry or who feared claiming status in the United States given that country's polices of recognition, detention, and deportation (Moore 2007). The impact of the agreement, then, was a sharp move towards harmonization of US-Canadian refugee policies in a more restrictive, or less accepting, manner. As part of this agenda, in 2002 Parliament also passed the Immigration and Refugee Protection Act, which tightened the conditions under which immigrants and refugees may acquire status in Canada, and extended the use of "security certificates" for detaining and deporting terrorist suspects, often based on secret evidence. Through such measures, immigration policy became "Canada's prime counter-terrorism instrument" in the wake of 9/11 (Roach 2011, 396).

On the same day they announced the Safe Third Country Agreement, Canada and the United States also established a Bi-National Planning Group (BPG 2006, iii) to "enhance bi-national military planning, surveillance, and support to civil authorities." Composed of approximately twenty-five defence and security officials from each country, the BPG worked alongside the US Northern Command (USNORTHCOM) and NORAD to plan future defence arrangements for North America under the assumption that continental security is *indivisible*. In its final report, the BPG praised the convergence of continental security structures, including those between Canada Command and the US Department of Defense and between the Canadian Department of Public Safety and Emergency Preparedness and the US Department of Homeland Security.

More broadly, the BPG (ibid., 7) argued that "Canada and the United States must continue to act as partners ... to shape the future of North American defense and security, using all of the instruments of diplomatic, economic, informational and military power." To this end, the BPG proposed a "Comprehensive Defence and Security Agreement," which would update and advance previous agreements on military cooperation in North America. For military planners, the goal of this project was not to subordinate, but to empower, the Canadian state within continental security structures, which would otherwise be directed by USNORTHCOM on a unilateral basis (Lagasse 2003).

The deep integration agenda was advanced in other ways during this period. At the regional summit in Waco, Texas, in March 2005, the governments of Canada, Mexico, and the United States agreed upon a Security and Prosperity Partnership (SPP), which formalized the Security and Prosperity Initiative of the CCCE. Through this process, the North American Competitiveness Council (NACC) was established as the organizational nexus of continental business interests (see Chapter 3). In conjunction with the SPP, the NACC called for a common external tariff and outer security perimeter; a North American border pass with biometric information; a unified border action plan; the coordination of law enforcement and the sharing of intelligence; and a common economic space in which resources, capital, and labour would move freely (Council on Foreign Relations 2005). Although the Martin Liberal government first supported this initiative, the Harper government further developed it until US President Barack Obama cut the project amid the US economic crisis and growing popular protest. The SPP has since been reconstituted, however, through more discreet and piecemeal measures – for example, through the "Beyond the Border Declaration" (Obama and Harper 2011) and the Regulatory Cooperation Council, both of which have been endorsed by leading corporate interests on both sides of the border.

The key point is that, through various modes of continental integration, the Canadian state has transformed itself in ways demanded by dominant class interests. In the process, it has built a continental security system for the protection of US primacy and the expanded reproduction of Canadian capital. The building of "Fortress North America," though, is linked to *other* interests of the state and power bloc. In particular, it serves as a bridge between the national project of centralizing the state for neoliberal market enforcement and the international project of imposing global exploitation through disciplinary militarism. As a result, *the making of "Fortress North America" is only one dimension of a multiscale project of armoured neoliberalism.*

The National Security State

The second element of the new imperial state is the building of a national security apparatus. As part of this agenda, the security institutions of the Canadian state have been thoroughly transformed. The starting point of this process was the December 2001 federal budget, which, as noted above, invested nearly $8 billion in new security spending, with $92 billion in fresh funding for security and defence projects allocated over the next decade (Macdonald 2011).

With access to such resources, the new national security apparatus has come to permeate the entire state structure, incorporating the gamut of federal agencies and departments. Indeed, it now includes a National Security Advisor and Advisory Council to the Prime Minister; the Borders Task Force and the International Assessment Staff of the Privy Council Office; the Cabinet Committee on National Security; the Department of Public Safety, which works closely with DFAIT; the Canadian Air Transport Security Authority; the Immigration Intelligence Branch of the Canada Border Services Agency (CBSA); the Integrated Border Enforcement and National Security Teams and Sections of the Royal Canadian Mounted Police (RCMP), as well as its National Operations Centre and National Security Community Outreach program; the Integrated Threat Assessment Centre; the Global Operations Centre of CSIS; the Canadian Cyber Incident Response Centre; the Financial Transactions and Reports Analysis Centre; the Government Operations Centre based in Public Safety Canada; the Integrated Terrorism Assessment Centre of the RCMP; the Operations Centre of DFAIT; the Marine Security Operations Centre; the Justice Emergency Team; and the US-Canada Integrated Border Enforcement Teams.

The securitization of the state has extended into other departments and services, including the Department of Finance, Transport Canada, the Canada Revenue Agency, the CBSA, Health Canada, Citizenship and Immigration Canada, Correctional Services, the Public Prosecution Service of Canada, and the Canadian Air Transport Security Authority (Canada 2004, 2012a). By infusing comprehensive security measures into this range of departments and agencies, the Canadian state has transformed itself into a *thoroughly armoured entity*. In the process, it has also become more integrated with the national, continental, and international structures of US global primacy (Lennox 2007, 2009).

At the policy level, the new security agenda has been supported by key pieces of legislation, including the Smart Borders Act (2001); the Charities Registration (Security Information) Act (2001); the Public Safety Act (2002); the Immigration and Refugee Protection Act (2002, amended 2008); the Anti-Terrorism Act (2002); the Canada Border Services Agency Act (2005); the Department of Public Safety and Emergency Preparedness Act (2005); and the Emergency Management Act (2007). The Anti-Terrorism Act, in particular, has affected a wide range of other Canadian laws, including the Canada Evidence Act, the Proceeds of Crime (Money Laundering) Act, and the Security of Information Act (replacing the Official Secrets Act). More than this, it has "introduced new and potentially dangerous legal concepts such as investigative hearings, preventive arrests, broad motive-based crimes based on participation in or contribution to terrorist groups at home and abroad, as well as new powers to list terrorist groups, take their property, and deprive suspected terrorists of sensitive security information in their trials and appeals" (Roach 2002, 895, quoted in Lennox 2009, 120).

Through these new legal structures, state power has been centralized in the security apparatus; Canadian law has converged with US law and become more amenable to executive prerogative and Crown discretion; and domestic dissent and protest have been classified as national security threats (Daniels, Macklem, and Roach 2001; Forcese 2009; Lennox 2007; Monaghan and Walby 2012). As part of this, a new culture of Islamophobia has been inculcated in civil society, particularly for grounding the "global war on terrorism" (Razack 2008). Prime Minister Harper's public warning of the "major threat" of "Islamicism" has been, perhaps, the most direct example of state targeting of Muslims (CBC 2011).[11]

Furthermore, as Jeffrey Monaghan and Kevin Walby (2012, 141) reveal, the new security establishment is increasingly focused not on genuine terrorist activity, but on *social movements of the left*, which have been classified in official threat assessments as "ideologically motivated extremist entities," warranting surveillance and possible suppression. In this context, "[t]he centralization of intelligence has resulted in a new framework for anti-terror policing where subversive and simply suspicious conduct is lumped under the categories of terrorism and extremism" (ibid., 146). For example, under the Harper government, the National Energy Board has worked closely with CSIS, the RCMP, and Canadian energy corporations to monitor and gather intelligence on anti-oil-sands activism (Millar 2013).

As part of building a new imperial capacity, the intelligence branches of the Canadian state have also been restructured and recapitalized. For example, funding for Communications Security Establishment Canada (CSEC), a federal agency that operates a "vast electronic eavesdropping system that works with allies ... to analyze intelligence on foreign adversaries," increased dramatically from $140 million in 2001 to $422 million in 2013. With new responsibilities for global signals-intelligence, the CSEC is building a new headquarters at the cost of $1.2 billion (S. Bell 2006; Davis 2012; Weston 2013). As requested by federal departments and agencies such as the RCMP, CSIS, DND, and the CBSA, the CSEC is engaged in domestic communications monitoring and shares information with intelligence agencies of the other "Five Eyes" group of countries – the United States, the United Kingdom, New Zealand, and Australia (CBC 2013; Mitrovica 2013). Under recent Liberal and Conservative governments, the CSEC has also operated a surreptitious metadata surveillance program that monitors telephone records and Internet usage internationally as well as in Canada (Freeze 2013, 2014). In support of Canadian mining and energy companies, it has also engaged in industrial espionage abroad (Lukacs and Groves 2013). In addition, the CSEC has established covert spying operations for the US National Security Agency in "approximately 20 high-priority countries" (Weston, Greenwald, and Gallagher 2013).

Since 2001, the operations of CSIS have also expanded internationally, and the agency has received a funding increase of more than 150 per cent, reaching $506 million in fiscal year 2010/11. Along with the CSEC, CSIS has been highly active in the "global war on terror" – for example, through new forms of communications monitoring in Canada, as well as international surveillance in Iraq and Afghanistan. In the process, CSIS has been implicated in the detention, rendition, and torture of Canadian citizens, including Maher Arar, Abousfian Abdelrazick, Omar Khadr, Abdullah Almalki, Ahmad Abou-Elmaati, and Muayyed Nurredin (Iacobucci 2010). In Afghanistan, CSIS played a "crucial and longstanding role as interrogators of captured Taliban fighters," many of whom were tortured by Afghan security personnel at some stage in the detention process (Brewster and Bronskill 2010). More broadly, CSIS maintains information-sharing agreements with dozens of countries that have a record of using torture. Under the Harper government, the Office of the Inspector General of CSIS has been closed to avoid unwanted scrutiny, and CSIS itself has been given permission to use information derived by torture from other intelligence services (Forcese 2014; Mitrovica 2012a,b). On the domestic front, CSIS monitors the global justice and peace movements in Canada (CSIS 2004, 2005) and has been accused by indigenous communities, mosques, and migrant groups of using guilt by association, racial profiling, bribery, blacklists, entrapment, and manipulation of evidence (People's Commission Network 2012). Although CSIS has a record of spying on and harassing trade unions and social movements in Canada, it is now more than ever a political policing mechanism for dominant class interests at home and abroad (Whitaker, Kealey, and Parnaby 2012).

In these ways, then, a national security state has been established in Canada to advance and protect the economic and political interests of the new power bloc.

The Foreign Policy Apparatus

CIDA, DFAIT, and the DND have also been reorganized institutionally, financially, and politically in accordance with the power bloc's interests. For example, funding for CIDA rose rapidly between fiscal years 2000/01 and 2006/07 from $2.6 billion to $4.23 billion (CIDA 2009, 3). This budget increase allowed CIDA to expand its range of operations, most notably in Afghanistan and Haiti – two key sites of Canadian military intervention. However, while CIDA gained new financial resources, it lost policy autonomy in relation to the means and targets of development spending. As part of the 3D strategy, CIDA projects have been subordinated to the security, military, and commercial objectives of DFAIT, the DND, and the Prime Minister's Office. According to Stephen Brown (2008, 92), "[g]reater policy integration and the increased politicization of aid have reduced CIDA's autonomy and capacity to fight poverty and actually promote development." Moreover, the 3D approach "contradicts the notion of a human rights-based approach to development, which focuses on the rights of recipients instead of the interests of the donor" (ibid., 100).

For these reasons, CIDA operations since 9/11 have extended and replicated long-standing problems in aid delivery, including the "tying" of aid to commercial profit and geopolitical objectives (Morrison 1998). For example, in fiscal year 2004/05, Canada tied more than 40 per cent of official development assistance (ODA) funds to the purchase of goods from Canadian sources (OECD 2007, table 23, cited in Brown 2008, 93). Under pressure to change this policy, though, the Harper government diminished the level of tied aid to 7.4 per cent in 2010 (OECD 2011, table 23), and promised to reduce that amount even further.

At the same time, CIDA's mandate to "lead Canada's international effort to help people living in poverty" is limited by other economic and political dynamics. First, Canadian transnational corporations import greater sums of investment income from developing countries than the Canadian state reciprocates through annual aid disbursements. Second, Canada often spends more on domestic agricultural subsidies than it spends on ODA (Gordon 2013, 222). Third, despite an increase in CIDA funding, ODA in 2011 accounted for only 0.31 per cent of Canada's gross national income (GNI), far less than the pledge of 0.7 per cent Canada made in 1970, when ODA was 0.4 per cent of GNI. Finally, CIDA funding has been hitched to the internationalization of Canadian capital, with the aim of making developing countries "trade and investment ready" (Fantino 2012).

CIDA funding, for example, is now part of a whole-of-government approach to expanding Canada's mining sector in the periphery (Mackrael 2014). To this end, CIDA provides funding for revising mining codes and royalty rates, building infrastructure, rewriting investment legislation, and supporting exploration and reclamation in Third World countries. Indeed, so important has mining become to CIDA that approximately three-quarters of its twenty "Countries of Focus" are home to vast mineral deposits, suggesting a torquing of aid in support of Canadian mining interests. In pursuit of this, CIDA works closely with Export Development Canada, Natural Resources Canada, and DFAIT as part of an integrated strategy for Canadian mining expansion (Blackwood and Stewart 2012, 227–32). As a result, CIDA is now engaged more than ever in neoliberal market enforcement as a means of internationalizing Canada's extractive sector. In the process, it has become an active player in resource conflicts in developing countries – that is, in the growing struggles over land rights, water use, deforestation, poverty, and dispossession in the contested zones of global mining (Arango 2013; Blackwood and Stewart 2012; Gordon and Webber 2008).[12]

For its part, DFAIT was restructured in the early 1980s when foreign affairs and international trade were combined for the purpose of "commercializing" Canadian foreign policy (Clarkson 2002, 396). In the 1990s, DFAIT supervised the integration of Canada and the world market through NAFTA, the World Trade Organization, the Free Trade Area of the Americas, and other trade and investment agreements. More recently, the Martin and Harper governments instructed DFAIT to establish closer, more agreeable ties with Washington in matters of trade, security, and foreign affairs. Although DFAIT has experienced funding cuts by recent Liberal and Conservative governments, and has been relatively sidelined by the DND and the Prime Minister's Office in the context of the "global war on terror" (Noble 2008; Stein and Lang 2007), it provided key ideological support for the whole-of-government mission in Kandahar, especially by way of authoring the IPS. DFAIT was also tasked by the Harper government with coordinating the 3D strategy in Afghanistan, reviewing relations with India and China, and developing a new "Strategy for the Americas" in the context of growing Canadian direct investment in the hemisphere (Noble 2008).[13] Since 2007, DFAIT has also negotiated foreign investment protection agreements with Bahrain, China, India, Jordan, Kuwait, Latvia, Madagascar, Mali, Peru, Romania, Senegal, Slovakia, and Tanzania; and free trade agreements with Colombia, Honduras, Jordan, Panama, Peru, and, most recently, the European Union. Furthermore, with the DND and the Canadian Commercial Corporation, DFAIT has participated in a whole-of-government effort at increasing Canadian arms exports, often in conjunction with trade missions undertaken by the Canadian Association of Defence and Security Industries (Meyer 2011; Pugliese 2011a).[14] In such ways, DFAIT has enabled the new grand strategy of armoured neoliberalism.

The DND has also been restructured in accordance with the planning documents cited above. In 2005, the Canadian Forces were reorganized into four integrated command structures, including Canada Command, the Canadian Expeditionary Force Command, the Canadian Special Operations Forces Command, and the Canadian Operational Support Command.[15] Likewise, the 2005 federal budget allowed for a $12.8 billion increase in new funding over five years, while the 2006 budget increased funding by another $5 billion. By increasing the automatic escalator in defence funding to 2 per cent, the 2008 budget envisioned an augmentation of military spending from $18 billion at the time to over $30 billion in fiscal year 2027/28. As a result, by 2011, Canadian defence spending had nearly doubled from the level of 2001, reaching $22 billion, the highest total since the Second World War (Staples 2011). In this context, Canada became, in 2012, the sixth-highest military spender among NATO countries and the fourteenth-highest in the world.

With these new resources, the DND has been able to increase regular and reserve personnel to 100,000 and to order new weapons systems, including C-17 Globemaster aircraft, C-130J Hercules tactical lift aircraft, replacement destroyers and frigates, fighter jets, unmanned aerial drones, and Leopard tanks and tactical armoured patrol vehicles. As an integrated package, these weapons systems indicate the qualitative shift in Canadian foreign policy away from peacekeeping and Middle Power functions towards a global method of disciplinary militarism, focused on counterinsurgency, terrorism, and rogue states. For example, the original purpose of the F-35 fighter aircraft purchase was to command what the DND calls an "away fleet" of stealth jets that would be able to participate in US-led bombing and patrol missions abroad (Leblanc 2012). For such types of operations, the DND is also seeking to establish seven overseas operational support hubs to "project combat power/security assistance and Canadian influence rapidly and flexibly anywhere in the world," according to a 2010 directive signed by then Chief of Defence Staff Walter Natynczyk (Berthiaume 2012a).

With such a focus on disciplinary militarism, Canada's role in United Nations peacekeeping missions has shrunk dramatically. In September 2012, Canada ranked fifty-seventh in terms of the total number of peacekeepers deployed, with only 148 on various missions, far below its contributions of past decades. This turn away from peacekeeping is the result of Canada's growing participation in NATO- and US-led operations and of the new organizational emphasis on "interoperability" and "JIMP" (joint, interagency, multinational, and public) operations, as evident in Afghanistan, Haiti, and Libya. Canada's foreign military training programs have also shifted from peacekeeping to counterinsurgency under DND's Special Operations Regiment and in conjunction with US military missions (Pugliese 2011b). With this "revolution in military affairs," the DND has become a leading site of strategy formation inside the Canadian state, especially with regards to current and future security trends and military deployments (see Canada 2008b, 2010). In this thinking, a new investment in disciplinary militarism is critical for securing the state and its economic interests in national, continental, and international markets.[16] From this standpoint, UN peacekeeping only inhibits the new grand strategy of the state and power bloc.

The DND has also become a key transmitter of US grand strategies into other branches of the Canadian state, in ways that often challenge the democratic principle of civilian control of the military. As Bruno Charbonneau and Wayne Cox (2008, 320) observe, "[i]t seems that throughout more than 60 years of integrated defense with the United States, the Canadian military has become a more autonomous actor – that is, autonomous from the Canadian state. At the same time, however, that autonomy is partially reflected by an organization that views its interest as shared with those of America's hegemonic strategic culture." In fact, since 9/11, the DND has worked as a conveyor belt for US imperialism in Canada, driving a policy of forward military force projection in Afghanistan and other flashpoints in the "global war on terror" (Stein and Lang 2007).

Under the Harper government, the DND has also worked to inculcate a new culture of militarism in civil society. As Ian McKay and Jamie Swift (2012, 280, 284) observe, "militarization is a process through which the state reorganizes society to realize a specific vision of Canada, one of money for arms, more respect for soldiers, and more muscularity in foreign policy," in addition to extending "martial values into completely new spheres." This has been achieved through a "state-orchestrated cultural revolution" involving yellow ribbon campaigns, fallen soldier ceremonies, war commemorations, recruitment drives, and military spectacles at professional sporting events (see also McCready 2010).

In accordance with the planning documents, then, the Canadian state has built the security, diplomatic, and military apparatus that dominant class interests have demanded. It has repositioned the national security and foreign policy agenda around an armoured, neoliberal strategy. In the process, it has sought a secondary role in the US-led Empire of Capital.

Conclusion: Social Relations, the State, and Empire

In the aftermath of 9/11, the Canadian state has been armoured as part of a new imperial project. Designed by a new power bloc of corporate, state, and military actors, this project is dedicated to neoliberal market enforcement, continental securitization, stratified multilateralism, cooperative specialization with US primacy, and disciplinary militarism towards the Third World. Codified in key planning documents, these principles have been used to restructure the state as a vessel of class domination at home and abroad. In the process, they have worked to securitize the economic interests of Canadian capital at national, continental, and international scales, and to position the state as a secondary power in the US-led Empire of Capital. As a result, they have formed the axes of a new imperial strategy.

In the account told here, it is the *social relations* of transnational neoliberalism that underpin new state policies and practices. Indeed, the Canadian state has forged a new grand strategy not simply in response to the balance-of-power and security environment, but also in relation to transnational class dynamics. In the process, it has crystallized the economic interests of capital in new state structures and strategies. It has consolidated a *social structure of power*.

What this means in terms of social science research – indeed, in terms of political practice – is that the new imperial state is an expression of key transformations in the political economy and class structure of

Canada. It reflects the transnational relations of accumulation and class formation that attend the internationalization of capital. As a result, it is unlikely to be changed or transformed in the absence of mass social movements against transnational neoliberalism. With this in mind, social movements in Canada would be wise to align with global campaigns for peace and social justice, for it is the social relations of global capital that drive and impel the new imperial project. To address this reality, the task of mapping the social content of Canadian state power will be of critical importance.

7 One of the Big Boys: Canada in Afghanistan and Haiti

We're not trying to be one of the big boys, we are one of the big boys and we have to start acting like it.

– Rick Hillier,
Chief of Defence Staff, Canadian Forces, 2008

To hear the big fellows talk, they wage war from fear of God and for all things bright and beautiful, but just look into it, and you'll see they're not so silly: they want a good profit out of it.

– Bertolt Brecht,
Mother Courage and her Children (1939)

In his 1993 book on Canadian foreign policy, Tom Keating concluded with an unusual warning. "Policy-makers," he argued, "[will] have to make a difficult choice in the future between their desire to be part of the [global] elite and the need to protect the institutions and norms that the vast majority of nations must rely on." As Keating observed, Canadian foreign policy-makers had begun "to move in more elite circles," and were increasingly aligned with US priorities in North America and around the world. For Keating, this new alignment "raise[d] questions about the future direction of Canada's multilateralist orientation" (Keating 1993, 248).

Two decades later, Keating's observations stand out for their prescience. Over this period, the goals and methods of Canadian foreign policy have shifted in fundamental ways. The Canadian state has abandoned the Middle Power strategy of the Cold War period and the corresponding practice of peacekeeping. In turn, Canada has begun to play a more powerful role in the economic, political, and military clubs of empire. For example, Canada has been a key actor in the "global war on terrorism" and a primary advocate of neoliberal economics in international trade bodies. Canada supported military activities in Haiti (2004, 2010), Afghanistan (2001–14), Serbia (1999), Somalia (1994), Iraq (1991–2002), and Libya (2011), and changed course on diplomatic issues such as nuclear disarmament and the Israel-Palestine conflict (Byers 2007; McQuaig 2007). This new foreign policy approach has become a flashpoint of debate at home and abroad, and is likely to feature more prominently in future elections.

As the last chapter demonstrated, these shifts in Canadian foreign policy are the outcome of a new grand strategy, one dedicated to neoliberal market enforcement, continental securitization, stratified multilateralism, cooperative specialization with US primacy, and disciplinary militarism towards the Third World. This strategy accords with the class interests of the new power bloc, and has guided the institutional restructuring of the state, particularly since 9/11. As such, it is neither a short-term policy preference of governments in Ottawa nor an internal reflex to external pressures. It is, instead, a hegemonic effort to position the state as a secondary power in the new imperialism. It is a logical expression of the internationalization of capital and of the recomposition of the power bloc around dominant class interests.

To advance these arguments, in this chapter I examine the new Canadian foreign policy in action since 2001. Using two case studies, I demonstrate the implementation of the new grand strategy abroad. In the first section, I consider the war in Afghanistan as the primary front of the new Canadian imperialism over the past decade. In the second section, I look at Canada's shifting role in Haiti since the coup of 2004 and the earthquake of 2010. By examining these cases, I confirm the thesis of this book – namely, that Canada's new grand strategy is a global practice of exploitation and domination, and thus is a hegemonic effort at *joining empire*.

Empire's Ally: Canada and the War in Afghanistan

The war in Afghanistan was a critical experiment for the new Canadian foreign policy. The common understanding of the war is that Canada joined the international effort to bring democracy, development, and security to Afghanistan in the wake of 9/11. Most studies also emphasize Canada's economic dependence on the United States as a secondary factor in driving the mission (Lennox 2009; Stein and Lang 2007). These factors alone, however, cannot explain the war and Canada's role in it. The Canadian state did indeed feel obliged to support US policies and practices, but it also viewed the war as a means to other ends. In particular, the war was conducive to military spending increases, new forms of interoperability with the forces of the United States and other members of the North Atlantic Treaty Organization (NATO), and training in disciplinary militarism for other global conflicts.[1] The war also advanced the internationalization of capital in Afghanistan and the wider region. As such, it was a key testing ground for the new grand strategy of the state and power bloc.

Occupying Afghanistan: State-Building, Development, and War

From the start, the Canadian government was quick to endorse the US plan for war in Afghanistan. In the days after 9/11, Prime Minister Jean Chrétien stated that Canada would stand "shoulder to shoulder" with the United States, while Foreign Affairs Minister John Manley asserted that Canada was then "at war with terrorism" (Lennox 2009, 92). With this kind of support from the Canadian state and other NATO allies, the United States refused multiple offers of negotiation from the Taliban government, and launched a war of aggression on 7 October 2001 (Cohn 2005; Duffy 2005; Mandel 2004; Williamson 2009). The US-led mission – entitled Operation Enduring Freedom – was supported on the ground by the United Islamic Front for the Salvation of Afghanistan (the "Northern Alliance"), a network of ethnic militias that had fought the Taliban government since the mid-1990s. Supported by the US Central Intelligence Agency (CIA) and NATO Special Forces, the Northern Alliance conquered the country over a two-month period. The Taliban leadership fled to Pakistan, several al-Qaeda training camps were destroyed, and warlords and other criminal elements quickly filled the power vacuum across the country. As international aid and human rights workers predicted at the time, hundreds of civilians were killed directly by the war and several thousand more died indirectly from hunger, displacement, illness, and disease (Klassen 2013, 141–3).

As the fighting subsided, the United States and the United Nations put forward a nation-building project for Afghanistan. The "Bonn Process" of building a new state was the first dimension of this project, and was designed to "end the tragic conflict in Afghanistan and [to] promote national reconciliation, lasting peace, stability and respect for human rights" (Agreement on Provisional Arrangements 2001). The state that emerged, however, was not reflective of these principles, but of the external interests of the United States and NATO, and the internal interests of the Northern Alliance.

For example, through a series of interim governments and constitutional assemblies, the United States and NATO helped to establish a centralized state dominated by President Hamid Karzai and his cabinet of Northern Alliance warlords. The process of building a state through elections was further compromised by widespread corruption, violence, and sectarianism, and by the exclusion of democratic, secular parties. For these reasons, the Bonn Process failed to achieve a democratic state with popular legitimacy. Instead, it recreated the forms of internal hierarchy and external domination that have plagued the country for more than two decades (Dorronsoro 2005; Klassen 2013; Ruttig 2006; Warnock 2013). The presidential election of 2009 and the parliamentary election of 2010 were both marred by violence and corruption, and symbolized the structural faults of the Bonn Process.

The second dimension of the nation-building project involved security sector reform as well as aid and development funding. The security sector reform project was designed to create a national army and police corps to maintain order and allow development programs to proceed. As part of these efforts, the Afghan National Police (ANP) was set to reach 160,000 members in 2014, while the Afghan National Army (ANA) was intended to total 260,000 in 2015. Tens of billions of dollars have been allocated to these projects, yet both the ANP and ANA have been hampered by structural weaknesses. As the ANP and ANA were being organized in 2002, they incorporated the militias and command structures of the Northern Alliance; as a result, they internalized sectarian divisions in their organizational hierarchies and deployment operations. In particular, Tajik commanders of the Northern Alliance, rather than majority Pashtuns, were ensconced at the head of the new security structures (Dorronsoro 2005, 337–8; see also International Crisis Group 2010, 10). Then, the ANP and ANA were misused as counterinsurgency tools against the Taliban and their Pashtun base, which was marginalized by the Bonn Process (Sedra 2004). For these reasons, the Afghan national security forces have been targeted by the insurgency, and have suffered high casualty and desertion rates (Giustozzi 2007, 181; Oxfam International 2011; United States 2010e, 26). In response, the western coalition and the Afghan government have worked to diversify the ethnic composition of the Afghan national security forces, which, as a result, have largely held the territory gained vis-à-vis the insurgency since the US military "surge" of 2009 (International Crisis Group 2010, 11). At the same time, the Afghan national security forces remain highly dependent on the United States and NATO, especially for training, financing, military hardware, and logistics support. As a result, it is unclear how the Afghan security services will perform after the bulk of western forces withdraw in 2014 (see Dorronsoro 2012).

The aid and development project has been troubled by similar dynamics. Through a host of plans and initiatives, including the Tokyo Agreement (2002), the National Development Framework (2002), the Afghan Reconstruction Trust Fund (2002), the National Solidarity Project (2003), the Afghan National Development Strategy (2005), and the Afghanistan Compact (2006), a neoliberal model of development was imposed on Afghanistan, designed by foreign experts who sought to privatize government assets, deregulate the Afghan economy, and integrate the country into transnational patterns of trade, investment, and finance (Klassen 2013, 158–62; Podur 2013, 354–5).[2] To these ends, the Afghan state was systematically handicapped at both the macro and micro levels. For example, international donors controlled the aims and directions of aid and development funding, and non-governmental organizations (NGOs) established independent service networks that were not coordinated with the state. In this context, the majority of aid funding was tied to donor-country purchases or funnelled into consultant contracts, executive salaries, security services, or corporate profits (Waldman 2008, 1–7).

Furthermore, as the Taliban insurgency gained momentum, the United States and NATO began to use aid and development funds as weapons on the battlefield. By tying aid to military objectives, NATO employed an *expeditionary economics*, which many international aid organizations condemned (ActionAid et al. 2010; InterAction 2003; Oxfam International et al. 2009). Even though billions of dollars of aid have poured into Afghanistan, the country remains one of the poorest in the world, with 70 per cent of the population living in extreme poverty and health vulnerability, and with thirty thousand children dying annually from malnutrition and related diseases (Bhandari 2012; World Health Organization 2011).

The problem here has not been a paucity of wealth or resources, but a *political structure* of corruption, abuse, and outside domination. As the United Nations Office of the High Commissioner for Human Rights (2010, iii, 4) put it, "[a]ll development indicators show that poverty reduction efforts have had little impact on the daily life of most Afghans." The reason is that "[a] key driver of poverty in Afghanistan is the abuse of power," with new warlords and politicians using "their influence to drive the public agenda for their own personal or vested interests." Moreover, by working with such "mistrusted Afghan power-holders," the international community has served to entrench "abusive, dysfunctional, and corrupt political structures," which obstruct or impede a human development agenda. Hence, "[p]overty is neither accidental, nor inevitable in Afghanistan: it is both a cause and consequence of a massive human rights deficit including widespread impunity and inadequate investment in, and attention to, human rights."

The war against the Taliban has been the third aspect of the US-led nation-building project. Although the Taliban were willing to work with the new government in 2001–02, the marginalization of the Pashtun population and the use of violence by warlords and NATO forces catalysed a new guerrilla movement (Gopal 2010; Klassen 2013). From 2005 onward, the Taliban inflicted major casualties on US and NATO forces, and built an insurgency of thousands of fighters, operating in four-fifths of the country. In response, the United States and NATO increased force levels, occupied every province of Afghanistan, and used counterinsurgency methods such as detentions, night raids, targeted killings, drone strikes, battlefield executions, and village razings – all of which amounted to an "almost industrial-scale counterterrorism killing machine," as retired US lieutenant-colonel John Nagl put it (PBS 2011).[3] Foreign forces were also complicit in the detention and torture of Afghan prisoners, who experienced beatings, sleep deprivation, sexual assault, electrocution, water boarding, and dog attacks by NATO and Afghan security personnel (Rashid 2008, chap. 14). Although the Taliban lack support to govern as they did in the 1990s, they have waged a "nationalist Islamist insurgency" (Gopal 2010, 2), and forced the United States and NATO to plan a partial withdrawal date of 2014.

Warrior Nation: Canada in Afghanistan

With this in mind, how did Canada participate in the political, economic, and military project of the US-led mission in Afghanistan? To begin, in fall 2001, Canada sent naval units to the Indian Ocean and deployed Special Forces of the Joint Task Force 2 (JTF2) as part of Operation Enduring Freedom. It also worked to bring NATO into Afghanistan through the invocation of Article 5 of the North Atlantic

Treaty. In January 2002, regular forces were dispatched to Kandahar on a stabilization mission. In 2004, Canada took command of the UN-mandated International Security Assistance Force (ISAF) in Kabul, and in 2005 deployed combat infantry, Special Forces, and aid workers to Kandahar as part of a counterinsurgency operation. After more than five years of fighting, however, Canadian soldiers were withdrawn from Kandahar without having defeated the Taliban movement. Between May 2011 and March 2014, Canadian security personnel were involved in training Afghan security forces in Kabul.

Throughout the war, the Canadian state used what the Liberal government of Paul Martin termed a "3D" approach to stabilization and reconstruction: a political intervention combining defence, developmental, and diplomatic responsibilities. The same strategy was relabelled a "whole-of-government" approach by the Conservative government of Stephen Harper. The aim of this strategy was to integrate the branches of the foreign policy apparatus as part of fighting a war, building a state, and reconstructing a country. To these ends, the Department of National Defence (DND), the Department of Foreign Affairs and International Trade (DFAIT), and the Canadian International Development Agency (CIDA) jointly operated a combat mission and a Provincial Reconstruction Team (PRT) in Kandahar, as well as a Strategic Advisory Team (SAT) within the Presidential Office of Hamid Karzai. Through such efforts, Canada spent more than $18 billion in Afghanistan, the vast majority of which was dedicated to military operations. In the process, 158 Canadians were killed, and thousands more wounded. In 2001 and 2002, a majority of the Canadian public supported the military intervention. By 2006, however, a majority was polling against the war, and by 2011 a strong plurality believed that the cost of the mission had not been worth the effort (Angus Reid 2010; CTV 2006c; EKOS Research Associates 2009; Leger Marketing Poll 2011).

Nevertheless, the war was of vital importance to the redirection of Canadian foreign policy – and to the implementation of the new grand strategy. Indeed, the war was critical for changing the form and function of the Canadian military, as well as the organizational hierarchy of the Canadian foreign policy apparatus, the patterns of military spending and weapons procurement, and the nature of US-Canadian relations. In these ways, the war effected what Alexander Moens (2008) calls a "revolution in Canadian foreign policy." At the same time, the mission was a failure in terms of meeting the goals of the 3D strategy. In fact, none of the stated goals of the mission was achieved. Rather, in matters of diplomacy, defence, and development, the Canadian mission reproduced the broader contradictions of the war and occupation.

Consider, first, the role of the Strategic Advisory Team. The highly discreet SAT was created through a bilateral agreement between Canada and Afghanistan, and gave sixteen armed DND officials inside access to Karzai's office and cabinet for the purposes of drafting legislation, setting priorities, and monitoring communications (Taylor 2007a). The SAT was "[m]andated by President Karzai personally to go anywhere in the country and investigate anything." It was allowed "to work at the ministerial level across all ministries and [to] deal with the United Nations, the World Bank, key donor nations, and NATO/ISAF on almost a daily basis" (Pigott 2007, 114). As a result, "[n]o other country [was] as strategically placed as Canada with respect to influencing Afghanistan's development," according to SAT member, Lieutenant-Commander Rob Ferguson. For example, the SAT was deeply involved in drafting and implementing the Afghanistan Compact and the National Solidarity Program, both of which were key elements of the neoliberal development model (St-Louis 2009). The SAT also managed the Karzai government's communications strategy, and in September 2006 wrote Karzai's speech to the Canadian Parliament (Freeman 2007). In this context, the SAT was "Canada's smallest and arguable most influential group in Afghanistan," allowing it to shape and dictate the political economy of that country (Blatchford 2008; see also Fenton and Elmer 2013). Through the SAT, then, Canada supported the state-building project in Afghanistan – in particular, the centralization of foreign and domestic power in President Karzai's office.

As part of the Kandahar deployments, the Canadian state also worked with local networks of political, economic, and military power. From 2001 to 2011, Canada supported – without public reservation – a series of governors who were involved in corruption, torture, drug trafficking, and human rights abuses. These governors included Gul Agha Sherzai (2001–03), a warlord who dominated Kandahar during the civil war years and who was accused by Human Rights Watch of committing crimes against humanity; Asadullah Khalid (2005–08), a former member of the Northern Alliance who was implicated in the drug trade and in the torture and abuse of detainees in secret jails in Kandahar; Major General Rahmatullah Raufi (2008), a former commander of the ANA who was sacked after challenging local drug lords; and Tooryalai Wesa (2008–present), an ex-patriot acquaintance of President Karzai who has been accused by the Afghan Independent

Human Rights Commission of ordering the "politically motivated" beating of local journalist Mohammad Yar (Hutchinson 2009; Johnson and Leslie 2008, 68; Rennie 2009; Smith 2010a,b; Zia-Zarifi 2004, 7).

In Kandahar province, Canada also collaborated with a number of warlords, including Mullah Naqib, a former Taliban supporter whose militia operated Canadian-made checkpoints north of Kandahar City; Abdul Hakim Jan, a former agent of the Northern Alliance whose militia controlled the police force and water supply of Kandahar; and Gul Agha Sherzai, whose militia filled the power vacuum in Kandahar in 2001. The DND granted large contracts to several of these warlords, including $900,000 to Company Sherzai for "transportation services" and $240,000 for "defence" and "research and development" (Blanchfield and Mayeda 2007; CTV 2007; Taylor 2007b). Canada also worked with the late Ahmed Wali Karzai, a drug trafficker and CIA asset who was known as "the most powerful and feared figure in the Afghan south" (Filkins, Mazzetti, and Risen 2009; Saunders 2008). Throughout the Kandahar deployment, Canadian personnel also worked, albeit with some reservations, with Kandahar police commander Abdul Raziq, a warlord known for drug trafficking, torture, and extrajudicial killings (Aikins 2011; Brewster 2010; Cavendish 2010; Watson 2011, 2012b).

In these ways, Canada supported the *political logic* of the US-led mission. Through the SAT in Kabul and through links to warlords and various governors in Kandahar, Canadian policy had the effect of reinforcing a *neocolonial occupation* – one in which political power was concentrated in the office of President Karzai and in provincial networks of warlords, criminals, and factional leaders (Klassen 2013). In supporting this structure of power, Canada embedded itself within the US-led occupation regime and compromised the goals of the Bonn Process.

Canada's development work in Afghanistan suffered for similar reasons. Before 2005, CIDA's work in Afghanistan focused on long-term development projects unhinged from any particular military mission. With this understanding, CIDA was involved in funding the Afghan National Development Strategy, the Afghan Reconstruction Trust Fund, the Micro Finance Investment Support Facility, the National Area Development Program, the Mine Action Project, and the operational budget of the Afghan government (Joya 2013; Stein and Lang 2007). In 2005, however, CIDA came under pressure from the DND and DFAIT to engage in short-term, quick-impact projects in Kandahar, where Canadian soldiers were engaged in counterinsurgency warfare. By 2007, roughly 50 per cent of CIDA funds were earmarked for Kandahar province, focused primarily on security, basic services, humanitarian aid, border control, national institutions, and reconciliation. As part of Canada's PRT, CIDA also funded three signature projects in education, irrigation, and polio eradication. In these ways, CIDA's work was integrated into the political calculus of the war and occupation. Indeed, CIDA became "a useful counterinsurgency tool," according to Lieutenant-Colonel Tom Doucette, former head of Canada's PRT in Kandahar (CTV 2006b).

Although CIDA funding for demining and disarmament was quite successful (Joya 2013, 295–6), other projects were far less so. For example, the National Solidarity Program, to which CIDA contributed $13 million, created "new village institutions for women" and produced "tangible improvements in access to drinking water and electricity," but did not "appear to have any impact on the access of villagers to infrastructure or result in any changes in economic activity, levels of community trust, or the likelihood of a village suffering a dispute or an attack" (Beath et al. 2010, vii). Similarly, CIDA's allocation of $50 million to the Canadian corporation SNC-Lavalin to rebuild the Dahla dam and irrigation system was an abject failure. As journalist Paul Watson (2012a) discovered, "Afghan farmers and officials complain that the project wasted money, taught villagers to expect handouts and lined corrupt people's pockets." Furthermore, by 2012, the dam's reservoir was "so full of silt that it [could not] hold enough water to get crops through the driest months." In Kandahar, Watson (2012a,b) also found that "the schools Canada built [were] plagued by shoddy construction" and that "[the province] is still called the world's capital of polio."[4] After CIDA cut funding for a girls' school in Kandahar (Watson 2012c), the one legacy of Canada's mission is a fifteen-kilometre stretch of gravel road built in Panjwayi district, for which the Canadian Forces paid more than $1 million in compensation for damaged agricultural goods and property (*Canadian Press* 2011b).

For these reasons, CIDA's practice of aid and development work was not just "divorced from reality," as classified government documents suggest, but incorporated broader contradictions of the military occupation and neoliberal development plan (Blackwell 2012). Indeed, evidence suggests that the aid program was compromised by military objectives; limited by a top-down, outside-in methodology; out of touch with local needs; ineffective at accomplishing goals; linked to warlords and suspect contractors; and possibly designed for public consumption – and political positioning – back home.[5] With this mind, Nipa Banerjee, the former head of CIDA operations in Afghanistan, argues that Canada's development work in Kandahar was a "total" waste. As her fieldwork has since revealed, "[a]ll the projects have failed" and "[n]one of them have been successful" (ibid.).

Canadian corporations, however, *were* successful at winning contracts and making investments in Afghanistan. For example, in the largely untapped Afghan mining sector, which the Pentagon values at more than $1 trillion (Risen 2010), Canadian companies have been highly active. Indeed, with a consortium of Indian firms, Canada's Kilo Mines has laid claim to Afghanistan's Hajigak iron ore deposit, the largest in the world.[6] Canadian companies such as Canaccord Financial Inc., SRK Consulting, and Heenan Blaikie LLP have also advised the Afghan Ministry of Mines on investment, licensing, royalties, tenders, and other legal matters (Johnson 2012). Likewise, Canada's Appleton Consulting, directed by a former colonel of the Canadian Forces, has been involved in contracting projects for numerous Canadian companies, including one for a $179 million apartment complex in Kabul (Proussalidis 2013). Furthermore, at military bases in Kandahar and Kabul, Canadian firms were able to cash in on providing security, food services, transportation, engineering, construction, and accommodations management through the Canadian Forces Contractor Augmentation Program (Engler 2009, 148–51; Perry 2007). To cite one example, SNC-Lavalin, Canada's largest engineering firm, received hundreds of millions of dollars for a range of operations such as rebuilding the Dahla dam and providing information and communications technology to the Canadian Forces in Kandahar province. In 2013, Canadian companies Canarail and Appleton Consulting also signed a $3.7 million contract with the Ministry of Public Works in Afghanistan to conduct a railway feasibility study in northern Afghanistan (*Railway Gazette* 2013). The Canadian defence industry was also able to profit off the war, exporting more than $500 million of weapons and ammunition after 2006 (Berthiaume 2013a). More broadly, the war served as a vehicle for Canadian corporate expansion into Central Asia, particularly in the mining and energy sectors (Foster 2008; Gordon 2013, 219–20). In these ways, the internationalization of Canadian capital worked in conjunction with the internationalization of disciplinary militarism.

Canada's role in the military conflict, though, was the most contentious aspect of the mission. Soon after Canada established the Kandahar PRT, the Senlis Council (2006, 18) reported that "some locals stated that they see the Canadian troops as overly aggressive, indifferent, militaristic, and lacking communication skills" (see Joya 2013, 296). In 2008, journalist Graeme Smith (2008a) found that Canadian soldiers were conducting night raids on villages and residential compounds, inciting "strong resentment among villagers." In his observation, "[t]he combination of abusive behaviour and violent breaking and entry into civilians' homes in the middle of the night stoke[d] almost as much anger and resentment ... as the more lethal air strikes." Journalist Hugo de Grandpré (2006) also reported that Canadian soldiers were kicking down doors in the middle of the night as part of counterinsurgency raids. In light of this activity, the United Nations criticized Canada for refusing to investigate the possible role of JTF2 commandos in "hunt and kill" operations with US and British Special Forces (CBC 2008a).

The Canadian military was also involved in large-scale infantry conflict. In August and September 2006, Canada launched Operation Medusa against Taliban fortifications outside Kandahar City. According to one Canadian officer, "[w]e destroyed infrastructure, tore up villages, to trap the Taliban ... We antagonized the local population, but we didn't rout the Taliban. They were back at us the next day. We lost face with the locals" (Stein and Lang 2007, 220). In June 2009, Canadian soldiers in Nakhoney launched a similar operation, during which they fired tank rounds into a school with the hope of killing Taliban bomb-makers. After failing to find evidence of any bombmaking there, the soldiers targeted a nearby residential compound, "blew open the blue metal gate," and "systematically smashed in the locked doors and searched every room, finding only a neat array of domestic items" (Perkel 2009). According to the United Nations, this type of fighting displaced tens of thousands of people in Kandahar, swelling the size of refugee camps (IRIN 2006). On a more regular basis, Canadian soldiers patrolled Kandahar City, "shooting in the air, like cowboys" (Smith 2008c). As Corporal Paul Demetrick (2008) revealed, "we respond[ed] to hostile fire by indiscriminate bombing and shelling of villages, killing innocent men, women and children; we fire[d] white phosphorus shells (a chemical weapon outlawed by the Geneva Conventions due to the horrific way it burns human beings) into vineyards where it was known Afghan insurgents were deployed; we hand[ed] over prisoners of war to Afghan authorities, who torture[d] them; and we [shot] and kill[ed] a 2-year-old Afghan boy and his 4-year-old sister." Indeed, Canadian soldiers were guilty of killing civilians, including children, on a regular basis. Consider the following examples:

- on 14 March 2006, Canadian forces fired into a taxi, killing Nasrat Ali Hassan (CBC 2006);
- on 22 August 2006, Canadian personnel killed a ten-year-old boy on a motorcycle (Smith 2006a);
- on 12 December 2006, Canadian troops killed a ninety-year-old man at a checkpoint (CTV 2006a);
- on 17 February 2007, Canadian forces shot and killed an unarmed man near Kandahar City (CBC 2007a);
- on 16 November 2007, Canadian soldiers shot and killed an Afghan civilian in a taxi (CBC 2007c);
- on 30 January 2008, Canadian soldiers fired into a civilian vehicle, killing a man and wounding others (*La Presse canadienne* 2008);
- on 27 February 2008, Canadian soldiers killed a man in his car in Kandahar City (Benlon 2008);
- on 27 July 2008, Canadian troops shot and killed a four-year-old girl and her two-year-old brother in Panjwayi district (CBC 2008b);
- on 18 September 2008, Canadian troops shot at a civilian vehicle, killing an occupant (CBC 2008c);
- on 24 February 2009, three children were killed after allegedly playing with artillery shells left behind by Canadian artillery units (Brewster 2009);
- on 22 July 2009, Canadian soldiers killed a young girl after firing on a motorcycle driver approaching their patrol (CBC 2009a).

As many journalists disclosed, Canadian military operations often engendered public demonstrations, including a number of "death to Canada" protests in Kandahar (CBC 2007b, 2009b; Panetta 2008b; Smith 2006b). In addition, school-aged children often pelted Canadian patrols with rocks, and by 2009 a polled majority in Kandahar wanted US and Canadian troops to leave (*Canadian Press* 2008a; Cordesman 2009, 32; Freeze 2009). In this context, the Taliban took control of most of Kandahar province, and Canadian troops were forced to abandon three outposts in Mushan and Panjwayi districts (Smith 2008b).

Despite these failures, Canadian officials maintained a posture of aggressive confidence and, indeed, racism. Throughout the mission, DND spokespeople described the Taliban as "detestable murderers and scumbags," "predators," "radical murderers and killers," a "threat to nations around the world," "Indian[s]," "Nazis," "hornets," "snakes," "rats," "[m]ole[s]," "dead dogs," and "terrorists," who are "insidious by their nature," "detest our freedoms," and want to "break our society" (Campion-Smith 2005; CBC 2008d; Evans 2005; Freeze 2009; Koring 2006; Leblanc 2005; Montpetit 2010; Stein and Lang 2007, 200, 233; Wattie 2003). As the mission spiralled downward, the DND spied on public critics of the war and refused to acknowledge many access to information requests (Armstrong et al. 2009; Berthiaume 2012b; Esau 2008; Pugliese 2007). Under the leadership of Chief of Defence Staff General Rick Hillier, it also blamed the democratic debate in Canada, instead of the mission itself, for the escalation of violence in Kandahar (*Canadian Press* 2008b).[7]

The DND was also implicated in the torture and abuse of detainees in Afghanistan (Razack 2013). In January 2002, Canadian soldiers handed over three detainees to the US military without prisoner-of-war assurances. As the DND prepared for the mission in Kandahar in 2005, Hillier co-signed a detainee agreement with his Afghan counterpart – outside the norms of inter-state agreement-making – that failed to include monitoring rights and Red Cross approval (Stein and Lang 2007, chap. 14). In April 2007, the *Globe and Mail* published interviews with thirty former detainees who had experienced savage beatings, electrocution, whippings, extreme cold, and choking at the hands of Afghan authorities (Smith 2007). In September 2007, reports surfaced that Canada could not account for fifty prisoners previously transferred to Afghan officials. According to classified documents, the Harper government knew that detainees faced "extrajudicial executions, disappearances, torture and detention without trial," yet repeatedly argued in public that such complaints were "allegations of the Taliban" (Koring 2007; Panetta 2008a). Between September 2007 and February 2008, the Canadian government also was aware that the governor of Kandahar, Asadullah Khalid, was running secret jails in which detainees were abused and tortured (Koring 2008). Afghan journalist Jawed Yazamy also accused Canadian soldiers of having him arrested as an "enemy combatant" by US forces, who inflicted torture and abuse on the journalist over a ten-month period (Blackwell 2008; Weber 2008). According to a fact-finding report by the United Nations Assistance Mission to Afghanistan (2013, 5), "evidence of torture was most prevalent in [the National Directorate of Security] and ANP facilities in Kandahar," the key province in which Canada was engaged in counterinsurgency and security sector programming and support. In April 2008, Canadian soldiers themselves were accused of roughing up prisoners before transferring them to Afghan authorities, and in October 2008 a Canadian soldier killed an unarmed suspect the day after being quoted in the media as saying, "I imagine we'll do some aggressive patrolling, some defensive work and try and root out the Taliban and kill and capture them" (Armstrong et al. 2009).

The Canadian practice of counterinsurgency, then, fit into a wider pattern of violence and repression in Afghanistan. Canadian troops were engaged in a constant war against the Taliban and their popular base in Kandahar, and were implicated in a spectrum of problematic activities, from killing civilians and raiding homes to abusing detainees and transferring them to torture. In doing so, the Canadian Forces collaborated with various warlords and failed to effect development through aid or PRT projects. For these reasons, Canada's mission was a microcosm of the broader failures of the war and occupation. More than this, it was an expression of the bona fide *imperialism* of the US-led mission – and of the new grand strategy of the state and power bloc in Canada. As such, it was a pro-active effort at joining empire.

Damming the Flood: Haiti and the New Imperialism

On 29 February 2004, the elected government of Haiti was toppled by an armed insurgency backed by US, French, and Canadian military forces. On that day, Haiti's president, Jean-Bertrand Aristide, was forced onto a plane by US Marines, who flew him to the Central African Republic.[8] Over the next several years, Canadian security personnel were stationed in Haiti on successive UN missions. After the 2010 earthquake, Canadian soldiers were again sent to Haiti on a security and reconstruction deployment. As part of these missions, Canadian governments allocated more than $1 billion in aid and development funding. In this context, Haiti became the second-most-important site of Canadian foreign policy practices over the past decade, and thus vital to the new grand strategy of the state and power bloc. How did the new Canadian foreign policy work in Haiti? What were the driving forces of this policy, how was it implemented, and what were the results?

Haiti and the Empire of Capital

Canada's role in Haiti must be viewed in the context of history. Once the pride of French colonialism, since the early 1800s Haiti has suffered from economic dependency, military occupation, political authoritarianism, ecological destruction, racial hierarchies, and civil wars. For example, after waging the first and only successful slave revolution in history, the Haitian people were forced – under the threat of a French naval blockade in 1825 – to pay an indemnity of 150 million francs – a debt that was paid off only in 1947. Under duress, the new Haitian republic was also forced to discount taxes on French shipping activities, resulting in a major loss of income for such a trade-dependent economy. The revolution itself destroyed the agricultural basis of the country, and up to one-third of the population was killed. Throughout the nineteenth century, diplomatic isolation, internal racial conflicts, devastating hurricanes and earthquakes, local protests and rebellions, and economic penetration by foreign capital further restricted Haiti's development. Taken together, these factors positioned the country on a path of economic and political dependence (Fatton 2006; James 1989).

Locked in this position, Haiti was subject to new patterns of exploitation and domination – now under the aegis of the American empire. By the late 1800s, US capital was highly invested in Haiti, especially in the sugar and fruit industries. To protect this property, the US Navy entered Haitian waters twenty-four times between 1849 and 1913. In 1915, US Marines occupied Haiti, where they would remain for nearly two decades. During this period, the United States dominated nearly every facet of Haiti's political economy. It imposed a new constitution, suppressed democratic institutions, legalized foreign ownership of land, instituted labour conscription, privatized the national bank, vetted and vetoed all government policies, nurtured authoritarian leaders, built infrastructure projects for trade, and established a national guard *cum* national army (Schmidt 1995). Upon leaving Haiti in 1934, the US military also secured a twenty-five-year banana contract for US Standard Fruit and Steamship Company (Podur 2012, 13–14).

In 1950, the Haitian army staged a military coup, replacing the authoritarian yet populist government of Dumarsais Estimé with the anti-communist government of Paul Magloire. In 1957, François "Papa Doc" Duvalier took control of the regime, which he would dominate until his death in 1971. Backed by the United States, his government killed tens of thousands of people (and exiled many thousands more), tortured prisoners, and expropriated millions of public funds for personal use. After the death of Papa Doc, his son Jean-Claude "Baby Doc" Duvalier extended the regime until February 1986, when popular protests drove him to France on a US Air Force jet. The protests were led by the *Lavalas* (the Creole word for "flood") movement of Aristide, a

Catholic priest in the liberation theology tradition. The politics of *Lavalas* involved democratic transformation, economic and legal justice, and an end to corruption (R. Robinson 2007). To contain this movement, the United States helped establish a National Governing Council and Intelligence Service, which ruled Haiti, often with extreme violence, after Baby Doc's departure. Nevertheless, the popular movement escalated over the next four years, forcing a presidential election on 16 December 1990. In the country's first fair and free election, Aristide swept to power with 67 per cent of the vote, against the 14 per cent won by the US-favoured candidate, Marc Bazin, a former World Bank official. The poor majority of Haiti thus voted en masse for the leader of *Lavalas* and its popular program.

Aristide's tenure – however brief – was true to the social movements out of which he emerged (R. Robinson 2007). Indeed, before he was overthrown in a military coup, Aristide managed to balance the budget and rationalize the federal service, while keeping his commitments to *Lavalas* and its social base. For example, he launched investigations of past human rights abuses, began dismantling the security services, and subsidized basic goods for poor people. These policies, though, were too threatening to Haitian elites, who backed the 30 September 1991 coup. Over the next three years, the military government murdered more than five thousand people and generated a refugee crisis. Although the United States formally opposed, and even partially embargoed, the military government, through the CIA it worked to fund the death squad, FRAPH (*Front Révolutionnaire Armé pour le Progrès d'Haiti*, later called the *Front pour l'Avancement et le Progrès Haitien* [Front for the Advancement and Progress of Haiti]), which targeted *Lavalas* and its supporters (Hamm 1994; Nairn 1995; Whitney 1996). The military government, however, was unable to stabilize the country or repress the popular movements, much to the ire of Washington.

In this context, the Bill Clinton administration decided to reinstate Aristide under Marine occupation in 1994. In the UN-mediated agreement, Aristide was forced to accept several concessions, including the privatization of state-owned enterprises, the reduction of tariffs on imported food, a government of national unity, an end to his term in February 1996, and the prime ministership of US ally, Smarck Michel. Yet, back in office, Aristide maintained the program of *Lavalas*. He refused to privatize state assets, increased taxes on the wealthy, instituted land reform, raised the minimum wage, re-established ties with Cuba, funded literacy campaigns, established a truth commission on human rights, and dismantled the Haitian National Army and the FRAPH. He also stood aside during the 1996 presidential elections, which were won by René Préval, a more neoliberal candidate but one who also belonged to Aristide's *Lavalas* movement and had a popular base.

For all of these reasons, Aristide was elected, on 26 November 2000, to a second term that commenced on 7 February 2001.[9] Over the next three years, as the *Washington Post* noted, he "pushed with mixed success a populist agenda of higher minimum wages, school construction, literacy programs, higher taxes on the rich and other policies that have angered an opposition movement run largely by a mulatto elite that has traditionally controlled Haiti's economy" (Wilson 2003). Aristide also demanded from France a reimbursement of the post-revolution indemnity, worth US$21 billion at the time (Farmer 2004). In such efforts, *Fanmi Lavalas*, the political party of Haiti's social movements, supported Aristide. *Fanmi Lavalas* had won decisive majorities in the May 2000 legislative and local elections, described by the Organization of American States (OAS 2000) as "a great success for the Haitian population, which turned out in large and orderly numbers to chose both their local and national governments."[10]

As the power structures and class composition of the state began to shift, though, a new opposition emerged to Aristide and *Fanmi Lavalas* from both internal and external sources. First, the United States and its allies launched a destabilization campaign against the Haitian government, particularly by blocking foreign aid. For example, under US pressure, the Inter-American Development Bank froze four pre-approved loans for Haiti (Burron 2012, 73), and the US government itself terminated bilateral aid payments. Deprived of these resources, the Haitian government and economy were severely handicapped. As the Bank reported at the time, "the major factor behind [Haiti's] economic stagnation is the withholding of both foreign grants and loans, associated with the international community's response to the critical political impasse" (Engler and Fenton 2005, 49). In the words of Jeffery Sachs (2004), the aid embargo was "squeezing Haiti's economy dry and causing untold suffering for its citizens," through "a balance-of-payments crisis, a rise in inflation, and a collapse of living standards."[11]

Second, an internal opposition was mobilized with critical foreign backing (Bogdanich and Nordberg 2006). This opposition included the Democratic Convergence, a coalition of parties funded by the International Republican Institute, and the Group of 184, a coalition of middle-class NGOs, business elites, and religious figures who opposed

Aristide and *Fanmi Lavalas*. The combined opposition demanded an annulment of the 2000 elections, and encouraged protests in the streets, leading to several clashes with government supporters.[12] As leaders of the Democratic Convergence told the *Washington Post*, the goal of the opposition was to provoke a US invasion, "this time to get rid of Aristide and rebuild the disbanded Haitian Army." Alternatively, it hoped for the CIA to "train and equip Haitian officers exiled in the neighbouring Dominican Republic so they could stage a comeback themselves" (Hallward 2004).

In this context, the fall of 2003 became a watershed for both the government and the opposition. The national economy was in crisis, the government was starved of resources, foreign-backed NGOs were serving the bulk of living requirements,[13] and former military and death squad members were launching armed attacks from the Dominican Republic. On 5 February 2004, the insurgency began a full-scale invasion, and carried out violent attacks government institutions and civilian infrastructure *en route* to Port-au-Prince (Human Rights Watch 2004b,c). Although the capital was surrounded by the end of February, the insurgency had little capacity to capture the city or to hold the towns and villages it had overrun previously. It lacked support among the poor majority, and failed to spark an insurrection in the capital. For these reasons, the militaries of the United States, France, and Canada were impelled to invade Haiti. Indeed, it was only through the invasion of the UN-sanctioned and US-led Multilateral Interim Force that the government was toppled and the coup secured.

The coup broke with Haiti's constitution and allowed a "Council of the Wise" to establish an interim government led by Gérard Latortue, a Haitian businessman who had been living in Florida. The coup was condemned by both the Caribbean Community (CARICOM) and the African Union, but the United States, the European Union, and the UN Security Council recognized the new government. *Fanmi Lavalas*, the most popular party in Haiti, was excluded from the government and soon became a target of political repression.

In fact, the coup unleashed a wave of violence against *Lavalas* and the poor communities in which it was based. As Human Rights Watch (2004a) documented, the armed gangs of the insurgency carried out "reprisal killings of Aristide supporters in Port-au-Prince." Furthermore, "U.S., French and Canadian forces ... [showed] little indication of challenging the rebels' control over the city." Over the next month, up to a thousand politically motivated murders occurred in the capital and elsewhere (Podur 2012, 65). A broader campaign of repression also targeted unions, strikers, workers' co-ops, and other institutions of the popular movements. US Marines used live fire to disperse protests in Port-au-Prince and even launched armed raids in the *Lavalas* neighbourhoods of Bel Air and Cité Soleil, killing dozens of people (ibid., 60). According to *The Lancet*, in the twenty-two months following the coup, Port-au-Prince experienced approximately eight thousand murders, thirty-five thousand rapes, and thousands of armed threats, many of which were orchestrated by coup forces (Kolbe and Hutson 2006). As Human Rights Watch (2005) observed, "the interim government's failure to restore stability left a power vacuum allowing armed groups to flourish." Indeed, "[t]he rampant violence in the capital ... left hundreds of persons killed and wounded." The US State Department (United States 2006) concurred, finding evidence of "arbitrary killings" and "disappearances" by the Haitian National Police, "overcrowding and poor sanitation in prisons," "prolonged pretrial detention and legal impunity," "widespread corruption in all branches of government," and "use of excessive – and sometimes deadly – force in making arrests or controlling demonstrations." The coup thus *precipitated* a human rights debacle in Haiti; it unleashed a global class war that suppressed democracy and killed thousands of people.

In April 2004, the UN Security Council authorized 6,700 troops and 1,622 civilian police for the UN Stabilization Mission in Haiti, known by the French acronym MINUSTAH. The formal purpose of MINUSTAH was to secure the peace for the interim government. However, as US Ambassador Janet Sanderson wrote in a classified embassy cable, "the UN Stabilization Mission in Haiti [became] an indispensable tool in realizing the core USG [US government] policy interests." These interests included suppressing "resurgent populist and anti-market economy political forces" and a possible "exodus of seaborne migrants," while maintaining "foreign and domestic investment." In these regards, MINUSTAH was "a financial and regional security bargain for the USG." In particular, it helped relieve US military forces for "military commitments elsewhere." In addition, it "help[ed] other major donors – led by Canada and followed up by the EU, France, Spain, Japan and others – justify their bilateral assistance *domestically*." Indeed, "[w]ithout [MINUSTAH], we would be getting far less help from our hemispheric and European partners in *managing Haiti*" (United States 2008, emphases added).

Re-imposing a neoliberal program was the ultimate aim of this "managing" project. For example, during this period, the US government worked with contractors for Hanes, Levi's, and Fruit of the Loom to block a minimum wage increase for Haiti's textile workers, the lowest paid in the hemisphere. In a classified cable, Ambassador Sanderson wrote that "[a] more visible and active engagement ... may be critical to resolving the issue of the minimum wage and its protest 'spin-off' – or risk the political environment spiraling out of control" (Coughlin and Ives 2011). In 2006, the US Congress also passed the Haitian Hemispheric Opportunity through Partnership Encouragement (HOPE) Act, offering Haitian manufacturing exporters preferential trade incentives. After the coup, the World Bank also issued loans to Haiti, including US$52.6 million for debt servicing. As the Bank put it at the time, "[t]he Transitional Government provide[s] a window of opportunity for implementing economic governance reforms ... that may be hard for a future government to undo" (Podur 2012, 64, 87). In March 2005, the Inter-American Development Bank (2005) also released US$270 million in previously blocked funding. The goal of these efforts, it seems, was to maintain Haiti's role as a low-wage export platform in the region and to secure the interim government for the neoliberal project of its international backers.

Although polls "showed that Aristide was still the only figure in Haiti with a favorability rating above 50%," as US Ambassador James Foley explained in another classified cable (Ives and Herz 2011), the United States and the UN worked aggressively to prevent his return and to organize new elections without Lavalas's participation. In this context, Lavalas was forced to back René Préval in the presidential election of 7 February 2006. The election was compromised by systematic irregularities, which appeared designed to force a run-off with the candidate of choice of the United States. However, after Haitians protested across the country, Préval was eventually declared the winner with 50.15 per cent of the vote (Podur 2012, 119–21). Once again, the poor majority played a critical role in securing the election, albeit in a highly repressive environment.

The earthquake of 12 January 2010, however, destroyed any vestige of popular sovereignty in Haiti. Although no serious security threat existed at the time,[14] the United States responded with a military invasion of twenty-two thousand troops. In the process, the US military took command of the Port-au-Prince airport, gave priority to US military landings, and turned away flights from the World Food Program and Doctors

Without Borders. On 22 January, the Haitian government granted the US military formal control of all ports, roads, and airports in the country. In these ways, the United States led an international response that was "militarized, controlled from without, and given in such a way as to undermine Haitian capacity and sovereignty" (ibid., 139).

The reconstruction program evinced similar features. At an international donors conference in March 2010, US$5.3 billion was promised for aid and reconstruction in Haiti. A year later, though, only US$1.28 billion had been delivered. Over this period, "[n]ot a cent of the $1.15 billion the U.S. promised for rebuilding [had] arrived" (Katz and Mendoza 2010).[15] As a result, 90 per cent of the rubble had yet to be cleared, and 800,000 people were still living in temporary camps (Podur 2012, 140). In this context, more than 8,000 people were killed by a cholera epidemic that was brought to Haiti by UN military forces (Sontag 2012).

As the human crisis persisted, transnational capital sought new claims on Haiti. As then-US Ambassador Kenneth Merten remarked in a secret cable, "The Gold Rush Is On!" "As Haiti digs out from the earthquake," he explained, "different [US] companies are moving in to sell their concepts, products and services." Working with USAID, these companies accessed nearly US$200 million in relief and reconstruction contracts – only 2.5 per cent of which went to Haitian firms (Herz and Ives 2011). For the US State Department (United States 2011, 29), the purpose of reconstruction was "to lay the foundations for small and medium size businesses to prosper and to attract modern companies into competitive industrial parks to take advantage of Haiti's workforce and nascent economic potential."[16] To this end, the United States established the Interim Haitian Recovery Commission (IHRC), which took command of Haiti's domestic budget and foreign aid funds. According to Haitian-American sociologist Alex Dupuy (2011), the IHRC, co-chaired by Bill Clinton and Haitian Prime Minister Max Bellerive, "effectively displaced the Haitian government and [took] charge of setting priorities for reconstruction" (see also Edmonds 2013). As Dupuy (2011) elaborates:

the IHRC has not done much. Less than 10 per cent of the $9 billion pledged by foreign donors has been delivered, and not all of that money has been spent. Other than rebuilding the international airport and clearing the principal urban arteries of rubble, no major infrastructure rebuilding – roads, ports, housing, communications – has begun. According to news reports, of the more than 1,500 U.S. contracts doled out worth [US]$267 million, only 20, worth [US]$4.3 million, have gone to Haitian firms. The rest have gone to U.S. firms, which almost exclusively use U.S. suppliers. Although these foreign contractors employ Haitians, mostly on a cash-for-work basis, the bulk of the money and profits are reinvested in the United States ... That same logic applies to the 1,000 or so foreign NGOs that are operating in Haiti.

The earthquake thus consolidated what Canadian academic Justin Podur (2012) calls the "new dictatorship" in Haiti: a structure of domination and exploitation that bridges the political and economic interests of domestic and foreign elites. In this structure, little space exists for popular sovereignty; foreign militaries impose order with domestic security agencies, global NGOs deliver basic services for survival, elections are corrupted by political repression, and transnational corporations operate without limitations. Through such mechanisms of exploitation and domination, the US-led mission has "managed Haiti." With this in mind, how has Canada engaged Haiti since 2001?

A "Duty to Protect"? Canada's Role in "Managing Haiti"

The academic literature on Canadian foreign policy in Haiti tends to offer two perspectives. One submits that Canada's interventions since 2001 were in genuine support of humanitarian assistance and peace-building (Gordon 2004; Shamsie 2006, 2012). The other argues that Canada's role was more reactive or subservient to US dictates, especially in the wake of the war in Iraq (Stein and Lang 2007, 126–7). Both perspectives are inadequate, however, to understanding Canada's role in the coup and its aftermath. In particular, they ignore Canada's active role in plotting the coup, suppressing the resistance, and imposing the "new dictatorship" on Haiti. In these ways, Canadian foreign policy was more in tune with a class-based strategy of empire.

This strategy was implemented in five key ways. First, Canada worked with allied partners to undercut the legitimacy of Aristide's presidency – in particular, by recognizing the opposition's political agenda and by negotiating plans for new elections.[17] For example, between 2001 and 2004, Canada worked through the OAS to "mediate talks between Aristide and opposition groups" (Shamsie 2006, 212). It also endorsed a CARICOM proposal for a new round of voting to follow a series of "short-term, confidence-building measures" (ibid.).

Furthermore, as the armed insurgency gained traction, Canada ignored Aristide's request for international peacekeepers, declined to criticize the opposition's intransigence, and gave "tacit approval" to the US policy of regime change (ibid., 213).

Second, Canada participated in the US-led destabilization campaign – for example, by supporting the US effort to block loans to Haiti from the Inter-American Development Bank (CHRGJ et al. 2008, 14; Ramachandran and Walz 2012, 3). In doing so, Canada took the position, according to a DFAIT memorandum dated 25 January 2002, that "[t]he [Inter-American Development Bank] (with the support of Canada as a member of the Council) continues to require a green light from the OAS ... before supporting the resumption of large scale assistance [to Haiti]." At the OAS, this minority position was taken with full knowledge that "Aristide must access blocked foreign aid or continue to lose ground," as an Intelligence Assessment from the Privy Council Office stated a month later (Fenton 2008).

Unlike the United States, however, Canada maintained a bilateral aid program for Haiti, but cut it drastically after 2000 and sought out new, non-governmental recipients. In particular, CIDA funding underwent "a shift in support to civil society" in Haiti (CIDA 2004, 8). Indeed, in the years before the coup, CIDA delivered $67.3 million to a network of NGOs linked to the Group of 184 as well as to other "small organizations and coalitions that represented Haiti's small middle class" (Burron 2012, 79). It also funded several Canadian-based NGOs, which later would endorse both the coup and the military intervention (Barry-Shaw and Jay 2012, 112–34).[18] As CIDA (2004, 12) reported on these efforts, "emphasis on non-governmental actors ... contributed to the establishment of parallel systems of service delivery, eroding legitimacy, capacity and will of the state to deliver key services." In CIDA's (ibid., 9) assessment, "by identifying a *change driver* (issue or sector with broad support), engaging *a coalition of key players*, and providing *sufficient resources*," Canada's support for "civil society initiatives and Canadian NGO partners produced relatively good qualitative results." In these ways, Canada worked to isolate the Haitian state from international financial networks, while providing material support to the political opposition on the ground. As CIDA itself recognized, these efforts undermined the Aristide government and empowered the opposition.

Third, Canada played an active role in planning the coup. On 31 January and 1 February 2003, the Canadian government hosted a meeting of foreign ministers from Europe, the United States, and Latin America (excluding Haiti) at Meech Lake, Quebec. Hosted by Liberal MP Denis Paradis, then Secretary of State for Latin America, Africa and the Francophonie, the so-called Ottawa Initiative was focused on "the current political situation in Haiti," and was "envisaged to be of a restricted and intimate nature ... in order to facilitate a free exchange of views and brainstorming among the invited participants." According to journalist Michel Vastel (2003), the participants agreed that Aristide "must go," that the Haitian army must be reconstituted, and that a "Kosovo-model" trusteeship might be organized for "protecting civilians."[19] On 5 February, Liberal cabinet minister Pierre Pettigrew met in Montreal with Paul Arcelin, a key figure of the Haitian opposition who helped coordinate both the insurgency and the coup (Bogdanich and Nordberg 2006; McCarthy, Sallot, and Knox 2004; Montgomery 2004; Podur 2012, 53).

Canada's role in planning the coup was evident in other ways as well. For example, on 11 February, Kenneth Cook, Canada's ambassador to Haiti, sent a confidential memo titled "Meeting with US Ambassador" to the Privy Council Office and DFAIT. In it, he implied that the United States and Canada were discussing the possibility of a military intervention under the mantle of a "duty to protect" civilians.[20] As he put it, "[t]he situation we face is not only one of a struggle for power, it involves a humanitarian crisis and the potential to permanently change the course of Haitian history. President Aristide is clearly a serious aggravating factor in the current crisis and unless he gives dramatic early signs that he is implementing the CARICOM road map, then the OAS, CARICOM and possibly UN will have to consider the options including whether a case can be made for the duty to protect" (Fenton and Jay 2006). In short, the evidence suggests that Canada was directly engaged in planning scenarios for a military intervention and political transition. Although Canada had been arguing publicly for a power-sharing arrangement between the government and the opposition in Haiti, it was also working on surreptitious plans for regime change and military engagement. In these efforts, Canada used the notion of the "responsibility to protect" as a justification for these policies.

Fourth, Canada played an instrumental role in effecting the coup and securing the interim government. As the coup began on 29 February 2003, Canada's JTF2 special commandos secured the airport for US military forces, which flew Aristide out of the country (CBC 2010). In the aftermath of the coup, up to five hundred Canadian troops also deployed in Port-au-Prince. In this role, they built a base for US military forces and oversaw the repression of *Lavalas* by armed insurgents, who were not disarmed or reined in by the Multilateral Interim Force (Podur 2012, 60). Over the following year, Canadian security personnel engaged in counterinsurgency operations against the *Lavalas* movement. According to a November 2004 study by the School of Law at the University of Miami, Canadian police officers were "engaged in daily guerrilla warfare" in Port-au-Prince (Griffin 2004, 40). Canada's draft counterinsurgency manual (Canada 2008b, 3.18) also acknowledged that Canadian forces were "conducting [counterinsurgency] operations ... in Haiti in early 2004." In the years that followed, Canada also worked to reconstitute the Haitian national police, particularly through the UN Civilian Police Force commanded by David Beer of the Royal Canadian Mounted Police. Indeed, CIDA dedicated tens of millions of dollars to this project, which integrated former military and paramilitary elements into new security services.[21]

Canada worked to stabilize the interim government in other ways as well. For example, in July 2004, Canada pledged $147 million for Haiti at a donor's conference in Washington (CIDA 2004, 22). As part of these efforts, it played a leading role in creating the Interim Cooperation Framework (ICF), which coordinated more than $1 billion in new aid for Haiti, particularly for organizations of the Group of 184 and for numerous international NGOs (Burron 2012, 84; Shamsie 2006, 216). As Yasmine Shamsie (2009) reveals, the ICF was focused primarily on attracting foreign investment into Haiti's low-wage export-processing zones, and ignored issues of rural reform and agricultural development. Canada also released $1 million for democratic institution building in Haiti through La Francophonie (Podur 2012, 62–3). As part of its focus on security sector reform, CIDA paid the salary of Haiti's deputy justice minister, Philippe Vixamar, for months after the coup (Griffin 2004, 32). In 2006, Canada established a Country Development Programming Framework in Haiti for allocating $555 million of reconstruction and development funding over a five-year period, particularly for state institution building (Burron 2012, 85). In the same year, CIDA also supported the widely compromised presidential elections. As Neil Burron (ibid., 86) explains, "[w]hile CIDA's technical and financial support ... to organize the elections were not in themselves objectionable, Canada's silence on the electoral process's shortcomings was. Despite funding an international observation mission, Canada and its partners failed to call international attention to numerous issues throughout the electoral process, including the imprisonment of Lavalas leader Father Gérard Jean-Juste, insufficient voter registration centres, and pro-government forces attacking Lavalas rallies." In all of these ways, Canada worked to certify and cement the post-coup order in Haiti, in alliance with the United States, Haitian elites, and international NGOs.

Finally, Canada's intervention involved a project of neoliberal market enforcement. For instance, in December 2004, CIDA (2004, 22) reported that "some Canadian companies are looking to shift garment production to Haiti." Among these was Montreal-based Gilden Activewear, which employed approximately eight thousand workers in Haiti's export manufacturing zones. Soon after the coup, Canadian mining companies KWG Resources and St. Genevieve Resources began prospecting for copper and gold in Haiti. Beyond supporting these particular corporate interests, the Canadian state worked with allies to advance a broader program of neoliberal transformation in Haiti, including "strengthening the private sector, which [was] viewed as the primary engine of economic growth," and "re-establishing Haiti's assembly manufacturing export sector" (Shamsie 2006, 216). In 2005, the World Bank noted that Canada was also working on "decentralizing" – that is, privatizing – Haiti's electrical system (Engler and Fenton 2005, 96, 98). Furthermore, CIDA (2004, 22) identified a long list of "potential business opportunities" for Canadian firms in Haiti, including "agriculture and agri-food, automotive parts and equipment, building products, education, energy, health and medical industries, information and communication technologies, maritime transportation and ports, services industries, capital projects (road construction and improvement) and tourism." CIDA (2006) also assisted the preparation of Haiti's Poverty Reduction Strategy Paper, and then boasted that Haiti "had achieved the zero-deficit objectives of the International Monetary Fund" (Gordon 2013, 228).

Before the earthquake, then, Canada's role in Haiti was characterized by active forms of disciplinary militarism, cooperative specialization with US policies, selective engagement with multilateral processes, and neoliberal market enforcement. In the process, Canadian policies worked against the stated goals of peacebuilding, development, and humanitarian assistance; on the contrary, they worked *for* the exploitation and domination of Haiti by leading factions of capital in the country and around the world.

After the quake, the same agenda was pursued in a prime example of what Naomi Klein (2007) calls "disaster capitalism." For instance, when the earthquake struck, Canada deployed two thousand troops as part of an expanded UN mission. It also hosted a "Friends of Haiti" meeting on 25 January 2010 to coordinate assistance measures. To the public, Foreign Affairs Minister Lawrence Cannon claimed that Canada's involvement was "all about solidarity ... all about helping this country [Haiti] in its hour of need" (Harris 2010). According to classified DFAIT documents, however, Ottawa's real concern was that "[political] fragility has increased the risks of a popular uprising [in Haiti], and has fed the rumour that ex-president Jean-Bertrand Aristide, currently in exile in South Africa, wants to organize a return to power." To avert these scenarios, Canada's mission was "to contain the risks of a popular uprising." In addition, it was to pursue a neoliberal reconstruction effort – one that would effect a "real paradigm shift" and "involve a fundamental, structural rebuilding of society and its systems from the ground up, beginning with the very fabric of society" (Montpetit 2011). Perhaps because of these calculations, the Canadian state's interest in aid and relief efforts was languid and sluggish. Indeed, nearly a year after the quake, the Canadian government had released only 35 per cent of the funds it had promised to deliver – that is, only $65.15 million out of the $220 million pledged (Minsky 2010). Although, by September 2012, Canada had disbursed $657 million in humanitarian and recovery assistance, 97 per cent of these funds bypassed the Haitian government, going instead to the UN, the Red Cross, and international NGOs (Canada 2012b). In such ways, Canada worked with US grand strategies for Haiti and compounded that country's political, economic, and social crises.[22]

Conclusion

Canada's interventions in Afghanistan and Haiti reveal much about the new Canadian foreign policy. In particular, they illuminate the concrete application of a new grand strategy by the state and power bloc – a strategy of disciplinary militarism, stratified multilateralism, cooperative specialization with US global primacy, and neoliberal market enforcement. In both cases, these elements of the new grand strategy were manifest as integrated components of a new imperial policy.

For example, in both Afghanistan and Haiti, the Canadian state engaged in disciplinary militarism in the form of counterinsurgency and Special Forces operations. It also engaged in selective multilateralism by supporting UN or NATO initiatives that worked in conjunction with US grand strategies or dominant class interests in Canada. In both conflicts, the Canadian state also offered specialized functions to the broader project of regime change or military occupation – for instance, by allocating aid and development funding, training police and security forces, and financing elections of limited legitimacy. In Afghanistan and Haiti, the Canadian state also advanced a policy of neoliberal market enforcement through drafting free market development models, writing procedures for transnational investment, privatizing government assets, and funding NGOs as an alternative to social program spending.

Through such mechanisms, the Canadian state sought to consummate a new grand strategy. It reinforced the internationalization of capital as well as the structures of exploitation and domination that constitute the world order. It worked to position itself as a secondary power in the hierarchy of states and to consolidate a machinery of government for capitalist class power at home and abroad. In doing so, it engaged in a class-based project of *joining empire* – of making Canada "one of the big boys" in the economic, political, and military structures of global capitalism.

At the same time, Canada's missions in Afghanistan and Haiti were clear-cut failures. In Afghanistan, for instance, the Canadian military was unable to defeat the Taliban insurgency or to achieve any notable political victories. In this context, the majority of Canadians – and of Afghans in Kandahar – came to oppose the military mission (see Klassen and Albo 2013). In a similar way, Canada's strategy for Haiti failed to advance a consensual – let alone a democratic – process of state-building and development.[23] To some extent, then, the "new dictatorship" in Haiti is a sign of fundamental policy failures and of a *weak hegemony* in Canadian state practices at home and abroad. For these reasons, one should expect to observe new patterns of contentious resistance, not just in Haiti and Afghanistan, but across the Empire of Capital in which Canadian foreign policy operates.

Conclusion: Canada and Empire –
The Counterconsensus

In November 2012, Canada's *CBC News* released details of a classified "foreign policy plan" that the federal Conservative government had been drafting for more than a year (Weston 2012). The plan was comprehensive in terms of linking the political, economic, and military dimensions of Canadian foreign policy. But the primary concern was with the competitive reach of Canadian capital in emerging market economies. As the government put it, "[w]e need to be frank with ourselves – our influence and credibility with some of these new and emerging powers is not as strong as it needs to be and could be." In fact, "Canada's record over past decades has been to arrive late in some key emerging markets. We cannot do so in the future."

To address this problem, the new foreign policy plan outlined a four-fold strategy. First, "Canada's trade and investment relations with new economies, leading with Asia, must deepen, and as a country we must become more relevant to our new partners." Second, "[t]o succeed we will need to pursue political relationships in tandem with economic interests even where political interests or values may not align." Third, "[w]hile Canada may participate, with its allies, in international security missions for broader strategic or other reasons, security and development engagements in key countries of interest will seek to address Canada's domestic security, economic and other priorities." And fourth, to achieve all of the above, "the U.S. will remain our bedrock partner." Indeed, "it is critical that we do not lose sight of the fact that our relationship with the United States is overall highly beneficial, and the vast majority of our trade is irritant-free."

As this book has demonstrated, these facets of a new foreign policy are natural extensions of a changing political economy and class

structure in Canada. In particular, they express a logic of internationalization in the economic, social, and political structures of the country,
a logic that dictates a full engagement with the global economy and
American empire. Viewed in this light, the four prongs of the draft plan
are consistent with the neoliberal project for Canada. They are commensurate with the global expansion of Canadian capital, the recomposition
of the corporate network around transnational actors, and the restructuring of the state in line with dominant class interests.

The argument I have presented in this book is that all these factors
have combined to generate a new foreign policy agenda. In the 1980s,
the Canadian state and corporate community embraced a strategy
of continental neoliberalism to restructure the national economy in a
regional system of production and trade. In the 1990s, this strategy was
rescaled as part of the globalization agenda, imposing the discipline
of transnational neoliberalism on the Canadian state and social formation. Canadian governments of all stripes have played an active role in
advancing this project and thus have facilitated the global integration
of the Canadian economy.

The core result has been an internationalization of capital in Canada.
Over the past three decades, the circuits of capital in the national setting
have been interlaced with circuits of capital in a global setting, creating a transnational system of production and exchange. In this context,
Canada's capitalist class has become embedded in global patterns of
exploitation, or in those traversing the world economy and nation-state
system, and thus has come to view the production of profit in fundamentally global terms. For governments in Ottawa, the globalization
process has had the effect of securing a secondary position for the Canadian state in the chain of value added in the world economy. For this
reason, the neoliberal agenda has been fully embraced by the governing
parties in Ottawa and by the domestic power blocs that support them.

It is vital to recognize that, as the national economy has been globalized, a transnational capitalist class has come to anchor Canada's power
bloc. The internationalization of capital has produced an internationalization of the corporate power structure in several key ways. First,
Canadian firms with operations spanning the globe are now central to
the national corporate network. Second, these same firms have under-
gone a process of exteriorization in terms of interlocking with firms in
the global network of capitalist class power. Indeed, the leading agents
of the corporate elite have become more engaged in transnational interlocking, particularly on boards of directors in the United States and

Europe. Finally, the national network has been diversified by the interiorization of Europe-based directors, who have begun to complement
the role of US directors in the Canadian corporate network. In these
ways, the rudiments of a transnational capitalist class have emerged in
Canada.

On this foundation, the corporate community has found a vested
interest in a new foreign policy strategy. After 9/11, the Canadian corporate elite began to advocate a deep integration of the North American bloc and a global military force projection against terrorist groups,
rogue states, and weapons of mass destruction. In this endeavour, it was
supported by the defence lobby, which began to mobilize for a new foreign policy of cooperative specialization with US global primacy, selective engagement with multilateral institutions, and counterinsurgency
warfare in failed or rogue states. Over the past decade, this alliance
between the corporate community on the one hand and the defence
lobby on the other has produced a new power bloc, or constellation of
social forces, in the Canadian political economy. Through the policy
groups and think tanks of this new power bloc, a grand strategy for the
state has been articulated, one of neoliberal market enforcement, continental securitization, stratified multilateralism, cooperative specialization with US foreign policy, and disciplinary militarism towards the
Third World. These elements of a new grand strategy are critical to the
expanded reproduction of Canadian capital in the world economy and
to the relative rise of Canadian state power in the nation-state system.
As such, they are integral to a *class-based effort at joining empire*.

As this book has documented, the Canadian state has internalized –
and managed in its own ways – the hegemonic strategies of the new
power bloc. Under Liberal and Conservative governments, the Canadian state has built an apparatus of power for the deep integration of
North America, the global expansion of Canadian capital, and the political management of the nation-state system. In doing so, it has transformed itself as an institutionalization of dominant class forces in the
Empire of Capital. It has crystallized a structure of governance – what I
have termed a *new imperial state* – for the internationalization of capital
in Canada and beyond.

Over the past decade, Canada's interventions in Afghanistan and
Haiti were testing grounds for this new grand strategy of armoured
neoliberalism. In both these countries, a practice of neoliberal market
enforcement, stratified multilateralism, disciplinary militarism, and
cooperative specialization with US global primacy was advanced. In

Afghanistan, for instance, Canada supported the Bonn Process through which President Hamid Karzai came to manage a centralized structure of power in conjunction with the Northern Alliance and the US-led military occupation. Under this framework, Canada engaged in a military project of counterinsurgency warfare and an economic project of neoliberal transformation. In doing so, Canada also supported the primacy strategies of US foreign policy in the region (Hanieh 2013; Skinner 2013). For these reasons, Canada's war was guided less by goals of democratization and development and more by goals of geopolitical and geo-economic positioning. Given the strength of the Taliban insurgency, however, it appears that Canada failed to achieve any strategic goals in Afghanistan.

In Haiti, the methods of empire were not dissimilar. In this case, Canada joined a US-led effort to destabilize and remove the Aristide government and to impose a "new dictatorship" of transnational capital on the country. In the process, a wide spectrum of foreign policy tools was used, including the redirection of aid for political purposes, the selective use of multilateralism and human rights law, the deployment of Special Forces in US-led military interventions, and a focus on elections and security sector reform as part of stabilization operations. In these ways, Haiti was "managed" by Canada as a secondary power in the Empire of Capital. Canada, however, was unable to broker or impose a hegemonic settlement in Haiti, thus opening the door to future rounds of popular protest and outside intervention.

How, then, should one theorize the new Canadian foreign policy? I have attempted to show in this book that a focus on *social relations* is necessary for understanding and mapping the structural shifts in Canadian foreign policy. Indeed, it is the social relations of Canadian capitalism – in both their national and their international dimensions – that form the material substratum of Canadian state power in the world order today. More specifically, it is the social ties of global exploitation that structure the accumulation of capital and the exercise of state power in the Canadian political economy. For this reason, I have argued that Canada's new foreign policy is an active embrace of empire – of transnational relations of economic exploitation and political domination – by the state and capitalist class.

For students of politics and policy in Canada, this analysis can help explain the lack of variance in Ottawa on matters of national security, continental integration, foreign economic relations, and war and militarism since 2001. As we have seen, the recomposition of Canadian capitalism has created a new rationality for a class-based project of armoured neoliberalism at the level of the state. To this end, the Liberal and Conservative parties increasingly have formed a de facto coalition in Parliament. In fact, with few exceptions, both parties have forged agreement, if not coordination, on major issues of Canadian foreign policy, including the deployments to Afghanistan and Haiti, the free trade agreement with Colombia, the foreign investment protection treaty with China, the extraction and export of oil sands bitumen, the global expansion of Canadian mining capital, the deep integration of continental security platforms, support for the expansion of the North Atlantic Treaty Organization (NATO) "out of area," and the embrace of Israeli positions on the Middle East.

If one difference between them persists, though, it pertains to multilateralism. Whereas Conservatives tend to view it as a tactic for advancing "national" interests alone, Liberals tend to view it as a vital strategy for balancing US primacy, creating stability for the world market, and multiplying the points of influence for Canadian statecraft abroad. This difference aside, the two parties share a commitment to globalizing capital and arming the state for this purpose. Although the Liberal Party has shied away from the militaristic nationalism of the Conservative Party, it has supported both the military missions and the defence spending projects that have allowed such a culture to grow in Canada.

During the period of neoliberalism, the New Democratic Party (NDP), the traditional party of social democracy in Canada, has also shifted ground, embracing elements of the new grand strategy of the state and power bloc. In 1999, for example, the NDP initially endorsed the unsanctioned NATO bombing of Serbia. In 2001, after first voting against a Canadian deployment to Afghanistan, the NDP swung behind the mission so far as it fell under UN and parliamentary auspices. Although the NDP later adopted a "troops out" position, the federal leadership refused to campaign or mobilize around this issue (O'Keefe 2013). In 2004, the NDP leadership also dismissed the party's long-standing opposition to NATO, and despite pressure from solidarity activists, refused to condemn the coup in Haiti, calling instead for an investigation into "Aristide's departure" (Beverly 2011). Furthermore, in 2011, the NDP voted twice to endorse Canada's role in NATO's "no fly" zone over Libya, a tactic that worked directly for regime change. Moreover, in 2013, the NDP endorsed Canada's military mission in Mali, particularly the use of a C-17 Globemaster III transport plane in support of French military forces. Finally, the NDP has accepted the escalation of defence spending since 2001, and NDP analysts have critiqued recent navy ship procurement delays for ruling out "force" as "an option for Canada" in "the Baltic, the Eastern Mediterranean, and even the Western Pacific" with the United States and NATO (Byers 2014). In all of this, the NDP has sought to position the new Canadian militarism in a "human rights," "multilateral," or "sovereignty" discourse, against the more principled opposition to capitalist imperialism by peace and social justice movements in Canada and around the world. Likewise, on the economic front, the NDP has taken a strong stance against foreign takeovers of Canadian corporations, but has virtually ignored the internationalization of Canadian capital abroad. In the process, it has further abandoned a class analysis of the Canadian political economy.

Since 2001, then, a near-consensus has emerged in Ottawa on the globalization of Canadian capital and the militarization of Canadian foreign policy. The many failures of this strategy, though, have yet to register an open break in Parliament or in policy discourse more generally. The reason for this, as Paul Kellogg (2013, 206) observes, is that the Canadian state is now "rooted in an economic architecture whose very logic points towards imperialism and militarism." In this context, the state has become increasingly immune to democratic accountability, working instead for the rule of capital in Canada and beyond. In doing so, it has reproduced the many contradictions of global capitalism and failed to gain legitimacy on foreign and domestic fronts.

Given this, what can we expect of Canadian foreign policy in the future? Much will depend, of course, on the structural dynamics of the world economy and nation-state system – in particular, on the future of US primacy vis-à-vis the "rise of the rest" (Zakaria 2012; see also Layne 2012). What I have demonstrated in this book, though, is that the class relations of Canadian capitalism tend to shape and determine the policy options of governments in Ottawa. For this reason, one might glean the vectors of Canadian foreign policy by noting debates of the corporate community. As a case in point, John Manley, the new chair of the Canadian Council of Chief Executives, recognizes the failures of the "global war on terror," but defends the general trend of militarization in Canadian foreign policy. As he told the 2013 Ottawa Conference on Defence and Security, "Canada is not neutral ... When there's something that matters we're prepared if necessary to bear arms" (Day 2013). For the upper echelons of the corporate community, then, the further project of globalizing capital likely will involve a supplementary project of disciplinary militarism.

On this assumption, Canada's defence lobby has begun to focus on the future threat that China might pose to the US-led structure of empire. In fact, calls for a "Pacific pivot" by the Royal Canadian Navy (RCN) and the Royal Canadian Air Force (RCAF) have become more pronounced in defence lobby statements and studies. The key thinking, as one paper by the Canadian Defence and Foreign Affairs Institute puts it, is that "Canada should not expect to make windfall profits from the positive outcomes of Asian markets if it is completely unwilling to invest in the security and stability that creates the positive environment for these very markets to flourish" (Girouard 2012, 3). With this in mind, the Canadian Forces have begun to test the waters of the Asia-Pacific. In 2012, for instance, the RCN and RCAF participated in the biannual RIMPAC, or Pacific war games, off Hawaii – the largest in history. Furthermore, in 2013, an RCAF officer was posted to US Pacific Command, the RCN made an unprecedented port call to the Philippines, Canada hosted a working group of naval officials from Australia, Malaysia, Japan, and the Philippines, and the RCN launched a drive for recruiting Chinese-Canadians (Chiang 2013; Fisher 2013; McDonough 2013). Although such efforts so far have been partial and cautious, they are signs of an early embrace of the US pivot to Asia and of a strategy to match the internationalization of Canadian capital in the Asia-Pacific with a new military posture and position. Yet, whether Canada will be able to expand economic ties with the region while seeking to enforce a US-led security system will be a contradiction worth watching. At stake will be Canada's role in the future fault lines of the capitalist world system.

If Canada's foreign policy is inextricable from such dynamics of empire, what is the alternative? Worth considering is the "counterconsensus" on Canadian foreign policy that Cranford Pratt identified three decades ago. As Pratt (1983/4, 100, 118) observed,

> there has emerged in Canada a substantial number of internationally minded public interest groups which are in serious opposition to many components of the present consensus which underlies Canadian foreign policy. These anti-consensus groups are an interesting and important development in Canadian public life. While in no way marginal to Canadian society, they are certainly peripheral to decision-making in Canadian public life and have very little impact upon it ... These groups are not special interest groups which take positions reflecting their own economic interests or ethnic background. Rather they are groups which oppose on

ethical grounds important elements of Canadian foreign policy. During the past fifteen years in which these groups have multiplied, they have tended to focus on specific issues. Nuclear disarmament, human rights, international equity, and solidarity with oppressed peoples have been the most frequent themes. However, there has gradually emerged a recognition that they are united in support of a consensus counter to that which currently sustains Canadian foreign policy. This counter-consensus involves a new view of the sources of international tension and how these tensions can be managed and a different sense of Canada's opportunities and responsibilities internationally.

Since the early 1980s, the counterconsensus has expanded by integrating struggles for peace, global justice, environmental sustainability, migrant rights, and self-determination for oppressed nations and indigenous peoples. In the process, it has moved beyond a moral critique of Canadian foreign policy to a structural analysis of Canadian capitalism in its local and global dimensions – that is, to an *immanent critique of Canadian imperialism*. As Greg Albo (2013, 266–8) points out, this new perspective was forged through the antinuclear and feminist struggles of the 1980s, the antiglobalization protests of the 1990s, the anti-war and international solidarity movements of the 2000s, and the more recent movements around migrants' rights, climate justice, and indigenous sovereignty. For these converging social movements, the political tasks are numerous: ending the war in Afghanistan and withdrawing from military alliances such as NATO; reassessing the North American Free Trade Agreement and other institutions of neoliberal globalization; rebalancing ties in the Middle East and supporting Palestinian self-determination; limiting hydrocarbon development as a means of halting climate change; demilitarizing the Canadian foreign policy apparatus and cutting defence spending levels; ceasing belligerence against left-wing governments and social movements in Latin America and the Caribbean; regulating the foreign direct investments of Canadian corporations, especially in the mining, energy, and financial sectors; and remaking the UN and other multilateral institutions to advance peace and equality in world affairs. As Albo (ibid., 268) contends, this "minimum program ... would reinforce democratic sovereignty and advance the struggle for an equalizing world order. It stands opposed to the neoliberal system built around the internationalization of capital and the disciplinary militarism of ... western [states]."

In the long run, however, the struggle for peace and global justice will have to confront, and radically transform, the social relations of Canadian capitalism. As the ultimate source of Canada's new imperialism, the social forms of capital will have to be replaced by democratic modes of production and exchange – that is, by a socialist transformation of state and society. To this end, the further building of a counterforce to empire, and with it, a program of *antiracist, working-class politics*, will be of vital importance, not just in Canada, but around the world as well.

Appendix

The issue of foreign ownership and control has long preoccupied social science in Canada. During the period of neoliberalism, as foreign direct investment (FDI) flooded into Canada, these concerns were raised anew. But has the increase in FDI sidelined Canadian capital and created new conditions of national dependence? In particular, has Canada become a "rich dependency," as argued by left-nationalist political economy? And have Canadian capitalists been forced, as a result, to specialize in non-productive circuits of capital?

These questions can be answered in two ways. First, the level of FDI in Canada can be compared with the level in other advanced capitalist states. Second, the real level of foreign ownership can be compared with the real level of Canadian ownership, both over time and by country and sector. When one makes these comparisons, it becomes clear that, first, there is nothing abnormal about the level of FDI in Canada and, second, that foreign ownership has not undermined the accumulation base of Canadian capital.

Consider, first, the ways in which FDI in Canada compares with FDI in other member countries of the Organisation for Economic Co-operation and Development (OECD). The ratio of FDI to gross domestic product (GDP) is an important measure of foreign control because it suggests the power of global capital in the national economy. According to OECD data (OECD 2012b), the stock of FDI in Canada equaled 35.6 per cent of GDP in 2010. Although such a ratio is often viewed as a sign of dependence, Canada has a lower FDI-to-GDP ratio than Spain (42.9 per cent) and the United Kingdom (48.4 per cent), compares positively with that of France (37.4 per cent), and is slightly higher than that of Germany (28.9 per cent). Thus, although Canada has a higher FDI-to-GDP ratio than Japan, Italy, and the United States, its ratio is comparable to that of other OECD countries. The data suggest, therefore, that the stock of FDI in the Canadian economy is not a clear sign of dependence and that, rather, Canada has a large home market outside the control of foreign capital.

One limitation of this OECD measure, however, is that it fails to account for reinvested earnings, and thus underestimates the real level of foreign ownership and control. As a result, one must examine the data collected by Statistics Canada on FDI and reinvested earnings. These data cover foreign ownership over time and by industry and nationality, and provide a more accurate picture of foreign control of the Canadian economy.

To begin, it is important to emphasize that there has been a *decline in foreign control in nearly all sectors of the Canadian economy since 1970* (see Klassen 2007, 184–93). This decline is commonly attributed to the national policies of Liberal governments under Pierre Trudeau and to the slowdown in US investment in the 1970s and 1980s. On the eve of the free trade period, then, foreign capital occupied a much smaller share of the domestic economy than it had traditionally.

Interestingly, the level of foreign control has remained relatively constant over the past twenty years. Despite two decades of transnational neoliberalism, foreign control of assets has declined, while foreign control of operating revenues has risen only slightly. As Figure 22 reveals,

Figure 22. Foreign Control of Assets and Operating Revenues, Canada, 1988–2010

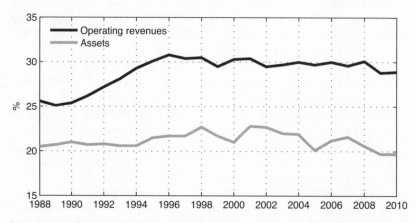

Source: Author's calculations, from Statistics Canada, *Corporation Returns Act* (various issues).

between 1988 and 2010, foreign control of assets decreased from 20.5 per cent to 19.7 per cent, while foreign control of operating revenues rose from 25.6 per cent to 28.9 per cent. The global integration of the Canadian economy, then, has not precipitated a new takeover of Canadian capitalism. Foreign control is still significant, but it has not crowded-out Canadian capital or increased dramatically during the period of neoliberalism.

The evidence on foreign control by industry reveals the same pattern. Statistics Canada's *Corporations Returns Act*, which collects data from annual surveys of Canadian- and foreign-controlled firms and accounts for both FDI – which is registered in the balance of payments – and reinvested earnings, provides the most accurate picture of foreign control in the Canadian economy. As Table 10 shows, foreign control is highest in manufacturing, at 53.1 per cent, with the United States and the European Union accounting for 29.7 and 17.5 per cent, respectively, of total assets. Likewise, foreign control is 35.0 per cent in the oil and gas sector, with the United States claiming 22.2 per cent of total assets. Finally, in the mining and wholesale trade sectors, foreign control is 32.8 per cent and 42.8 per cent, respectively. Although these numbers are significant, they do not indicate a new "silent surrender" of the Canadian economy. Canadian capital controls 47.0 per cent of manufacturing assets, 65.0 per cent of oil and gas assets, 67.2 per cent of mining assets, and 57.2 per cent of wholesale trade assets. Canadian capital, then, has not been undermined in these circuits of productive and commercial capital. Indeed, 73.3 per cent of the non-financial sector is under domestic control, and US capital controls only 15.2 per cent. Similarly, of the economy as a whole, only 19.7 per cent is controlled by foreign capital and only 10.3 per cent is controlled by Americans.

The evidence suggests, then, that, although foreign control is high in certain sectors, especially in manufacturing, oil and gas, and wholesale trade, Canadian capital has not been displaced from these sectors or from the economy as a whole. In value terms, Canadian capital has not been pushed from the circuit of productive capital into circuits of money and commodity capital. On the contrary, Canadian capital continues to control the majority of assets in nearly all sectors, and operates across the chain of value-added production. As a result, the overall level of foreign – especially US – control does not support the theory of Canadian dependence. Rather, the opposite is true: national firms are the strongest force in the Canadian market, and although foreign control is significant, it has not reduced the capacity of Canadian capital to compete in all sectors of the economy. A more appropriate view of this

Table 10. Canadian and Foreign Control of Assets by Industry, Canada, 2010

| Industry | Foreign | | | | Canadian | | |
	United States	European Union	Other	Total	Private	Public	Total
				(per cent)			
Agriculture, forestry, fishing, hunting	0.2	0.4	0.8	1.4	×	×	98.6
Oil and gas	22.2	×	×	35.0	×	×	65.0
Mining	×	9.3	×	32.8	×	×	67.2
Utilities	5.8	×	×	8.5	25.6	65.9	91.5
Construction	3.0	2.6	0.3	×	×	×	94.1
Manufacturing	29.7	17.5	5.8	53.1	×	×	47.0
Wholesale trade	21.9	13.2	7.6	42.8	×	×	57.2
Retail trade	22.5	1.6	0.5	24.5	74.1	1.4	75.5
Transportation and warehousing	4.0	4.4	1.3	9.8	80.9	9.3	90.2
Information and cultural industries	5.1	0.8	×	6.3	×	×	93.7
Non-depository credit intermediation	30.7	5.8	7.0	43.4	11.5	45.1	56.6
Insurance	7.6	15.0	3.3	25.8	70.7	3.5	74.2
Other financial	7.8	1.4	1.7	10.8	×	×	89.2
Depository credit intermediation	1.9	4.5	0.6	7.0	×	×	93.0
Real estate	4.1	1.9	2.2	8.2	91.1	0.6	91.8
Professional, scientific, technical services	16.5	6.8	1.5	24.8	×	×	75.2
Waste management	12.7	3.4	1.6	17.7	×	×	82.3
Education, health, social assistance	1.0	×	×	1.5	98.5	×	98.5
Arts, entertainment, recreation	×	×	×	13.5	66.3	20.3	86.5
Accommodation and food services	8.7	2.3	5.4	16.4	×	×	83.6
Repair, maintenance, personal services	8.5	0.9	0.6	9.9	90.1	×	90.1
Total financial	5.9	5.6	1.6	13.1	78.7	8.2	86.9
Total non-financial	15.2	7.0	4.5	26.7	67.4	5.9	73.3
Total all	10.3	6.3	3.0	19.7	73.3	7.1	80.3¯

Source: Statistics Canada (2012).

Note: The "x" marks are provided by Statistics Canada, and I interpret them to mean that the data are unavailable or cannot be released to the public.

relationship, then, involves foreign and Canadian firms competing as relative equals in a common space of accumulation. Canadian capital does not command a fully enclosed base of accumulation, but neither is it asymmetrically dependent on foreign capital in all sectors of the economy. On the contrary, in most sectors there is effective competition between equally strong capitals of different national origins, including, most importantly, Canadian capital.

Notes

Introduction

1 The issue of transnational class formation is a major theme of recent scholarship on globalization (see Chapter 5). For some, this process involves a denationalization of capital – a superseding of any moorings to national economic spaces or corporate communities. In this book, however, I use a more nuanced conceptualization – unless specified otherwise, "transnational" connotes a global expansion or "internationalization" of capital. In other words, I analyse how Canadian capital is undergoing a process of global expansion without necessarily losing its national moorings.

2 Canada has a long history of imperial relations, first within the British Empire and then within the American empire after the Second World War. In this book, the notion of "joining empire" refers to the new modalities of Canada's integration with global structures of economic, political, and military power. Thus, although Canada's new grand strategy builds upon and extends past practices of international statecraft, it includes numerous innovations in military, diplomatic, and economic thinking in line with the internationalization of capital and the recomposition of the corporate power bloc.

3 As Coates (1999) points out, the absence of a full-fledged bourgeoisie undercut the insurrectionary movements, making a "bourgeois revolution" near-impossible.

4 Gustavus Myers (1913) demonstrated how the fur trade or staples economy created a "primitive accumulation" of capital, which eventually was invested in capitalist industries such as railway transport and manufacturing, under the guidance of the state.

5 Admittedly, the link between internal colonialism and external imperialism is underexplored in this book. Canada's colonial past and present underlie all projections of corporate and state power abroad. For example, Canada would not rank as a global mining power without the expropriation of the land of indigenous peoples. With this in mind, the growing links between indigenous movements in Canada and anti-mining campaigns around the world is a key front of anti-imperialist resistance. See Blackwood and Stewart (2012) and Gordon (2010).

6 Starting with the 1910 Immigration Act, Canada had a de facto "white only" immigration policy. The act granted cabinet the power to exclude "immigrants belonging to any race deemed unsuited to the climate or requirements of Canada." The political project of nation building was therefore tightly linked to racialized forms of settlement and colonization; see Boyko (1995).

7 The principle of "functionalism" held that countries should gain representation and decision-making influence in accordance with their contribution to the war effort.

8 The Colombo Plan was a development assistance program for the former British colonies of South Asia, including India, Pakistan, and Sri Lanka. Its primary goal was to prevent communist or leftist forces from gaining power.

9 This new Canadian nationalism was apparent in the Diefenbaker years, the Gordon, Watkins, and Grey Reports, George Grant's *Lament for a Nation*, the Waffle, the Committee for an Independent Canada, and the labour and social movements of the 1960s and 1970s.

10 Although Trudeau recognized the People's Republic of China and befriended Cuba's Castro, he later deployed US cruise missiles in Canada.

11 Hart's argument is highly problematic for linking terrorism and Islam, and for spreading fear and xenophobia about Muslims in Europe and elsewhere. In 2011, Conservative prime minister Stephen Harper made a similar argument in stating that the "the biggest threat [to Canada] is still Islamicism," a threat that exists "all over the world" (CBC 2011). This perspective does not just border on racism; it ignores scholarship on the *political* motivations of many "radical Islamist" groups, including the original al-Qaeda. As Mohamedou (2006) and Pape (2005) demonstrate, the key political issues for many Islamist groups include the occupations of Iraq, Afghanistan, and Palestine, and western support for oil despots in the Arab world. These political realities often have been more important than religion in explaining the wide diversity of resistance, including terrorism, to western foreign policies in the Arab and Muslim worlds.

12 Carroll (1986, 28–9) shows that Clement misinterpreted his own data.

13 The same mistake occurs in contemporary work on the Alberta oil sands, which are viewed not as a highly advanced form of industrial capital, but as just another "staple" industry, dependent on exports to the American empire. For McCullum (2006), it is the oil commodity itself that binds Canada in a dependent continental relationship. This kind of commodity fetishism ignores the production of oil through capitalist class methods, and the wider process of internationalization in the circuits of capital (see Chapter 4).

14 See, for example, Dewitt and Kirton (1983); Eayrs (1981); and Lyon and Tomlin (1979). None of these studies includes a theory of accumulation, but instead proceed from a random selection of empirical or "material stock" variables.

15 In the activist press, Yves Engler (2009) and Todd Gordon (2010) have published critiques of Canadian foreign policy and its links to corporate interests. In the scholarly field, Linda Freeman (1997) has explored the same themes regarding Canadian-South African relations. However, as John Saul (1999) points out, her study is not grounded in a fully developed class analysis.

1. Understanding Empire: Theories of International Political Economy

1 For Robert Gilpin (1981, 23), imperialism is nothing but the "conquest of territory in order to advance economic, security, and other interests." As Campbell Craig (2004, 165) elaborates: "Our realist definition of empire stipulates that a dominant power engages in imperialism when its expansionist foreign policies cannot plausibly be attributed to security requirements and when in fact that expansionism comes to damage its security." In this framework, then, imperialism is not a factor in international relations except as an aberrant policy of territorial domination by adventurist states.

2 The same is true of some strands of realism today. For instance, John Mearsheimer (2001, 402) believes that "the United States has a profound interest in seeing Chinese economic growth slow considerably in the years ahead."

3 As Mark Rupert (1995, 6) points out, "[t]he social bases of state power, the historically specific ideologies and socially productive practices which sustain it, are placed outside the scope of inquiry, supplanted by formal calculations of interest and comparative assessments of the putatively power-bearing resources possessed by states."

4 As Richard Ashley (1984, 238) argues, "[t]he proposition that the state might be essentially problematic or contested is excluded from neorealist theory."

5 As Alexander Wendt (1995, 81) puts it, "neorealist ethics come down to 'sauve qui peut'."

6 In the words of Wendt (1995, 78): "Anarchy as such is not a structural cause of anything. What matters is its social structure."

7 As Mearsheimer (2001, 17) admits, "[r]ealism tends to emphasize the irresistible strength of existing forces and the inevitable character of existing tendencies, and to insist that the highest wisdom lies in accepting, and adapting oneself to these forces and these tendencies."

8 Generally speaking, postcolonial theory is the academic project of deconstructing the culture of colonialism in western art, literature, politics, philosophy, and discourses of the Third World. At various points in this book, I draw upon postcolonial theory to buttress my arguments about Canadian foreign policy and political culture. In Chapter 1, however, I do not include postcolonial theory as a major social science because it tends to lack a positive research program. As Robert Young (1998, 5) argues, "postcolonialism offers a politics rather than a coherent theoretical methodology. Indeed you could go so far as to argue that strictly speaking there is no such thing as postcolonial theory as such." With this in mind, I keep to integrating numerous insights of postcolonial theory into my own research framework and methodology.

9 Doyle's choice of terms is imprecise: many "non republics" are democracies, while many "republics" have non-representative forms of government.

10 As the United Nations (UNDP 2010, 4, 72) observes, the world economy has witnessed "no convergence in income ... because on average rich countries have grown faster than poor ones over the past 40 years. The divide between developed and developing countries persists: a small subset of countries has remained at the top of the world income distribution, and only a handful of countries that started out poor have joined that high-income group." Furthermore, "[w]ithin countries, rising income inequality is the norm: more countries have a higher Gini coefficient now than in the 1980s. For each country where inequality has improved in the last 20-30 years, it has worsened in more than two." Using household surveys, Branko Milanovic (2012) shows that global inequality, regardless of nationality, has also increased over the past several decades.

11 See Amnesty International (2013); Chomsky (2002); Klassen and Albo (2013); Prashad (2012); and Tirman (2011).

12 For Marx ([1894] 1990), the *rate of exploitation* is the ratio of surplus labour time, S, to paid labour time, V. The former creates surplus value or profit; the latter stands for wages, or what Marx termed "variable capital."

13 As Marx points out, the history of capitalism begins with the separation of producing classes from the means of production. In particular, it begins with the sixteenth-century dispossession of the English peasantry, culminating in the private ownership of the land, the marketization of the means of subsistence, and the making of a propertyless working class. The "primitive accumulation of capital" was also aided by colonialism. In fact, "[t]he colonies provided a market for the budding manufactures, and a vast increase in accumulation which was guaranteed by the mother country's monopoly of the market. The treasures captured outside Europe by undisguised looting, enslavement, and murder flowed back to the mother country and were turned into capital there" (Marx [1867] 1990, 918). Although Marx in his early writings saw a progressive side to British imperialism, he later became a strong opponent of colonialism, racism, and national oppression, supporting the Chinese side in the Second Opium War, the Sepoy uprising in India, the abolitionist cause in the US Civil War, the Polish uprising of 1863, and Irish independence. As Kevin Anderson (2010) reveals, such struggles became central to Marx's political strategy for human emancipation.

14 Marx ([1867] 1990) recognized that rising real wages are possible under capitalism, but that they are always tempered by the technological displacement of workers and by the subsequent formation of a "relative surplus population" as a general law of accumulation.

15 For Marx, the rate of profit is defined by the formula, $S/(C + V)$, where S is surplus value, C is constant capital, and V is variable capital. Although Marx identifies countertendencies to a falling rate of profit, he reveals how crises are rooted in production, not in exchange.

16 As Marx observed in *Capital* ([1867] 1990, 918): "The colonies provided a market for the budding manufactures, and a vast increase in accumulation which was guaranteed by the mother country's monopoly of the market. The treasures captured outside Europe by undisguised looting, enslavement and murder flowed back to the mother-country and were turned into capital there."

17 In his first outline for *Capital*, Marx planned to write distinct volumes on the state, foreign trade, and the world market and crisis, but these volumes were never written; see Rosdolsky (1989).

18 At the same time, the Prebisch hypothesis of declining terms of trade between primary products and manufactured goods was accurate at the time, and has been confirmed recently (see Arezki et al. 2013).

19 See Arrighi (1978); Baran (1957); Gunder Frank (1966); and Wallerstein (1979).
20 As Robert Brenner (2006b, 83) observes, the state is "dependent upon capital, because those who govern (whoever they might be) will tend to find that the realization of their own interests (whatever they are) depends on the promotion of capitalist profits and capital accumulation, as the latter are the sine qua non for economic growth and financial solvency, and thus for stability domestically and strength internationally."

2. Hegemonic Liberalism: The Political Economy of US Primacy

1 For my own take on the US decline debate, see Klassen (2014).
2 Council on Foreign Relations (1940); see Shoup and Minter (2004, 130).
3 Council on Foreign Relations (1941); see Shoup and Minter (2004, 136).
4 As wartime Secretary of State Cordell Hull put it: "Leadership toward a new system of international relationships in trade and other economic affairs will devolve very largely upon the United States because of our great economic strength. We should assume this leadership, and the responsibility that goes with it, primarily for reasons of pure national self-interest" (Kolko 1968, 251).
5 Stewart (1992, 188) elaborates that, "[b]eginning with the Reciprocal Trade Agreement in 1935, running through the economic and trade cooperation during the World War II period, and culminating in the Free Trade Agreement in 1988, American policy [towards Canada] was dedicated to encouraging economic integration and facilitating the common exploitation of the continental market and natural resources."
6 In March 1948, Lester Pearson, then undersecretary for external affairs, represented Canada at top-secret talks with the United States and Britain on the possibility of founding a North Atlantic alliance. The following year, Pearson told the House of Commons that "[t]he power of the communists, wherever that power flourishes, depends upon their ability to suppress and destroy the free institutions that stand against them. They pick them off one by one: the political parties, the trade unions, the churches, the schools, the universities, the trade associations, even the sporting clubs and the kindergartens. The North Atlantic Treaty Organization is meant to be a declaration to the world that *this kind of conquest from within* will not in the future take place amongst us"; see Engler (2012, emphasis added).
7 US positions at the 1954 Geneva Conference were key obstacles to a peace treaty. In particular, the United States opposed North Korean proposals

for nation-wide elections to create a new Korean government; instead, the United States and South Korea insisted on new elections for the North only.

8 Reflecting on his wartime experience, Secretary Hull noted that, "[a]t no time ... did we press Britain, France, or the Netherlands for an immediate grant of self-government to their colonies. Our thought was that it would come after an adequate period of years, short or long" (Kolko 1968, 276).

9 For the CIA, the aim of the coup, as part of Operation AJAX, was to "bring to power a government which would reach an equitable oil settlement" and "vigorously prosecute the dangerously strong Communist Party" (Wilber 1954, iv).

10 Rather than reducing Third World debt, the economics of global finance have expanded it from US$540 billion in 1980 to US$3,360 billion in 2007. Between 1985 and 2007, the net transfer of this debt – that is, the difference between loans and payments – was a negative US$759 billion, the equivalent of 7.5 Marshall Plans from the South to the North. See Millet and Toussaint (2009).

11 On oligarchic forces, see Bender (2014) and Kramer (2014). On fascist and ultra-nationalist elements, see BBC (2014b) and English (2014). The high degree of US involvement was revealed in a leaked phone call between Assistant Secretary of State Victoria Nuland and the US Ambassador to the Ukraine, Geoffrey Pyatt; see BBC (2014a). For context on how the United States bears primary responsibility for the "New Cold War" with Russia, see Cohen (2009, chap. 7).

3. Continental Neoliberalism and the Canadian Corporate Elite

1 This chapter draws upon my authored sections of Carroll and Klassen (forthcoming).

2 Corporate boards in the United States and Canada have diminished in size to enhance accountability and shareholder value; see Carroll (2004).

3 At the time, profit rates were sinking, unit labour costs were rising, productivity growth was stalled, and trade deficits were mounting (D. Robinson 2007, 270).

4 As Gordon Stewart (1992, 188) reveals, CAFTA helped realize the long-term goals of US strategy towards Canada: "encouraging economic integration and facilitating the common exploitation of the continental market and natural resources."

5 In September 1985, the Canadian government's communications strategy was leaked. It stated: "Our communications strategy should

rely less on educating the general public than on getting across the message that the trade initiative is a good idea. In other words, a selling job ... [A] substantial majority of the public may be willing to leave the issue in the hands of the government and other interested groups, if the government maintains communications control of the situation. Benign neglect from a majority of Canadians may be the realistic outcome of a well-executed communications program" (quoted in Brownlee 2005, 83–4).

6 The election was called after the Liberal-dominated Senate delayed passage of CAFTA.

7 The opposition parties won more votes, but lost the election due to Canada's first-past-the-post parliamentary system.

8 In 1992, corporate profits before taxes had dropped to only 4.6 per cent of GDP (author's calculation, from Statistics Canada, CANSIM II database, V646928, V498086).

9 Author's interview with Thomas d'Aquino, 7 May 2012; this interview is the source of the remainder of the paragraph.

10 Ibid.

11 In 2001, the BCNI changed its name to the CCCE in order to present a more global profile.

12 Author's interview with d'Aquino, 7 May 2012.

13 Accessed online from the US National Association of Manufacturers, 17 October 2011.

14 Author's interview with d'Aquino, 7 May 2012.

4. The Internationalization of Canadian Capital

1 According to Gill (1995, 415), "[n]ew constitutionalism is a macro-political dimension of the process whereby the nature and purpose of the public sphere ... has been redefined in a more privatized and commodified way, with its economic criteria defined in a more globalised and abstract frame of reference."

2 Author's interview with Thomas d'Aquino, 7 May 2012.

3 Ibid.

4 Adam Hanieh (2011) develops a similar approach to studying capitalism and class formation in the Gulf Cooperation Council.

5 The notion of "fractions of capital" is contentious in Marxist theory because ownership cuts across circuits of capital. General Motors, for example, operates in production, finance, and exchange. With this in mind, I mark out different forms of internationalization in the circuits of capital

but refrain from drawing any strong conclusions on class fractions in Canada.

6 In fact, the world economy can be periodized by the stages of internationalization in the circuits of capital. If mercantilism globalized the commodity circuit, and classical imperialism globalized the money circuit, the post–Second World War period – particularly from the 1980s onward – globalized the productive circuit.

7 For example, according to the United Nations (2005, 75), net transfers of financial resources for developing countries were negative between 1997 and 2004, and reached US$350 billion in 2004 alone. As the *New York Times* reports, "[a]ccording to the United Nations, in 2006 the net transfer of capital from poorer countries to rich ones was [US]$784 billion, up from [US]$229 billion in 2002" (Rosenburg 2007).

8 Nominal GDP is calculated using prevailing exchange rates, but it does not account for differences in the cost of living or in the number of people living and working in each country. PPP GDP takes into account the relative cost of living and inflation rates between countries, while GDP at PPP per capita calculates the value of all final goods and services produced within a nation in a given year divided by the average population for the same year, with GDP dollar estimates taken from PPP calculations.

9 See International Monetary Fund, *World Economic Outlook Database* (Washington, DC), available online at https://www.imf.org/external/pubs/ft/weo/2011/02/weodata/index.aspx.

10 Jim Stanford (2006b, 7) has noted, for instance, that of all new corporate profits generated across Canada in 2005, "a stunning 70% were in Alberta."

11 The OECD definition of value added is different than a Marxian one (see Chapter 1). For the OECD, value added is "the value of output less the value of intermediate consumption; it is a measure of the contribution to GDP made by an individual producer, industry or sector; gross value added is the source from which the primary incomes of [production] are generated and is therefore carried forward into the primary distribution of income account." See https://stats.oecd.org/glossary/detail.asp?ID=1184. The key point here is not the conceptual discrepancy but the basic comparison between countries.

12 Author's calculations, from Statistics Canada, CANSIM II database, table 3860006, V114277, V114278, V114279, V114280, V114281, V114282, V114283, V114331, V114332, V114333, V114334, V114335, V114336, V114337.

13 If Canada were to run a long-term deficit in the current account, it would be a sign that domestically based capitalists were realizing comparatively

less surplus value in foreign markets than vice versa. As a result, Canada's overall competitiveness would decline.

14 Between 2008 and 2013, Canada registered four years of overall trade deficits due to declining demand in the United States and rising imports from the European Union and non-OECD states. Yet Canada has continued to run a strong trade surplus with the United States. See http://www.statcan.gc.ca/tables-tableaux/sum-som/l01/cst01/gblec02a-eng.htm.

15 In fact, "[o]ne quarter of U.S. imports from Canada consist of value added from the United States itself" (Koopman et al. 2010, 7).

16 See United States (2010f); and Statistics Canada, CANSIM II database, table 510006, V35.

17 Author's calculations, from Statistics Canada, CANSIM II database, table 510037, V29850343, and table 510006, V16.

18 Statistics Canada, CANSIM II database, table 3760060, V2171184, V21711845; and UNCTAD 2011, Annex, table 34.

19 See UNCTAD, *UNCTADStat*, available online at http://unctadstat.unctad.org/.

20 Author's calculations, from Statistics Canada, CANSIM II database, table 3760014, V112908, V112909, V112910, V112911, V112912, V112913, V112914.

21 See Toronto Mining Index, available online at http://www.tmx.com/en/listings/sector_profiles/mining.html, accessed 8 March 2014.

22 Worth noting is that Canadian financial capital in the Caribbean owns approximately 60 per cent of the region's banking assets (Greenwood 2013).

23 Author's calculations, from Statistics Canada, CANSIM II database, table 3760053, V20143969, V20143970, V20143971, V20143972, V20143973, V20143974.

24 As Chapter 3 demonstrates, the share of before-tax corporate profit in GDP rose from 4.6 per cent in 1992 to more than 13 per cent in 2007. Over the same period, as this chapter demonstrates, the labour share of national income fell by five percentage points (see OECD 2012a).

5. Transnational Class Formation: Globalization and the Canadian Corporate Network

1 This chapter first appeared as Klassen and Carroll (2011).

2 The UNCTAD "transnationality index" represents an average of FDI inflows as a percentage of gross fixed capital formation, FDI inward stocks as a percentage of GDP, the value added of foreign affiliates

as a percentage of GDP, and the employment of foreign affiliates as a percentage of total employment; see UNCTAD (2009). For data on trade and investment in Canada, see OECD (2009, 65).

3 In compiling the C250, the main source for data on firm size was the *Financial Post 500* listings, published in July 1997 and 2007. To qualify for the C250, a corporation could not be wholly owned by another Canadian corporation. However, wholly owned Canadian subsidiaries of foreign TNCs (such as Walmart Canada, Honda Canada, Ford Motor Co. of Canada, Toyota Canada) were included in the C250 if they met the size criteria. Data on board composition was sourced from the annual reports of the corporations, available at company web sites or at the Mergent Online database. To maintain consistency throughout the analysis, we restricted ourselves to companies for which we were able to obtain complete data on firm size and board composition.

4 Data for G500 companies are from Carroll's (2009a) study. In compiling each G500, Carroll employed the same criteria as ours for the C250, but doubled the number, selecting the four hundred largest non-financials (ranked by revenue) and the one hundred largest financials (ranked by assets). To qualify for the G500, a corporation could not be wholly owned by another corporation. Names of directors of G500 corporations were taken mainly from corporate annual reports. See Carroll (2009a) for details. We analysed the Canadian-based corporations that qualified for both the C250 and G500 (nine in 1996, fifteen in 2006) as members of the C250, not G500 – that is, the G500 contains only companies that, from a Canadian standpoint, are foreign based.

5 Data on foreign subsidiaries of C250 firms were gleaned from Dunn and Bradstreet's *Who Owns Whom* (1997 and 2007 editions), whose listings enable counts of companies that are majority-owned by a given firm and by all subsidiaries of that firm – that is, the total number of subsidiaries (direct and indirect) of each firm. The domicile of every parent and subsidiary is indicated, enabling the assignment for each C250 firm of its subsidiaries to specific national domiciles. Since *Who Owns Whom* displays intercorporate ownership relations as nested hierarchies, we were able to assess each firm's subsidiaries (categorized by domicile of the subsidiary) by examining companies listed underneath it in the hierarchy of ownership. This applied not only to firms that were ultimate parents, but also to Canadian subsidiaries of foreign-based companies.

6 Data on country of control were taken from the *Financial Post 500* listings, supplemented where necessary by the *Financial Post InfoMart* database (http://www.fpinfomart.ca). We categorized a company as under

foreign control if 50 per cent or more of its share capital is held outside Canada or if the largest block of shares comprising at least 20 per cent of share capital is owned by a single foreign investor. Canadian-controlled companies are firms that do not meet these thresholds for foreign control. In practice, foreign control nearly always involves majority ownership of a corporation's share capital.

7 Counting subsidiaries implicitly weights each one equally, with the result that a firm with five foreign subsidiaries, each with revenues of $20 million, appears as five times more transnationalized than one with a single foreign subsidiary with revenues of $100,000. This measure of transnationality is not nearly as sensitive as the UNCTAD "transnationality index," yet it is the best we can do with available data.

8 These proportions are the values of Eta-squared based on one-way analyses of variance, with transnationality as the independent variable and revenue as the dependent variable. In this context, Eta-squared indicates the proportion of the total variance in revenue that is attributable to between-group differences in transnationality.

9 The contingency coefficient for the 1996 data in Table 8 is 0.359; for the 2006 data, it is 0.298.

10 The Eta-squared values, with national degree as the criterion, are 0.250 in 1996 and 0.199 in 2006.

11 Not evident in Figures 16 and 17 are three kinds of statistically deviant cases. (1) In 1996, the category of near-TNCs controlled in Europe had two members. One of them – Shell Canada – was interlocked with two non-Canadian G500 firms; thus, the mean degree for this very small category was 1.0. (2) In contrast, in the same year, nationally bound firms controlled by interests outside the North Atlantic made up a more substantial category of eight firms (see Table 8), all subsidiaries of Japanese parents, and in several cases linked to multiple members of Japanese-based corporate sets – accounting for the unusually high mean transnational degree of 1.6 (on corporate sets in Japan (see Scott 1997, 181–95). (3) By 2006, three firms with continental investments, each controlled in Europe, showed an elevated national degree of interlocking: Shell Canada, with thirteen such interlocks; Imperial Tobacco Canada, with four; and St. Lawrence Cement, with six.

12 In both 1996 and 2006, Canadian TNCs under domestic control engaged in far more transnational interlocking than the few TNCs under foreign control. In 2006, mean degrees were 1.04 for Canadian-controlled TNCs and 0.20 for foreign-controlled TNCs.

13 ANOVA-based eta-squared = .005.

14 By way of comparison, the proportion of all domestic interlocks involving Canadian TNCs held steady through the decade (820 of 2,204 domestic interlocks in 1996; 413 of 1,128 domestic interlocks in 2006, comprising 36.6 per cent of all domestic ties).

15 Included among these companies were the Canadian subsidiaries of Toyota; Nissan; Honda; Mitsubishi; Mitsui; Itochu; and Bank of Tokyo (all based in Japan); McDonald's; Sears, Roebuck; Costco; Gulf's parent; A&P's parent; Textron's parent; and Weyerhaeuser (all based in the United States); LaFarge; and Société Générale (based in France); and HSBC (based in the United Kingdom).

16 By 2006, these firms tend to link across the Atlantic to European parents, rather than continentally to US or across the Pacific to Japanese parent companies. Canadian subsidiaries with transnational interlocks to their G500 parents in 2006 included GlaxoSmithKline, Standard Life, Wolseley Insurance, and HSBC (all controlled in the United Kingdom); AXA Canada and Aviva Canada (controlled in France); ING Bank and TransAmerica (controlled in the Netherlands); Sears Canada, Apache Canada, and Tim Hortons (controlled in the United States); Sony Canada and Honda Canada (controlled in Japan); and Husky Energy (controlled in Hong Kong).

17 In 1996, AMOCO Canada and Nexen were controlled in the United States; in 2006, Inco was controlled in Brazil and Teck Corporation was (partially) controlled in Japan, with Sumitomo Metal Mining as a dominant shareholder, alongside the (Canadian) Keevil family.

18 In 1996, Power Corporation of Canada was already networked across the Atlantic, but although its investments in and beyond Canada were substantial, it did not qualify as a TNC; see Carroll (2004, 64–5).

6. Armoured Neoliberalism: The Power Bloc and the New Imperial State

1 In his critique of Hegel's *Philosophy of Right*, Karl Marx ([1843] 1970) demonstrated how the capitalist state is not a consummation of freedom, but an expression of the contradictions of civil society.

2 Carroll (2010) makes the critical point that the transnational capitalist class is anchored by corporations of North America and Europe, and thus perpetuates an uneven structure of corporate power and capital accumulation in the world economy.

3 According to Thomas d'Aquino, former president of the CCCE, both he and the CCCE were "very closely consulted" on "certainly anything involving North American security" after 9/11 and were "heavily

involved" in the "most important" foreign policy issues between 1980 and 2010; author's interview with Thomas d'Aquino, 7 May 2012.

4 For more on this concept, see Albo (2013).

5 For Albo (2013, 244), the "stratified multilateralism" of Canadian foreign policy follows a double logic: "on the one hand, using a degree of policy autonomy in pursuit of diplomatic initiatives and extra-market state assistance for the internationalization of Canadian capital and, on the other, facilitating and buttressing US and western hegemony over the world order."

6 See Albo (2013) and Klassen and Albo (2013) for more on this concept.

7 These documents include the *National Security Policy* (Canada 2004), the *International Policy Statement* (Canada 2005b), the *Canada First Defence Strategy* (Canada 2008a), the *Global Commerce Strategy* (Canada 2008c), the *Counter-Terrorism Strategy* (Canada 2012a), the *Global Markets Action Plan* (Canada 2013), and various reports by standing committees of Parliament.

8 On Canada's indirect support for CIA extraordinary renditions, see Open Society Foundations (2013, 70–1).

9 Canada's corporate elites, policy groups, and think tanks were strongly in favour of the US-led war on Iraq, and hoped that Canada would participate in it, if only to maintain economic ties with the United States (Donolo 2006). In April 2003, the CCCE organized a trip of one hundred Canadian business executives to Washington to smooth over relations with US political and economic leaders (Veenbaas 2003).

10 As Mohamedou (2006) reveals, al-Qaeda's primary impetus was responding to what it perceived as unjust American policies towards Muslims in the Middle East, especially in Palestine. The United States' support for the Gulf Arab regimes has been another key grievance of al-Qaeda. In the Canadian context, one member of the Toronto 18 has made a similar point, stating that "[i]t was Canadian foreign policy specifically in Afghanistan" that motivated his involvement in the bombing plot (Davison and Thomson 2014).

11 On 18 January 2014, a spokesperson for the Prime Minister's Office also made an unfounded accusation against the National Council of Canadian Muslims, saying that "[w]e will not take seriously criticism from an organization with documented ties to a terrorist organization such as Hamas" (Chase 2014).

12 To consolidate all of these shifts in CIDA operations and to further enhance the political direction of development funding and programming, the Harper government announced in March 2013 that CIDA would be folded into a new Department of Foreign Affairs, Trade and Development (Mackrael 2013).

13 As Peter McKenna's (2012) anthology makes clear, the Strategy for the·
    Americas is designed to support Canadian corporate expansion, bolster
    conservative governments in the hemisphere, and garner clout in
    Washington. According to a secret US embassy cable from Ottawa (dated
    15 April 2009), the Strategy was designed specifically to gain influence with
    the United States "by emphasizing its relations in its own neighborhood."
    In 2014, Export Development Canada (EDC) opened an office in Bogota,
    Colombia, to help Canadian firms "link into the supply chains of upcoming
    infrastructure, oil and gas, and mining project opportunities," according
    to Rajesh Sharma, senior vice-president for international business
    development at EDC. Sharma adds that "[t]he capital-intensive demands
    of large infrastructure projects present a number of opportunities for EDC
    to bring its significant financing capacity to the region, to the benefit of
    Canadian companies operating there" (Isfeld 2014).
14 The transformation of the Canadian Commercial Corporation, a Crown
    corporation that promotes Canadian exports, is another sign of the
    making of a new imperial state. According to Carl Meyer (2011), under the
    Harper government, "the Canadian Commercial Corporation has been
    transformed from a low-profile Canadian intermediary agency to a major
    player in promoting Canadian global arms sales."
15 On 5 October 2012, the Canadian Forces were further reorganized into two
    command structures: the Canadian Joint Operations Command (merging
    Canada Command, the Canadian Expeditionary Force Command, and
    the Canadian Operational Support Command) and the Canadian Special
    Operations Forces Command.
16 In the wake of the Afghanistan War, the DND has sought a "Global
    Engagement Strategy" of "defence diplomacy" with old and new
    allies, involving everything from "high-level engagement and visits, to
    international personnel placements, Canadian defence attachés, ship
    and aircraft visits, joint exercises and capacity-building initiatives"
    (Berthiaume 2013b).

7. One of the Big Boys: Canada in Afghanistan and Haiti

 1 In 2009, Ben Rowswell, Canada's diplomatic representative in Kandahar,
    indicated that Canada and the United States were working on
    counterinsurgency "at full integration," adding, "[w]e are cheek by jowl …
    The best way to integrate is to integrate completely" (Fenton 2009).
 2 As the World Bank (2005) argued, "[a] dynamic private sector will be
    essential for Afghanistan to achieve the robust, sustained economic growth

that is necessary for national poverty reduction, state building, and other reconstruction objectives" (see also Podur 2013, 355).

3 At the 2010 Global Investigative Journalism Conference in Geneva, Switzerland, journalist Seymour Hersh reported that "battlefield executions are taking place" in Afghanistan. His keynote speech is available online at https://www.youtube.com/watch?v=IRltBu-oFjk. Matthieu Aikins (2013) has also reported on such dirty war tactics in Afghanistan for *Rolling Stone*.

4 Reporting from Kandahar province, the *Canadian Press* (2011a) found other problems in Canada's school-building efforts: "[s]chools in Kandahar that were built or renovated on the Canadian government's dime have far fewer students than official roll numbers suggest … The findings call into question the efficacy of one of the Conservative government's legacy projects in southern Afghanistan."

5 According to Lieutenant-Colonel Hope, Canada's counterinsurgency tried to win "the confidence of the people" of Kandahar in order to increase "public will" back home for the war (Podur 2013, 350).

6 After the wining bid was announced, Ed Fast, Canada's Minister for International Trade, stated: "Canada is strongly committed to helping Afghans rebuild their country, and this investment by Kilo Goldmines will create jobs for Afghans and Canadians alike" (Skinner 2013, 127).

7 As Canada's Senate Standing Committee on National Security and Defence (Canada 2007, 9) observed, "[t]hings may be improving in some parts of [Afghanistan], but where Canada is trying to have its biggest impact – in Kandahar – life is clearly *more perilous because we are there*."

8 Aristide insists that he was kidnapped during the coup. As he told CNN: "I called it a *coup d'état* because it [was] a modern kidnapping" (CNN 2004).

9 The opposition boycotted the election because of controversy surrounding the counting mechanism for the May 2000 senate elections; see endnote 10 below. In the presidential election, Aristide received 91.7 per cent of the vote, with a turnout of roughly 50 per cent; see Hallward (2004).

10 At the same time, the OAS criticized the counting methods of Haiti's Provisional Electoral Council regarding ten senate seats. According to the OAS, the winning candidates did not receive a strict majority of total votes, but only a majority of votes cast for the top four candidates in each race in question. The OAS (2000) concluded that "the highest electoral authority of the country violated its own constitution and electoral law." In this context, the opposition parties boycotted the run-off elections

of 9 July 2000, and the United States terminated bilateral aid payments
to Haiti and also blocked the Inter-American Development Bank from
dispensing hundreds of millions of aid dollars. As Peter Hallward
(2004) notes, however, "[t]he OAS had itself been closely involved in the
development of this form of [electoral] calculation, and there is no good
reason to believe that the balance of power in the Senate would have
been any different whatever method was used." Furthermore, "[i]n 2001,
a bankrupt Aristide agreed to virtually all of the concessions demanded
by his opponents: he obliged the winners of the disputed Senate seats to
resign, accepted the participation of several ex-Duvalier supporters in his
new government, agreed to convene a new and more opposition-friendly
[Provisional Electoral Council] and to hold another round of legislative
elections several years ahead of schedule. But the US still refused to lift its
aid embargo."

11 In 2001, a US Army War College Strategy Paper (Loesch 2001, 16) outlined
the neoliberal logic of US policy towards Haiti: "By keeping initial aid out
of the hands of the Haitian government, the United States can ensure that
corruption is minimized, while limiting the power of the Government of
Haiti (GOH). Reduced corruption could be accomplished by bypassing
the GOH in handling any USAID funds, working instead directly with
[NGOs] to provide needed aid. Not only would this reduce corruption, but
it would also demonstrate to the Haitian population that the power of the
GOH is limited."

12 For context and analysis, see Hallward (2004, 2008); and Podur (2012, 24–5).

13 In 2004, a CIDA report (2004, 9) noted that "non-governmental actors
(for-profit and not-for-profit) provided almost 80 per cent of [Haiti's] basic
services."

14 According to a US embassy cable dated 16 January, the priorities of the
Préval government were not security related but humanitarian – for
example, re-establishing telephone communications, clearing debris and
bodies, providing food and water to the population, burying the dead,
treating the injured, and so on. Préval did not mention insecurity as a major
concern, nor did he request military support. See United States (2010d).

15 According to the US Government Accountability Office (United States
2013), as of 31 March 2013, only 45 per cent of USAID money pledged for
Haiti had been dispensed since the earthquake.

16 Oxford economist Paul Collier (2009) argues that, with wages on par with
China, Haiti should develop into a globally competitive garment export-
processing zone.

17 See endnotes 9 and 10 above.

18 Some of these Canadian-based NGOs included Concertation Pour Haiti, Development and Peace, Entraide Missionaire, and Rights & Democracy (Burron 2012, 80).

19 In a subsequent interview, Paradis asserted that "there was one thematic that went under the whole meeting ... the 'Responsibility to Protect'" (Fenton 2004). The "responsibility to protect" is an evolving yet highly contentious norm at the United Nations that seeks to justify military interventions in sovereign states. In the final report of the Canada-led International Commission on Intervention and State Sovereignty (2001, xi), the norm asserts that "the principle of non-intervention yields to the international responsibility to protect" when civilians are victims of human rights abuses. However, the UN has neither legalized nor codified this evolving norm.

20 Since the notion of a "duty to protect" is *directly* associated with military interventions by western states, if Canadian officials were seeking to invoke such a "duty" in Haiti, they were *clearly anticipating a military intervention.*

21 In February 2013, the UN Human Rights Council reported serious problems with the Haitian national police, including "illegal and arbitrary police arrests, extended pretrial detention at certain police headquarters or stations, refusal to issue certificates in cases of rape, police harassment and ill-treatment, and police brutality." Furthermore, "[p]rison conditions ... continue to amount to cruel, inhuman and degrading treatment within the meaning of the Convention against Torture." See Forst (2013).

22 In January 2013, Haiti's prime minister, Laurent Lamothe, argued that Canada's aid funding was "routed directly to NGOs ... and Canadian firms" and that such practices "weakened our institutions" (Blatchford 2013).

23 For example, on 30 September 2013, massive protests occurred in Port-au-Prince criticizing the current government and supporting Aristide and *Fanmi Lavalas.*

Bibliography

Aaronson, Susan. 1991. "How Cordell Hull and the Postwar Planners Designed a New Trade Policy." *Business & Economic History II* 20: 171–9.

Acheson, Dean. 1952. "The Secretary of State to the Embassy in France." 19 September 1952. Foreign Relations of the United States, 1952–1954, Volume 5, Part 1, Western European Security, Document 174.

Acheson, Dean. 1969. *Present at the Creation: My Years in the State Department.* New York: W.W. Norton.

ActionAid et al. 2010. "Quick Impact, Quick Collapse: The Dangers of Militarized Aid in Afghanistan." Oxford: Oxfam International. January.

Agence France-Presse. 2012. "No compensation for seized Canadian mine: Bolivia." 3 October.

"Agreement on Provisional Arrangements in Afghanistan Pending the Re-Establishment of Permanent Government Institutions." 5 December 2001.

Aikins, Matthieu. 2011. "Our Man in Kandahar." *Atlantic*, November.

Aikins, Matthieu. 2013. "The A-Team Killings." *Rolling Stone*, 6 November.

Albo, Gregory. 1994. "'Competitive Austerity' and the Impasse of Capitalist Employment Policy." In *The Socialist Register 1994: Between Globalism and Nationalism*, ed. Ralph Miliband and Leo Panitch. London: Merlin.

Albo, Gregory. 2004. "The Economics of the Old and New Imperialism." In *The Socialist Register 2004: The New Imperial Challenge*, ed. Leo Panitch and Colin Leys. London: Merlin.

Albo, Gregory. 2005. "Contesting the 'New Capitalism'." In *Varieties of Capitalism, Varieties of Approaches*, ed. David Coates. London: Palgrave.

Albo, Gregory. 2013. "Fewer Illusions: Canadian Foreign Policy since 2001." In *Empire's Ally: Canada and the War in Afghanistan*, ed. Jerome Klassen and Greg Albo. Toronto: University of Toronto Press.

Albright, Madeleine. 1998. *Today*. National Broadcasting Company. 19 February.

Ambrose, Stephen E. 1988. *Rise to Globalism: American Foreign Policy since 1938*, 5th ed. New York: Penguin.

Amnesty International. 2013. *Iraq: A Decade of Abuses*. London: Amnesty International.

Anderson, Kevin. 2010. *Marx at the Margins: On Nationalism, Ethnicity, and Non-Western Societies*. Chicago: University of Chicago Press.

Angus Reid. 2010. "Three-in-five Canadians oppose Afghan mission." 20 June.

Anievas, Alex, ed. 2010. *Marxism and World Politics*. London: Routledge.

Anievas, Alex. 2012. "1914 in World Historical Perspective: The 'Uneven' and 'Combined' Origins of the First World War." *European Journal of International Relations* 1 March: 1–26.

Arango, Santiago Ortega. 2013. "Canadian mining companies subject of worldwide protests." Special to *CBC News*, 3 April. Available online at http://www.cbc.ca/news/business/story/2013/04/02/f-mining-protests -canada-abroad.html.

Arezki, Rabah, et al. 2013. "Testing the Prebisch-Singer Hypothesis since 1650: Evidence from Panel Techniques that Allow for Multiple Breaks." International Monetary Fund Working Paper 13/180. Washington, DC: IMF.

Arkin, William M. 2002. "Secret plan outlines the unthinkable." *Los Angeles Times*, 10 March.

Armstrong, Jane, et al. 2009. "Soldier's murder charge raises question about secrecy." *Globe and Mail*, 3 January.

Armstrong, Philip, Andrew Glyn, and John Harrison. 1991. *Capitalism since 1945*. New York: John Wiley & Sons.

Arneil, Barbara. 1994. "Trade, Plantations, and Property: John Locke and the Economic Defense of Colonialism." *Journal of the History of Ideas* 55 (4): 591–609.

Arrighi, Giovanni. 1978. *Geometry of Imperialism*. London: New Left Books.

Arrighi, Giovanni. 2005. "Hegemony Unravelling." *New Left Review* 32 (March-April): 23–80.

Arrighi, Giovanni. 2009. *Adam Smith in Beijing: Lineages of the 21st Century*. London: Verso.

Arthurs, Harry W. 2000. "The Hollowing Out of Corporate Canada?" In *Globalizing Institutions: Case Studies in Regulation and Innovation*, ed. J. Jenson and B. de Sousa Santos. Burlington, VT: Ashgate.

Ashley, Richard K. 1984. "The Poverty of Neorealism." *International Organization* 38 (2): 225–86.

Associated Press. 2013. "55 wounded, 80 detained in clashes at Canadian mine in Kyrgyzstan." 31 May.

Axworthy, Lloyd. 2003. *Navigating a New World: Canada's Global Future.* Toronto: Alfred A. Knopf.

Ayres, Jeffrey. 2004. "Power Relations under NAFTA: Reassessing the Efficacy of Contentious Transnationalism." *Studies in Political Economy* 74 (Autumn): 101–23.

Ayres, Jeffrey, and Laura Macdonald, eds. 2009. *Contentious Politics in North America: National Protest and Transnational Collaboration under Continental Integration.* London: Palgrave Macmillan.

Ayres, Jeffrey, and Laura Macdonald. 2012a. "Democratic Deficits and the Role of Civil Society in North America: The SPP and Beyond." In *North America in Question: Regional Integration in an Era of Economic Turbulence,* ed. Jeffrey Ayres and Laura Macdonald. Toronto: University of Toronto Press.

Ayres, Jeffrey, and Laura Macdonald. 2012b. "Introduction: North America in Question." In *North America in Question: Regional Integration in an Era of Economic Turbulence,* ed. Jeffrey Ayres and Laura Macdonald. Toronto: University of Toronto Press.

Bacevich, Andrew. 2002. *American Empire: The Realities and Consequences of U.S. Diplomacy.* Cambridge, MA: Harvard University Press.

Baldwin, J., and G. Gellatly. 2007. "Global Links: Multinationals in Canada: An Overview of Research at Statistics Canada." Cat. no. 11-622-MIE2007014. Ottawa: Statistics Canada.

Baldwin, John R., and Wulong Gu. 2008. *Basic Trends in Outsourcing and Offshoring in Canada.* Ottawa: Statistics Canada.

Balkin, Jack M. 2008. "The Constitution in the National Surveillance State." *Minnesota Law Review* 93 (1): 1–25.

Baragar, Fletcher, and Mario Seccareccia. 2008. "Financial Restructuring: Implications of Recent Canadian Macroeconomic Developments." *Studies in Political Economy* 82 (Autumn): 61–83.

Baran, Paul. 1957. *The Political Economy of Growth.* New York: Monthly Review Press.

Barlow, Maude. 2000. "The Free Trade Area of the Americas (FTAA) and the Threat to Social Programs, Environmental Sustainability and Social Justice in Canada and the Americas." Ottawa: Council of Canadians.

Barlow, Maude. 2005. *Too Close for Comfort: Canada's Future within Fortress North America.* Toronto: McClelland and Stewart.

Barry-Shaw, Nikolas, and Dru Oja Jay. 2012. *Paved with Good Intentions: Canada's Development NGOs from Idealism to Imperialism.* Halifax, NS: Fernwood.

BBC. 2014a. "Ukraine crisis: Transcript of leaked Nuland–Pyatt call." 7 February. Available online at http://www.bbc.com/news/world-europe-26079957.

BBC. 2014b. "Ukraine's revolution and the far right." 6 March. Available online at http://www.bbc.com/news/world-europe-26468720.

BCNI (Business Council on National Issues). 1993. "The North American Free Trade Agreement: Why It Is in Canada's interest." Submission to the Senate Standing Committee on Foreign Affairs. Ottawa, 25 May.

BCNI. 1997. "Six APEC Leaders, 20 Ministers to Address APEC CEO Summit in Vancouver." 20 November. Available online at http://www.ceocouncil.ca/news-item/six-apec-leaders-20-ministers-to-address-apec-ceo-summit-in-vancouver-15.

Beard, Charles A. [1913] 2004. *An Economic Interpretation of the Constitution of the United States.* Mineola, NY: Dover.

Beath, Andrew, et al. 2010. *Estimates of Interim Program Impact from First Follow-Up Survey.* [n.p.]: National Solidarity Program. Available online at http://www.nsp-ie.org.

Beckley, Michael. 2011/12. "China's Century? Why America's Edge Will Endure." *International Security* 36 (3): 41–78.

Beier, J. Marshall, and Lana Wylie, eds. 2010. *Canadian Foreign Policy in Critical Perspective.* Don Mills, ON: Oxford University Press.

Bell, Colleen. 2006. "Surveillance Strategies and Populations at Risk: Biopolitical Governance in Canada's National Security Policy." *Security Dialogue* 37 (2): 147–65.

Bell, Stewart. 2006. "Listening in on the enemy." *National Post*, 15 April, A1.

Bello, Walden. 2006. "The Capitalist Conjuncture: Over-accumulation, Financial Crises, and the Retreat from Globalization." *Third World Quarterly* 27 (8): 1345–67.

Bender, Yuri. 2014. "In the wake of turmoil, the role of Ukraine's oligarchs is under scrutiny." *Financial Times*, 27 March.

Benlon, Brodie. 2008. "MacKay defends soldiers in Afghan shooting." *Globe and Mail*, 28 July.

Bercuson, David, et al. 2003. *National Defence, National Interest: Sovereignty, Security and Canadian Military Capability in the Post 9/11 World.* Calgary: Canadian Defence and Foreign Affairs Institute.

Bernier, Gérald, and Daniel Salée. 1992. *The Shaping of Québec Politics and Society: Colonialism, Power, and the Transition to Capitalism in the 19th Century.* Washington, DC: Crane Russak.

Berthiaume, Lee. 2012a. "Outposts key to projecting power abroad." *Postmedia News*, 20 July.

Berthiaume, Lee. 2012b. "Tories closely tracked F-35 coverage." *Postmedia News*, 11 December.

Berthiaume, Lee. 2013a. "Canadian arms exports hit $12 billion last year – $4 billion sent to Saudi Arabia." *Ottawa Citizen*, 23 February.

Berthiaume, Lee. 2013b. "Military carrying diplomatic torch as Foreign Affairs struggles to stay above water." *Postmedia News*, 7 June.

Berthiaume, Lee. 2014. "Canada looks to weapons sales to developing countries to maintain domestic arms industry." *Postmedia News*, 5 January.

Bespoke Investment Group. 2012. "Changes in Share of World Market Cap." Available online at http://www.bespokeinvest.com/thinkbig/2012/5/11/changes-in-share-of-world-market-cap.html.

Beverly, Graham. 2011. "Canada: How the NDP Facilitates Imperialist War." *World Socialist Website*, 23 August. Available online at https://www.wsws.org/en/articles/2011/08/cana-a23.html.

Bhandari, Subel. 2012. "Drought hits Afghanistan's malnourished children." *Deutsche Presse-Agentur*, 17 February.

Black, Jeff. 2011. "Germany's future rising in east as exports to China eclipse U.S." *Bloomberg News*, 6 April. Available online at http://www.bloomberg.com/news/2011-04-06/germany-s-future-rising-in-east-as-exports-to-china-eclipse-u-s-.html.

Blackwell, Tom. 2008. "Canadian Forces just as guilty, says journalist," *Province*, 25 September.

Blackwell, Tom. 2012. "Canada's $1.5B Afghanistan aid effort 'divorced from reality,' according to damning, previously unreleased documents." *National Post*, 12 October.

Blackwood, Elizabeth, and Veronika Stewart. 2012. "CIDA and the Mining Sector: Extractive Industries as an Overseas Development Strategy." In *Struggling for Effectiveness: CIDA and Canadian Foreign Aid*, ed. Stephen Brown. Montreal; Kingston, ON: McGill-Queen's University Press.

Blanchfield, Mike, and Andrew Mayeda. 2007. "1.1 million dollar contract of Canadian military with a company of infamous warlord." *Ottawa Citizen*, 19 November.

Blatchford, Andy. 2013. "Haiti PM responds: Give our government more say over Canadian aid." *Canadian Press*, 8 January.

Blatchford, Christie. 2008. "'Bureaucratic jealousy' threatens military team." *Globe and Mail*, 14 January.

Block, Sheila, and Grace-Edward Galabuzi. 2011. *Canada's Colour Coded Labour Market: The Gap for Racialized Workers*. Ottawa: Canadian Centre for Policy Alternatives.

Bogdanich, Walt, and Jenny Nordberg. 2006. "Mixed U.S. signals helped tilt Haiti toward chaos." *New York Times*, 29 January.

Boot, Max. 2003. "American imperialism? No need to run away from label."
    USA Today, 5 May.
Boukalas, Christos. 2014. "No Exceptions: Authoritarian Statism. Agamben,
    Poulantzas and Homeland Security." *Critical Studies on Terrorism* 7 (1): 112–30.
Bourgeault, Ron G. 1988. "Race and Class under Mercantilism: Indigenous
    People in Nineteenth-century Canada." In *Racial Oppression in Canada*, 2nd
    ed., ed. B. Singh Bolaria and Peter S. Li. Toronto: Garamond.
Bow, Brian. 2012. "Immovable Object or Unstoppable Force? Economic
    Crisis and the Social Construction of North America." In *North America in
    Question: Regional Integration in an Era of Economic Turbulence*, ed. Jeffrey
    Ayres and Laura Macdonald. Toronto: University of Toronto Press.
Boyko, John. 1995. *Last Steps to Freedom: The Evolution of Canadian Racism.*
    Toronto: Watson and Dwyer.
BPG (Bi-National Planning Group). 2006. *Final Report on Canada and the United
    States (CANUS) Enhanced Military Cooperation.* Peterson Air Force Base, CO.
Brenner, Robert. 1977. "The Origins of Capitalist Development: A Critique of
    Neo-Smithian Marxism." *New Left Review* I/104 (July-August): 25–92.
Brenner, Robert. 1998. "Uneven Development and the Long Downturn: The
    Advanced Capitalist Economies from Boom to Stagnation, 1950–1998."
    New Left Review 229.
Brenner, Robert. 2006a. *The Economics of Global Turbulence.* London: Verso.
Brenner, Robert. 2006b. "What Is, and What Is Not, Imperialism?" *Historical
    Materialism* 14 (4): 79–105.
Brewer, Anthony. 1990. *Marxist Theories of Imperialism: A Critical Survey*,
    2nd ed. New York: Routledge.
Brewster, Murray. 2009. "3rd child in Afghan blast dies." *Canadian Press*,
    24 February.
Brewster, Murray. 2010. "NATO bullish, Canadians wary about brutal
    effectiveness of Afghan warlord Razik." *Associated Press*, 27 December.
Brewster, Murray, and Jim Bronskill. 2010. "Prisoners interrogated by CSIS:
    transcripts." *Globe and Mail*, 8 March, A10.
Brzezinski, Zbigniew. 1997. *The Grand Chessboard: American Primacy and its
    Geostrategic Imperatives.* New York: Basic Books.
Brzezinski, Zbigniew. 2009. "An Agenda for NATO: Toward a Global Security
    Web." *Foreign Affairs* 88 (5): 5–20.
Brodie, Janine, and Jane Jenson. 1988. *Crisis, Challenge and Change: Party and
    Class in Canada Revisited.* Ottawa: Carleton University Press.
Bromley, Simon. 2006. "The Logic of American Power in the International
    Capitalist Order." In *The War on Terror and the American Empire after the Cold
    War*, ed. Alejandro Colás and Richard Saull. New York: Routledge.

Brown, Stephen. 2008. "CIDA under the Gun." In *Canada Among Nations 2007: What Room for Manoeuvre?* ed. Jean Daudelin and Daniel Schwanen. Montreal; Kingston, ON: McGill-Queen's University Press.

Brownlee, Jamie. 2005. *Ruling Canada: Corporate Cohesion and Democracy.* Halifax, NS: Fernwood.

Brunelle, Dorval, and Sylvie Dugas. 2009. "Civil Society Organizations against Free Trade in North America." In *Contentious Politics in North America: National Protest and Transnational Collaboration under Continental Integration,* ed. Jeffrey Ayres and Laura Macdonald. London: Palgrave Macmillan.

Bukharin, Nikolai. 1917. *Imperialism and World Economy.* London: Martin Lawrence.

Burgess, Bill. 2000. "Foreign Direct Investment: Facts and Perceptions about Canada." *Canadian Geographer* 44 (2): 98–113.

Burron, Neil A. 2012. *The New Democracy Wars: The Politics of North American Democracy Promotion in the Americas.* Burlington, VT: Ashgate Publishing.

Bush, George W. 2001. Speech to Congress. 20 September. Available online at http://articles.cnn.com/2001-09-20/us/gen.bush.transcript_1_joint -session-national-anthem-citizens/2?_s=PM:US.

Byers, Michael. 2007. *Intent for a Nation: What Is Canada For?* Toronto: Douglas & McIntyre.

Byers, Michael. 2014. "Sorry NATO – we're fresh out of warships." *National Post,* 12 March.

Callinicos, Alex. 2001. "Periodizing Capitalism and Analyzing Imperialism: Classical Marxism and Capitalist Evolution." In *Phases of Capitalist Development: Booms, Crises and Globalizations,* ed. Robert Albritton et al. New York: Palgrave Macmillan.

Callinicos, Alex. 2002. "Marxism and Global Governance." In *Governing Globalization: Power, Authority and Global Governance,* ed. David Held and Anthony McGrew. Oxford, UK: Blackwell.

Callinicos, Alex. 2009. *Imperialism and Global Political Economy.* Cambridge, UK: Polity Press.

Cameron, Maxwell A., and Brian W. Tomlin. 2000. *The Making of NAFTA: How the Deal was Done.* Ithaca, NY: Cornell University Press.

Campion-Smith, Bruce. 2005. "Canada urged to go after 'scumbags'." *Toronto Star,* 15 July.

Canada. 1985. Royal Commission on the Economic Union and Development Projects for Canada. *Report.* 3 v. Ottawa: Minister of Supply and Services.

Canada. 1996. Royal Commission on Aboriginal Peoples. *Report.* Ottawa: Minister of Supply and Services.

Canada. 2001. Parliament. House of Commons. Standing Committee on
Foreign Affairs and International Trade. *Towards a Secure and Trade-Efficient
Border*. Ottawa.

Canada. 2002a. Parliament. Senate. Standing Committee on National Security
and Defence. *Defence of North America: A Canadian Responsibility*. Ottawa.

Canada. 2002b. Parliament. House of Commons. Standing Committee
on Foreign Affairs and International Trade. *Partners in North America:
Advancing Canada's Relations with the United States and Mexico*. Ottawa.

Canada. 2004. *Securing an Open Society: Canada's National Security Policy*.
Ottawa: Privy Council Office.

Canada. 2005a. Parliament. House of Commons. Standing Committee on
Foreign Affairs and International Trade. *Elements of an Emerging Market
Strategy*. Ottawa, June.

Canada. 2005b. *A Role of Pride and Influence in the World: Canada's International
Policy Statement*. 4 v. Ottawa.

Canada. 2005c. Parliament. Senate. Standing Committee on National Security
and Defence. *Wounded: Canada's Military and the Legacy of Neglect*. Ottawa.

Canada. 2006. Parliament. Senate. Standing Committee on National Security
and Defence. *Managing Turmoil: The Need to Upgrade Canadian Foreign Aid
and Military Strength to Deal with Massive Change*. Ottawa.

Canada. 2007. Parliament. Senate. Standing Committee on National Security
and Defence. *Canadian Troops in Afghanistan: Taking a Hard Look at a Hard
Mission (An Interim Report)*. Ottawa.

Canada. 2008a. Department of National Defence. *The Canada First Defence
Strategy*. Ottawa.

Canada. 2008b. Department of National Defence. *Counter-Insurgency Operations*.
Ottawa.

Canada. 2008c. *Seizing Global Advantage: A Global Commerce Strategy for
Securing Canada's Growth and Prosperity*. Ottawa: Minister of Public Works
and Government Services Canada.

Canada. 2010. Department of National Defence. *The Future Security Environment,
2008–2030*. Ottawa.

Canada. 2011a. Citizenship and Immigration Canada. 2011. *Facts and Figures
2010*. Ottawa.

Canada. 2011b. Department of Foreign Affairs and International Trade
Canada. *Report on Exports of Military Goods from Canada, 2007–2009*. Ottawa.

Canada. 2011c. Department of Foreign Affairs and International Trade. *State of
Trade 2011*. Ottawa.

Canada. 2012a. *Building Resilience against Terrorism: Canada's Counter-Terrorism
Strategy*. Ottawa: Department of Public Safety.

Canada. 2012b. Office of the Special Envoy to Haiti. 2012. "Canada: Post-earthquake Assistance to Haiti as of September 2012." Available online at http://www.haitispecialenvoy.org/download/Home/Donor_Status/canada.pdf.

Canada. 2013. *Global Markets Action Plan: The Blueprint for Creating Jobs and Opportunities for Canadians through Trade*. Ottawa.

Canadian Press. 2008a. "Assessing Afghan security no easy task for troops," 21 October.

Canadian Press. 2008b. "Hiller calls for Afghan mission extension," 22 February.

Canadian Press. 2011a. "Afghan enrollment grades fail to make grade," 10 February.

Canadian Press. 2011b. "Panjwaii road dubbed 'dagger' in insurgency heart: A lasting Canadian legacy?" 1 May.

Carchedi, Guglielmo. 1991. *Frontiers of Political Economy*. London: Verso.

Carchedi, Guglielmo. 2001. *For Another Europe: A Class Analysis of European Economic Integration*. London: Verso.

Carpentier, Michel. 2007. "Canada and 9/11: Border Security in a New Era." Master's thesis, Department of Political Science, University of Saskatchewan.

Carroll, William K. 1986. *Corporate Power and Canadian Capitalism*. Vancouver: University of British Columbia Press.

Carroll, William K. 1989. "Neo-liberalism and the Recomposition of Finance Capital in Canada." *Capital & Class* 38: 81–112.

Carroll, William K. 1990. "Restructuring Capital, Reorganizing Consent: Gramsci, Political Economy, and Canada." *Canadian Review of Sociology and Anthropology* 27 (3): 390–416.

Carroll, William K. 1993. "Canada in the Crisis: Transformations in Capital Structure and Political Strategy." In *Restructuring Hegemony in the Global Political Economy*, ed. Henk Overbeek. London: Routledge.

Carroll, William K. 2004. *Corporate Power in a Globalizing World: A Study in Elite Social Organization*. Don Mills, ON: Oxford University Press.

Carroll, William K. 2008. "The Corporate Elite and the Transformation of Finance Capital: A View from Canada." *Sociological Review* 56 (S1): 44–63.

Carroll, William K. 2009a. "Transnationalists and National Networkers in the Global Corporate Elite." *Global Networks* 9 (3): 289–314.

Carroll, William K. 2009b. "World Trade Organization (WTO) Protests, Quebec City, 2001." In *International Encyclopedia of Revolution and Protest*, ed. Immanuel Ness. New York: Blackwell.

Carroll, William K. 2010. *The Making of a Transnational Capitalist Class*. London: Zed Books.

Carroll, William K., and Jerome Klassen. 2010. "Hollowing Out Corporate Canada? Changes in the Corporate Network since the 1990s." *Canadian Journal of Sociology* 35 (1): 1–30.

Carroll, William K., and Jerome Klassen. Forthcoming. "Continental neoliberalismo y la elite corporativa de Canada." In *America del Norte se marchitan?* ed. Elisa Davalos. Mexico City: National Autonomous University of Mexico Press.

Carroll, W.K., and J.P. Sapinski. 2011. "Corporate Elites and Intercorporate Networks." In *Handbook of Social Network Analysis*, ed. J. Scott and P. Carrington. London: Sage.

Carroll, William K., and Murray Shaw. 2001. "Consolidating a Neoliberal Policy Bloc in Canada, 1976 to 1996." *Canadian Public Policy* 27 (2): 195–217.

Castells, Manuel. 2000. *The Rise of the Network Society*, 2nd ed. Oxford: Wiley-Blackwell.

Cavendish, Julius. 2010. "In Afghanistan war, government corruption bigger threat than Taliban." *Christian Science Monitor*, 12 April.

CBC (Canadian Broadcasting Corporation). 2006. "Canadian soldiers fatally shoot taxi driver," 15 March.

CBC. 2007a. "Canadian troops kill unarmed Afghan civilian." 17 February.

CBC. 2007b. "'Death to Canada', outraged Afghans chant." 26 September.

CBC. 2007c. "Fifth Bullet: Canadian troops involved in Afghan shooting death." 16 November.

CBC. 2008a. "Canadian military silent on Afghan civilian deaths: UN investigator." 26 June.

CBC. 2008b. "Canadian troops kill 2 children after car nears convoy." 28 July.

CBC. 2008c. "Man dies after Canadian troops fire on Afghan civilian truck." 19 September.

CBC. 2008d. "Sophistication of deadly Taliban attack concerning: Natynczyk." 4 September.

CBC. 2009a. "Afghan girl's death by stray Canadian bullet angers family." 24 July.

CBC. 2009b. "Crowd blames Canadians for deaths of 2 children in Afghanistan." 23 February.

CBC. 2010. "Joint Task Force 2: Canada's Elite Fighters." 15 September.

CBC. 2011. "Harper says 'Islamicism' biggest threat to Canada." 6 September.

CBC. 2013. "What do we know about Canada's eavesdropping agency? Communications Security Establishment mines metadata of phone calls and emails." 14 June.

CCCE (Canadian Council of Chief Executives). 2003. *The North American Security and Prosperity Initiative*. Ottawa.

CCCE. 2004. *New Frontiers: Building a 21st Century Canada-United States Partnership in North America.* Ottawa.

CCCE. 2005. "Think well beyond ballistic missile defence business leader tells audiences in five U.S. cities." 3 March. Available online at http://www.ceocouncil.ca/news-item/think-well-beyond-missile-defence-business-leader-tells-audiences-in-five-u-s-cities-165.

CCCE. 2011. "From Vision to Action – Advancing the Canada – United States Partnership." Submission to the Beyond the Borders Working Group. Ottawa, May.

CCCE. n.d. "Defense and Security." Available online at http://www.ceocouncil.ca/en/canada/defence.php, accessed 10 January 2007.

CDAI (Conference of Defence Associations Institute). 2002. *A Nation at Risk: The Decline of the Canadian Forces.* Ottawa.

CDAI. 2004. *Canada's National Security and Defence Policy in the 21st Century.* Ottawa.

Cellucci, Paul. 2003. Speech to the Economic Club of Toronto, 25 March.

Cerny, Philip G. 2005. "Political Globalization and the Competition State." In *Political Economy and the Changing Global Order*, 3rd ed., ed. Richard Stubbs and Geoffrey R.D. Underhill. Don Mills, ON: Oxford University Press.

Chang, Ha-Joon. 2002. *Kicking Away the Ladder: Development Strategy in Historical Perspective.* London: Anthem Press.

Chang, Ha-Joon. 2007. *Bad Samaritans: The Myth of Free Trade and the Secret History of Capitalism.* New York: Bloomsbury Press.

Chapnick, Adam. 2000. "The Canadian Middle Power Myth." *International Journal* 55 (2): 188–206.

Charbonneau, Bruno, and Wayne S. Cox. 2008. "Global Order, US Hegemony, and Military Integration: The Canadian-American Defense Relationship." *International Political Sociology* 2 (4): 305–21.

Chase, Steven. 2008. "Think tank's funding tied to getting good press." *Globe and Mail*, 16 May.

Chase, Steven. 2014. "Muslim group demands an apology from Harper, chief spokesman over 'terrorist' comment." *Globe and Mail*, 28 January.

Chesterman, Simon, Michael Ignatieff, and Ramesh Thakur, eds. 2005. *Making States Work: State Failure and the Crisis of Governance.* Tokyo: United Nations University Press.

Chiang, Chuck. 2013. "Canadian navy looks to Pacific and to a multi-cultural future." *Vancouver Sun*, 22 September.

Chivers, C.J., and Eric Schmitt. 2013. "Arms airlift to Syria rebels expands, with aid from C.I.A." *New York Times*, 24 March.

Chomsky, Noam. 1985. *Turning the Tide: U.S. Intervention in Central America and the Struggle for Peace*. Boston: South End Press.

Chomsky, Noam. 2002. *The New Military Humanism: Lessons from Kosovo*. Monroe, ME: Common Courage Press.

Chomsky, Noam. 2003. *Hegemony or Survival: America's Quest for Global Dominance*. New York: Metropolitan Books.

Chomsky, Noam, and Edward S. Herman. 1979. *The Washington Connection and Third World Fascism*. Boston: South End Press.

Chowdry, Geeta, and Sheila Nair, eds. 2004. *Power, Postcolonialism, and International Relations: Reading Race, Class, and Gender*. New York: Routledge.

CHRGJ (Center for Human Rights and Global Justice) et al. 2008. *Wòch nan Soley: The Denial of the Right to Water in Haiti*. New York: New York University School of Law.

CIDA (Canadian International Development Agency). 2004. "Canadian Cooperation with Haiti: Reflecting on a Decade of 'Difficult Partnership'." Ottawa, December.

CIDA. 2006. "Canada-Haiti Cooperation – Interim Cooperation Framework – Result Summary." Ottawa.

CIDA. 2009. *Statistical Report on International Assistance: Fiscal Year 2006–2007*. Ottawa.

Clark, Wesley. 2003. *Winning Modern Wars: Iraq, Terrorism and the American Empire*. New York: Public Affairs.

Clark-Jones, Melissa. 1987. *A Staple State: Canadian Industrial Resources in the Cold War*. Toronto: University of Toronto Press.

Clarkson, Stephen. 2002. *Uncle Sam and Us: Globalization, Neoconservatism and the Canadian State*. Toronto: University of Toronto Press.

Clarkson, Stephen. 2008. *Does North America Exist? Governing the Continent after NAFTA and 9/11*. Toronto: University of Toronto Press.

Clarkson, Stephen, and Matto Mildenberger. 2011. *Dependent America? How Canada and Mexico Construct U.S. Power*. Toronto: University of Toronto Press.

Clement, Wallace. 1975. *The Canadian Corporate Elite: An Economic Analysis of Power*. Toronto: McClelland and Stewart.

Clement, Wallace. 1977. *Continental Corporate Power: Economic Linkages between Canada and the United States*. Toronto: McClelland and Stewart.

Clement, Wallace, and Leah H. Vosko, eds. 2003. *Changing Canada: Political Economy as Transformation*. Montreal; Kingston, ON: McGill-Queen's University Press.

Clement, Wallace, and Glen Williams, eds. 1989. *The New Canadian Political Economy*. Montreal; Kingston, ON: McGill-Queen's University Press.

Clinton, Hillary. 2011. "America's Pacific Century." *Foreign Policy* (November). Available online at http://www.foreignpolicy.com/articles/2011/10/11/americas_pacific_century.

CNN. 2004. "Aristide: 'I call it a coup d'état'." *CNN.com*, 1 March. Available online at http://www.cnn.com/2004/WORLD/americas/03/01/cnna.aristide/index.html.

COAT (Coalition to Oppose the Arms Trade). 2011. "WikiWeapons Canada Database." Available online at http://coat.ncf.ca/research/WikiWeaponsCanada.xls, accessed 13 August 2012.

Coates, Colin M. 1999. "The Rebellions of 1837–38, and other Bourgeois Revolutions in Quebec Historiography." *International Journal of Canadian Studies* 20 (Fall): 19–34.

Coburn, Elaine. 2011. "Resisting Neoliberal Capitalism: Insights from Political Economy." In *Relations of Global Power: Neoliberal Order and Disorder*, ed. Stephen McBride and Gary Teeple. Toronto: University of Toronto Press.

Cohen, Stephen F. 2009. *Soviet Fates and Lost Alternatives: From Stalinism to the New Cold War*. New York: Columbia University Press.

Cohn, Marjorie. 2005. "United States Violations of International Law in Yugoslavia, Afghanistan, and Iraq." In *Challenges of Multi-Level Constitutionalism*, ed. J. Nergelius, P. Policastro, and K. Urata. Chicago: Polpress.

Colás, Alejandro, and Richard Saull, eds. 2006. *The War on Terrorism and the American "Empire" after the Cold War*. New York: Routledge.

Coleman, William, and Tony Porter. 2003. "'Playin' Along': Canada and Global Finance." In *Changing Canada: Political Economy as Transformation*, ed. Wallace Clement and Leah F. Vosko. Montreal; Kingston, ON: McGill-Queen's University Press.

Collier, Paul. 2009. "Haiti: From Natural Catastrophe to Economic Security: A Report for the Secretary-General of the United Nations." Oxford: Oxford University. January.

Conference Board of Canada. 2007. *Canada's Changing Role in Global Supply Chains*. Ottawa.

Cooney, Paul. 2004. "Towards an Empirical Measurement of International Transfers of Value." In *The New Value Controversy and the Foundations of Economics*, ed. Alan Freeman et al. London: Edward Elgar.

Cooper, Robert. 2002. "The new liberal imperialism." *Observer*, 7 April.

Cordesman, Anthony H. 2009. *Afghan Public Opinion and the Afghan War: Shifts by Region and Province*. Washington, DC: Center for Strategic and International Studies.

Coughlin, Dan, and Kim Ives. 2011. "WikiLeaks Haiti: Let them live on $3 a day." *Nation*, 1 June.

Council on Foreign Relations. 1940. Economic and Financial Group. "Memorandum E-B19." New York, October.

Council on Foreign Relations. 1941. Economic and Financial Group. "Memorandum E-B34." New York, 24 June.

Council on Foreign Relations. 2005. *Building North America: Report of An Independent Task Force*. New York.

Cox, Robert W. 1981. "Social Forces, States and World Orders: Beyond International Relations." *Journal of International Studies - Millennium* 10 (2): 126–55.

Cox, Robert W. 1987. *Production, Power and World Order*. New York: Columbia University Press.

Coyne, Christopher J. 2008. *After War: The Political Economy of Exporting Democracy*. Redwood City, CA: Stanford University Press.

Craig, Campbell. 2004. "American Realism versus American Imperialism." *World Politics* 57 (1): 143–71.

Crosby, Ann Denholm. 2007. "Myths of Canada's Human Security Pursuits: Tales of Tool Boxes, Toy Chests, and Tickle Trunks." In *Readings in Canadian Foreign Policy: Classic Debates and New Ideas*, ed. Duane Bratt and Christopher J. Kukucha. Don Mills, ON: Oxford University Press.

Crosby, Ann Denholm. 2010. "Canada-US Defence Relations: Weapons of Mass Control and a Praxis of Mass Resistance." In *Canadian Foreign Policy in Critical Perspective*, ed. J. Marshall Beier and Lana Wylie. Don Mills, ON: Oxford University Press.

Cross, P., and Z. Ghanem. 2008. "Tracking Value-added Trade: Examining Global Inputs to Exports." *Canadian Economic Observer*, February.

CSIS (Canadian Security Intelligence Service). 2004. "From Anti-Globalization to 'Alter-Globalization': A Canadian Perspective." CSIS Intelligence Brief (Secret). Ottawa, 18 November.

CSIS. 2005. "The Creation of a New Peace Movement?" CSIS Intelligence Brief (Secret). Ottawa, 20 January.

CSTB (Coalition for Secure and Trade-Efficient Borders). 2001. "Rethinking Our Borders: Statement of Principles." 1 November.

CSTB. 2005. "Rethinking Our Borders: A New North American Partnership." n.p.

CTV. 2006a. "Afghan accidentally killed by Canadian troops." *CTV.ca*, 13 December.

CTV. 2006b. "Afghan leaders work with Cdn. development agency." *CTV.ca*, 21 May.

CTV. 2006c. "Most Canadians Oppose Afghanistan Deployment: poll." *CTV.ca*, 6 May.

CTV. 2007. "Taliban preparing for attack on Afghan warlord." *CTV.ca*, 16 September.

Cullather, Nicholas. 1994. "Operation PBSUCCESS: The United States and Guatemala, 1952–1954." Central Intelligence Agency History Staff Document. Washington, DC.

Cumings, Bruce. 2011. *The Korean War: A History*. New York: Modern Library.

Daniels, Ronald J., Patrick Macklem, and Kent Roach. 2001. *The Security of Freedom: Essays on Canada's Anti-Terrorism Bill*. Toronto: University of Toronto Press.

d'Aquino, Thomas. 1987. "'Truck and Trade with the Yankees': The Case for a Canada-United States Comprehensive Trade Agreement." Paper presented to a Conference on Canadian-American Free Trade, Montreal, 19 March.

d'Aquino, Thomas. 2001. "Beyond September 11: A Time for Prudence, Creativity and Unity of Purpose." Presentation to the Standing Committee on Finance, House of Commons, Parliament of Canada, Ottawa, 25 September.

d'Aquino, Thomas. 2003. "Security and Prosperity: The Dynamics of a New Canada-United States Partnership in North America." PowerPoint presentation, 14 January. Available at: http://www.ceocouncil.ca, accessed 10 January 2007.

Daschuk, James. 2013. *Clearing the Plains: Disease, Politics of Starvation, and the Loss of Aboriginal Life*. Regina, SK: University of Regina Press.

Davis, Jeff. 2012. "Canada's cybersecurity agency CSEC full of secrets." *Postmedia News*, 18 April.

Davison, Janet, and Janet Thomson. 2014. "Homegrown terrorist: Toronto 18 bomb plotter Saad Khalid recalls his radicalization." *CBC News*, 16 April.

Day, Adam. 2013. "Canada is not a neutral country, conference told." *Legion Magazine*, 12 May.

de Graaff, Nan'a, and Bastiaan van Apeldoorn. 2010. "Varieties of US Post-Cold War Imperialism: Anatomy of a Failed Hegemonic Project and the Future of US Geopolitics." *Critical Sociology* 37 (4): 403–27.

de Grandpré, Hugo. 2006. "Les soldats Canadiens en Afghanistan pour tuer." *La Presse*, 22 June.

Demetrick, Paul. 2008. "Soldier says it's time to end Afghanistan war." *Toronto Star*, 8 October.

Deneault, Alain, and William Sacher. 2012. *Imperial Canada Inc.: Legal Haven of Choice for the World's Mining Industries*. Vancouver: Talon Books.

Desai, Radhika. 2007. "The Last Empire? From Nation-building Compulsion to Nation-wrecking Futility and Beyond." *Third World Quarterly* 28 (2): 435–56.

Desai, Radhika. 2013. *Geopolitical Economy: After US Hegemony, Globalization, and Empire*. London: Pluto Press.

Dewitt, David B., and John J. Kirton. 1983. *Canada as a Principal Power: A Study in Foreign Policy and International Relations.* Toronto: John Wiley and Sons.

Dillon, Douglas. 1958. "A Report by the Assistant Secretary for Economic Affairs to the Draper Committee; Moderating the African-Asian Revolution." 22 December 1958. Box 9, Records of the US President's Committee on Military Assistance Programs, DDEL.

Dobbin, Murray. 2003. *Paul Martin: CEO for Canada?* Toronto: James Lorimer.

Dobbin, Murray. 2009. "Canada must forge its own economic fate: the SPP is dead." *Tyee* (Vancouver), 24 September. Available online at http://thetyee.ca/Opinion/2009/09/24/EconomicFate, accessed 13 October 2011.

Dobson, Wendy. 2002a. "Shaping the Future of the North America Economic Space: A Framework for Action." *C.D. Howe Institute Commentary* 162. Toronto: C.D. Howe Institute.

Dobson, Wendy. 2002b. "Wanted: A big idea for the U.S. relation." *Globe and Mail*, 16 April.

Domhoff, G. William. 2006. *Who Rules America? Power, Politics & Social Change*, 5th ed. New York: McGraw-Hill.

Donolo, Peter. 2006. "Why Jean Chrétien was right to stay out of Iraq." *Globe and Mail*, 21 March.

Dorronsoro, Gilles. 2005. *Revolution Unending: Afghanistan 1979 to the Present.* New York: Columbia University Press.

Dorronsoro, Gilles. 2012. "Waiting for the Taliban in Afghanistan." Washington, DC: Carnegie Endowment for International Peace.

Doyle, Michael W. 1986. "Liberalism and World Politics." *American Political Science Review* 80 (4): 1151–69.

Doyle, Michael W. 1999. "A Liberal View: Preserving and Expanding the Liberal Pacific Union." In *International Order and the Future of World Politics*, ed. T. Paul and J. Hall. Cambridge: Cambridge University Press.

Drache, Daniel. 1977. "Staple-ization: A Theory of Canadian Capitalist Development." In *Imperialism, Nationalism, and Canada: Essays from the Marxist Institute of Toronto*, ed. Craig Heron and John Saul. Toronto: New Hogtown Press.

Drohan, Madeleine. 1991. "Canada invited to talks; Gulf stance called key to Mexico." *Globe and Mail*, 12 January.

Duffy, Helen. 2005. *The "War on Terror" and the Framework of International Law.* Cambridge: Cambridge University Press.

Duménil, Gerard, and Dominique Lévy. 2004. *Capital Resurgent: Roots of the Neoliberal Revolution.* Cambridge, MA: Harvard University Press.

Dupuis-Déri, Francis. 2010. "History of the Word 'Democracy' in Canada and Quebec: A Political Analysis of Rhetorical Strategies." *World Political Science Review* 6 (1): 1–23.

Dupuy, Alex. 2011. "One year after the earthquake, foreign help is actually hurting Haiti." *Washington Post*, 7 January.

Eayrs, James. 1981. "Defining a New Place for Canada in the Hierarchy of World Power." *International Perspectives* (November-December): 3–9.

Economist. 2003. "The Shadow Men." 24 April.

Edgar, Alistair D., and David G. Haglund. 1995. *The Canadian Defence Industry in the New Global Environment*. Montreal; Kingston, ON: McGill-Queen's University Press.

Edmonds, Kevin. 2013. "Beyond Good Intentions: The Structural Limitations of NGOs in Haiti." *Critical Sociology* 39 (3): 439–52.

Eichengreen, Barry. 2008. *Globalizing Capital: A History of the International Monetary System*. Princeton, NJ: Princeton University Press.

EKOS Research Associates. 2009. 'Decisive opposition to Canada's Afghan mission.' 16 July.

Emmanuel, Arghiri. 1972. *Unequal Exchange: A Study of the Imperialism of Trade*. New York: Monthly Review Press.

Engler, Yves. 2009. *The Black Book of Canadian Foreign Policy*. Halifax, NS: Fernwood.

Engler, Yves. 2012. "NATO enforces Western politics, economics." *Embassy Magazine*, 15 August.

Engler, Yves, and Anthony Fenton. 2005. *Canada in Haiti: Waging War on the Poor Majority*. Halifax, NS: Fernwood.

English, Robert. 2014. "Ukraine's threat from within." *Los Angeles Times*, 13 March.

Esau, Jeff. 2008. "Defence department flouting information policy, Globe finds." *Globe and Mail*, 26 January.

Evans, Patrick. 2005. "Maj. Gen. Andrew Leslie warns that our troops in Afghanistan will face 'predators'." *Toronto Star*, 8 August.

Fantino, Julian. 2012. "Reducing Poverty – Building Tomorrow's Markets." Speech, Toronto, 23 November.

Farmer, Paul. 2004. "Who Removed Aristide?" *London Review of Books* 26 (8): 28–31.

Fast, Travis. 2005. "Disparate Models, Desperate Measures: The Convergence of Limits." In *Varieties of Capitalism, Varieties of Approaches*, ed. David Coates. London: Palgrave.

Fatton, Robert. 2006. "Haiti: The Saturnalia of Emancipation and the Vicissitudes of Predatory Rule." *Third World Quarterly* 27 (1): 115–33.

Fennema, Meindert, and Huibert Schijf. 1985. "The Transnational Network." In *Networks of Corporate Power*, ed. F.N. Stokman, R. Ziegler, and J. Scott. Cambridge, UK: Polity Press.

Fenton, Anthony. 2004. "Quebec MP Paradis interviewed about Haiti coup." 11 September. Available online at http://www2.webster.edu/~corbetre/haiti-archive-new/msg23287.html, accessed 20 December 2012.

Fenton, Anthony. 2008. "Haiti and the Danger of the Responsibility to Protect (R2P)." *Upside Down World*, 22 December. Available online at http://upsidedownworld.org/main/haiti-archives-51/1638-haiti-and-the-danger-of-the-responsibility-to-protect-r2p-.

Fenton, Anthony. 2009. "Canada: 'Cheek by jowl' with U.S. on COIN in Afghanistan." *Inter Press Service*, 15 December.

Fenton, Anthony, and Jon Elmer. 2013. "Building an Expeditionary Force for Democracy Promotion." In *Empire's Ally: Canada and the War in Afghanistan*, ed. Jerome Klassen and Greg Albo. Toronto: University of Toronto Press.

Fenton, Anthony, and Dru Oja Jay. 2006. "Declassifying Canada in Haiti: Part I." *Dominion*, 7 April. Available online at http://www.dominionpaper.ca/foreign_policy/2006/04/07/declassify.html.

Ferguson, James. 2010. *Canada and Ballistic Missile Defence, 1954–2009: Déjà Vu All Over Again*. Vancouver: UBC Press.

Ferguson, Niall. 2003. "The Empire Slinks Back." *New York Times Magazine*, 27 April.

Ferguson, Thomas. 1984. "From Normalcy to New Deal: Industrial Structure, Party Competition, and American Public Policy in the Great Depression." *International Organization* 38 (1): 41–94.

Filkins, Dexter, Mark Mazzetti, and James Risen. 2009. "Karzai's brother is said to be on CIA payroll." *New York Times*, 27 October.

Financial Times. 2012. "Chinese exports by type of enterprise." 10 September. Available online at http://blogs.ft.com/beyond-brics/2012/09/10/chart-of-the-week-who-is-making-chinas-exports/chinese-exports-by-type-of-enterprise-sep-2012/.

Fine, Ben, and Dimitris Milonakis. 2008. *From Political Economy to Economics: Method, the Social and the Historical in the Evolution of Economic Theory*. New York: Routledge.

Fischer, Fritz. 1967. *Germany's Aims in the First World War*. New York: W.W. Norton.

Fisher, Mathew. 2013. "Time for the gloves to come off when dealing with China." *Postmedia*, 22 February.

Foote, Christopher, et al. 2004. "Economic Prospects and Policy in Iraq." *Journal of Economic Perspectives* 18 (3): 47–70.

Forbes. 2012. "Global 2000." Available online at http://www.forbes.com/global2000/, accessed 14 August 2012.

Forcese, Craig. 2009. "Canada's National Security 'Complex': Assessing the Secrecy Rules." *IRPP Choices* 15 (5).

Forcese, Craig. 2014. "Touching Torture with a Ten Foot Pole." *Osgoode Hall Law Journal* 52 (1).

Forst, Michel. 2013. *Report of the Independent Expert on the Situation of Human Rights in Haiti*. 7 February. New York: United Nations Human Rights Council.

Foster, John. 2008. *A Pipeline through a Troubled Land: Afghanistan, Canada, and the New Great Energy Game*. Ottawa: Canadian Centre for Policy Alternatives.

Fravel, M. Taylor. 2008. "China's Search for Military Power." *Washington Quarterly* 31 (1): 125–41.

Freeman, Alan. 2007. "Military wrote Karzai's speech, NDP says." *Globe and Mail*, 26 September.

Freeman, Linda. 1997. *Ambiguous Champion: Canada and South Africa in the Trudeau and Mulroney Years*. Toronto: University of Toronto Press.

Freeze, Colin. 2009. "A boy throws a stone, and Gen. Vance teaches a lesson in counterinsurgency." *Canadian Press*, 22 June.

Freeze, Colin. 2013. "Data-collection program got green light from MacKay in 2011." *Globe and Mail*, 10 June.

Freeze, Colin. 2014. "Spy agency's work with CSIS, RCMP fuels fears of privacy breaches." *Globe and Mail*, 31 January.

Froese, Marc D. 2010. *Canada at the WTO: Trade Litigation and the Future of Public Policy*. Toronto: University of Toronto Press.

Fukuyama, Francis. 1992. *The End of History and the Last Man*. New York: Penguin.

Gabriel, Christina, and Laura Macdonald. 2004. "Of Borders and Business: Canadian Corporate Proposals for North American 'Deep Integration'." *Studies in Political Economy* 74 (Fall): 79–100.

Galabuzi, Grace-Edward. 2006. *Canada's Economic Apartheid: The Social Exclusion of Racialized Groups in the New Century*. Toronto: Canadian Scholars Press.

Gamble, Andrew. 1988. *The Free Economy and the Strong State: The Politics of Thatcherism*. London: Macmillan.

Gereffi, Gary. 2005. "The New Offshoring of Jobs and Global Development." *ILO Social Policy Lectures*. Geneva: ILO Publications.

Gereffi, Gary, John Humphrey, and Timothy Sturgeon. 2005. "The Governance of Global Value Chains." *Review of International Political Economy* 12 (1): 78–104.

Germain, Randall, with Abdulghany Mohamed. 2012. "Global Economic Crisis and Regionalism in North America: Region-ness in Question?" In *North America in Question: Regional Integration in an Era of Economic Turbulence*, ed. Jeffrey Ayres and Laura Macdonald. Toronto: University of Toronto Press.

Gewen, Barry. 2004. "Kill the empire! (or not)." *New York Times*, 25 July.

Ghanem, Z., and P. Cross. 2008. "Loonie Tunes: Industry Exposure to the Rising Exchange Rate." *Canadian Economic Observer*, March.

Gilbert, Emily. 2012. "Borders and Security in North America." In *North America in Question: Regional Integration in an Era of Economic Turbulence*, ed. Jeffrey Ayres and Laura Macdonald. Toronto: University of Toronto Press.

Gill, Stephen. 1991. *American Hegemony and the Trilateral Commission*. Cambridge: Cambridge University Press.

Gill, Stephen. 1995. "Globalisation, Market Civilisation, and Disciplinary Neoliberalism." *Millennium – Journal of International Studies* 24 (3): 399–423.

Gill, Stephen. 2003. *Power and Resistance in the New World Order*. New York: Palgrave Macmillan.

Gill, Stephen. 2005. "The Contradictions of U.S. Supremacy." In *The Socialist Register 2005: The Empire Reloaded*, ed. Leo Panitch and Colin Leys. London: Merlin.

Gilmore, Jason. 2009. *The 2008 Canadian Immigrant Labour Market: Analysis of Quality of Employment*. Ottawa: Minister of Industry.

Gilpin, Roger. 1981. *War and Change in World Politics*. Cambridge: Cambridge University Press.

Girouard, Roger. 2012. *China's Shadow: A Canadian Concern?* Calgary: Canadian Defence and Foreign Affairs Institute.

Giustozzi, Antonio. 2007. *Koran, Kalashnikov and Laptop: The Neo-Taliban Insurgency in Afghanistan*. London: Hurst.

Golob, Stephanie R. 2012. "*Plus ca change*: Double-Bilateralism and the Demise of Trilateralism." In *North America in Question: Regional Integration in an Era of Economic Turbulence*, ed. Jeffrey Ayres and Laura Macdonald. Toronto: University of Toronto Press.

Gopal, Anand. 2010. *The Battle for Afghanistan: Militancy and Conflict in Kandahar*. Washington, DC: New America Foundation.

Gordon, J. King, ed. 1966. *Canada as a Middle Power*. Toronto: Canadian Institute of International Affairs.

Gordon, Nancy. 2004. "Humanitarian Challenges and Canadian Responses." In *Canada Among Nations 2004: Setting Priorities Straight*, ed. David Carment, Fen Osler Hampson, and Norman Hillmer. Montreal; Kingston, ON: McGill-Queen's University Press.

Gordon, Todd. 2010. *Imperialist Canada*. Winnipeg: Arbeiter Ring.

Gordon, Todd. 2013. "Canada and the Third World: The Political Economy of Intervention." In *Empire's Ally: Canada and the War in Afghanistan*, ed. Jerome Klassen and Greg Albo. Toronto: University of Toronto Press.

Gordon, Todd, and Jeffrey R. Webber. 2008. "Imperialism and Resistance: Canadian Mining Companies in Latin America." *Third World Quarterly* 29 (1): 63–87.

Gowan, Peter. 1999. *The Global Gamble: Washington's Faustian Bid for Global Dominance*. London: Verso.

Gowan, Peter. 2003. "US Hegemony Today." *Monthly Review* 55 (3): 30–50.

Gramsci, Antonio. 1971. *Selections from the Prison Notebooks of Antonio Gramsci*, ed. and trans. Quentin Hoare and Geoffrey Nowell Smith. London: Lawrence and Wishart.

Granatstein, J.L., ed. 1993. *Canadian Foreign Policy: Historical Readings*. Toronto: Copp Clark Pitman.

Grandin, Greg. 2006. *Empire's Workshop: Latin America, the United States, and the Rise of the New Imperialism*. New York: Metropolitan Books.

Greenwood, John. 2013. "Canadian banks' Caribbean mystery: Little known about how giants make money in paradise." *Financial Post*, 13 December.

Grieco, Joseph M. 1988. "Anarchy and the Limits of Cooperation: A Realist Critique of the Newest Liberal Institutionalism." *International Organization* 42 (3): 485–507.

Griffin, Thomas. 2004. *Haiti Human Rights Investigation, November 11–21*. Coral Gables, FL: University of Miami School of Law, Center for the Study of Human Rights.

Grinspun, Ricardo, and Yasmine Shamsie, eds. 2007. *Whose Canada? Continental Integration, Fortress North America, and the Corporate Agenda*. Montreal; Kingston, ON: McGill-Queen's University Press.

Gulalp, H. 1986. "Debate on Capitalism and Development: The Theories of Samir Amin and Bill Warren." *Capital & Class* 28: 139–59.

Gunder Frank, Andre. 1966. *The Development of Underdevelopment*. New York: Monthly Review Press.

Hall, Peter A., and David Soskice, eds. 2001. *Varieties of Capitalism: The Institutional Foundations of Comparative Advantage*. Oxford: Oxford University Press.

Hallward, Peter. 2008. *Damming the Flood: Haiti and the Politics of Containment*. London: Verso.

Hallward, Peter. 2004. "Option Zero in Haiti." *New Left Review* 27 (May–June): 23–47.

Hamm, Lisa M. 1994. "U.S. promoted FRAPH in Haiti, says magazine." *Associated Press*, 6 October.

Hanieh, Adam. 2006. "Praising Empire: Neoliberalism under Pax Americana."
In *The New Imperialists: Ideologies of Empire*, ed. Colin Mooers. Oxford:
Oneworld.

Hanieh, Adam. 2009. "Khaleeji Capital: Class formation and the Gulf
Cooperation Council." PhD diss., York University.

Hanieh, Adam. 2011. *Capitalism and Class in the Gulf Arab States*. New York:
Palgrave Macmillan.

Hanieh, Adam. 2013. "A 'Single War': The Political Economy of Intervention
in the Middle East and Central Asia." In *Empire's Ally: Canada and the War
in Afghanistan*, ed. Jerome Klassen and Greg Albo. Toronto: University of
Toronto Press.

Hardt, Michael, and Antonio Negri. 2000. *Empire*. Cambridge, MA: Harvard
University Press.

Harris, Jerry. 2005. "To Be or Not to Be: The Nation-centric World Order under
Globalization." *Science & Society* 69 (3): 329–40.

Harris, Kathleen. 2010. "Canada to take lead building 'New Haiti'." *Toronto
Sun*, 17 January.

Harris, Richard G., and David Cox. 1983. *Trade, Industrial Policy and Canadian
Manufacturing: Report from the Ontario Economic Council*. Toronto: University
of Toronto Press.

Hart, Michael. 2008. *From Pride to Influence: Towards a New Canadian Foreign
Policy*. Vancouver: UBC Press.

Hart-Landsberg, Martin. 2011. "The Chinese Reform Experience: A Critical
Assessment." *Review of Radical Political Economics* 43 (1): 56–76.

Hart-Landsberg, Martin. 2013. *Capitalist Globalization: Causes, Consequences, and
Resistances*. New York: Monthly Review Press.

Harvey, David. 1990. *The Condition of Postmodernity*. Cambridge, UK: Blackwell.

Harvey, David. 2003. *The New Imperialism*. Oxford: Oxford University Press.

Harvey, Frank P. 2004. *Smoke and Mirrors: Globalized Terrorism and the Illusion of
Multilateral Security*. Toronto: University of Toronto Press.

Healy, Teresa. 2007. "North American Competitiveness Council and the
SPP: *Les agents provocateurs* at the Montebello Leaders' Summit." Research
Paper 44. Halifax, NS: Canadian Labour Congress. Available online at
http://www.canadianlabour.ca/sites/default/files/pdfs/NACC__SPP
_MontebelloSummit-RP44.pdf, accessed July 3, 2013.

Healy, Teresa. 2012. "North American Community from Above and from
Below: Working-Class Perspectives on Economic Integration and Crisis."
In *North America in Question: Regional Integration in an Era of Economic
Turbulence*, ed. Jeffrey Ayres and Laura Macdonald. Toronto: University of
Toronto Press.

Hearden, Patrick J. 2002. *Architects of Globalism: Building a New World Order during World War II*. Fayetteville: University of Arkansas Press.

Heemskerk, Eelke M. 2007. *Decline of the Corporate Community: Network Dynamics of the Dutch Business Elite*. Amsterdam: Amsterdam University Press.

Held, D., and A. McGrew. 2003. "The Great Globalization Debate: An Introduction." In *The Global Transformations Reader*, ed. D. Held and A. McGrew. Cambridge, UK: Polity Press.

Helleiner, Eric. 1995. "Explaining the Globalization of Financial Markets: Bringing the State Back in." *Review of International Political Economy* 2 (2): 515–41.

Helleiner, Eric. 1996. *States and the Reemergence of Global Finance*. Ithaca, NY: Cornell University Press.

Heron, Craig. 1996. *The Canadian Labour Movement*, 2nd ed. Toronto: James Lorimer.

Heron, Craig, ed. 1998. *The Workers' Revolt in Canada, 1917–1925*. Toronto: University of Toronto Press.

Herz, Anse, and Kim Ives. 2011. "WikiLeaks Haiti: The post-quake 'gold rush' for reconstruction contracts." *The Nation*, 15 June.

Hilferding, Rudolf. [1910] 1981. *Finance Capital: A Study of the Latest Phase of Capitalist Development*. London: Routledge & Kegan Paul.

Hirst, Paul, and Grahame Thompson. 1999. *Globalization in Question: The International Economy and the Possibilities of Governance*, 2nd ed. Cambridge, UK: Polity Press.

Hobson, John A. [1902] 1972. *Imperialism: A Study*. Ann Arbor: University of Michigan Press.

Hobson, John M. 1998. "The Historical Sociology of the State and the State of Historical Sociology in International Relations." *Review of International Political Economy* 5 (2): 284–320.

Hoffman, Stanley. 1977. "An American Social Science: International Relations." *Daedalus* 106 (3): 41–60.

Hobsbawm, Eric. 1987. *The Age of Empire, 1875–1914*. New York: Pantheon Books.

Holmes, John W. 1979. *The Shaping of Peace: Canada and the Search for World Order*. Toronto: University of Toronto Press.

Hufbauer, Gary Clyde, and Jeffrey J. Schott. 2005. *NAFTA Revisited: Achievements and Challenges*. Washington, DC: Institute for International Economics.

Human Rights Watch. 2004a. "Haiti: International Forces Must Assert Control: More Troops Urgently Needed to Protect Human Rights." New York, 3 March.

Human Rights Watch. 2004b. "Haiti: Rebel Leaders' History of Abuses Raises Fears." New York, 27 February.

Human Rights Watch. 2004c. "Letter to Secretary Powell and Secretary Rumsfeld." New York, 11 March.

Human Rights Watch. 2005. "Haiti: Hundreds Killed Amid Rampant Impunity." New York, 14 April. Available online at http://www.hrw.org/news/2005/04/13/haiti-hundreds-killed-amid-rampant-impunity.

Human Rights Watch. 2011. "Gold's Costly Dividend: Human Rights Impacts of Papua New Guinea's Porgera Gold Mine." New York.

Hunt, Krista, and Kim Rygiel. 2006. (En)gendering the War on Terror: War Stories and Camouflaged Politics. Burlington, VT: Ashgate.

Huntington, Samuel P. 1993. "Why International Primacy Matters." International Security 17 (4): 68–83.

Hurtig, Mel. 2003. The Vanishing Country: Is it too late to save Canada? Toronto: McClelland & Stewart.

Hurtig, Mel. 2006. "Selling Off Our Country: Takeovers Place Key Canadian Industries in Foreign Hands." Canadian Centre for Political Alternatives Monitor, April. Available online at http://www.policyalternatives.ca/MonitorIssues/2006/04/MonitorIssue1353/.

Hutchinson, Brian. 2009. "Afghanistan's election gets rough, and it hasn't even started." CanWest News Service, 5 May.

Hymer, Stephen. 1979. The Multinational Corporation: A Radical Approach. Cambridge: Cambridge University Press.

Iacobucci, Frank. 2010. "Internal Inquiry into the Actions of Canadian Officials in Relation to Abdullah Almalki, Ahmad Abou-Elmaati and Muayyed Nureddin: Supplement to Public Report." Ottawa: Minister of Public Works.

Idiong, Uduak. 1997. "The Third Force: Returned Soldiers in the Winnipeg General Strike of 1919." Manitoba History 34 (Autumn): 15–22.

Ignatieff, Michael. 2003. "The Burden." New York Times Magazine, 5 January.

Ikenberry, G. John. 2002. "America's Imperial Ambition." Foreign Affairs 81 (5): 44–60.

Ikenberry, G. John. 2006. Liberal Order and Imperial Ambition. Oxford: Polity Press.

InterAction. 2003. "Provincial Reconstruction Teams in Afghanistan: Position Paper." 23 April.

Inter-American Development Bank. 2005. "IDB approves Haiti transition strategy 2005–2006 for $270 million program of operations." Press release. Washington, DC. 14 March.

International Commission on Intervention and State Sovereignty. 2001. The Responsibility to Protect. Ottawa: International Development Research Centre.

International Crisis Group. 2010. *A Force in Fragments: Reconstituting the Afghan National Army.* Kabul; Brussels.

IRIN. 2006. "Afghanistan: Thousands displaced by fighting in Kandahar." 6 September.

Isaac, Jeffrey C. 2002. "Hannah Arendt on Human Rights and the Limits of Exposure, or Why Noam Chomsky Is Wrong about the Meaning of Kosovo." *Social Research* 69 (2): 263–95.

Isfeld, Gordon. 2014. "Export Development Canada opens Bogota office amid Central, South America push." *Financial Post*, 5 February.

Isitt, Benjamin. 2006. "Mutiny from Victoria to Vladivostok, December 1918." *Canadian Historical Review* 87 (2): 223–64.

Ives, Kim, and Ansel Herz. 2011. "WikiLeaks Haiti: The Aristide files." *The Nation*, 5 August.

Jackson, Andrew. 2007. "From Leaps of Faith to Hard Landings: Fifteen Years of 'Free Trade'." In *Whose Canada? Continental Integration, Fortress North America and the Corporate Agenda*, ed. Ricardo Grinspun and Yasmine Shamsie. Montreal; Kingston, ON: McGill-Queen's University Press.

James, C.L.R. 1989. *The Black Jacobins: Toussaint L'Ouverture and the San Domingo Revolution.* New York: Vintage.

Jenkins, Rhys. 1987. *Transnational Corporations and Uneven Development: The Internationalization of Capital and the Third World.* London: Methuen.

Jenson, Jane. 1989. "'Different' but not 'Exceptional': Canada's Permeable Fordism." *Canadian Review of Sociology & Anthropology* 26 (1): 69–94.

Jenson, Jane. 1990. "Representations in Crisis: The Roots of Canada's Permeable Fordism." *Canadian Journal of Political Science* 23 (4): 653–83.

Jockel, Joseph T., and Joel J. Sokolsky. 1999. "Canada's Cold War Nuclear Experience." In *Pondering NATO's Nuclear Options: Gambits for a Post-Westphalian World*, ed. David G. Haglund. Kingston, ON: Queen's Quarterly.

Johnson, Nicolas. 2012. "Canadian firms guide Afghan efforts to unlock mining 'treasure trove'." *Globe and Mail*, 7 March.

Johnson, Chris, and Jolyon Leslie. 2008. *Afghanistan: The Mirage of Peace.* London: Zed Books.

Joya, Angela. 2013. "Failed States and Canada's 3D Policy in Afghanistan." In *Empire's Ally: Canada and the War in Afghanistan*, ed. Jerome Klassen and Greg Albo. Toronto: University of Toronto Press.

Kagan, Robert D. 2014. "In Defense of Empire." *The Atlantic* (April).

Katz, Jonathan M., and Martha Mendoza. 2010. "Haiti still waiting for pledged U.S. aid." *Associated Press*, 29 September.

Kaufman, Michael. 1984. "The Internationalization of Canadian Bank Capital (with a Look at Bank Activity in the Caribbean and Central America)." *Journal of Canadian Studies* 19 (4): 61–81.

Kautsky, Karl [1914] 1970. "Ultra-Imperialism." *New Left Review* 59 (January–February).

Keating, Tom. 1993. *Canada and World Order: The Multilateralist Tradition in Canadian Foreign Policy.* Toronto: McClelland and Stewart.

Kellogg, Paul. 1990. "Arms and the Nation: The Impact of 'Military Parasitism' on Canada's Place in the World Economy." PhD diss., Queen's University, Kingston, ON.

Kellogg, Paul. 2005. "Kari Levitt and the Long Detour of Canadian Political Economy." *Studies in Political Economy* 76 (Autumn): 31–60.

Kellogg, Paul. 2013. "From the Avro Arrow to Afghanistan: The Political Economy of Canadian Militarism." In *Empire's Ally: Canada and the War in Afghanistan,* ed. Jerome Klassen and Greg Albo. Toronto: University of Toronto Press.

Kennan, George. 1947. "The Sources of Soviet Conduct." *Foreign Affairs* 25 (July): 566–82.

Kennan, George. 1948. "Memorandum by the Director of the Policy Planning Staff to the Secretary of State and the Under Secretary of State, Top Secret. PPS/23, 24 February." In United States, Department of State, *Foreign Relations of the United States,* 1948, vol. 1. Washington, DC: US Government Printing Office.

Kennedy, Paul. 1989. *The Rise and Fall of the Great Powers.* New York: Knopf Doubleday.

Kentor, Jeffrey. 2005. "The Growth of Transnational Corporate Networks: 1962–1998." *Journal of World-Systems Research* 11 (2): 263–86.

Kentor, Jeffrey, and Y.S. Jang. 2004. "Yes, There Is a (Growing) Transnational Business Community: A Study of Global Interlocking Directorates, 1983–98." *International Sociology* 19 (3): 355–68.

Kiely, Ray. 2010. *Rethinking Imperialism.* London: Palgrave Macmillan.

Kindleberger, Charles P. 1973. *The World in Depression, 1929–1939.* Berkeley: University of California Press.

Klare, Michael T. 2002. *Resource Wars: The New Landscape of Global Conflict.* New York: Holt.

Klassen, Jerome. 2007. "Canada, Globalization, Imperialism: Rethinking Canada's Role in a Neoliberal World." PhD diss., York University.

Klassen, Jerome. 2009. "Canada and the New Imperialism: The Economics of a Secondary Power." *Studies in Political Economy* 83 (Spring): 163–90.

Klassen, Jerome. 2013. "Methods of Empire: State Building, Development, and War in Afghanistan." In *Empire's Ally: Canada and the War in*

Afghanistan, ed. Jerome Klassen and Greg Albo. Toronto: University of Toronto Press.

Klassen, Jerome. 2014. "Hegemony in Question: US Primacy, Multi-Polarity, and Global Resistance." In *Polarizing Development: Alternatives to Neoliberalism and the Crisis*, ed. L. Pradella and T. Marois. London: Pluto Press.

Klassen, Jerome, and Greg Albo, eds. 2013. *Empire's Ally: Canada and the War in Afghanistan*. Toronto: University of Toronto Press.

Klassen, Jerome, and William K. Carroll. 2011. "Transnational Class Formation? Globalization and the Canadian Corporate Elite." *Journal of World-Systems Research* 17 (2): 379–402.

Klein, Naomi. 2007. *The Shock Doctrine: The Rise of Disaster Capitalism*. New York: Picador.

Kolbe, Athena R., and Royce A. Hutson. 2006. "Human Rights Abuse and Other Criminal Violations in Port-au-Prince, Haiti: A Random Survey of Households." *Lancet* 368 (9538): 864–73.

Kolko, Gabriel. 1968. *The Politics of War: The World and United States Foreign Policy, 1943–1945*. New York: Random House.

Kolko, Gabriel. 1969. *The Roots of American Foreign Policy*. Boston: Beacon Press.

Kolko, Gabriel. 1988. *Confronting the Third World: United States Foreign Policy, 1945–1980*. New York: Pantheon Books.

Kolko, Gabriel. 1994. *Anatomy of a War: Vietnam, the United States, and the Modern Historical Experience*. New York: New Press.

Kolko, Joyce, and Gabriel Kolko. 1972. *The Limits of Power: The World and United States Foreign Policy, 1945–54*. New York: Harper and Row.

Koopman, Robert, et al. 2010. "Give Credit Where Credit Is Due: Tracing Value Added in Global Production Chains." NBER Working Paper 16426. Cambridge, MA: National Bureau of Economic Research. Available online at http://www.nber.org/papers/w16426.

Koring, Paul. 2006. "More troops at risk, general warns." *Globe and Mail*, 31 October.

Koring, Paul. 2007. "What Ottawa doesn't want you to know." *Globe and Mail*, 25 April.

Koring, Paul. 2008. "Ottawa kept abuse charges against ally secret." *Globe and Mail*, 1 February.

Kramer, Andrew E. 2014. "Ukraine turns to its oligarchs for political help." *New York Times*, 2 March.

Krasner, Stephen D. 1978. *Defending the National Interest: Raw Materials Investments and U.S. Foreign Policy*. Princeton, NJ: Princeton University Press.

Krauthammer, Charles. 1990/1991. "The Unipolar Moment." *Foreign Affairs* 70 (1): 23–33.

Laclau, Ernesto. 1971. "Feudalism and Capitalism in Latin America." *New Left Review* I/67 (May–June).

LaFeber, Walter. 1993. *Inevitable Revolutions: The United States in Central America*, 2nd ed. New York: W.W. Norton.

Lagasse, Philippe. 2003. "Northern Command and the Evolution of Canada-US Defence Relations." *Canadian Military Journal* 4 (1): 15–22.

Lake, Anthony. 1993. "From Containment to Enlargement." Speech, Johns Hopkins University, Baltimore, 21 September.

Lake, Anthony. 1994. "Confronting Backlash States." *Foreign Affairs* 73 (2): 45–55.

Lal, Deepak. 2004a. *In Defense of Empires*. Washington, DC: AEI Press.

Lal, Deepak. 2004b. *In Praise of Empires*. New York: Palgrave Macmillan.

Langille, David. 1987. "The Business Council on National Issues and the Canadian State." *Studies in Political Economy* 24 (Autumn): 41–85.

Laxer, Gordon. 1989. *Open for Business: The Roots of Foreign Ownership in Canada*. Oxford: Oxford University Press.

Laxer, Jim. 1973. "Canadian Manufacturing and U.S. Trade Policy." In *(Canada) Ltd.: The Political Economy of Dependency*, ed. Robert Laxer. Toronto: McClelland and Stewart.

Laxer, Robert. 1973. "Foreword." In *(Canada) Ltd.: The Political Economy of Dependency*, ed. Robert Laxer. Toronto: McClelland and Stewart.

Layne, Christopher. 2006a. *The Peace of Illusions: American Grand Strategy from 1940 to the Present*. Ithaca, NY: Cornell University Press.

Layne, Christopher. 2006b. "The Unipolar Illusion Revisited: The Coming End of the United States' Unipolar Moment." *International Security* 31 (2): 7–41.

Layne, Christopher. 2012. "This Time It's Real: The End of Unipolarity and the Pax Americana." *International Studies Quarterly* 56 (1): 203–13.

Leblanc, Daniel. 2005. "JTF2 to hunt al-Qaeda." *Globe and Mail*, 15 July.

Leblanc, Daniel. 2012. "Canada needs 'away fleet' of fighter jets, says military." *Globe and Mail*, 4 May.

Leffler, Melvyn P. 1992. *A Preponderance of Power: National Security, the Truman Administration, and the Cold War*. Redwood City, CA: Stanford University Press.

Leffler, Melvyn P. 2013. "Defense on a Diet: How Budget Crises Have Improved U.S. Strategy." *Foreign Affairs* 92 (6): 65–76.

Leger Marketing Poll. 2011. "After nine years in Afghanistan, Canadian troops are finally pulling out. Which of the following best reflects your opinion?" 25–27 July.

Liebknecht, Karl. 1917. *Militarism*. Toronto: William Briggs.

Lenin, V.I. [1917] 1982. *Imperialism, the Highest Stage of Capitalism*. Moscow: Progress Publishers.

Lennox, Patrick. 2007. "From Golden Straitjacket to Kevlar Vest: Canada's Transformation to a Security State." *Canadian Journal of Political Science* 40 (4): 1017–38.

Lennox, Patrick. 2009. *At Home and Abroad: The Canada-US Relationship and Canada's Place in the World*. Vancouver: UBC Press.

Levitt, Kari [1970] 2002. *Silent Surrender: The Multinational Corporation in Canada*. Montreal; Kingston, ON: McGill-Queen's University Press.

Leys, Colin. 1977. "Underdevelopment and Dependency: Critical Notes." *Journal of Contemporary Asia* 7 (1): 92–107.

Linden, Greg, Kenneth L. Kraemer, and Jason Dedrick. 2007. "Who Captures Value in a Global Innovation System? The Case of Apple's iPod." Irvine: University of California, Personal Computing Industry Center.

Loesch, Jonathan E. 2001. "Averting Continuation of Failed US Policy with Haiti." Strategy Research Project, 1 April. Carlisle Barracks, PA: United States Army War College.

Lukacs, Martin, and Tim Groves. 2013. "Canadian spies met with energy firms, documents reveal." *Guardian*, 9 October.

Luxemburg, Rosa. [1914] 2003. *The Accumulation of Capital*. New York: Routledge.

Lundestad, Geir. 1986. "Empire by Invitation? The United States and Western Europe, 1945–1953." *Journal of Peace Research* 23 (3): 263–77.

Lyon, Peyton V., and Brian W. Tomlin. 1979. *Canada as an International Actor*. Toronto: Macmillan.

Macaluso, Grace. 2012. "Canada's ranking as global auto exporter slipping." *Windsor Star*, 25 April.

MacAskill, Ewan, and James Ball. 2013. "Portrait of the NSA: no detail too small in quest for total surveillance." *Guardian*, 2 November.

Macdonald, David. 2011. *The Cost of 9/11: Tracking the Creation of a National Security Establishment*. Ottawa: Rideau Institute.

Mackrael, Kim. 2013. "CIDA's sudden demise shifts control to PMO." *Globe and Mail*, 21 March.

Mackrael, Kim. 2014. "Commercial motives driving Canada's foreign aid, documents reveal." *Globe and Mail*, 8 January.

Magdoff, Harry. 1969. *The Age of Imperialism: The Economics of U.S. Foreign Policy*. New York: Monthly Review Press.

Magdoff, Harry. 2003. *Imperialism without Colonies*. New York: Monthly Review Press.

Mallaby, Sebastian. 2002. "The Reluctant Imperialist." *Foreign Affairs* 81 (2): 2–7.

Maloney, Sean M. 2002. *Canada and UN Peacekeeping: Cold War by Other Means, 1945–1970.* St. Catharines, ON: Vanwell Publishing.

Mandel, Ernest. 1983. *Late Capitalism.* London: Verso.

Mandel, Michael. 2004. *How America Gets Away with Murder: Illegal Wars, Collateral Damage and Crimes against Humanity.* London: Pluto Press.

Marx, Karl. [1843] 1970. *Critique of Hegel's Philosophy of Right.* Cambridge: Cambridge University Press.

Marx, Karl. [1867] 1990. *Capital: A Critique of Political Economy, Volume One.* New York: Penguin.

Marx, Karl. [1885] 1992. *Capital: A Critique of Political Economy, Volume Two.* New York: Penguin.

Marx, Karl. [1894] 1993. *Capital: A Critique of Political Economy, Volume Three.* New York: Penguin.

Marx, Karl. [1939] 1973. *Grundrisse.* Harmondsworth, UK: Penguin.

Marx, Karl, and Friedrich Engels. [1848] 1985. *The Communist Manifesto.* New York: Penguin.

McBride, Stephen. 2005. *Paradigm Shift: Globalization and the Canadian State.* Halifax, NS: Fernwood.

McCallum, John. 1980. *Unequal Beginnings: Agriculture and Economic Development in Quebec and Ontario until 1870.* Toronto: University of Toronto Press.

McCarthy, Shawn, Jeff Sallot, and Paul Knox. 2004. "Canada assailed for failing to step in and save Aristide." *Globe and Mail*, 2 March, A1.

McCormack, Geoffrey. 2014. "The Great Canadian Slump, 1990–92." *Historical Materialism* 22 (2): 1–45.

McCready, A.L. 2010. "'Tie a Yellow Ribbon Round Public Discourse, National Identity and the War: Neoliberal Militarization and the Yellow Ribbon Campaign in Canada." *Topia: Canadian Journal of Cultural Studies* 23–24: 28–51.

McCullum, David. 2006. *Fuelling Fortress America: A Report on the Athabasca Tar Sands and U.S. Demands for Canada's Energy.* Ottawa: Canadian Centre for Policy Alternatives.

McDonough, David S. 2013. "A Pacific pivot for the RCN?" *Vanguard*, February–March.

McInnis, Peter S. 2002. *Harnessing Labour Confrontation: Shaping the Postwar Settlement in Canada, 1943–1950.* Toronto: University of Toronto Press.

McKay, Ian, and Jamie Swift. 2012. *Warrior Nation: Rebranding Canada in an Age of Anxiety.* Toronto: Between the Lines.

McKenna, Barrie, and Richard Blackwell. 2014. "The world's newest creditor nation: Canada." *Globe and Mail*, 13 March.

McKenna, Peter, ed. 2012. *Canada Looks South: In Search of an America's Strategy.* Toronto: University of Toronto Press.

McNally, David. 1981. "Staples Theory as Commodity Fetishism: Marx, Innis and Canadian Political Economy." *Studies in Political Economy* 6 (Autumn): 35–63.

McNally, David. 2006. *Another World Is Possible: Globalization and Anti-Capitalism.* Winnipeg: Arbeiter Ring.

McQuaig, Linda. 2007. *Holding the Bully's Coat: Canada and the U.S. Empire.* Toronto: Doubleday.

Mearsheimer. John J. 2001. *The Tragedy of Great Power Politics.* New York: W.W. Norton.

Mearsheimer, John. 2014. "America unhinged." *The National Interest* (January–February).

Meyer, Carl. 2011. "CCC sees 'untapped' market for Canadian arms." *Embassy*, 15 June. Available online at http://www.embassynews.ca/news/2011/06/15/ccc-sees-untapped-market-for-canadian-arms/40395?absolute=1.

Milanovic, Branko. 2012. "Global Inequality Recalculated and Updated: The Effect of New PPP Estimates on Global Inequality and 2005 Estimates." *Journal of Economic Inequality* 10 (1): 1–18.

Milberg, William. 1994. "Is Absolute Advantage *Passe*? Towards a Keynesian/Marxian Theory of International Trade." In *Competition, Technology and Money, Classical and Post-Keynesian Perspectives*, ed. Mark A. Glick. Aldershot, UK: Edward Elgar.

Mill, John Stuart. 1859. "A Few Words on Non-Intervention." *Foreign Policy Perspectives* 8.

Millar, Matthew. 2013. "Harper government's extensive spying on anti-oil sands groups revealed in FOIs." *Vancouver Observer*, 19 November.

Millet, Damien, and Eric Toussaint. 2009. "Figures Relating to the Debt for 2009." Liège, Belgium: Committee for the Abolition of Third World Debt. Available online at http://cadtm.org/The-Debt-in-figures, accessed 10 July 2012.

Minsky, Amy. 2010. "Most aid still in Canada, CIDA reports." *Postmedia News*, 5 November.

Mitrovica, Andrew. 2012a. "Canada complicit in torture for decades." *Toronto Star*, 12 February.

Mitrovica, Andrew. 2012b. "CSIS freed from final shreds of oversight." *Toronto Star*, 30 April.

Mitrovica, Andrew. 2013. "Canada is part of the eavesdropping network." *Ottawa Citizen*, 7 June.

Moens, Alexander. 2008. "Afghanistan and the Revolution in Canadian Foreign Policy." *International Journal* 63 (3): 569–86.

Mohamedou, Mohammad Mahmoud. 2006. *Understanding Al Qaeda: The Transformation of War*. Ann Arbor, Michigan: University of Michigan Press.

Monaghan, Jeffrey, and Kevin Walby. 2012. "Making Up 'Terror Identities': Security Intelligence, Canada's Integrated Threat Assessment Centre, and Social Movement Suppression." *Policing and Society* 22 (2): 133–51.

Monteiro, Nuno P. 2011/12. "Unrest Assured: Why Unipolarity Is Not Peaceful." *International Security* 36 (3): 9–40.

Montgomery, Sue. 2004. "Mastermind tells how plot evolved: Former Montrealer leads political wing of group that overthrew Haiti's Aristide." *Montreal Gazette*, 9 March.

Montpetit, Jonathan. 2010. "Canadians target Taliban supply lines in Panjwaii, prompting counter-attack." *Canadian Press*, 30 October.

Montpetit, Jonathan. 2011. "Canada feared popular uprising in Haiti after last year's earthquake." *Canadian Press*, 30 March.

Moore, J.W. 2002. "Capital, Territory, and Hegemony over the *longue durée*." *Science & Society* 65 (4): 476–84.

Moore, Andrew F. 2007. "Unsafe in America: A Review of the U.S.-Canada Safe Third Country Agreement." *Santa Clara Law Review* 47 (2): 201–84.

Moore, Steve, and Debi Wells. 1975. *Imperialism and the National Question in Canada*. Toronto: Steve Moore.

Morgenthau, Hans J. [1948] 1985. *Politics Among Nations*, 6th ed. New York: Alfred A. Knopf.

Morgenthau, Hans J. 1964. *The Purpose of American Politics*. New York: Vintage.

Morrison, David R. 1998. *Aid and Ebb Tide: A History of CIDA and Canadian Development Assistance*. Waterloo, ON: Wilfrid Laurier University Press.

Murray, Joshua. 2014. "Evidence of a Transnational Capitalist Class-for-Itself: The Determinants of PAC Activity among Foreign Firms in the Fortune 500, 2000–2006." *Global Networks* 14 (2): 230–50.

Myers, Gustavus. 1913. *A History of Canadian Wealth*. Chicago.

NACC (North American Competitiveness Council). 2007. "Enhancing Competitiveness in Canada, Mexico and the United States: Private Sector Priorities for the Security and Prosperity Partnership (SPP); Initial Recommendations." February.

Nadeau, Marc, Simon Prefontaine, and Lili Mei. 2010a. "A Profile of Canadian Exporters." *Canadian Trade Review*. Ottawa: Statistics Canada.

Nadeau, Marc, Simon Prefontaine, and Lili Mei. 2010b. "A Profile of Canadian Importers, 2002 to 2007." *Canadian Trade Review*. Ottawa: Statistics Canada.

Nairn, Allan. 1995. "Our Payroll, Haitian Hit." *Nation Magazine*, 9 October.

Naylor, R.T. 1972. "The Rise and Fall of the Third Commercial Empire of the St. Lawrence." In *Capitalism and the National Question in Canada*, ed. Gary Teeple. Toronto: University of Toronto Press.

Naylor, R.T. 2006. *Canada in the European Age, 1453–1919*. Montreal; Kingston, ON: McGill-Queen's University Press.

Neubauer, Fred, Ulrich Steger, and Georg Radler. 2000. "The Daimler/Chrysler Merger: The Involvement of the Boards." *Corporate Governance* 8 (4): 375–87.

Neufeld, Mark. 2007. "Hegemony and Foreign Policy Analysis: The Case of Canada as Middle Power." In *Readings in Canadian Foreign Policy: Classic Debates and New Ideas*, ed. Duane Bratt and Christopher J. Kukucha. Don Mills, ON: Oxford University Press.

Niosi, Jorge. 1985a. *Canadian Multinationals*. Toronto: Garamond.

Niosi, Jorge. 1985b. "Continental Nationalism: The Strategy of the Canadian Bourgeoisie." In *The Structure of the Canadian Capitalist Class*, ed. Robert J. Brym. Toronto: Garamond.

Nkrumah, Kwame. 1965. *Neo-Colonialism, the Last Stage of Imperialism*. London: Thomas Nelson & Sons.

Noble, John J. 2008. "PMO/PCO/DFAIT: Serving the Prime Minister's Foreign Policy Agenda." In *Canada Among Nations 2007: What Room for Manoeuvre?* ed. Jean Daudlin and Daniel Schwanen. Montreal; Kingston, ON: McGill-Queen's University Press.

Nolan, Peter. 2012. *Is China Buying the World?* Cambridge, UK: Polity Press.

Nossal, Kim Richard. 1985. *The Politics of Canadian Foreign Policy*. Scarborough, ON: Prentice-Hall.

Nossal, Kim Richard. 2004. "Canada and the Search for World Order: John W. Holmes and Canadian Foreign Policy." *International Journal* 59 (4): 749–60.

OAS (Organization of American States). 2000. "The OAS Observation Mission in Haiti: Chief of Mission Report to the OAS Permanent Council." Washington, DC. 13 July.

Obama, Barack, and Stephen Harper. 2011. "Beyond the Border: A Shared Vision for Perimeter Security and Economic Competitiveness." 4 February.

OECD (Organisation for Economic Co-operation and Development). 2007. *Statistical Annex of the 2006 Development Cooperation Report: Tying Status of ODA by Individual DAC Members*. Paris.

OECD. 2008. *OECD Factbook 2008*. Paris.

OECD. 2011. *Statistical Annex of the 2011 Development Cooperation Report: Tying Status of ODA by Individual DAC Members*. Paris.

OECD. 2012a. *Employment Outlook 2012: Canada*. Paris. Available online at http://www.oecd.org/canada/Canada_final_EN.pdf.

OECD. 2012b. *Handbook of Statistics 2011–2012*. Paris.

Ohlin, Bertil. 1933. *Inter-Regional and International Trade*. Cambridge, MA: Harvard University Press.

Ohmae, Kenichi. 1990. *The Borderless World*. London: Collins.

O'Keefe, Derrick. 2013. "Bringing Ottawa's Warmakers to Heel: The Anti-War Movement in Canada." In *Empire's Ally: Canada and the War in Afghanistan,* ed. Jerome Klassen and Greg Albo. Toronto: University of Toronto Press.

Open Society Foundations. 2013. *Globalizing Torture: CIA Secret Detention and Extraordinary Rendition*. New York.

Overbeek, Henk, and Kees van der Pijl. 1993. "Restructuring Capital and Restructuring Hegemony: Neoliberalism and the Unmaking of the Postwar Order." In *Restructuring Hegemony in the Global Political Economy: The Rise of Transnational Neo-Liberalism in the 1980s*, ed. Henk Overbeek. London: Routledge.

Oxfam International et al. 2009. "Caught in the Conflict: Civilians and the International Security Strategy in Afghanistan." Oxford. April.

Oxfam International. 2011. "No Time to Lose: Promoting the Accountability of the Afghan National Security Forces." Oxford, UK, 10 May.

Palloix, Christian. 1977. "Conceptualizing the Internationalization of Capital." *Review of Radical Political Economics* 9 (2): 17–28.

Panetta, Alexander. 2008a. "Government can't be trusted on Afghanistan, lawyers argue." *Canadian Press*, 24 January.

Panetta, Alexander. 2008b. "Rage follows slaying by Canadians." *Canadian Press*, 28 July.

Panitch, Leo. 1977. "The Role and Nature of the Canadian State." In *Imperialism, Nationalism, and Canada: Essays from the Marxist Institute of Toronto*, ed. Craig Heron and John Saul. Toronto: New Hogtown Press.

Panitch, Leo. 1981. "Dependency and Class in Canadian Political Economy." *Studies in Political Economy* 6 (Autumn): 7–33.

Panitch, Leo. 1994. "Globalisation and the State." In *The Socialist Register 1994: Between Globalism and Nationalism*, ed. Leo Panitch and Ralph Miliband. London: Merlin.

Panitch, Leo. 2000. "The New Imperial State." *New Left Review* II (March–April): 5–20.

Panitch, Leo, and Sam Gindin. 2004. "Global Capitalism and American Empire." In *The Socialist Register 2004: The New Imperial Challenge*, ed. Leo Panitch and Colin Leys. London: Merlin Press.

Panitch, Leo, and Sam Gindin. 2005a. "Finance and American Empire." In *The Socialist Register 2005: The Empire Reloaded*, ed. Leo Panitch and Colin Leys. London: Merlin Press.

Panitch, Leo, and Sam Gindin. 2005b. "Superintending Global Capital." *New Left Review* 35 (September–October): 101–23.

Panitch, Leo, and Colin Leys, eds. 2000. *The Socialist Register 2001: Working Classes, Global Realities*. London: Merlin Press.

Panitch, Leo, and Donald Swartz. 1993. *From Consent to Coercion: The Assault on Trade Union Freedoms*. Toronto: Garamond.

Pape, Robert. 2005. *Dying to Win: The Strategic Logic of Suicide Terror*. New York: Random House.

PBS. 2011. "Kill/Capture." *Frontline*, 10 May.

Peck, Jamie. 2001. *Workfare States*. New York: Guilford Press.

Pentland, H. Clare. 1959. "The Development of a Capitalistic Labour Market in Canada." *Canadian Journal of Economics and Political Science* 25 (4): 450–61.

Pentland, H. Clare. 1981. *Labour and Capital in Canada, 1650–1860*. Toronto: James Lorimer.

People's Commission Network. 2012. "CSIS targeted for profiling and intimidation." Montreal, 29 March. Available online at http://www .peoplescommission.org/en/csis/, accessed 7 November 2012.

Perkel, Colin. 2009. "Canadian troops storm Afghan town." *Canadian Press*, 25 June.

Perry, David. 2007. "Contractors in Kandahar, eh? Canada's 'Real' Commitment to Afghanistan." *Journal of Military and Strategic Studies* 9 (4): 1–23.

Picciotto, Sol. 1991. "The internationalisation of the state." *Capital & Class* 15 (1): 43–63.

Pierson, Paul, ed. 2001. *The New Politics of the Welfare State*. New York: Oxford University Press.

Pigott, Pierre. 2007. *Canada in Afghanistan: The War So Far*. Toronto: Dundurn Press.

Piketty, Thomas, and Emmanuel Saez. 2007. "Income and Wage Inequality in the United States, 1913–2002." In *Top Incomes Over the Twentieth Century: A Contrast between Continental European and English Speaking Countries*, ed. A.B. Atkinson and Thomas Piketty. Oxford: Oxford University Press.

Podur, Justin. 2012. *Haiti's New Dictatorship: The Coup, the Earthquake and the UN Occupation*. London: Pluto Press.

Podur, Justin. 2013. "Incompatible Objectives: Counterinsurgency and Development in Afghanistan." In *Empire's Ally: Canada and the War in Afghanistan*, ed. Jerome Klassen and Greg Albo. Toronto: University of Toronto Press.

Porter, Michael E. 1990. "The Competitive Advantage of Nations." *Harvard Business Review* (March–April): 73–91.

Portes, Alejandro, and John Walton. 1981. *Labor, Class, and the International System*. New York: Academic Press.

Posen, Barry. 2003. "Command of the Commons: The Military Foundation of US Hegemony." *International Security* 28 (1): 5–46.

Poulantzas, Nicos. 1978a. *Classes in Contemporary Capitalism*. London: Verso.

Poulantzas, Nicos. 1978b. *Political Power and Social Classes*. London: Verso.

Pozo-Martin, Gonzalo. 2007. "Autonomous or materialist geopolitics?" *Cambridge Review of International Affairs* 20 (4): 551–63.

Prashad, Vijay. 2007. *The Darker Nations: A People's History of the Third World*. New York: New Press.

Prashad, Vijay. 2012. *Arab Spring, Libyan Winter*. Oakland, CA: AK Press.

Pratt, Cranford. 1983/4. "Dominant Class Theory and Canadian Foreign Policy: The Case of the Counter-Consensus." *International Journal* 39 (Winter): 99–135.

Pratt, Cranford. 2007. "Competing Rationales for Canadian Development Assistance: Reducing Global Poverty, Enhancing Canadian Prosperity and Security, or Advancing Global Human Security." In *Readings in Canadian Foreign Policy: Classic Debates and New Ideas*, ed. Duane Bratt and Christopher J. Kukucha. Don Mills, ON: Oxford University Press.

Pratt, Larry. 1982. "Energy: The Roots of National Policy." *Studies in Political Economy* 7 (Winter): 27–59.

Prebisch, Raúl. 1950. *The Economic Development of Latin America and Its Principal Problems*. New York: United Nations.

Prebisch, Raúl. 1959. "Commercial Policy in the Underdeveloped Countries." *American Economic Review* 49 (May): 251–73.

La Presse canadienne. 2008. "Enquête sur une fusillade entre soldats canadiens et civils afghans," 11 February.

Proussalidis, Daniel. 2013. "Canadian consultant wins bid for Afghanistan housing project." *Quebecor Media*, 5 June.

Public Policy Forum. 2003. *Canada in Transition*. Ottawa.

Pugliese, David. 2007. "DND kept tabs on left-wing analyst, planned counter views to his speeches." *Ottawa Citizen*, 27 July.

Pugliese, David. 2011a. "Canadian Association of Defence and Security Industries leads military and security equipment trade mission to Kuwait." *Ottawa Citizen* (Defence Watch Blog), 10 December. Available online at http://blogs.ottawacitizen.com/2011/12/10/canadian-association-of-defence-and-security-industries-leads-military-and-security-equipment-trade-mission-to-kuwait/.

Pugliese, David. 2011b. "Canadian teams to expand international training role." *Defensenews.com*, 4 April.

Railway Gazette. 2013. "Afghan government commissions east-west rail study."
11 December. Available online at http://www.railwaygazette.com/news/
news/asia/single-view/view/afghan-government-commissions-east-west
-rail-study.html.

Ramachandran, Vijaya, and Julie Walz. 2012. "Haiti: Where Has All the
Money Gone?" Policy Paper 004. Washington, DC: Center for Global
Development.

Rashid, Ahmed. 2008. *Descent into Chaos: The United States and the Failure of
Nation Building in Pakistan, Afghanistan, and Central Asia*. London: Penguin.

Razack, Sherene. 2004. *Dark Threats and White Knights: The Somalia Affair,
Peacekeeping, and the New Imperialism*. Toronto: University of Toronto Press.

Razack, Sherene. 2008. *Casting Out: The Eviction of Muslims from Western Law
and Politics*. Toronto: University of Toronto Press.

Razack, Sherene. 2013. "Canada's Afghan Detainee Torture Scandal: How
Stories of Torture Define the Nation." In *Empire's Ally: Canada and the War
in Afghanistan*, ed. Jerome Klassen and Greg Albo. Toronto: University of
Toronto Press.

Renaud, Benoit, and Jessica Squires. 2013. "Québec Solidaire and the Anti-war
Movement." In *Empire's Ally: Canada and the War in Afghanistan*, ed. Jerome
Klassen and Greg Albo. Toronto: University of Toronto Press.

Rennie, Steve. 2009. "Afghan Canadian to be new Governor of Kandahar."
Canadian Press, 29 April.

Resnick, Philip. 1984. *Parliament vs. People: An Essay on Democracy and Canadian
Political Culture*. Vancouver: New Star Books.

Resnick, Philip. 1990. *The Masks of Proteus: Canadian Reflections on the State*.
Montreal; Kingston, ON: McGill-Queen's University Press.

Reuters. 2013. "Barrick's Pascua-Lama gold project frozen for at least 1–2 years:
Chile regulator." 30 May.

Reynolds, David. 1994. *The Origins of the Cold War in Europe: International
Perspectives*. New Haven, CT: Yale University Press.

Ricardo, David. [1817] 1963. *The Principles of Political Economy and Taxation*.
Homewood, IL: Richard D. Irwin.

Richardson, Jack. 1982. "'Merchants against Industry': An Empirical study of
the Canadian Debate." *Canadian Journal of Sociology* 7 (3): 279–96.

Richardson, Jack. 1988. "'A Sacred Trust': The Trust Industry and Canadian
Economic Structure." *Canadian Review of Sociology and Anthropology* 25 (1): 1–19.

Richardson, Jack. 1992. "Free Trade: Why Did It Happen?" *Canadian Review of
Sociology and Anthropology* 29 (3): 307–28.

Ripsman, Norrin M., and T.V. Paul. 2010. *Globalization and the National Security
State*. Montreal; Kingston, ON: McGill-Queen's University Press.

Risen, James. 2010. "U.S. identifies vast mineral riches in Afghanistan." *New York Times*, 13 June.

Roach, Kent. 2002. "Did September 11 Change Everything? Struggling to Preserve Canadian Values in the Face of Terrorism." *McGill Law Journal* 47: 893–947.

Roach, Kent. 2011. *The 9/11 Effect: Comparative Counter-Terrorism*. Cambridge: Cambridge University Press.

Robinson, David. 2007. "All Pain, No Gain: Canadian Labour in the Integrated North American Economy." In *Whose Canada? Continental Integration, Fortress North America and the Corporate Agenda*, ed. Ricardo Grinspun and Yasmine Shamsie. Montreal; Kingston, ON: McGill-Queen's University Press.

Robinson, Randall. 2007. *An Unbroken Agony: Haiti, From Revolution to the Kidnapping of a President*. New York: Basic Civitas Books.

Robinson, William I. 2004. *A Theory of Global Capitalism: Production, Class, and State in a Transnational World*. Baltimore: Johns Hopkins University Press.

Rosdolsky, Roman. 1989. *The Making of Marx's Capital*. London: Pluto.

Rosenberg, Justin. 1996. "Isaac Deutscher and the Lost History of International Relations." *New Left Review* (Series 1) 215 (January–February): 2–15.

Rosenburg, Tina. 2007. "The way we live now: Reverse foreign aid." *New York Times*, 25 March.

Rotberg, Robert I., ed. 2008. *China into Africa: Trade, Aid, and Influence*. Washington, DC: Brookings Institution Press.

Rowthorn, Robert, and Ramana Ramaswamy. 1997. *Deindustrialization: Its Causes and Implications*. Washington, DC: International Monetary Fund.

Roy, F. 2006. "Canada's Place in World Trade 1990–2005." *Canadian Economic Observer*, March.

Ruggie, John Gerard. 1982. "International Regimes, Transactions, and Change: Embedded Liberalism in the Postwar Economic Order." *International Organization* 36 (Spring): 379–415.

Rupert, Mark. 1995. *Producing Hegemony: The Politics of Mass Production and American Global Power*. Cambridge: Cambridge University Press.

Rutherford, Tod D., and John Holmes. 2007. "'We simply have to do that stuff for our survival': Labour, Firm Innovation and Cluster Governance in the Canadian Automotive Parts Industry." *Antipode* 39 (1): 194–221.

Rutherford, Tod D., and John Holmes. 2008. "'The flea on the tail of the dog': Power in Global Production Networks and the Restructuring of Canadian Automotive Clusters." *Journal of Economic Geography* 8 (4): 519–44.

Ruttig, Thomas. 2006. *Islamists, Leftists – and a Void in the Center: Afghanistan's Political Parties and Where They Come From (1902–2006)*. Berlin: Konrad Adenauer Foundation.

Ryerson, Stanley B. 1976. *Unequal Union: Roots of Crisis in Canada, 1815–1973.* Toronto: Progress Books.

Sanders, Richard. 2009. "Fueling Wars! Canadian Arms Exports at Work." *Press for Conversion* 64 (November).

Sachs, Jeffrey D. 2004. "From his first day in office, Bush was ousting Aristide." *Los Angeles Times*, 4 March.

Sassen, Saskia. 2005. "The Global City: Introducing a concept." *Brown Journal of World Affairs* 11 (2): 27–43.

Sassen, Saskia. 2007. "Introduction: Deciphering the Global." In *Deciphering the Global: Its Scales, Spaces and Subjects*, ed. Saskia Sassen. New York: Routledge.

Satzewich, Vic, and Terry Wotherspoon. 2000. *First Nations: Race, Class, and Gender Relations.* Regina, SK: University of Regina Press.

Saul, John. 1999. "A Class Act: Canada's Anti-Apartheid Effort." *Southern Africa Report* 14.2 (March).

Saunders, Doug. 2008. "Corruption eats away at Afghan government." *Globe and Mail*, 3 May.

Scahill, Jeremy. 2013. *Dirty Wars: The World Is a Battlefield.* New York: Nation Books.

Schlesinger Jr., Arthur. 1967. "Origins of the Cold War." *Foreign Affairs* 46 (1): 22–52.

Schmidt, Hans R. 1995. *The United States Occupation of Haiti, 1915–1934.* New Brunswick, NJ: Rutgers University Press.

Schramm, Carl J. 2010. "Expeditionary Economics: Spurring Growth after Conflicts and Disasters." *Foreign Affairs* 89 (3): 89–99.

Scoffield, Heather. 2006. "Canada hollowing out? It's a world beater." *The Globe and Mail*, 5 December.

Scott, John. 1997. *Corporate Business and Capitalist Classes.* Oxford: Oxford University Press.

Scott, R.E., C. Salas, and B. Campbell. 2001. "Revisiting NAFTA: Still Not Working for North America's Workers." EPI Briefing Paper 173. Washington, DC: Economic Policy Institute.

Seabrooke, Leonard. 2001. *US Power in International Finance.* New York: Palgrave.

Seccareccia, Mario. 2007. "Critical Macroeconomic Aspects of Deepening North American Economic Integration." In *Whose Canada? Continental Integration, Fortress North America and the Corporate Agenda*, ed. Ricardo Grinspun and Yasmine Shamsie. Montreal; Kingston, ON: McGill-Queen's University Press.

Sedra, Mark. 2004. "Security Sector Reform in Afghanistan." Working Paper 143. Geneva: Center for the Democratic Control of Armed Forces.

Seidman, Stephen. 1983. "Network Structure and Minimum Degree." *Social Networks* 5 (3): 269–87.

Senlis Council. 2006. *Canada in Kandahar: No Peace to Keep, a Case Study of the Military Coalitions in Southern Afghanistan*. London. June.

Shaikh, Anwar. 1979/80. "Foreign Trade and the Law of Value: Part One." *Science & Society* 43 (3): 281–302.

Shaikh, Anwar. 1983. "Concentration and Centralization of Capital." In *A Dictionary of Marxist Thought*, ed. Tom Bottomore. Oxford, UK: Basil Blackwell.

Shaikh, Anwar. 2005. "The Economic Mythology of Neoliberalism." In *Neoliberalism: A Critical Reader*, ed. Alfredo Saad-Filho and Deborah Johnston. London: Pluto.

Shaikh, Anwar, ed. 2007. *Globalization and the Myths of Free Trade: History, Theory, and Empirical Evidence*. New York: Routledge.

Shaikh, Anwar, and E. Ahmet Tonak. 1994. *Measuring the Wealth of Nations*. Cambridge: Cambridge University Press.

Shamsie, Yasmine. 2006. "It's Not Just Afghanistan or Darfur: Canada's Peacebuilding Efforts in Haiti." *Canada Among Nations, 2006: Minorities and Priorities*, ed. Andrew F. Cooper and Dane Rowlands. Montreal; Kingston, ON: McGill-Queen's University Press.

Shamsie, Yasmine. 2009. "Export Processing Zones: The Purported Glimmer in Haiti's Development Murk." *Review of International Political Economy* 16 (4): 649–72.

Shamsie, Yasmine. 2012. "Canadian Assistance to Haiti: Some Sobering Snags in a Fragile-State Approach." In *Canada Looks South: In Search of an Americas Policy*, ed. Peter McKenna. Toronto: University of Toronto Press.

Sharma, Nandita Rani. 2006. *Home Economics: Nationalism and the Making of "Migrant Workers" in Canada*. Toronto: University of Toronto Press.

Shields, John, and Stephen McBride. 1997. *Dismantling a Nation: The Transition to Corporate Rule in Canada*, 2nd ed. Halifax, NS: Fernwood.

Shoup, Lawrence H., and William Minter. 2004. *Imperial Brain Trust: The Council on Foreign Relations and United States Foreign Policy*. Lincoln, NB: Authors Choice Press.

Singh, Ajit. 1977. "UK Industry and the World Economy: A Case of De-industrialization?" In *Welfare Aspects of Industrial Markets*, ed. A.P. Jacquemin and H.W. de Jong. New York: Springer.

Singh, Ajit. 2007. "Capital Account Liberalization, Free Long-term Capital Flows, Financial Crises, and Economic Development." In *Globalization and the Myths of Free Trade: History, Theory, and Empirical Evidence*, ed. Anwar Shaikh. New York: Routledge.

Skinner, Michael. 2013. "The Empire of Capital and the Latest Inning of the Great Game." In *Empire's Ally: Canada and the War in Afghanistan*, ed. Jerome Klassen and Greg Albo. Toronto: University of Toronto Press.

Sklair, Leslie. 2001. *The Transnational Capitalist Class*. Oxford, UK: Blackwell.

Sklair, Leslie, and Peter T. Robbins. 2002. "Global Capitalism and Major Corporations from the Third World." *Third World Quarterly* 23 (1): 81–100.

Sloan, Elinor C. 2005. *Security and Defence in the Terrorist Era: Canada and North America*. Montreal; Kingston, ON: McGill-Queen's University Press.

Smardon, Bruce. 2010. "Rethinking Canadian Economic Development: The Political Economy of Canadian Fordism, 1880–1914." *Studies in Political Economy* 85 (Spring): 179–208.

Smiley, Donald V. 1975. "Canada and the quest for a national policy." *Canadian Journal of Political Science* 8.1 (March): 40–62.

Smith, Adam. [1776] 1994. *An Inquiry into the Nature and Causes of the Wealth of Nations*. New York: Modern Library.

Smith, Graeme. 2006a. "Calm prevails in Kandahar one day after Canadian soldier killed boy at roadblock." *Globe and Mail*, 24 August.

Smith, Graeme. 2006b. "Taking blame for Afghan carnage," *Globe and Mail*, 16 June.

Smith, Graeme. 2007. "From Canadian custody into cruel hands," *Globe and Mail*, 23 April.

Smith, Graeme. 2008a. "Report slams tactic of night raids on Afghan homes." *Globe and Mail*, 23 December.

Smith, Graeme. 2008b. "Taliban control more of Kandahar: analysis." *Globe and Mail*, 15 July.

Smith, Graeme. 2008c. "Top soldier denies significant increase in violence." *Globe and Mail*, 14 July.

Smith, Graeme. 2010a. "Bondage, beatings and a few questions from the governor." *Globe and Mail*, 10 April.

Smith, Graeme. 2010b. "House of pain: Canada's connection with Kandahar's ruthless palace guard." *Globe and Mail*, 10 April.

Sontag, Deborah. 2012. "In Haiti, global failures on a cholera epidemic." *New York Times*, 31 March.

Sontag, Susan. 2004. "What have we done?" *Guardian*, 24 May.

Souare, Malick, and Weimin Wang. 2009. "Are Canadian Industries Moving Up the Value Chain?" Working Paper Series. Ottawa: Statistics Canada.

Stairs, Denis, et al. 2003. *In the National Interest: Canadian Foreign Policy in an Insecure World*. Calgary: Canadian Defence and Foreign Affairs Institute.

Stanford, Jim. 2006a. "Modeling North American Integration: Pushing the Envelope of Reality." In *Living with Uncle: Canada-US Relations in an Age of Empire*, ed. Bruce Campbell and Ed Finn. Toronto: James Lorimer.

Stanford, Jim. 2006b. "A Tale of Two Economies: Gap between Alberta and Rest of Canada Now a Yawning Chasm." *CCPA Monitor* 13 (2).

Stanford, Jim. 2008. "Staples, Deindustrialization, and Foreign Investment: Canada's Economic Journey Back to the Future." *Studies in Political Economy* 82 (Autumn): 7–34.

Staples, Steven. 2007. "Fortress North America: The Drive towards Military and Security Integration and Its Impact on Canada." In *Whose Canada? Continental Integration, Fortress North America, and the Corporate Agenda*, ed. Ricardo Grinspun and Yasmine Shamsie. Montreal; Kingston, ON: McGill-Queen's University Press.

Staples, Steven. 2011. "Canada Is Overspending on Defence." *Embassy*, 16 November.

Statistics Canada. 2012. *Corporations Returns Act 2010*. Ottawa.

Steil, Benn. 2013. *The Battle of Bretton Woods: John Maynard Keynes, Harry Dexter White, and the Making of a New World Order*. Princeton, NJ: Princeton University Press.

Stein, Janice, and Eugene Lang. 2007. *The Unexpected War: Canada in Kandahar*. Toronto: Viking.

Stewart, Gordon T. 1992. *The American Response to Canada since 1776*. East Lansing: Michigan State University Press.

St-Louis, Michel-Henri. 2009. "The Strategic Advisory Team in Afghanistan – Part of the Canadian Comprehensive Approach to Stability Operations." *Canadian Military Journal* 9 (3): 58–67.

Stokes, Doug. 2002. "Better Lead than Bread? A Critical Analysis of the US' Plan Colombia." *Civil Wars* 4 (2): 59–78.

Stokes, Doug. 2005. *America's Other War: Terrorizing Colombia*. London: Zed Books.

Stokes, Doug, and Sam Raphael. 2010. *Global Energy Security and American Hegemony*. Baltimore: Johns Hopkins University Press.

Strange, Susan. 1994. *States and Markets*, 2nd ed. London: Continuum.

Sui, Sui, and Zhihao Yu. 2013. "The Dynamics of Expansion to Emerging Markets: Evidence from Canadian Exporters." *Review of Development Economics* 17 (3): 510–22.

Taylor, Scott. 2007a. "The Strategic Advisory Team: Canadian Military Officers Discreetly Build a Government in Afghanistan." *Esprit de Corps*, 8 February.

Taylor, Scott. 2007b. "The Warlords Return to Kandahar." *Esprit de Corps*, 8 February.

Teeple, Gary. 2000. *Globalization and the Decline of Social Reform: Into the Twenty-First Century*. Toronto: University of Toronto Press.

Thürer, Daniel. 1999. "The 'Failed State' and International Law." *International Review of the Red Cross* 81 (836): 731–60.

Tirman, John. 2011. *The Deaths of Others: The Fate of Civilians in America's Wars*. Oxford: Oxford University Press.

Trotsky, Leon. [1932] 1961. *The History of the Russian Revolution*. New York: Pathfinder.

Tsoukalas, Konstantinos. 1999. "Globalisation and the Executive Committee: Reflections on the Contemporary Capitalist State." In *The Socialist Register 1999: Global Capitalism vs. Democracy*, ed. Leo Panitch and Colin Leys. London: Merlin Press.

UNCTAD (United Nations Conference on Trade and Development). 2009. *World Investment Report 2008*. New York; Geneva: United Nations.

UNCTAD. 2011. *World Investment Report 2011*. New York; Geneva: United Nations.

UNCTAD. 2012. *UNCTAD Handbook of Statistics 2011*. New York; Geneva: United Nations.

UNDP (United Nations Development Programme). 2010. *Human Development Report 2010: The Real Wealth of Nations*. New York: United Nations.

UNEP (United Nations Environment Programme). 2009. *From Conflict to Peacebuilding: The Role of Natural Resources and the Environment*. Nairobi: UNEP.

United Nations. 2005. *World Economic and Social Survey 2005*. New York: United Nations, Department of Economic and Social Affairs.

United Nations Assistance Mission to Afghanistan. 2013. *Treatment of Conflict-Related Detainees in Afghan Custody: One Year On*. Kabul: UNAMA.

United Nations Office of the High Commissioner for Human Rights. 2010. "Human Rights Dimension of Poverty in Afghanistan." March.

United States. 1945. Department of State. *Foreign Relations of the United States: Diplomatic Papers 1945*, vol. 8, *The Near East and Africa*. Washington, DC: US Government Printing Office.

United States. 1948. Central Intelligence Agency. "ORE-25-48: The Break-up of the Colonial Empires and Its Implications for U.S. Security." Washington, DC. 3 September.

United States. 1950. National Security Council. "United States Objectives and Programs for National Security." Washington, DC. 14 April.

United States. 1953a. National Security Council. "Directive 144/1." Washington, DC. 18 March.

United States. 1953b. National Security Council. "Review of Basic National Security Policy." Memorandum 162/1. Washington, DC. October 30.

United States. 1954. National Security Council Directive 5428. "United States Objectives and Policies with Respect to the Near East." Washington, DC. 23 July.

United States. 1990. *The National Security Strategy of the United States of America*. Washington, DC: White House.

United States. 1992. Department of Defense. *Draft FY 94–99 Defense Planning Guidance*. Washington, DC.

United States. 1995. *United States Security Strategy for the East Asia-Pacific Region*. Washington, DC: Office of the Secretary of Defense.

United States. 1997. *The Report of the Quadrennial Defense Review*. Washington, DC: Department of Defense.

United States. 1999. *Annual Report of the Secretary of Defense to the President and the Congress*. Washington, DC. Available online at http://www.fas.org/man/docs/adr_00/index.html.

United States. 2000. Joint Chiefs of Staff. *Strategic Vision 2020*. Washington, DC.

United States. 2001. *Quadrennial Defense Review Report*. Washington DC: Department of Defense.

United States. 2002a. Air Force Space Command. "Strategic Master Plan (SMP) FY04 and Beyond." Peterson AFB, CO. 5 November.

United States. 2002b. *The National Security Strategy of the United States of America*. Washington, DC: White House.

United States. 2006. Department of State. "U.S. Department of State Country Report on Human Rights Practices 2005, Haiti." Washington, DC. 8 March. Available online at http://www.unhcr.org/refworld/docid/441821ae11.html, accessed 18 December 2012.

United States. 2008. Embassy, Port-au-Prince. 2008. "Why We Need Continuing Minustah Presence in Haiti." 8 October. Available online at http://wikileaks.org/cable/2008/10/08PORTAUPRINCE1381.html.

United States. 2010a. Joint Forces Command. *The Joint Operating Environment 2010*. Washington, DC: Department of Defense.

United States. 2010b. *The National Security Strategy of the United States*. Washington, DC: White House.

United States. 2010c. Department of Defense. *Nuclear Posture Review*. Washington, DC: Department of Defense.

United States. 2010d. Embassy, Port-au-Prince. "Préval Annouces GOH Priorities." 16 January. Available online at http://wikileaks.org/cable/2010/01/10PORTAUPRINCE50.html.

United States. 2010e. Department of Defense. *Report on Progress toward Security and Stability in Afghanistan*. Washington, DC.

United States. 2010f. Department of the Army. *Special Forces Unconventional Warfare*. Washington, DC.

United States. 2010g. Department of Homeland Security. *Yearbook of Immigration Statistics: 2010*. Washington, DC. Available online at http://www.dhs.gov/files/statistics/publications/LPR10.shtm, accessed 20 December 2011.

United States. 2011. Department of State. *Post-Earthquake USG Haiti Strategy: Toward Renewal and Economic Opportunity*. Washington, DC, 3 January.

United States. 2013. Government Accountability Office. *Haiti Reconstruction: USAID Infrastructure Projects Have Had Mixed Results and Face Sustainability Challenges.* Washington, DC, 18 June.

United States Central Command. 1995. "Combatant Commands Informational Series, Chapter 1, Strategic Environment." Available online at http://web .archive.org/web/20011114230326/tuvok.au.af.mil/au/database/projects/ ay1995/acsc/95-002/chap1/stratgic.htm, accessed 10 July 2012.

Useem, Michael. 1984. *The Inner Circle: Large Corporation and the Rise of Business Political Activity in the U.S. and U.K.* New York: Oxford University Press.

Van Alphen, Tony. 2011. "Auto sector roaring back." *Toronto Star*, 26 July. Available online at http://www.thestar.com/wheels/article/1030748--auto -sector-roaring-back.

van Apeldoorn, Bastiaan. 2002. *Transnational Capitalism and the Struggle over European Order.* London: Routledge.

van der Pijl, Kees. 1997. *The Making of an Atlantic Ruling Class.* London: Verso.

van der Pijl, Kees. 2005. "A Theory of Global Capitalism, Feature Review." *New Political Economy* 10 (2): 273–7.

Van Kirk, Sylvia. 1983. *Many Tender Ties: Women in Fur-trade Society, 1670–1870.* Ottawa: University of Ottawa Press.

Vastel, Michel. 2003. "Haiti mise en tutelle par l'ONU?" *L'Actualité*, 15 March.

Veenbaas, Jim. 2003. "Iraq war divides business." *Alberta Venture*, 1 December.

Waldman, Mark. 2008. *Falling Short: Aid Effectiveness in Afghanistan.* Kabul: Agency Coordinating Body for Afghan Relief.

Wallerstein, Immanuel. 1979. *The Capitalist World-Economy.* Cambridge: Cambridge University Press.

Waltz, Kenneth. 1979. *Theory of International Politics.* Long Grove, IL: Waveland Press.

Warnock, John. 1970. *Partner to Behemoth: The Military Policy of a Satellite Canada.* Toronto: New Press.

Warnock, John. 2013. "Afghanistan and Empire." In *Empire's Ally: Canada and the War in Afghanistan*, ed. Jerome Klassen and Greg Albo. Toronto: University of Toronto Press.

Watkins, Melville H. 1963. "A Staple Theory of Economic Growth." *Canadian Journal of Economics and Political Science* 29 (2): 141–58.

Watkins, Mel. 1968. *Foreign Ownership and the Structure of Canadian Industry: Report of the Task Force on the Structure of Canadian Industry.* Ottawa.

Watson, Paul. 2011. "Credibility eludes Kandahar police force." *Toronto Star*, 20 June.

Watson, Paul. 2012a. "Canada's Afghan legacy: failure at Dahla dam." *Toronto Star*, 14 July.

Watson, Paul. 2012b. "Canada's Afghan legacy: shoddy school buildings and sagging morale." *Toronto Star*, 15 July.

Watson, Paul. 2012c. "U.S. rushes in to fund Afghan school for girls after CIDA failed to renew funding." *Toronto Star*, 30 September.

Wattie, Chris. 2003. "We'll be your friends, troops tell villagers." *CanWest News Service*, 15 September.

Weber, Bob. 2008. "Afghan journalist says Canadian tip-off was behind his arrest, imprisonment." *Canadian Press*, 24 September.

Weeks, John. 1981. "The Differences between Materialist Theory and Dependency Theory and Why They Matter." *Latin American Perspectives* 8 (3–4): 118–23.

Weiss, Linda. 2000. "Globalization and State Power." *Development and Society* 29 (1): 1–15.

Welsh, Jennifer. 2004. *At Home in the World: Canada's Global Vision for the 21st Century*. Toronto: Harper Collins.

Wendt, Alexander E. 1987. "The Agent-Structure Problem in International Relations Theory." *International Organization* 41 (3): 335–70.

Wendt, Alexander E. 1995. "Constructing International Politics." *International Security* 20 (1): 71–81.

Westad, Odd Arne. 2007. *The Global Cold War: Third World Interventions and the Making of Our Times*. Cambridge: Cambridge University Press.

Weston, Greg. 2011. "Canada offered to aid Iraq invasion: Wikileaks." *CBC News*, 15 May.

Weston, Greg. 2012. "Secret document details new Canadian foreign policy." *CBC News*, 19 November.

Weston, Greg. 2013. "Inside Canada's top-secret billion-dollar spy palace." *CBC News*, 8 October.

Weston, Greg, Glenn Greenwald, and Ryan Gallagher. 2013. "Snowden document shows Canada set up spy posts for NSA." *CBC News*, 9 December.

Whitaker, Reg, Gregory S. Kealey, and Andrew Parnaby. 2012. *Secret Service: Political Policing in Canada from the Fenians to Fortress America*. Toronto: University of Toronto Press.

Whitney, Kathleen Marie. 1996. "SIN, FRAPH, and the CIA: U.S. Covert Action in Haiti." *Southwestern Journal of Law and Trade in the Americas* 3 (2): 303–32.

Wilber, Donald N. 1954. "Overthrow of Premier Mossadeq of Iran. November 1952–August 1953." Central Intelligence Agency, Clandestine Services History. Washington, DC. March.

Williams, Glen. 1988. "On Determining Canada's Location in the International Political Economy." *Studies in Political Economy* 25 (Spring): 107–40.

Williams, Glen. 1994. *Not for Export: The International Competitiveness of Canadian Manufacturing*. Toronto: McClelland and Stewart.

Williams, Kristian. 2006. *American Methods: Torture and the Logic of Domination*. Cambridge, MA: South End Press.

Williams, William Appleman. 2009. *The Tragedy of American Diplomacy*. New York: W.W. Norton.

Williamson, Myra. 2009. *Terrorism, War, and International Law: The Legality of the Use of Force against Afghanistan in 2001*. Burlington, VT: Ashgate.

Wilson, Scott. 2003. "Armed attacks increase pressure on Haitian leader; Civilian opposition movement targets popular Aristide." *Washington Post*, 21 November.

Winch, Donald. 1965. *Classical Political Economy and Colonies*. London: G. Bell.

Winternitz, J. 1949. "The Marxist Theory of Crisis." *Modern Quarterly* 4 (4).

Wissin, Markus, and Ulrich Brand. 2011. "Approaching the Internationalization of the State: An Introduction." *Antipode* 43 (1): 1–11.

Wohlforth, William C. 1999. "The Stability of a Unipolar World." *International Security* 24 (2): 5–41.

Wood, Ellen Meiksins. 1995. *Democracy against Capitalism: Renewing Historical Materialism*. Cambridge: Cambridge University Press.

Wood, Ellen Meiksins. 1999. "Unhappy Families: Global Capitalism in a World of Nation-States." *Monthly Review* 51 (3): 1–12. Available online at http://monthlyreview.org/1999/07/01/unhappy-families.

Wood, Ellen Meiksins. 2005. *Empire of Capital*, 2nd ed. London: Verso.

World Bank. 2005. *Afghanistan – State Building, Sustained Growth, and Reducing Poverty: A World Bank Country Study*. Washington, DC.

World Health Organization. 2011. "Country Cooperation Strategy at a Glance: The Islamic Republic of Afghanistan." Geneva. May.

Wyman, Diana. 2007. "Trading with a Giant." *Canadian Economic Observer*, November.

Young, Robert J.C. 1998. "Ideologies of the Postcolonial." *Interventions: International Journal of Postcolonial Studies* 1 (1): 4–8.

Young, Robert J.C. 2009. "What Is the Postcolonial?" *ARIAL: A Review of International English Literature* 40 (1): 13–25.

Zakaria, Fareed. 2012. *The Post-American World: Release 2.0*. New York: W.W. Norton.

Zia-Zarifi, Sam. 2004. *Losing the Peace in Afghanistan*. New York: Human Rights Watch.